165901

LAW MAKERS, LAW BREAKERS
and
UNCOMMON TRIALS

Robert Aitken and Marilyn Aitken

SECTION *of* LITIGATION
AMERICAN BAR ASSOCIATION

Defending Liberty
Pursuing Justice

Cover design by ABA Publishing.

The materials contained herein represent the opinions and views of the authors and/or the editors, and should not be construed to be the views or opinions of the law firms or companies with whom such persons are in partnership with, associated with, or employed by, nor of the American Bar Association or the Section of Litigation unless adopted pursuant to the bylaws of the Association.

Nothing contained in this book is to be considered as the rendering of legal advice, either generally or in connection with any specific issue or case. Nor do these materials purport to explain or interpret any specific bond or policy, or any provisions thereof, issued by any particular franchise company, or to render franchise or other professional advice. Readers are responsible for obtaining advice from their own lawyers or other professionals. This book and any forms and agreements herein are intended for educational and informational purposes only.

Printed in the United States of America.

Library of Congress Cataloging-in-Publication Data

Aitken, Robert.
   Law makers, law breakers and uncommon trials / Robert Aitken and Marilyn Aitken.
      p.   cm.
   Includes bibliographical references and index.
   ISBN 978-1-59031-880-5
   1. Trials—United States.   2. Trials—Great Britain.   3. Trials—Ireland.
   I. Aitken, Marilyn.   II. Title.
   K540.A38   2007
   345.73'07—dc22   2007029819

Discounts are available for books ordered in bulk. Special consideration is given to state bars, CLE programs, and other bar-related organizations. Inquire at Book Publishing, ABA Publishing, American Bar Association, 321 N. Clark, Chicago, Illinois 60610-4714.

www.ababooks.org

To Doug

CONTENTS

FOREWORD

The success of television series and movies about trial lawyers, their clients, and their travails (including my favorite, *Rumpole of the Bailey*), illustrates the attraction most of us have for courtroom drama. But fictional accounts often pale in comparison to the excitement involved, year in and year out, in real-life courtroom trials.

From the time of my entry into law school more than half a century ago, I have been fascinated by the legal controversies, both civil and criminal, that have formed the basis of so much of the colorful history of the Western world. The circumstances that precipitated these cases, and the unusual personalities so often involved, offer insightful views not only of compelling personal stories but of the important events that have shaped the United States. A great number of these events have evolved from litigation and court rulings that remain powerful in our society to this day. One shining example recounted in this book is the momentous opinion written in 1803 by Chief Justice John Marshall, which announced the bedrock principle that the Supreme Court has power to declare invalid statutes enacted by Congress and approved by the president that the Court deems inconsistent with the Constitution.

Marilyn and Bob Aitken's *Law Makers, Law Breakers and Uncommon Trials* contains a treasure trove of material about a number of intriguing cases and their resolutions. Their effortless, easy-to-read style is accessible to all and avoids legalistic parlance. They have unearthed many little-known facts and events that led parties into court. The diversity of material they have explored contributes to a deeper understanding of past lives and times, which, in turn, have helped shaped our own.

The legal lore contained here is not limited solely to that of the United States. Historic cases are examined from England and

Ireland, including an example of masterful cross-examination by Sir Edward Carson, whose questioning brought high-flying Irish poet and playwright Oscar Wilde down to earth and eventually landed him in Reading Gaol. There are also accounts of a number of cases resulting from World War II atrocities in France and Italy. Additionally, the authors examine the defamation suit brought against novelist Leon Uris for his description in *Exodus* of the horrific conduct of an Auschwitz doctor. Let me offer a few other examples of what is in store:

1. The events leading to the infamous 1856 ruling of the Supreme Court in the *Dred Scott* case, which dehumanized African-Americans and helped foster the Civil War, and the saga of Rosa Parks, whose lonely act of courage presaged the movement for civil rights in the 1960s.
2. Several extraordinary trials in the early days when the West was being settled, including the trial of the man who killed Wild Bill Hickok, as well as the trials arising from the 1857 massacre of the Fancher party in the Utah Territory.
3. Courtroom battles involving works of art and literature that were looked upon with disdain when they first appeared but now are regarded as among the finest achievements. These accounts include the trial resulting from customs officials' confiscation of *Ulysses* on the basis that James Joyce's masterpiece was an obscene book, as well as the suit that artist James Whistler brought against critic John Ruskin for having trashed his paintings as third-rate art.

I once read that a positive view of life will not solve all our problems but will annoy enough people to make it worthwhile. Accordingly, I express my optimistic hope and expectation that Marilyn and Bob Aitken will continue to plumb the archives and favor us in later volumes with more delightfully engrossing accounts of remarkable trials and the folks enmeshed in them.

Thomas P. Sullivan
Jenner & Block LLP
Chicago, Illinois
March 19, 2007

PREFACE

Life may be random, ever-changing, non-linear, and prone to decay, but we dust our furniture and wash our windows to maintain an illusion of stability. We try on a larger scale to bring order out of chaos. From the makers of the Constitution to Rosa Parks's protest against discrimination, our history is replete with stories of our long search for justice under law. Against this setting, law breakers also flourish. Murder seldom can be prevented. War rewards a clash of wills with human dust and vast destruction. We are not perfect, but we bumble on, living our all too human lives, stubbornly opposing each other's ideas, but continually hoping for the best. Here are 25 examples of people involved in uncommon trials and events—and of the enduring power of the past.

ACKNOWLEDGMENTS

Thank you to everyone at *Litigation* during the 12 years we have written "Legal Lore" articles—especially to former editors-in-chief Mark Neubauer, who launched our project, Ken Nolan, Larry Vilardo, Gary Sasso, Judge Jeffrey Cole, and Chuck Tobin, who enthusiastically supported it, and to our current editor-in-chief, Joyce Meyers, and executive editor Steve Good. Thanks also to Tony Murray and Mike Tigar, who led the way to the ABA "Litigation Section." Applause for managing editors, first, Cie Armstead, and now Annemarie Micklo, of the hard work and outrageous puns. Marjean Blinn, Joyce Graman, Lanny Swallow and Larry Tominaga at the Palos Verdes Peninsula Library were exceptionally helpful. James M. Russ and Ed Retzler saved us from error. Dr. Roy Halpern scrutinized each article, and Maryellen Halpern was his co-conspirator. They have earned our appreciation. Frank Brummett gave us expert advice and help, as did Jack Walrad. While researching, we also called upon Phil Simon, Mike McHale, Paul Burg, Chris Moore, Lisa Ackerman and other friends over coffee at Malaga Cove Plaza. Doug Aitken offered awesome inspiration. Peter Baird suggested the book and cheered us on. Shirley Retzler, Robert McKee, Phil and Karen Madden, Cynthia Scheer, Gemma Ponsa, Judge Roderic and Carol Duncan, Anne Wittels, Kermit and Catharine Wagner, Glen and Noel Garrett, Sam and Jane Salmon, Captain Howard Skidmore USN (ret.), the Kendricks, Cuddigans and most of all, Deborah, Bill, Arlene, John and Heather Aitken patiently listened to our tales. Patrice and Butch Hutton of Page, Arizona, shared an article in the evening with campers they took on a Grand Canyon raft trip, and teacher Bruce Halpern read a story to his elementary school class. Maynard Garrison, Judge John Conway and Stan Ackerman offered to distribute their favorite "Lores." Edna

Epstein encouraged us to apply to the ABA Book Board. Jim Archibald suggested the "Sedition Act" article and recommended the Francis Wharton book. The wonderfully helpful Tim Brandhorst and Denise Eichhorn took over from there. Jeff Cole told us of his friendship with legendary lawyer Tom Sullivan, a fan of Dickens and Rumpole, who, to our amazement, also likes our work and wrote the foreword. We thank Tom and "notable, quotable" Bill and Mary Hangley, Tom McDermott, Susan Wise and Mark Hermann. Our best to John McCrae, Mary Ann Stevenson-Petrillo, Ann Harrison Walli and the high school class whose reunion we missed while proofreading. No doubt we have absentmindedly omitted others we should acknowledge, and we apologize. Finally, we would like to thank you, dear reader, for opening this book.

ABOUT THE AUTHORS

Robert and Marilyn Aitken's collaboration began in Michigan when Bob, who was visiting his cousin at a cottage at Saginaw Bay, came to the McKees' cottage nearby to borrow their boat. Marilyn opened the door. They were married three years later after Marilyn graduated from Michigan State University with high honors in English and Bob entered the University of Michigan Law School.

After graduation, they came to California, where Bob joined the Long Beach law firm of Ball, Hunt and Hart and became a partner. He has served as chair of the Executive Committee of the Litigation Section of the State Bar of California and as editor-in-chief of their journal, *California Litigation*. Bob is the author of *California Evidentiary Objections* (West, 1989) and *Handling Expert Witnesses in California Courts* (CEB, 2006). As Associate Editor of *Litigation*, the journal of the ABA Section of Litigation, he has been the editor of *Legal Lore* and *Literary Trials*. He is a fellow of the American College of Trial Lawyers.

Marilyn has written articles for the *Los Angeles Times* and was associate editor of *South Bay* magazine. Their son, Doug, is an international artist. They live in Palos Verdes Estates, California.

SECTION I

Making a Nation

Created from the sturdy fabric of English law, the words of the Constitution endure. Some actions of the founders were less worthy. In a masterstroke, Supreme Court Chief Justice John Marshall made a solid contribution, establishing the power of judicial review.

1

The King Who Lost His Head
The Trial of Charles I

Claiming the divine right of kings, English monarch Charles Stuart insisted upon absolute power and meddled in religion once too often. In 1649, a rump faction of Parliament's House of Commons decided to oust him. They had no legal precedent, but they winged it with a trial, a conviction, and a beheading. When the American founders wrote the Constitution the following century, they studied the story of Charles I.

The concept of divine right was based on the belief that God had anointed a particular family and its heirs to rule a nation. England had been ruled by a succession of dynasties. When Queen Elizabeth I, the Virgin Queen, died in 1603, ending the Tudor dynasty, James VI of Scotland, son of Elizabeth's enemy, Mary, Queen of Scots, became James I of England, the first Stuart king. Hard-drinking, big-spending, and too fond of his dashing favorite, George Villiars, Duke of Buckingham, James was a learned man who wrote books advancing his argument for absolutism. In 1610, James told Parliament: "The state of monarchy is the supremest thing upon earth. . . . Kings are justly called Gods, for that they exercise a manner or resemblance of divine power upon earth." James VI & I, *The True Law of Free Monarchies* (1599).

In contrast, England's Parliament had developed its political power incrementally over several centuries. In the Magna Carta, signed by King John I at Runnymede after the barons' revolt in 1215, the nobles insisted on a government in which no free man should be punished "but by lawful judgment of his peers or by the law of the land." Parliament, which began in 1295 under Edward I, grew not from lofty principles, but from the monarch's need for money. The word "parliamentum"—a talking together—had been used for meetings of the Great Council when king, bishops, and barons discussed big issues. The king convened Parliament when he required funds to maintain his household or to finance a war. Parliament remained subservient to the king.

King Edward I began to invite wealthy men from the communities to Parliament, and they later became the House of Commons. As they controlled the purse strings, they expected political power. Much of the country's wealth was held by gentry surrounded by sheep and by merchants trading in textiles. No one spoke for the tenant farmers who cultivated the land. J. Thorn, R. Lockyer & D. Smith, *A History of England* (1961).

Conflicts emerged during the reign of James I, who had already successfully ruled Scotland and was adamant that Parliament should have no control over his foreign policy. He tried to create a balance of power. The problems were complicated by religion. King Henry VIII had split from the Vatican because of his divorce and established the Church of England. The Reformation swept in from Europe and added Protestants to the mix. James reigned over the kingdoms of Anglican England, Presbyterian Scotland, and Catholic Ireland. Fiercely anti-Catholic, Parliament was furious when James attempted to arrange a marriage between his son, Charles, and the daughter of Philip III of Spain. When that fell through, he managed a marriage between Charles and the Catholic princess Henrietta Maria, daughter of Henry IV of France. James kept the peace, promoted the King James version of the Bible, and died in 1625.

Charles Stuart was 25 years old when he became king. He had been a fragile child with a lingering stammer, but he grew strong and athletic. Edward Hyde, a supporter and historian, described Charles: "He had a tenderness and compassion of nature which restrained him from ever doing a hard-hearted thing." Charles, a patron of the arts, had his portrait painted by Sir Anthony Van

4

Dyck. He was shy, fearless, and temperate. G. Edwards, *The Last Days of Charles I* (1999).

Raised in the old feudal and social codes, Charles was confronted by a dizzying array of sects and conflicting interests and morals. He was head of the Church of England, but he relaxed penal laws against Catholics and allowed his new queen to practice her religion. Charles became a loving husband and father of six children. No scandal touched him. Poet John Milton said Charles's only vice was reading too much Shakespeare. But his personal happiness was not reflected in his relationship with Parliament, where sources of contention were religion, money, and the law. C. Carlton, *Charles I* (1941).

Shortly after his succession, Charles opened his first Parliament, which he expected would finance a war against Spain. Commons provided inadequate funding and limited his right to levy tonnage and poundage (export and import duties) to a one-year term. Charles dissolved Parliament two months later. In 1626, after joining with the Duke of Buckingham in an unsuccessful attack on Spain at Cadiz, Charles was almost bankrupt. He called his second Parliament, but it was dissolved after impeaching Buckingham and without voting funds. In 1628, his third Parliament listed its grievances in a Petition of Right, a constitutional landmark. The king could no longer arbitrarily commit his subjects to prison, quarter the military with them, or subject them to martial law. The king also required Parliament's consent to assess taxes. W.&A. Durant, *The Story of Civilization*, vol. 7 (1961).

Charles, ever wary of relinquishing his authority, reluctantly signed the petition. In return, he expected Commons to vote him money and grant him tonnage and poundage duties. Instead, they voted the Remonstrance, declaring that by collecting duties, Charles had violated the law. Parliament requested the king to dismiss the rash Buckingham. He refused. The issue became moot when an ex-soldier walked 60 miles to London and stabbed Buckingham to death. Commons, dominated by Presbyterians, continued its attack, condemning High Church Arminianism, which asserted that man is saved by good works as well as faith. Instead, Commons promoted the Calvinist doctrine of predestination, which maintained that God had already decided who would be saved and who would be damned.

Charles's vision of an orderly world coincided with the Arminian view. Alarmed that Catholic monarchies had grasped power throughout Europe, Commons proposed a strictly Calvinistic interpretation of the Thirty-Nine Articles, the founding statement of the Church of England. Charles insisted on the king's absolute right to rule. He claimed that the alternative was anarchy, and he ordered Parliament to adjourn. Parliament refused until the king's troops approached. Charles ordered nine members imprisoned for sedition. Thorn, Lockyer & Smith, *supra*; J.N. Larned, *A History of England* (1900).

In 1629, Charles dissolved Parliament and ruled as an absolute monarch for 11 years. During this period, he took advantage of the undefined term "taxes" in the petition and levied tonnage and poundage on shippers without Parliament's consent. He extended a ship money tax to inland areas, convened the court of Star Chamber for non-jury trials to punish his enemies, and imposed enormous fines. Yet the 1630s were peaceful, and the arts flourished. Architect Inigo Jones built the Banqueting House in Whitehall, where the ceiling was decorated by Rubens. In the distance was civil war and Charles's death outside this magnificent structure. E.W. Knappman, ed., *Great World Trials* (1997).

Religion continued to be the most explosive issue. Charles supported the Anglican bishops, but Parliament was afraid that under William Laud, archbishop of Canterbury, the Church of England was growing closer to its Roman Catholic roots. Laud, with Charles's support, began imposing a standard plan of worship on the clergy. Puritans who had simplified the ceremonies and decor were taken to court, while the Star Chamber punished those who distributed Puritan tracts. Many Puritans emigrated to settlements in New England.

Laud also attempted to bring the Scottish church under his control. In July 1637, Charles's insistence on forcing a new Anglicized prayer book on the Scottish Presbyterian kirk caused riots in Edinburgh. Although Charles abandoned the prayer book, thousands of Scots signed a National Covenant to defend the Presbyterian faith. The Scots demanded an ouster of bishops, but Charles refused. His father had said, "No bishop, no throne." Their support was essential. The Scots took up arms. Queen Henrietta Maria, later, as an exiled widow in France, realized that Laud's actions had led to civil war and referred to "that fatal book." Carlton, *supra*; B. Axner & E. Sagarin, *World's Great Trials* (1985).

In 1640, the "Short Parliament" was called by Charles, who hoped Commons would help subdue the Scots. John Pym, who controlled Commons, smothered that hope, and Parliament was dissolved. Charles summoned the English peers, who reluctantly provided a motley army. The Scots easily won at Newburn and marched into England. Charles agreed to an armistice in which the Scottish troops would occupy England's northern counties and be paid 860 pounds per day until a peace treaty was signed. Charles was humiliated. J. Miller, *The Stuarts* (2004).

The fifth, or "Long Parliament," met in November and forced the king to agree that the Parliament could not be dissolved without its consent. Commons had ensured its future. Pym, leading extremists including Oliver Cromwell, made a list of complaints against Charles—a Grand Remonstrance—and attacked the Anglican Church. That was too much for moderates. Led by Edward Hyde, they fought passage of the bill because they believed it would transfer executive power to Parliament and leave the king impotent. Cromwell later said that if the bill had failed, he would have taken a ship to America. But Pym won by 11 votes and introduced a militia bill, giving Parliament control of army appointments. The conflict between king and Parliament reached a crisis in 1642 when Charles forced his way into Commons in a vain attempt to arrest five members, including Pym, accusing them of treason. Charles resolved to fight. He thought he could rally most of the peers and a third of Commons. Thorn, Lockyer & Smith, *supra*; Durant, *supra*.

Civil War

In August 1642, civil war broke out at Nottingham between the Royalists, known as Cavaliers, and the Parliamentarians, called Roundheads. Cromwell convinced Parliament to pass a "Self-Denying Ordinance" in which all members, including lords, gave up their commissions. The superior New Model army was created. It was commanded by Thomas Fairfax. Cromwell was second in command. The New Model defeated the main royal army at Naseby in 1645. Fairfax and Cromwell removed pockets of resistance in country houses. At Basing House, Cromwell battered the walls with cannons. The army removed its treasures and took the clothes from 70-year-old Inigo Jones, leaving him only a blanket. It was the end of Cavalier England. Thorn, Lockyer & Smith, *supra*.

Charles was tossed like a hot potato from one side to another. He surrendered to the Scots in 1646, ending the first civil war. He attempted to negotiate with his fellow countrymen. The Scots offered help if he would sign the Presbyterian Covenant and make

7

the Presbyterian Church compulsory throughout Britain. Charles refused. Parliament paid the Scots to return home, and they delivered Charles as a prisoner to English commissioners. The Presbyterian majority in Parliament, who felt threatened that the Independents (Puritans) controlled the army, hastily negotiated with the king in 1645. They almost reached an agreement to restore him if he accepted the Presbyterian Covenant for a three-year period.

It was too late. The New Model army was owed back pay and refused to disband. Cromwell ordered Charles to be taken to army headquarters. The army formed a Grand Council composed of officers and men. It claimed to speak for the English people. But the army was divided. Most officers, led by Cromwell, who came from a comfortable background, wanted to improve the traditional English government. Some officers and most men, a group called Levelers, wanted to remove the king and the House of Lords and give every man a right to vote. Cromwell quieted the dissenters. In August, the troops entered London, bringing Charles with them. Cromwell maintained order in the city. Thorn, Lockyer & Smith, *supra*.

Charles escaped to the Isle of Wight, where Scottish commissioners secretly promised him an army if he would adopt the Presbyterian faith and suppress other religions. They would accept Charles's offer of a three-year trial period. Parliament was alarmed when it saw itself subordinated to Scotland and quickly made peace with Cromwell. Charles was again taken prisoner by the army on December 1, 1648, after the army had subdued some local revolts in the "second civil war" and Cromwell's force had crushed the Scots. Some army leaders vowed that it was their duty to call Charles Stuart to account for the bloodshed.

The plot twisted and turned. Parliament, saved from the Scots by the army, now attempted to free itself of the army by reopening negotiations with Charles. Presbyterian success was unacceptable to the Puritans. Early in December, Cromwell ordered Colonel Thomas Pride and a file of musketeers to purge the Presbyterian and Royalist members from Commons. He arrested about 40 members of Parliament and kept out about 60. Many members protested by staying away. A minority, mostly Puritan Independents, remained. This small group was disparagingly called the Rump, but it claimed the full authority of Parliament. Larned, *supra*; Thorn, Lockyer and Smith, *supra*; Durant, *supra*; Miller, *supra*.

The Rump passed an ordinance accusing the king of treason. Three judges and 135 commissioners were appointed to try Charles. The commission was composed of Parliament members, army officers, aldermen, and county gentlemen. On January 1, 1649, the House of Lords, with twelve members voting, rejected the ordinance. Five days later, in a close vote, Commons approved an Ordinance for Trial. The three judges refused to participate.

One commissioner told Cromwell that they had no legal authority to try the king. Cromwell lost patience. "I tell you," he replied, "we will cut off his head with the crown upon it." The army tried once more to avoid regicide. They offered to acquit Charles if he would sell the bishops' lands and give up the power to veto parliamentary ordinances. Charles refused, saying he had sworn to be faithful to the Church of England. Edwards, *supra*; Durant, *supra*.

Trial

On Saturday afternoon, January 20, 1649, the trial began. Charles was arraigned for committing treason. It was the only time in history that a king of England was publicly tried by his subjects. Only 67 of the commissioners sat as judges. John Bradshaw, an obscure lawyer, became lord president. Bradshaw spoke directly to the king and read the indictment:

> Charles Stuart, King of England, the Commons in England assembled in Parliament, being sensible of the evils and calamities that have been brought upon this nation and of the innocent blood that hath been shed in it, have resolved to make inquisition for this blood, and according to the debt they owe to God, to Justice, the kingdom and themselves, and according to that fundamental power that is vested, and trust reposed in them by the People (other means failing through your default) have resolved to bring you to trial and judgment, and have therefore constituted this high court of justice. . . . Where you are to hear your charge, upon which the court will proceed according to justice.

As John Cook, the acting attorney general and prosecutor, showed the charge to the court and spectators, the king tapped Cook with his cane and said, "Hold." Bradshaw answered, "The court commands the charge shall be read: if you have anything to say, after, the court will hear you." Cook continued: "High Treason

9

and other High Crimes . . . for and on behalf of the people of England against Charles Stuart, King of England." He passed the charge to the court clerk.

Cook continued: "The king has attempted . . . to erect and uphold in himself an unlimited and tyrannical power, to rule according to his will and to overthrow the rights and liberties of the people . . . and hath traitorously and maliciously levied war against the present Parliament and the people therein represented." Charles was accused of causing the civil wars in which "much innocent blood of the free people of this nation hath been spilt, many families have been undone, the public treasure wasted and exhausted, trade destructed and miserably decayed, vast expense to the nation incurred and many parts of the land spoiled, some of them even to desolation."

The king was charged as a tyrant, traitor, murderer, and public and implacable enemy to the Commonwealth of England. Charles laughed at this accusation. He represented himself and attacked the court's jurisdiction. Charles reminded Parliament that the English monarchy was not elective but hereditary for a thousand years. He said, "I will stand for the privilege of the Commons, rightly understood, as any man whatsoever. . . . I see no House of Lords here that may constitute a Parliament." Charles was unyielding: "I am your king. . . . I have a trust committed to me by God, by old and lawful descent. I will not betray that trust to answer to a new unlawful authority. I stand more for the liberty of my people than any here that sitteth to be my judge."

Charles's position never changed. Each day he appeared alone, adamant in his defense that he ruled by divine right. As king, he was above the law. Charles claimed the court's authority rested only on force, and if he, as king, submitted. "I do not know what subject . . . can be sure of his life or anything he calls his own. . . . I do plead for the liberties of the people of England."

Divine right was explained by Henry of Bracton, an English judge, who wrote that English monarchs were anointed with holy oils by the archbishop of Canterbury, ordaining them to monarchy. Bracton referred to the earlier writings of Augustine of Hippo and Paul of Tarsus. Charles's claim to absolute power was bolstered by the philosophy of Thomas Hobbes. Henry of Bracton, *On the Laws and Customs of England* (c. 1265); T. Hobbes, *Leviathan* (1651); B. Russell, *A History of Western Philosophy* (1945).

It became obvious that Charles would never accept Parliament's jurisdiction, and the trial proceeded. The prosecution presented witnesses who testified that Charles had acted against the interests of the English people. On January 29, Charles, convicted as a tyrant and enemy of the nation, was sentenced to death by "severing his head from his body." After sentence was passed, Charles wanted to speak, but Bradshaw ordered guards to remove him. "I am not suffered to speak," Charles commented. "Expect what justice other people will have." Edwards, *supra*; Thorn, Lockyer & Smith, *supra*.

The next day, Tuesday, January 30, 1649, Charles was taken to a scaffold covered in black cloth built outside his own Banqueting Hall at Whitehall. He spoke to the crowd: "For the people . . . truly I desire their liberty and freedom as much as anybody . . . but I must tell you that their liberty and freedom consist in having of government—those laws by which their lives and goods may be most their own. It is not for having a share in government . . . that is nothing pertaining to them. A subject and a sovereign are clean different things." He placed himself in an appropriate position so the executioner could strike his neck and sever his head with one blow, and he indicated by stretching out his hands that he was ready. After his death, his body lay at St. James Palace until he was buried at St. George's Chapel, Windsor, on February 7. Charles I's trial marked the end of unchallenged absolute monarchy.

Afterword

On February 5, 1649, the Scots proclaimed Charles I's son, the Prince of Wales, as King Charles II. Unlike his father, Charles II took the covenant of the reformed Calvinistic Kirk of Scotland. In March, Commons abolished the monarchy and the House of Lords. It declared a commonwealth, a republic governed by a Council of State. John Milton was the Latin (foreign) secretary.

In 1650, Cromwell, who became lord general, led a successful invasion of Scotland, and the next year, he defeated Charles II and his forces at Worcester. Charles II escaped to France. Cromwell's military success was blemished by massacres of Catholic rebels in Ireland. Cromwell believed in religious liberty only for the "godly." In December 1653, Cromwell established a protectorate that remained in place until his death in 1658, when his son Richard, known as "Tumble-down Dick," became protector. Richard was weak, and when the monarchy was restored in 1660, Charles II became king. R. Kee, *The Green Flag, The Most Distressful Country* (1972); Edwards, *supra*.

Although Charles II called for pardons, reprisals occurred. Cromwell's body was exhumed, decapitated, and his skull was set on a spike. The Anglican Church was restored. Monarchs might continue to believe in divine right, but they owed their position to Parliament. Charles II, who had many mistresses but no heir, ruled until 1685.

His brother, the Catholic James II, succeeded him. Three years later, after Protestant leaders invited William of Orange to invade England, James II was allowed to escape to France. William's mother was Charles I's daughter, Mary, and William's wife, also named Mary, was a Protestant daughter of James II, so the kingdom remained linked to the family when King William III and Queen Mary II agreed in 1689 to rule as constitutional monarchs.

During this Glorious Revolution, Parliament's authority increased dramatically. The Habeas Corpus Act had been passed in 1679. Parliament passed the 1689 Bill of Rights, limiting the power of the Crown. Catholics were barred from the throne. A Toleration Act permitted Non-Conformists to hold services, and Catholics were denied freedom of worship but were no longer prosecuted. Non-Conformists and Catholics were banned from public service. Edwards, *supra*; Thorn, Lockyer & Smith, *supra*; N. Cantor, *Imagining the Law* (1997).

William III died in 1702 after he was thrown by his horse, and James II's daughter, Anne, an Anglican, became the final Stuart monarch. At the time of her death in 1714, property owners dominated Parliament, religious fervor had diminished, and the eighteenth century was becoming the Age of Reason. Miller, *supra*.

The eighteenth century also brought the American Revolution. Following the Declaration of Independence in 1776, the nation's founders created a government informed by their knowledge of English history. They protected individual freedom with constitutional safeguards such as habeas corpus, and they ensured the separation of church and state through the establishment clause of the First Amendment: "Congress shall make no law respecting an establishment of religion, or prohibiting the full exercise thereof." The phrase "a hedge or wall of separation" was first used by Roger Williams, founder of the Rhode Island Colony. It was popularized by Thomas Jefferson. A.R. Amar, *America's Constitution* (2005).

Parliament was a blueprint for the two houses of Congress. The Constitution stated that the members of Congress would meet annually, be elected for fixed terms, and be paid from the national treasury. Congress would decide where to locate the permanent national district. The powers of the legislative branch, the executive branch, and the federal courts were separated into Articles I, II, and III.

English common law contained no mechanism for removing a monarch, but the Constitution provided for a president to be impeached. By a majority vote, the House of Representatives, acting as a special grand jury, could impeach the president "for treason, bribery and other high crimes and misdemeanors." The Senate was empowered to try an impeached defendant with the chief justice presiding. President Andrew Johnson was impeached in 1868, as was President Bill Clinton in 1998, but both were acquitted. Neither was in danger of losing his head.

2

James Wilson
An Unknown American Founder

Wilson's mind is "one blaze of light."
————Benjamin Rush

America's founders are household names. George Washington, John Adams, Thomas Jefferson, and James Madison are known by almost everyone. All became presidents. Benjamin Franklin is world famous. Alexander Hamilton and Aaron Burr fought a notorious duel. John Hancock's signature remains iconic. But what about James Wilson?

Wilson was one of the major creators of the Constitution. "The outstanding legal theorist of America in the latter eighteenth century," he was the "Father of Article III." And he fought for popular sovereignty. Yet, Wilson is largely unknown in the country he helped design.

Although he provided the words "pursuit of happiness" instead of "property" in the Declaration of Independence, in later years his pursuit of property made Wilson a tragic figure. His public-spirited devotion to the formation of a new government competed with his private ambition to buy vast tracts of the new land. Wilson's vision of America has endured, but his identity as a Founding Father, tinged with scandal, has faded with time.

Born in 1742 in Caskardy, Scotland, the son of a farmer in the egalitarian county of Fifeshire, Wilson attended the Universities of St. Andrews, Edinburgh, and Glasgow. He studied Greek, Latin, philosophy, and mathematics. Wilson was exposed to the Scottish Enlightenment and the idea of earthly happiness replacing religious salvation. His devout Calvinist parents wanted him to prepare for the ministry, but when his father died, Wilson abandoned his studies. He tried tutoring and accounting. Finally, in 1765, the 23-year-old Scotsman borrowed money and sailed from Glasgow to New York City and then headed for Philadelphia, the largest and most cosmopolitan city of the 13 colonies. Wilson never returned to Scotland.

Wilson taught Greek, Latin, and rhetoric at the College of Philadelphia. Because he admired Cicero, he strove to become an orator, speaking in the ornate, flowery manner of the time. Wilson received an honorary master's degree in 1766, but he wanted to be a lawyer, so he apprenticed under John Dickinson, a champion of colonial rights. Through Dickinson, he was swept into the political maelstrom between American colonists and the British Empire. There was a new society to be created. Legal philosophy and history were now hot topics. This was a golden age of lawyers. Always happiest in his library working out abstract ideas, Wilson glowed with confidence.

No New Taxes

Intense friction had developed between Britain and the American colonies over taxation and was exacerbated by the enforcement of the Sugar Act of 1764. The earlier Molasses Act of 1733, which imposed a duty on imported molasses from countries other than the British West Indies, was accepted by Americans as a tariff regulating trade. Although the Sugar Act lowered the tax rate, it created a bureaucracy to ensure its collection and began doing so, to the chagrin of Americans—this was a tax meant not to regulate trade but to raise revenue.

Next, Britain's Parliament imposed the Stamp Act on "all legal documents, newspapers, pamphlets, almanacs, playing cards and dice." Then came the Townshend Duties, taxing manufactured imports, including tea. In New York City, Wilson saw riotous meetings and heard riotous talk everywhere of parliamentary tyranny. The lack of American representation in Parliament was an idea that stirred Wilson. He was part of this turbulent scene.

Time Out for Love

In 1767 he became a member of the bar and began his legal career in the industrial and trading town of Reading, Pennsylvania, 50 miles northwest of Philadelphia. Wilson, often pictured as an aloof, unromantic figure with soda-bottle eyeglasses and a white wig, soon found love. Before he left Philadelphia, Wilson and his friend William (Billy) White, who later became Pennsylvania's Episcopalian bishop, began writing a series of columns signed "The Visitant" for the *Pennsylvania Chronicle and Universal Advertiser*. The first article appeared on February 1, 1768, and the opening sentence declared, "Our happiness is the final end of our existence." Although later columns turned to erudite philosophical subjects, the most popular column assured readers of The Visitant's veneration for ladies and the qualities of the feminine mind.

Meanwhile, Wilson's law practice grew. He represented Reading's two most prominent citizens, Colonel John Patton and his stepson, Mark Bird, whose sister Rachel was a charming young heiress. Wilson visited Rachel at the family estate at Birdsboro and fell in love. Rachel resisted, saying she intended never to marry. After more than a year, Wilson won Rachel's consent. They were married on November 5, 1771, and moved to a house Wilson bought in a Scotch-Irish settlement in Carlisle, the seat of Cumberland County. In 1774 his political career began there, when he was elected to the Carlisle Committee of Correspondence, which voiced its resistance to British policy. C.P. Smith, *James Wilson* (1956); C. Cushman, ed., *The Supreme Court Justices* (1993).

Short Message

During this time, the fire of political debate surrounded Wilson. In 1768 Wilson made his own passionate argument against Parliament's authority over the colonies, writing "with the view and expectation of being able to trace some constitutional line between those cases in which we ought, and those in which we ought not, to acknowledge the power of Parliament over us." When his treatise, "Considerations on the Nature and Extent of the Legislative Authority of the British Parliament," was published in 1774, Wilson was recognized as an American constitutional leader.

R.G. McCloskey, vol. 1, *Justices of the United States Supreme Court, 1789–1969* (1969).

The treatise title was long, but the message was short. Wilson denied the "legislative authority of the British Parliament over the colonies . . . in every instance." The message resonated in the Continental Congress. In 1787 Wilson took his concept of "popular sovereignty" and "human rights" with him to the Constitutional Convention in Philadelphia. C. Becker, *The Declaration of Independence* (1969); B. Wilson, ed., *Works of James Wilson* (1804).

Unlike his more radical colleagues in Massachusetts and Virginia, Wilson stopped short of moving for total separation. He strove to maintain a link between the colonies and Great Britain and believed the American colonists owed their "obedience and loyalty" to "the Kings of Great Britain." His claim that Parliament had no power over American colonists because they were not represented, yet owed allegiance to the English monarch, foreshadowed Great Britain's Dominion (or Commonwealth) policy. Wilson's treatise was written before those by Adams and Jefferson, who authored their own polemics. A.H. Kelly & W.A. Harbison, *The American Constitution* (1955); M.D. Hall, *The Political and Legal Philosophy of James Wilson 1742–1798* (1997).

Independence

Tension rocketed as Britain and the American colonists faced immediate conflict. Wilson, lawyer and politician, now became Wilson, the officer. He received a commission as colonel in the Fourth Battalion of the County of Cumberland in 1775 and was promoted to brigadier general in 1782.

As violence heightened, Wilson, who had been elected to the Pennsylvania Assembly, was sent as a delegate to the 1776 Second Continental Congress. Pennsylvania was split between reconciliation and war. Militant Americans were determined to demand independence. In June Wilson supported a delay on the decision, but on July 2, Wilson joined Benjamin Franklin and John Morton to vote for the Declaration of Independence. They constituted a majority of the seven-member delegation because John Dickinson, Wilson's former mentor, and John Morris refused to appear, and two other members opposed the Declaration.

On July 4, 1776, more than a year after hostilities began, the Declaration of Independence was adopted. Jefferson, the author, used the phrase "life, liberty and the pursuit of happiness" instead of John Locke's "life, liberty and property." Wilson had stated in his treatise that government was founded "to increase the happiness of the governed." Wilson, Franklin, Morton, Morris, and five Pennsylvania delegates who were later added signed the Declaration of Independence. Dickinson and the two opposition members did not.

Constitutional Convention

Bickering continued among the 13 semi-autonomous states and made any assertion of federal sovereignty impossible. In 1787 the inadequacies of the Confederation led to the Constitutional Convention.

In May 1787, 55 delegates from 12 of the 13 states began to arrive at Independence Hall in Philadelphia. Twenty-four were lawyers. The deliberations lasted from May 25 to September 17. Several famous founding fathers were not present, including John Adams and Thomas Jefferson. Also absent were John Jay, Samuel Adams, John Hancock, Thomas Paine, Richard Henry Lee, and Patrick Henry.

Virginia (pop. 747,610) and Pennsylvania (pop. 484,373) led the large states. Small states such as Delaware (pop. 59,096) and Georgia (pop. 82,548) were reluctant to participate. Rhode Island not only did not attend but also did not ratify the Constitution until 1790, after Washington was inaugurated president.

Wilson led Pennsylvania's host delegation, which also included such major figures as Gouverneur Morris, Benjamin Rush, Jared Ingersoll, Robert Morris, and 81-year-old Benjamin Franklin. An imposing figure, Franklin was carried to the Convention in a sedan chair.

Among Virginia's seven delegates were George Washington, George Mason, Edmund Randolph, and James Madison. Washington was reluctant, but Madison implored him to attend, and he was unanimously elected the presiding officer. The delegates brought the Virginia Plan (Virginia Resolves)—and a strategy. They would convince the Convention delegates that America should be a nation with proportional representation, rather than a confederation.

Under the Articles of Confederation, each of the 13 states could cast one vote regardless of population. This was the "one state/one vote" rule. Coming into the Convention, the small states were fearful of losing this parity with the larger states.

With the backing of Pennsylvania, the Virginia delegation pushed its 15 Resolves. Its strong national government proposed a single executive, a unicameral legislature, and an independent judiciary. Wilson and Madison argued vociferously for this concept.

On June 14 William Paterson presented his state's New Jersey Plan, which advocated revising the Articles of Confederation rather than creating a new constitution. The Convention faced a crisis, but Connecticut's Roger Sherman structured a compromise: Each state would have two senators and one representative for each 30,000 inhabitants. This broke the impasse. The small states were placated by equal Senate representation. And the large states achieved popular sovereignty in the House of Representatives.

Wilson, Madison, Hamilton, and Gouverneur Morris formed a hard federalist bloc that was principally responsible for creating the Constitution. Wilson was a politically conservative revolutionary. His dogma was democratic nationalism. M.E. Bradford, *Founding Fathers* (1994).

The Sources

Wilson explored the incremental development of England's "unwritten" constitution, which benefited from a rich reservoir of about 565 writings dating from the Dooms of Aethelberht in 601 AD. These included:

- The writers: Locke (*Second Treatise on Government*, 1690); Coke (Institutes, common law); Glanville; Bracton (*On the Laws and Customs of England*); Milton; Harrington; Reid; Aristotle; Cicero; Bacon; Blackstone (*Commentaries on the Laws of England, 1765–1769*); Montesquieu (*Spirit of the Laws*, separation of powers); Rousseau (*Social Contract*); and Vattel (*Le Droit des Gens, 1758*).
- The most salient writings: Magna Carta (1215), Petition of Right (1628), Habeas Corpus Act (1679), Bill of Rights (1689), Toleration Act (1689), and the Triennial Act (1694).
- The English experience: political powers divided between the monarch (one), House of Lords (few), and House of Commons (many); evolution of binding legal precedence in following common law decisions; limitation of power by checks and balances; concept of natural rights; fundamental law written in a fixed document; evolution of the concepts of law of the land (1215) and due process (1348); limitation of the monarch's

power (1215); judicial review (1610); evolution of the rights to trial by jury and habeas corpus; and limitations on the government's power in search and seizure, religious freedom, and popular sovereignty. W.S. Churchill, *A History of the English-Speaking Peoples, The Birth of Britain* (1956); C.S. & F.G. Marcham, eds., *Sources of English Constitutional History* (1937).

- The American colonial experience: royal charters; state constitutions; the Virginia Bill of Rights; Mayflower Compact; Fundamental Orders of Connecticut (1748); concept of a written constitution; compact theory of the state; concept of constitutional supremacy and limited legislative capacity; American experience with federalism under the British Empire; and the Articles of Confederation. Kelly & Harbison, *supra*.

From these constitutional historical sources, Wilson created a template with popular sovereignty for the new American government. His solution was to divide political power among the legislative, executive, and judicial branches, using checks and balances to limit the power of each; and to create a judiciary that would be coequal with the legislative and executive branches, limiting the power of both.

Wilson's Ideas

Wilson's belief in popular sovereignty led to the substitution of "We the people of the United States . . ." for "We the people and the states . . ." in the Preamble. The American people were parties to the Constitution.

Wilson wanted a strong executive popularly elected by the people as the best safeguard against tyranny and ruled out other proposals, including one calling for a triumvirate. The delegates agreed to one executive but disagreed with direct elections. Wilson proposed the Electoral College as a compromise. Presidential electors selected in each state would meet and choose the executive. His proposal was accepted as a buffer against popular sovereignty. Although Wilson preferred a three-year term with the right to seek re-election, the delegates decided on four years. Kelly & Harbison, *supra*; C. Berkin, *A Brilliant Solution* (2002); M. Farrand, *Records of the Federal Convention of 1787* (four vols., 1911–37).

Wilson proposed the popular election of members of both the House of Representatives and the Senate. He won his battle with respect to representatives, but senators would be appointed by the state legislatures. Madison noted Wilson "entered elaborately into the defence [sic] of a proportional representation, stating for his first position that as all authority was derived from the people, equal numbers of people ought to have an equal number of representatives." Farrand, *supra*.

Allied with wealthy businessmen, Wilson had experienced mob violence in Philadelphia in 1778, and this may have influenced him to support the protections of the presidential veto and the principle of judicial review. Hall, *supra*.

Wilson fought against the use of hereditary titles. "Our manners, our laws, the abolition of entails and of primogeniture, the whole genius of the people are opposed to it," he noted. Wilson's efforts were rewarded. Article I, Sections 9 and 10 of the Constitution mandate: "No Title of Nobility shall be granted by the United States" and "No State shall . . . grant any Title of Nobility." Wilson's efforts also were significant in adding to Section 10, "No state shall . . . pass any . . . Law . . . impairing the Obligations of Contracts." C. Van Doren, *The Great Rehearsal* (1948).

Framer of Federal Judiciary

Wilson's greatest gift to America was the U.S. Supreme Court and the federal judiciary. He was called the Father of Article III, which created the judicial branch of the government. Wilson shaped a federal judiciary with appellate jurisdiction over state courts. He argued for judicial independence. He wanted lower federal courts with judicial appointments by the president. And he successfully argued against the president's right to remove justices. Smith, *supra*.

Most of all, Wilson wanted the right of judicial review. He believed that Congress, subject to prejudice and passion, might pass unconstitutional laws. Judicial review would be a check. In England Lord Coke had ruled in *Dr. Bonham's Case*, 8 Co. 113b, 118a, 77 Eng. Rep. 646, 652 (1610):

> And it appears in our books, that in many cases, the common law will controul [sic] Acts of Parliament, and sometimes adjudge them to be utterly void: for when an Act of Parliament is against common right and reason, or repugnant, or impossible to be performed, the common law will controul [sic] it, and adjudge such Act to be void.

C.J. Friedrich observes: "[O]ne can see here the clear basis for judicial review of legislative acts as it later became reality under the written constitution of the United States." Judicial review, accepted in colonial and state courts, however, never was written into the Constitution. Farrand, *supra*; C.J. Friedrich, *The Philosophy of Law in Historical Perspective* (1963).

Wilson opposed restrictions against foreigners sitting as federal judges and holding federal office. Seven of the Convention delegates including Wilson were immigrants from England, Scotland, Ireland, and the West Indies. Yet the restrictions were strongly debated. Wilson, who was ambitious to serve on the Supreme Court, considered such exclusion "one of the most galling chains which the human mind could experience to deprive the government of the talents, virtue and abilities of such foreigners as might choose to remove to this country."

Finally, the Convention agreed to require at least seven years of citizenship for representatives, nine for senators, but none for Supreme Court justices. Only the chief executive had to be native born or a citizen at the time the Constitution was adopted. Farrand, *supra*; R.G. Ferris & J.H. Charleton, *Signers of the Constitution* (1986); C.D. Bowen, *Miracle at Philadelphia* (1986); U.S. Constitution, art. I §§ 2, 3, art. II § 1.

Wilson also opposed both oaths and religious qualifications for officeholders. He claimed that a good government did not need oaths and "a bad one could not or ought not to be supported." Many states required officeholders to take a religious oath that discriminated against Catholics, Jews, unbelievers, and Deists. The delegates agreed to an oath to support the Constitution but rejected any religious qualification. Article VI states, "but no religious Test shall ever be required as a Qualification to any Office or public Trust under the United States." Bowen, *supra*.

Wilson had a major role in drafting the treason clause in Article III. As a lawyer, he had defended several Philadelphia Quaker Tory merchants charged with treason. Wilson argued that a conviction should require two witnesses to an overt act of treason. The judges, following English law, decided a lesser degree of proof was adequate. Three of Wilson's clients were acquitted; the others were found guilty and hanged. This had a profound impact on Wilson. He persuaded the Convention that the treason clause must require two witnesses to "the same overt act" rather than two witnesses to "an act." U.S. Constitution, art. III § 3; Farrand, *supra*; Smith, *supra*; Hall, *supra*.

Slavery

Slavery was sharply debated but not resolved. Claiming slavery's abolition was inevitable, Wilson wrote, "[A]nd though the period is more distant than I could wish, yet it will produce the same kind of gradual change for the whole nation as was pursued in Pennsylvania." He continued, "The day will come when the American people will turn their views to the great principles of humanity and demand that all slaves be freed." He forecast that Congress "would never allow slaves in any of the new states." He was wrong. Berkin, *supra*; Hall, *supra*; Smith, *supra*; Farrand, *supra*; Bradford, *supra*.

Final Draft

On July 26, Wilson, John Rutledge, Edmund Randolph, Nathaniel Gorham, and Oliver Ellsworth were appointed to the Committee of Detail to organize a final draft of the Constitution. Wilson was the committee's most active member and strongest nationalist. He was the probable draftsman of its final report. The states righters insisted on Article 1, Section 8, which enumerates the congressional powers. On August 6, when the delegates reconvened, the draft of the new Constitution was read. For the next five weeks, the delegates continued the debate. On September 8, the Convention finished its work and appointed a Committee on Style to "revise the stile [*sic*] and arrange the articles." Four days later, the final draft of the Constitution, written almost entirely by Gouverneur Morris, was complete.

On September 17, 1787, the Constitution was signed by 39 of the 55 delegates. Twenty-two signers, including Wilson, were lawyers. Seven signers were educated in Great Britain. Six signers, including Wilson, signed both the Constitution and the Declaration of Independence. Ferris & Charleton, *supra*.

Ratification

The Convention's final act was ratification by the states. Wilson successfully bypassed the state legislatures by joining with other federalists in urging the submission of the Constitution to popularly elected state conventions. But how many of the 13 state conventions would be required to ratify? Ratification by all 13 was impossible—Rhode Island had refused even to send a delegate. New York's Robert Yates and John Lansing had left the Convention on July 10.

Wilson argued that seven states could ratify. This caused immediate turmoil. Other delegates moved for 10 and nine. Wilson then
raised his number to nine. But if fewer than 13 states ratified, all
states would be under a Constitution that some had refused to accept. Wilson saw a way to win: "We must, in this case, go to the
original powers of society. The house on fire must be extinguished
without a scrupulous regard to ordinary rights." The Constitution
would apply only to the ratifying states. The Convention agreed.

The ratification process was tumultuous. Wilson began his pro-
ratification defense of the Constitution with his "State House Yard
Speech" on October 6, 1787. It rivaled the Federalist Papers in
popularity and was so effective, Washington had it reprinted for
use at other ratification conventions. It ultimately appeared in 34
newspapers in 12 states. Wilson's enemies derided his Scottish an-
cestry, calling him "James of Caledonia." Because of his efforts,
however, Pennsylvania became the second state to ratify, on December 12, 1787. When Wilson returned to Carlisle to celebrate at
an outdoor bonfire victory rally on December 27, anti-federalists
armed with clubs attacked him. Wilson fought back but was
knocked to the ground. Berkin, *supra*; Bowen, *supra*.

On June 21, 1788, New Hampshire became the ninth state to
ratify. The Constitution was now law.

Wilson Speaks

Wilson had resettled his family in Philadelphia in 1778. When
America's new government moved from New York to Philadelphia in 1790, the College of Philadelphia announced an introductory lecture by the Honorable James Wilson, Esq., to take place at
6 PM, December 15. Benjamin Franklin was a founder of the college, which became the University of Pennsylvania. Wilson was its
first law professor. President Washington, Vice President John
Adams, and members of the first Congress attended. Wilson was
awarded a Doctor of Laws degree. He considered this occasion
the apex of his career.

Wilson told his audience that America "has been eminently distinguished by the love of liberty and the love of law." He cautioned, however:

> Law and liberty cannot rationally become objects of our love,
> unless they first become the objects of our knowledge. . . . In-
> deed, neither of them can be known, because neither of them

can exist, without the other. Without liberty, law . . . becomes oppression. Without law, liberty . . . becomes licentiousness.

The language of the law was then, as now, a concern:

Some, (lawyers and judges) indeed, involve themselves in a thick mist of art; and use a language unknown to all, but those of the profession. By such, the knowledge of the law, like the mysteries of some ancient divinity, is confined to its initiated votaries; as if all others were in duty bound blindly to obey. But this ought not to be the case.

Smith, *supra*.

Associate Justice

Wilson sent a letter to President Washington requesting his appointment as Chief Justice of the U.S. Supreme Court. Instead, on September 24, 1789, Washington appointed him an associate justice. He was the first justice to be sworn in. On February 1, 1790, the U.S. Supreme Court convened in the Exchange Building in New York City. Smith, *supra*.

During his tenure on the Court, Justice Wilson's work was adequate. For the first three years, the Supreme Court had no cases to decide, but the federal circuit courts presided over by Supreme Court justices were busy. Wilson wrote 20 pages in his six decisions. His most noteworthy case was *Chisholm v. Georgia*, 2 Dall. 419 (1793). Wilson argued that a state was amenable to suit in a federal court by a citizen of another state. Two South Carolinians had sued the state of Georgia. Wilson said, "[A]s to the purposes of the Union, therefore, Georgia is not a sovereign state." The people had made a compact directly with the United States of America. The reaction to this decision led to the Eleventh Amendment to the Constitution in 1795, which denied this right to sue.

Wilson was on the Court when the case of *Hylton v. United States*, 3 Dall. 409 (1796), was heard. *Hylton* demonstrated the Supreme Court's concept of judicial review before *Marbury*. The issue was the constitutionality of the Carriage Tax Act of 1794, a federal statute. Wilson did not participate in the decision because he had presided over the case in the circuit court. In ruling the statute valid, Justice Samuel Chase alluded to the concept of judicial review, stating:

26

It is unnecessary, at this time, for me to determine, whether this court, constitutionally possesses the power to declare an act of Congress void, on the ground of its being made contrary to, and in violation of, the Constitution. . . . if the court have such power, I am free to declare that I will never exercise it, but in a very clear case.

R.P. Frankel, Jr., "Before *Marbury: Hylton v. United States* and the Origins of Judicial Review," *Journal of Supreme Court History* (2003).

Wilson's great desire to be Chief Justice was never fulfilled. Washington appointed John Jay the Court's first, and in 1795 Wilson again was bypassed when Washington appointed John Rutledge. After the Senate rejected Rutledge's appointment, Washington appointed Oliver Ellsworth. It is possible that Washington was offended by Wilson's brashness in asking for the appointment. Washington had hired Wilson to tutor his nephew, Bushrod, and some gossiped that Washington thought Wilson overcharged for the lessons. Later, when Bushrod Washington was 36, he was appointed to the U.S. Supreme Court by President John Adams.

More likely, it was the specter of Wilson's financial disaster as a land speculator that influenced Washington. Fear of disgrace upon the Court may have been the reason Wilson never won the top post.

Unhappy Ending

As the future of the nation was being secured, Wilson's personal life was collapsing. Wilson's pursuit of property had resulted in a huge, entangled mass of land-based debts. It was common knowledge that his financial empire was tottering.

In an earlier blow, Wilson had lost his wife Rachel, who died in Philadelphia on April 14, 1786, at the age of 39. Despite her early protest that she had no desire to marry, she had been a loyal wife and the mother of six children, the youngest an infant.

Wilson rode the Supreme Court circuit in the 1790s, sometimes with his friend and fellow Supreme Court Justice James Iredell of Edenton, North Carolina. In 1793 Wilson found a brief escape from his financial worries. He attended a church meeting in Boston and noticed a young lady sitting nearby. He was soon romancing 19-year-old Hannah Grey. Wilson was 51. He married Hannah, a strict Quaker, on September 19. His children welcomed her. Smith, *supra*.

Soon, Wilson plunged into new land schemes supported by high interest loans. Justice Iredell wrote his wife that Wilson might resign from the Court. He did not. His money crisis escalated, and his health deteriorated. Hannah, pregnant, delivered a son, Henry, on May 12, 1796.

There was a speculation panic. Businesses were failing, and prominent men were going to jail. Wilson and Hannah hid at Morris Tavern in Bethlehem, Pennsylvania, while his lawyer and his son Bird tried to settle judgments against him. Wilson went alone to Burlington, New Jersey, where a creditor found him. Unable to post bail, he was jailed. The future seemed bleak.

Bird raised money, and Wilson journeyed south. Hannah joined him in Edenton, North Carolina, at the Horniblow Tavern. Pierce Butler, a former senator from South Carolina, found him there, and Wilson again was incarcerated for reneging on a $197,000 debt. There was no money. Wilson came down with malaria and said he was hunted "like a wild beast."

Wilson's health briefly improved, and he wrote to Bird with new plans to settle with his creditors. But there was no time. Wilson relapsed and suffered a stroke. Hannah stayed at his bedside for three nights until Justice Iredell took her away. Wilson died on August 21, 1798, and was buried at Hayes Plantation in North Carolina, owned by Justice Iredell's father-in-law, because his family could not afford to have his body moved to Philadelphia. There was no eulogy by the Supreme Court. Hall, *supra*; Wilson, *supra*; Smith, *supra*; Cushman, *supra*.

In 1906 the James Wilson Memorial Committee arranged for Wilson's remains to be removed to Philadelphia for burial in the yard of Christ Church. A state funeral was held, with Justice Oliver Wendell Holmes, Jr., and Chief Justice Melville Fuller leading the funeral cortege. This time Justice D. Edward White of the U.S. Supreme Court and Andrew Carnegie gave eulogies. President Theodore Roosevelt said, "I can not do better than base my theory of governmental action upon the words and deeds of one of Pennsylvania's greatest sons, Justice James Wilson." Cushman, *supra*; Hall, *supra*; Historical Society of Pennsylvania, *Who Was Who During the American Revolution* (1976).

Afterword

Wilson's son Bird served as a Pennsylvania judge but resigned because of his opposition to capital punishment. He became an

Episcopal clergyman and editor of his father's works. Henry, Wilson's son with Hannah, died in infancy. D. Malone, *Story of the Declaration of Independence* (1975).

Self-government for colonies within the British Empire was established when dominion status was granted to Canada, Australia, New Zealand, and the Union of South Africa. Wilson had anticipated the British Foreign Office by more than 70 years. Hall, *supra*. Wilson's concept of a Supreme Court with judicial review became reality when Chief Justice John Marshall made his landmark decision in *Marbury v. Madison*, 1 Cranch 137, 2 L. Ed. 60 (1803). The Supreme Court became the protector of the Constitution. H.J. Abraham, *Justices, Presidents and Senators* (1999); Kelly & Harbison, *supra*; U.S. Constitution, art. III; Hall, *supra*.

The Electoral College still exists in presidential elections, but the states established popular election of presidential electors, and they now represent political parties. Kelly & Harbison, *supra*.

In 1861 secessionists claimed the Constitutional Convention had created a compact between the federal government and the states. But President Abraham Lincoln used Wilson's words in the Preamble, "We the People of the United States," not "We the People of the United States and the states," to prove the "people" and not the states had created an indissoluble bond with the federal government. They had executed a constitutional compact through their ratification conventions. Smith, *supra*; Kelly & Harbison, *supra*.

Although Wilson was successful in establishing popular sovereignty for elections to the House of Representatives, his efforts for popular sovereignty for the Senate were thwarted. Popular sovereignty for the Senate was established in 1913, with the passage of the Seventeenth Amendment.

In *Wesberry v. Sanders*, 376 U.S. 1 (1964), Justice Hugo Black looked back to Justice Wilson, stating:

> Soon after the Constitution was adopted, James Wilson of Pennsylvania, by then an Associate Justice of this Court, gave a series of lectures at Philadelphia in which, drawing on his experience as one of the most active members of the Constitutional Convention, he said: "[A]ll Elections ought to be equal."

Black quoted Wilson to support the one-man/one-vote principle in a case involving the constitutionality of Georgia's legislative apportionment system. R.G. McCloskey maintains, "Wilson was the only really helpful eighteenth century authority the Justice could invoke for the very good reason that he was the only one of the framers who had unequivocally expressed himself in favor of the principle." Smith, *supra*; McCloskey, *supra*.

As a result of Wilson's insistence on allowing foreigners to serve the government, six U.S. Supreme Court justices including Wilson were foreign born. The others were James Iredell, England; William Paterson, Ireland; David Brewer, Turkey; George Sutherland, England; and Felix Frankfurter, Austria.

Wilson, as a constitutional architect, had a message for future interpreters of the Constitution: "We should consider that we are providing a Constitution for future generations, and not merely for the peculiar circumstances of the moment." Smith, *supra*.

3

The 1798 Sedition Act
President's Party Prosecutes Press

Perhaps it is a universal truth that the loss of liberty at home is to be charged to provisions against danger, real or pretended, from abroad.
————James Madison, letter to Thomas Jefferson, May 1798

The best of times in the new United States of America was followed by the worst of times. The golden age of the founders ended with President George Washington's farewell address in 1796 warning of the dangers of foreign alliances and party politics. As with children left in a schoolroom without the teacher present, chaos ensued. Political parties appeared and attacked each other with vitriolic fervor. Foreign alliances divided the country. The notorious Alien and Sedition Act was passed.

France and Britain were at war. Vice President Thomas Jefferson and his Republican (later Democratic) Party embraced France and popular sovereignty. President John Adams, Washington's successor, and the Federalists despised the excesses of the French Revolution and tilted American neutrality toward Britain.

When President Adams sent three envoys to Paris to negotiate a treaty ending French attacks on American shipping, they were confronted by Talleyrand agents demanding bribes. The agents were referred to by initials, and the XYZ Affair helped the Federalist cause by arousing patriotism. Adams began a "half-war" against France, with Congress authorizing an expanded army and a Department of the Navy. Federalist popularity soared as fear of war increased. J.M. Smith, *Freedom's Fetters* (1956); A. Mapp Jr., *Thomas Jefferson* (1987).

Then the Federalists went too far. Dark forces prevailed. Congress passed the 1798 Alien and Sedition Act into law after debating its constitutionality along party lines. The Sedition Act punished anyone who conspired to oppose any measure of the government. More chilling, the act provided for the prosecution of persons writing, printing, uttering, or publishing "any false, scandalous and malicious writing" with intent to defame. This included material that brought the federal government, the Congress, or the president into contempt or disrepute, or that excited the hatred of the good people of the United States. It notably omitted Vice President Jefferson from its protection. Alexander Hamilton pushed for enforcement. No one was ever deported under the companion Alien Act. The Sedition Act was used as a political tool. A. Lewis, *Make No Law* (1991).

In the Sedition Act, truth could be used as a defense. Proof of malicious intent was required, and the jury would decide guilt. But Federalist judges did not require the government to prove statements false. No op-ed pieces were allowed under this law. Malice was presumed, and intent to defame was inferred from words that had a "bad tendency," as in the English common law of seditious libel. Juries were charged so that their only decision was whether the accused had published the offending statement. Punishment called for up to two years in prison and $2,000 in fines. The law's expiration date was March 3, 1801—the day before President Adams's term ended. E. Knappman, ed. *Great American Trials* (1994).

By that time, publishers of leading Republican newspapers had been tried, and other papers ceased publication. Writers were imprisoned. Adams's reputation was forever tainted. The Federalist Party came to an end. Fallout from the act continued after Jefferson became president. Flamboyant scandalmonger James Callender, who was tried under the law, had earlier spread the story of Alexander Hamilton's extramarital affair and would later turn on

Jefferson. U.S. Supreme Court Justice Samuel Chase, who presided at Callender's trial, was impeached by the Jeffersonian Congress, and Chase's acquittal preserved federal judicial independence. All this was dramatic proof of the unintended consequences of the misuse of partisan political power. Callender's trial, along with the trials of Matthew Lyon, Anthony Haswell, David Brown, and Thomas Cooper, highlighted the partisan bias of the Sedition Act. F. Wharton, *State Trials of the United States* (1849, reprinted 1970).

Benjamin Franklin Bache, named after his grandfather, was publisher of the Republican newspaper *Aurora* in Philadelphia. He prompted passage of the Sedition Act when he published a copy of a letter by Talleyrand, the French foreign minister, which convinced Federalists of a connection between Republicans and France. He was indicted under the prevailing common law for libeling Adams and his administration, but he died of yellow fever before his trial.

Matthew Lyon, a Republican congressman from Vermont, was the first to fall under the act. He was born in Ireland and fought in the Revolutionary War. The Green Mountain Boys endorsed his election. In January 1798, Federalist Roger Griswold of Connecticut confronted Lyon in the House of Representatives and attacked his war record. Lyon ignored him, but when Griswold grabbed his coat and repeated the insult, Lyon spit in his eye. Although the Federalists attempted to expel Lyon from the House, they lacked the necessary two-thirds vote. The sedition law settled the score. B. Neff, "Fracas in Congress," *Essays in History* 41 (1999).

In October 1799, Lyon was indicted on three charges. The first count, which asserted that his intent was to "stir up sedition and to bring the president and government of the United States into contempt," accused him of the following libelous matter in a letter to the editor of the *Vermont Journal* of Windsor, Vermont:

> As to the Executive, when I shall see the efforts of that power bent on the promotion of the comfort, the happiness, and accommodation of the people, that executive shall have my zealous and uniform support; but whenever I shall, on the part of the Executive, see every consideration of the public welfare swallowed up in a continual grasp for power, in an unbounded thirst for ridiculous pomp, foolish adulation, and selfish avarice; when I shall behold men of real merit daily

turned out of office, for no other cause but independency of sentiment; when I shall see men of firmness, merit, years, abilities, and experience, discarded in their applications for office, for fear they possess that independence, and men of meanness preferred for the ease with which they take up and advocate opinions, the consequence of which they know but little of—when I shall see the sacred name of religion employed as a state engine to make mankind hate and persecute one another, I shall not be their humble advocate.

The second count charged Lyon with publishing a letter said to be from a French diplomat. The letter included the statement that the president was "telling the world that although he should succeed in treating with the French, there was no dependence to be placed on any of their engagements, that their religion and morality were at an end, that they would turn into pirates and plunderers, and it would be necessary to be perpetually armed against them, though you were at peace: we wondered that the answer of both Houses had not been an order to send him to a mad house." The third count charged Lyon with aiding in this publication.

After the prosecution rested, Lyon said the court had no jurisdiction, the act of Congress being unconstitutional and void, if not so generally, at least as to writings composed before its passage. Second, the publication was innocent. Third, the contents were true. He called Supreme Court Justice William Paterson, the presiding circuit judge, and asked him whether he had not frequently dined with the president and observed his "ridiculous pomp and parade." The judge replied that he had sometimes, though rarely, dined with the president, but he had never seen any pomp or parade, but a great deal of plainness and simplicity. Wharton, *supra*.

Justice Paterson charged the jury that its only decision was whether Lyon's statement could have been made with "any other intent than that of making odious or contemptible the President and government, and bring them both into disrepute." The jury convicted Lyon, and he was sentenced to four months in prison, with a $1,000 fine and $60.96 in court costs.

Lyon became a populist folk hero and was reelected to Congress while in prison. When his sentence ended on February 9, 1799, he had no money and would have remained imprisoned, but Republican leaders contributed to a fund, and Senator Stevens T. Mason of Virginia ceremoniously paid the sum in gold to the court. Lyon exited the jail as a parade passed by in his honor. The Federalists lost the first round. More than 40 years later, on July 4, 1840, a bill to pay Lyon's fine with interest was passed by Congress, disavowing the Sedition Act. Lewis, *supra*; Wharton, *supra*.

Anthony Haswell, a supporter of Lyon, was indicted in May 1800 because of an advertisement in the *Vermont Gazette*, which he edited. Calling for the collection of funds to pay Lyon's fine, he wrote of the "oppressive hand of usurped power" that punished Lyon and "the indignities . . . heaped upon him from a hard-hearted savage." (Lyon had written a letter from jail recounting his bad treatment by the jailer.) Reprinted from the *Aurora* was a claim that Tories were holding government office. Justice Paterson again presided and charged the jury, which returned quickly with a verdict of guilty. Haswell was sentenced to a fine of $200 and two months' imprisonment. In 1844, as in Lyon's case, Congress passed legislation refunding this fine to the defendant's representatives with interest. Wharton, *supra*.

The 1800 trial of pamphleteer Thomas Cooper in Philadelphia with Justice Samuel Chase presiding was more remarkable for its aftermath than its proceedings. In his delightful account of the trials, Wharton footnotes the lives of the accused. Cooper, born in London in 1759, studied law but excelled in the natural sciences, especially chemistry. Arriving in the United States with Dr. Joseph Priestley, a famous scientist, he expected a government appointment. He was accused of turning against Adams when he did not receive it.

The libelous material read:

Nor do I see any impropriety in making this request of Mr. Adams. At that time he had just entered into office; he was hardly in the infancy of political mistake: even those who doubted his capacity thought well of his intentions. Nor were we yet saddled with the expense of a permanent navy, or threatened, under his auspices, with the existence of a standing army. Our credit was not yet reduced so low as to borrow money at eight per cent in time of peace, while the unnecessary violence of official expressions might justly have provoked a war.

He was also accused of writing that Adams had influenced the decisions of a court in delivering to Britain an American citizen, Jonathan Robbins, to be court-martialed. Justice Chase in his charge to the jury defended Adams and emphasized that Cooper must prove "to the marrow" every charge. He was found guilty, and the court sentenced him "to pay a fine of $400, to be imprisoned for six months, and then to find surety for his good behavior, himself in $1,000 and two sureties in $500 each."

Justice Chase's conduct was moderate compared to his actions in the Callender case. Cooper's defense, in which he reviewed the Adams administration, attracted great attention, and his imprisonment was a popular subject for Republicans in the election campaign. President Adams would have pardoned him, but Cooper sent a letter that he would not accept clemency unless it was accompanied by the president's acknowledgment of the breach of good faith the publication asserted. Cooper completed his sentence, and the fine was paid. Cooper's fine was repaid by Congress in 1850. His petition for repayment was introduced in nearly every Congress beginning in 1825. When he was dying, he insisted that his wife pledge to continue the campaign for a refund, and even in his will, he urged his "claim upon Congress may be pursued until recovered." J.D. Stevens, "Congressional History of the 1798 Sedition Law," *Journalism Quarterly* (1966).

Upon his release from prison, Cooper enjoyed high esteem in the newly dominant Republican Party. Five years after his prison term he became a judge, but five years later he was impeached before the Senate of Pennsylvania upon charges similar to those made against Justice Chase. Cooper rebounded. He won a post in chemistry and was made president of Columbia College in South Carolina. He became a states' rights advocate and published tracts on politics, divinity, and metaphysics; a treatise on the bankruptcy laws; a translation of Justinian; a treatise on political economy; a manual of chemistry; and a general compendium of useful information. Wharton, *supra*.

David Brown, a wandering orator in Massachusetts, offered a more pathetic story. After he spoke in Dedham in 1798, the citizens raised a liberty pole with a sign stating: "No Stamp Act, No Sedition, No Alien Bills, No Land Tax, downfall to the Tyrants of America, peace and retirement to the President, Long Live the Vice-President and the Minority; May moral virtue be the basis of civil government." Brown was charged with inspiring the pole raising. Justice Chase was at his partisan best. Brown pleaded guilty. Chase sentenced him to 18 months in prison and a fine of $480. When his prison term ended, Brown could not pay the fine and remained in prison until Jefferson became president and pardoned him. Lewis, *supra.*

Republican leaders were outraged that the Alien and Sedition Acts were aimed at their party, but they fought back, and the public responded to their appeal for "liberty of the press" and "freedom of speech." The laws were denounced as unconstitutional. Jefferson was not an idle bystander during these years. He gave money to anti-Federalist writers and publications. Adams and his wife, Abigail, had been close friends of Jefferson. Adams had suggested that Jefferson write the Declaration of Independence, but they split over their vision of America's future and became political enemies. Adams's Federalists wanted strong central authority, while Jefferson's Republicans, representing the rural South, demanded states' rights.

Jefferson believed that the Sedition Act was unconstitutional under the First Amendment, but as all three branches of the government were under Federalist control, he secretly worked with Madison on the Virginia and Kentucky Resolutions, which stated that the federal government was created by the states, so the states must be superior. A state could nullify a federal law. In November 1798, Kentucky adopted Jefferson's resolutions, and Virginia adopted Madison's milder version in December. These resolutions later became the basis for nullification and even secession by the Confederate States in the Civil War.

James Callender and Justice Chase were heavyweights matched in the most famous sedition law trial, which was held in the U.S. District Court in Richmond, Virginia, in 1800. When U.S. Supreme Court Chief Justice William Rehnquist gave a speech in 2003 at a symposium on judicial independence at the University of Richmond's law school, he described Samuel Chase as "more than six feet tall and correspondingly broad; his complexion was brownish-red, earning him the nickname, 'Old Bacon Face.' He was hearty, gruff and sarcastic." Callender was described by Justice Rehnquist as a "well-educated Scotsman, notorious hack writer and great drinker, who was indicted for publishing a book entitled *The Prospect Before Us*, in which it was said he brought President Adams into disrepute by accusing him of being a monarchist and a toady to British interests." Callender's chief lawyer was the highly respected William Wirt.

Callender had fled Scotland under indictment for sedition, and he fled Philadelphia when indictment under the sedition law

37

seemed imminent. In 1799, he began editing Virginia's leading Republican paper, the *Examiner*, while writing his book.

Justice Chase made his circuit ride, leaving a trail of judicial prosecution. In the Cooper trial he had agreed with the prosecutor that a conviction would deter administration critics, and in the John Fries trial, later cited in his impeachment proceedings, he so outraged the defendant's lawyers that they withdrew. Fries was found guilty, and Chase sentenced him to be hanged. Within a month, President Adams issued a full pardon. Chase then headed south to Virginia to apply a federal law in a state that held it unconstitutional. Smith, *supra*.

The material set out in Callender's indictment as libelous began:

> The reign of Mr. Adams has been one continued tempest of malignant passions. As President, he has never opened his lips, or lifted his pen without threatening and scolding; the grand object of his administration has been to exasperate the rage of contending parties, to calumniate and destroy every man who differs from his opinions. Mr. Adams has labored, and with melancholy success, to break up bonds of social affection, and under the ruins of confidence and friendship, to extinguish the only gleam of happiness that glimmers through the dark and despicable farce of life.

He continued in this manner until his conclusion that "in the midst of such a scene of profligacy and of usury the President has persisted as long as he dared, in making his utmost efforts for provoking a French war. . . . Take your choice, then, between Adams, war and beggary, and Jefferson, peace and competency." Wharton, *supra*.

The first witness called by the defense was Colonel John Taylor. Justice Chase insisted on a written statement of the questions he would be asked. Chase then declared Taylor's testimony inadmissible: "No evidence is admissible that does not go to justify the whole charge." Philip Nicholas, a defense lawyer, suggested it might be proper to prove one part of a specific charge with one witness, then prove another part with a different witness, thereby proving the whole charge, but Justice Chase did not agree. Chase's actions in this case would provide charges for his own impeachment trial. He constantly interrupted Callender's lawyers, and for the second time in two months, defense counsel withdrew from a Chase trial. After two hours of deliberation, the jury returned with a guilty verdict, and Callender was sentenced to a fine of $200 and an imprisonment of nine months. Callender received a refund in 1801, but the money was raised by private subscription from prominent Republicans. Jefferson donated $50. Wharton, *supra*; Stevens, *supra*.

Afterword

As soon as Jefferson was inaugurated, he pardoned all who had been convicted under the sedition law, but he refused Callender's request to appoint him postmaster at Richmond. Callender began writing scurrilous articles about Jefferson's administration. He continued his personal attacks, detailing Jefferson's relationship with his slave, Sally Hemings. Jefferson had given money to Callender, and he felt compelled to explain the reason in a letter to James Monroe. On July 15, 1802, he wrote that in 1798–1799 he was asked to contribute to Callender's relief and did so. He also gave him $50 on three occasions as charity. When Callender wished to become postmaster, Jefferson wrote, "I did not think the public offices were confided to me to give away as charities."

Jefferson wrote to Abigail Adams on July 22, 1804,

> I discharged every person under punishment or prosecution under the Sedition law, because I considered, and now consider, that law to be a nullity as absolute and as palpable as if Congress had ordered us to fall down and worship a golden image. It was done . . . without asking what the offenders had done, or against whom they had offended, but whether the pains they were suffering were inflicted under the pretended Sedition law. It was certainly possible that my motives for contributing to the relief of Callender . . . might have been to protect, encourage and reward slander; but they may also have been those which inspire ordinary charities to objects of distress, meritorious or not, or the obligation of an oath to protect the Constitution, violated by an unauthorized act of Congress. Which of these were my motives, must be decided by a regard to the general tenor of my life.

The irresistible Wharton described the end of Callender's life: "It remains to be added that, while this wretched libeler, who had now become an habitual sot, was disseminating his slanders and ribaldry with untiring virulence, he was, one morning, found drowned in James' River, where he had been bathing, it was supposed, in a state of intoxication." Wharton, *supra*.

39

Judicial review of the constitutionality of laws by the Supreme Court was not yet established when the sedition law was enforced. That happened in 1803 when Chief Justice John Marshall decided *Marbury v. Madison*, but the sedition law had already expired by then. What would Marshall have ruled? As a Congressional candidate in 1798–1799, he denounced the Virginia Resolutions and argued for the constitutionality of the Alien and Sedition Acts, claiming it was obvious that states should attend to local subjects and that the nation should attend to general affairs. He added that had he been in Congress, he would have voted against the Alien and Sedition Acts as "useless" and "calculated to create unnecessary discontents and jealousies."

Marshall, a moderate, was elected to Congress and became the only Federalist to join the new Republican majority in a vote to eliminate the oppressive wording in part four of the sedition law. His beliefs probably were best expressed years earlier when he joined his fellow envoys to France in informing Talleyrand: "The genius of the Constitution and the opinions of the people of the United States cannot be overruled by those who administer the government." A. Beveridge, *The Life of John Marshall*, vol. II (1916).

In January 1804, Justice Chase was impeached in the Jeffersonian-Republican–controlled House of Representatives. Chase had been appointed by President Washington to the U.S. Supreme Court. His courtroom tantrums, insolent behavior, and some unpopular judicial decisions made him a target. Five impeachment articles were based on Callender's trial. Wharton wrote that while on some articles, nothing saved him except his advanced age and the peculiar party sympathies of the Senate, from a conviction by the requisite majority of two-thirds,

[t]he fourth article (rude, contemptuous and indecent conduct during the trial), rested on the abuse of a discretionary power, not susceptible, perhaps of exact legal measurement, but the rejection of Mr. Taylor's testimony, on which the second article hung, was a palpable and unprecedented violation of the law of evidence.

Mr. Taylor was offered to prove the truth of one of the several allegations in the alleged libelous article; the Sedition Act provided that the defendant should be permitted to give the truth in evidence; Judge Chase refused to allow Mr. Taylor to be examined, because it was no defense to justify part of the libelous matter; it was necessary that there should be a justification of the whole. In other words, a witness was rejected, who proved a material part of the defendant's case, simply because the particular witness was not able to prove the whole of it.

Enough Republicans voted with the Federalists against conviction that the Senate acquitted Chase by four votes in March 1805. He is the only U.S. Supreme Court justice who has been impeached.

Just before Adams left office, Congress passed the Judiciary Act of 1801, packing the federal courts with Federalist judges. President Jefferson, alarmed, had encouraged the Chase impeachment proceedings. He disliked life appointments for federal judges, and Chase would serve as a test case. If he could impeach Chase, other Federalist judges, especially Chief Justice John Marshall, might follow. Republican vice president Aaron Burr presided over the impeachment trial. He gave Chase's lawyer, Luther Martin, full opportunity to defend his client. When Aaron Burr was tried for treason two years later, Marshall was a judge, and Martin was Burr's lawyer. *The American Experience, Samuel Chase*, www.pbs.org (2000); A.H. Kelly & W.A. Harbison, *The American Constitution* (1955).

In his Richmond speech, Chief Justice Rehnquist described the scene in the impeachment court with Aaron Burr, who was under indictment in New Jersey and New York for killing Alexander Hamilton in a duel, presiding. "One wag," Rehnquist said, "remarked that although in most courts the murderer was arraigned before the judge, in this court the judge was arraigned before the murderer." But, Rehnquist concluded, the significance of the outcome of the Chase trial cannot be overstated: "Chase's narrow escape from conviction exemplified how close the development of an independent judiciary came to being stultified. . . . The political precedent set by Chase's acquittal has governed that day to this: a judge's judicial acts may not serve as a basis for impeachment."

During the Civil War, President Abraham Lincoln was accused of curtailing civil liberties. Critics compared his policies to the Sedition Act of 1798, especially in the case of "Peace Democrat" Clement Vallandigham, who, like Matthew Lyon, had been a congressman. While Lyon had been reelected from jail, Vallandigham, convicted and then banished by Lincoln to the Confederacy, made his way to Windsor, Ontario, Canada, where he campaigned unsuccessfully to be governor of Ohio. According to New York Law

School dean emeritus and law professor James S. Simon, the comparison between Lincoln's restrictions and the oppressive 1798 Sedition Act is unfair. There was no comparable threat to liberties until the Civil War began. Though mail was censored and military commanders occasionally shut down a newspaper, no version of the Sedition Act was proposed. Yet the opposition press continued to attack the administration.

Simon contends that Lincoln's defense of Vallandigham's arrest and conviction is unconvincing. Nothing in the record shows "that he did more than criticize the administration's prosecution of the war. That is political speech and should have been protected under the First Amendment. But the civilian courts to which Vallandigham appealed were unresponsive. The federal circuit court judge hearing the appeal emphatically endorsed the military tribunal's judgment, and the U.S. Supreme Court refused to review the case on the merits." Simon notes that "the reluctance of the Supreme Court to declare the government's wartime policies unconstitutional continued through every major war of the twentieth century." J. Simon, *Lincoln and Chief Justice Taney* (2006).

The Sedition Act of 1798 was so unpopular that no sedition law emerged again until, at President Woodrow Wilson's urging during World War I, Congress passed the Sedition Act of 1918 as an amendment to the Espionage Act of 1917.

University of Chicago provost and law professor Geoffrey R. Stone wrote, "I have a simple thesis: In time of war—or, more precisely, in time of national crisis—we respond too harshly in our restriction of civil liberties, and then later regret our behavior." G.R. Stone, *Journal of the Supreme Court History*, vol. 28, no. 3 (2003).

4

Signed, Sealed, but Not Delivered

Marbury v. Madison

With one bold stroke, Chief Justice John Marshall gave the U.S. Supreme Court the power of judicial review. He took *Marbury v. Madison*, a petty, partisan squabble, and made it a constitutional landmark. Less noble but more human is the story behind the decision. *Marbury v. Madison* began with Marshall's mistake. As secretary of state for the Adams administration, Marshall neglected to give Marbury his judicial commission.

By the election year 1800, the two-party system, unforeseen by the Founding Fathers, had arrived. Thomas Jefferson defeated the incumbent Federalist President John Adams, and the Jeffersonian Republicans also won majorities in the House and Senate. It was a defeat from which the Federalists never recovered.

During the four months between the election of November 1800 and Jefferson's inauguration the following March, Adams and the defeated Federalist Congress were determined to retain judicial power by packing the courts with Federalist judges, including Abigail Adams's nephew and three of Marshall's relatives.

The lame-duck Congress passed the Judiciary Act of 1801, which reduced the size of the Supreme Court from six to five, eliminated the Supreme Court justices' circuit court duty, and created six new circuit courts with 26 new judgeships.

A week before Adams left office, Congress authorized him to appoint five-year terms for 45 justices of the peace for the unfinished, malarial swamp of the nation's new capital, Washington, D.C. Nominated on March 2, 1801, and confirmed by the Senate the next day, the 45 were the final group of Adams's "midnight justices." Jefferson's Republicans were furious. Jefferson wrote to a friend, "The Federalists have retired into the judiciary as a stronghold." *The Papers of John Marshall*, ed C.F. Hobson (1990); A.J. Beveridge, *The Life of John Marshall* (1919); J.E. Smith, *John Marshall: Definer of a Nation* (1996).

March 3, 1801

Adams sat at his desk until 9 PM on his last night in office, March 3, signing commissions brought to him by a State Department clerk. The clerk then took them back to the State Department, where the Great Seal of the United States of America was affixed on each commission, which then was to be delivered to the appointed justice. J.F. Simon, *What Kind of Nation* (2002).

John Marshall now enters. Marshall had been confirmed as Adams's secretary of state on May 13, 1800. He had hoped to work for a centrist coalition, but after Jefferson's inauguration, his service as the Federalist secretary of state would end. Adams appointed Marshall as chief justice of the U.S. Supreme Court on January 31, 1801, but Marshall continued to discharge the duties of secretary of state in the brief interval before Jefferson became president. It was Marshall who had affixed the Great Seal to the commissions. Smith, *supra.*

What happened next is uncertain. David Brent, a State Department clerk, recalled giving the commissions to John Marshall's brother James, who had just been appointed by Adams to the new Circuit Court of Appeals for the District of Columbia. However, not all of the commissions were delivered. Simon, *supra;* Smith, *supra.*

Adams left Washington by stage coach at 4 AM the next morning, eight hours before Jefferson was scheduled to take the oath of office.

March 4, 1801

Jefferson had written curtly to Marshall: "I propose to take the oath or oaths of office as President of the United States on

44

Wednesday the 4th [of March] at 12 o'clock in the Senate chamber. May I hope the favor of your attendance to administer the oath?" Marshall acerbically replied the same day, "I shall with much pleasure attend to administer the oath of office on the 4th, & shall make a point of being punctual." Simon, *supra.*

And so Thomas Jefferson became the third president of the United States. In his inaugural address, Jefferson was conciliatory: "We are all Republicans. We are all Federalists," he famously said. But amity was brief.

The following day, Jefferson appointed James Madison as secretary of state. Shortly after Jefferson took office, he was told that judicial commissions had been found lying on a table in the State Department. He told Levi Lincoln, the acting secretary of state, to withhold them because, like a deed or bond, the commissions were not valid until delivered. *The Papers of John Marshall, supra;* Smith, *supra.*

Jefferson, years later, explained his action:

[I]f there is any principle of law never yet contradicted, it is that delivery is one of the essentials to the validity of a deed. Although signed and sealed, yet as long as it remains in the hands of the party himself, it is *in fieri* [incomplete], it is not a deed, and can be made so [only] by its delivery.

Memoirs, Correspondence and Private Papers of Thomas Jefferson, T.J. Randolph, ed., 1829.

On March 18, John Marshall replied to his brother's query regarding the undelivered commissions, explaining, "I should . . . have sent out commissions which had been signed and sealed but for the extreme hurry of time and the absence of Mr. Wagner [State Department chief clerk]." Marshall added that he was not concerned and considered the commissions legally binding because Adams had signed them and the Great Seal had been affixed. "To withhold the Commissions of the justices," Marshall later wrote, "is an act of which I entertained no suspicion." *Papers of John Marshall, supra;* Smith, *supra.*

Of the 42 commissions Marshall left on the desk, Jefferson, seeking to moderate tension after the bitter election campaign, retained 25 and then added five more. Jefferson's final list did not contain the names of William Marbury and three others who decided to seek a writ of mandamus from the Supreme Court demanding delivery. Marshall and Jefferson's disagreement on the

45

validity of these inconsequential appointments culminated in Marshall's monumental decision in *Marbury v. Madison*.

Cousins

Marshall and Jefferson were well known to each other—they were second cousins. They were political enemies—Marshall with his Federalist loyalties favoring a strong central government with an affinity to the British and the bankers; and Jefferson, the Francophile, with his belief in an agrarian, states' rights democracy.

There were personal animosities as well. Both men's fathers were hardworking settlers. Both married into the wealthy Randolph family of Virginia. But Marshall's grandmother, Mary Randolph, whose father established the Tuckahoe plantation, was disinherited by the family, while Jefferson's forebears flourished with Randolph assistance. Thomas Jefferson's father, a surveyor and planter, became the administrator of the Tuckahoe estate and moved his family there. Jefferson spent his early childhood at the plantation that Marshall's grandmother, who eloped with a slave overseer, had fled. W.S. Randall, *Jefferson: A Life* (1993); Smith, *supra*.

Mary Randolph eventually married James Keith, an Anglican minister. He was Marshall's grandfather, but Marshall preferred to praise his father, whose position as surveyor and land agent for wealthy Lord Fairfax gave the family social and financial support.

Jefferson (born 1743) and later Marshall (born 1755) studied law under George Wythe. Jefferson appointed Wythe the first law professor in America, at the College of William and Mary. Jefferson closed his law practice and, inspired by Patrick Henry, plunged into revolutionary politics, ultimately writing the Declaration of Independence.

Marshall fought in the Revolutionary War, was promoted to captain, and spent the fierce winter of 1777 at Valley Forge with his longtime friend General George Washington. The convivial Marshall spent 20 years as a successful lawyer. S.H. Ash, *The Supreme Court and Its Great Justices* (1971); P. Irons, *A People's History of the Supreme Court* (1999); Beveridge, *supra*.

An unlikely link between Marshall and Jefferson resulted from a failed romance. As a tall, slender 20-year-old, Jefferson became infatuated with 16-year-old Rebecca Burwell but failed to pursue her. Rebecca married an older suitor, Jacquelin Ambler; eventually, their daughter Mary Willis Ambler—known as Polly—became

John Marshall's wife. S.G. Brown, *Thomas Jefferson* (1963); Beveridge, *supra*.

Polly Marshall soon became an invalid. Jefferson's wife, Martha, died young. Jefferson's interests in architecture, philosophy, science, and fine wine centered around Monticello, the Virginia mansion he designed, about two miles from Charlottesville and not far from Shadwell, the Albemarle County plantation established by his father. Marshall borrowed money to invest in a large tract of Fairfax land, but his Supreme Court terms were spent dining with his colleagues at a Washington boarding house.

In later years, Jefferson wrote irreverently that the "venality" of most lawyers "makes me ashamed that I was ever a member" of the bar. Jefferson taunted lawyers who "question everything, yield nothing and talk by the hour." He looked to a time when there would be a scientific approach to law. Randall, *supra*.

Two Political Parties

The ill will that Jefferson attempted to soften during his first days in office had grown violent in the midst of the election campaign. Jeffersonians were irate at Federalist judges who had strictly enforced the series of laws that were designed to stifle criticism of the Adams administration. The Naturalization Act substantially increased the residency period for citizenship. New citizens from France and Ireland almost invariably joined Jefferson's party. The Alien Act allowed the president to deport any alien he considered dangerous "to the peace and safety" of the United States with neither an explanation nor a jury trial. Jefferson, outraged, called this act "worthy of the eighth or ninth century." But the Sedition Act was met with even greater opposition. Both acts were to expire on the last day of Adams's term. Simon, *supra*.

Jefferson, protesting that this legislation violated the Constitution and would lead to monarchy, stated:

> They have brought into the lower house a sedition bill which, among other enormities, undertakes to make printing certain matters criminal, though one of the amendments to the Constitution has so expressly taken . . . printing presses . . . out of their coercion. Indeed, this bill and the alien bill both are so palpably in the teeth of the Constitution as to show they mean to pay no respect to it.

Simon, *supra*.

47

Marshall disliked the excesses of the Republican press, but he had been a member of the committee that drafted the First Amendment, framed to prohibit prosecution for seditious libel. Marshall distanced himself from the High Federalists who were responsible for the acts. He said the Constitution, sanctioned by the will of the people, was the rock of political salvation.

It was the unpopularity of the Alien and Sedition Acts that helped Jefferson defeat Adams. A year after Jefferson assumed office, he attacked Adams's attempt to pack the judiciary with Federalist judges. On March 8, 1802, the Jefferson Republican Congress repealed the Judiciary Act of 1801. On April 29, Jefferson signed the Judiciary Act of 1802, which restored the Supreme Court to six justices, giving himself the right to appoint an additional justice, and he abolished the new circuit court judgeships. The Federalists attacked the repealing statute as unconstitutional. In order to prevent reaction by Marshall's Supreme Court, the act also changed the schedule for Supreme Court sessions so it could not convene for 14 months. When it met again in February 1803, *Marbury v. Madison* was on the Supreme Court docket. Adams's most insignificant appointees still wanted their commissions. The stage was set. R.F. Cushman, *Cases in Constitutional Law.*

Marbury v. Madison

Marshall's close friend Charles Lee represented William Marbury. Lee had served as attorney general under both Washington and Adams. The other disappointed nominees who joined Marbury were Robert Hooe, Dennis Ramsay, and William Harper, all now lost to history. Lee had appeared before the Court on December 16, 1801, requesting an order for Secretary of State Madison to show cause why a writ of mandamus should not be issued directing Madison to deliver the justice of the peace commissions.

It was perceived as a minor matter, an attempt by embittered candidates to obtain lowly judicial offices. The four applicants were locally prominent Federalists. The posts they were seeking had a civil jurisdiction of $20 with no salary. Remuneration, if any, was recoverable only from collected fees. Lee told the Court, "The emoluments, or the dignity of the office, are no objects with the applicants." James Madison did not even send a lawyer in his own defense and passed up the chance to blame Marshall for his failure to deliver the commissions. Simon, *supra;* J. Appleby, *Thomas*

Jefferson (2003); P.C. Nagel, *The Lees of Virginia* (1990); *Marbury v. Madison*, 1 Cranch 137 (1803); Irons, *supra*.

Although the parties were Marbury and his fellow applicants against Madison, the real antagonists were Marshall and Jefferson. Had Marshall ordered Madison to deliver the commissions, Jefferson almost certainly would have told him not to do it. Marshall had no power to enforce such an order. If the Supreme Court's ruling were ignored, the judiciary would remain the ineffectual branch it had been since it began in 1790.

Because Marshall was directly involved in the case, questions have been asked about why he did not recuse himself. Two justices were unavailable so a quorum would not have been possible. Although that might have provided an excuse to avoid the case, Marshall remained on the bench.

Marshall's plan was to win by losing. First, he agreed with Lee that Marbury was entitled to his commission: "In the opinion of the Court by signing the Commission of Mr. Marbury, the President of the United States appointed him a justice of the peace." He affirmed, "The seal of the United States, affixed thereto by the Secretary of State" gave Marbury "a legal right to the office." Next, he answered Lee's question whether the law provided Marbury a remedy. Madison's refusal to deliver the commissions was "a plain violation of that right, for which the laws of his country afford him a remedy." Finally, was mandamus the remedy in Marbury's suit? Could the Court order Madison to deliver it? Irons, *supra*.

Here, Marshall forever secured his place in constitutional history. He decided that the Supreme Court had no jurisdiction to issue the writ of mandamus requested by Marbury under section 13 of the Judiciary Act of 1789, which stated, "The Supreme Court . . . shall have power to issue . . . writs of *mandamus*, in cases warranted by the principles and usages of law, to any courts appointed or persons holding office, under the authority of the United States." A congressional act granting the right of original jurisdiction to the Supreme Court was unconstitutional and, therefore, invalid. U.S. Statutes at Large, 1, 73; 1 Annals of Cong. 2d Sess. 2245; Randall, *supra*; Cushman, *supra*; Simon, *supra*; Smith, *supra*; Irons, *supra*.

Marshall recognized that Congress had granted the Supreme Court jurisdiction in cases such as *Marbury*, but the Supreme Court owed allegiance to a higher authority than Congress. That authority was the Constitution. Under Article III, the Constitution gave the Supreme Court original jurisdiction in all cases affecting ambassadors or other public ministers, and cases in which a state was a party. In all other cases, its jurisdiction was appellate. He asked whether the Supreme Court owed its primary allegiance to the fundamental law in the Constitution or to an ordinary act of legislation.

"The Constitution is either a superior paramount law, unchangeable by ordinary means, or it is on a level with ordinary legislative acts, and, like other acts, is alterable when the legislature shall be pleased to alter it," Marshall concluded. The Framers did not intend the legislature, as only one of three coequal branches of the federal government, to change the rules of constitutional democracy as it pleased. The Constitution was supreme.

Then, Marshall clinched his argument. The Supreme Court was charged with the responsibility to interpret the Constitution: "It is emphatically the province and duty of the judicial department to say what the law is." Otherwise, the justices who had sworn an oath to uphold the Constitution must ignore it: "Must the Court convict a citizen of treason on the basis of a confession made out of court when the Constitution explicitly requires that there be no conviction of treason unless on the testimony of two witnesses?" The answer: "No." Simon, *supra*.

Just as Jefferson condemned the power of Congress over the rights of states, Marshall refused to allow Congress to overrule the Constitution. Each attacked the authority of Congress from opposite directions. But Marshall's decision concentrated judicial power in the U.S. Supreme Court, a result Jefferson deplored.

Yet the criticism of Marshall's decision was focused on his opinion that Marbury was entitled to his commission, a writ of mandamus was the proper remedy, and the executive was properly subject to mandamus if the case was heard in the appropriate court. Judicial review went unchallenged.

Marshall never ordered Madison to deliver the commissions. Marbury had the right to take his request to a lower court. But now the Supreme Court had the power to declare legislation unconstitutional. Jefferson had won a minor victory, but he lost much more. Marshall's trivial mistake in not delivering the justice of the peace commissions resulted in Marshall's towering decision on February 24, 1803, which implemented the right of judicial review. *Marbury v. Madison* made the Supreme Court an equal partner with the executive and legislative branches. At the time, few understood the full impact of the decision. Marshall cited no precedent. In this young court that Marshall was creating, he was making precedents rather than following them. M. Smelser, *The Democratic Republic* (1968).

Six months later, a circuit court holding that another act of Congress was unconstitutional was not criticized. Jefferson wrote a letter in 1807 disagreeing with Marshall's decision, but he complained about Marshall's support of Marbury, not about the exercise of judicial review. Cushman, *supra;* Smith, *supra;* M.D. Hall, *The Political and Legal Philosophy of James Wilson 1742–1798* (1997).

Origins

Marshall's concept was not original. James Otis brought the doctrine of judicial review to the American colonies from Great Britain. Arguing in Boston in 1761 against the use of the writs of assistance in Lechmere's Case, Quincy Reports 51 (Mass. 1761), Otis cited Dr. Bonham's Case. There, Chief Justice Coke stated:

> And it appears in our books, that in many cases, the common law will controul [*sic*] Acts of Parliament, and sometimes adjudge them to be utterly void: for when an Act of Parliament is against common right and reason, or repugnant, or impossible to be performed, the common law will controul [*sic*] it, and adjudge such Act to be void.

8 Co. 113b, 118a, 77 Eng. Rep. 646 (1610). Otis widely circulated Coke's opinion throughout the colonies in his popular pamphlet *The Rights of the British Colonies Asserted and Proved*, published in Boston in 1765. B. Knollenberg, *Origin of the American Revolution* (1965).

Judicial review was so prevalent in America's early days that four American state courts (New Jersey, Virginia, New York, and Rhode Island) declared state statutes unconstitutional under their state constitutions. *Holmes v. Walton* (1799); *Commonwealth v. Caton* (1780); *Rutgers v. Waddington* (1784); *Trevett v. Weeden* (1787); B. Schwartz, *A History of the Supreme Court* (1993).

In *The Federalist Papers* (1788), Alexander Hamilton, an ardent Federalist, gave his vision of the judiciary's role in America:

> The interpretation of the laws is the proper and peculiar province of the courts. A constitution is, in fact, and must be regarded by the judges, as a fundamental law. It therefore belongs to them to ascertain its meaning, as well as the meaning of any particular act proceeding from the legislative body. If

51

there should happen to be an irreconcilable variance between the two . . . the Constitution ought to be preferred to the statute, the intention of the people to the intention of their agents.

R.P. Fairfield, ed., *The Federalist Papers* (1966); P.G. Kauper, *Constitutional Law* (1954).

In Hylton v. United States, 3 Dall. 409 (1796), the Supreme Court clearly foreshadowed *Marbury*. R.P. Frankel Jr., "Before Marbury: *Hylton v. United States* and the Origins of Judicial Review," *Journal of Supreme Court History* (2003).

Afterword

Fifty-four years passed after *Marbury v. Madison* with no exercise of federal judicial review. Then, the Supreme Court declared a federal statute (the Missouri Compromise) unconstitutional in the infamous *Dred Scott* case. (*Scott v. Sandford*, 19 Howard 393 (1857); A.H. Kelly & W.A. Harbison, *The American Constitution* (1955).

Long after Jefferson retired to Monticello, he gave a bitter assessment of Marshall's Federalist court: "The judiciary of the United States is the subtle corps of sappers and miners constantly working underground to undermine the foundations of our confederated fabric." Jefferson deplored Supreme Court decisions issued with "the silent acquiescence of lazy and timid associates, by the crafty chief judge who sophisticates the law to his own mind by the turn of his own reasoning. Irons, *supra*.

On June 13, 1804, Jefferson wrote to Abigail Adams:

I can say with truth that one act of Mr. Adams' life, and one only, ever gave me a moment of personal displeasure. I did consider his last appointments to office as personally unkind. . . . It seemed but common justice to leave a successor free to act by instruments of his choice.

L.J.F. Cappon, ed., *The Adams-Jefferson Letters* (1959); Smith, *supra*.

SECTION II

Dividing a Nation

If addressing slavery and uniting the states into a cohesive nation seemed difficult to the founders, it proved impossible as new states were added. The *Dred Scott* decision led to the Civil War, and the assassination of President Abraham Lincoln doomed the peace. Dr. Samuel Mudd and his descendants spent a century trying to establish his innocence in the murder. Confederate leader Judah Benjamin, in contrast, escaped to London as the war ended and won great success in his new legal career.

5

Justice Benjamin Curtis and *Dred Scott*

The most important decision ever made by the Supreme Court of the United States was pronounced yesterday . . . that negroes are not citizens of the United States . . . at one blow all the legislation of the country, from the formation of the Constitution to the present day, against the extension of slavery is swept away. . . . It is impossible to exaggerate the importance of this decision.
———*The New York Times*, March 7, 1857

Scott v. Sandford remains the most infamous of all the U.S. Supreme Court's decisions. In a one-two punch, the Taney Court denied citizenship to African-Americans under the Constitution and declared the Missouri Compromise of 1820 unconstitutional. Congress could not prohibit slavery in the American territories. But the opinion was not unanimous. Justices Benjamin R. Curtis and John MacLean dissented. Then, Curtis resigned from the Court.

Curtis was not an abolitionist. On April 9, 1855, he had been denounced in the New York *Tribune* as a "slave-catching judge, appointed to office as a reward for his professional support given to the Fugitive Slave Bill." Yet two years later, he clashed mightily with Chief Justice Roger Taney over *Dred Scott*. How did this happen?

Early Years

In the charming, stilted style of the time, Curtis's brother George wrote a two-volume memoir of the justice that was later edited by Benjamin R. Curtis, Jr. The Curtis family origins were in Essex, England. Their father, son of a Massachusetts surgeon, was in the merchant marine. Benjamin Robbins Curtis was born in 1809 and George Ticknor Curtis in 1812. When their father died at sea, their mother, Lois, a strong-minded woman, raised her two boys. She remained in her family's old home in Waterton, about seven miles from Cambridge, and earned money by running a circulating library from the house. Benjamin became an avid reader. Throughout his life, Benjamin exchanged letters with his uncle, George Ticknor, a Harvard professor, from which George Curtis included excerpts in the book.

Benjamin's earliest recorded writing, before he was 16, was an essay, "On the Origin of Evil." He attributed the origin of evil neither to an evil spirit nor the natural depravity of man. Instead, he concluded:

> [N]o one would do wrong merely for the sake of some pleasure or advantage that he imagined to be contained in it, and he would a thousand times rather have obtained the advantage without the sin if he could; but as he could not, the imagined pleasure or advantage outweighed his abhorrence of sin.

B.R. Curtis Jr., ed., *Memoir of Benjamin Robbins Curtis* (1879).

Benjamin's mother was determined to provide him with a college education and, through self-sacrifice, managed to provide his tuition to Harvard College. He entered Harvard Law School but left for a short time when he joined a law practice in the town of Northfield, Massachusetts. Benjamin hoped a small, assured income could hasten his marriage to his cousin Eliza Maria Woodward. He returned to Harvard and received his Bachelor of Laws in 1832. Benjamin married Eliza the next year.

Benjamin and Eliza set up housekeeping in Northfield and began their family. George relates that later, in Boston, Benjamin used his knowledge of special pleading against an astute opponent. When asked about his expertise, Benjamin replied that he had studied it a great deal while he was at Northfield, and knew by heart the whole series of declarations, pleas, replications, rebutters, sur-rebutters, . . . as given by Chitty on Pleading; that he had sometimes walked the floor of his nursery for hours in the night, with a sick child in his arms, repeating to it these forms; and that he found them as good a lullaby as anything in Mother Goose, and much more of a relief to his own mind.

Curtis, *supra*.

After three years of practice, Curtis accepted a lucrative offer to join the Boston law firm of a distant relative, Charles Pelham Curtis. There, his practice grew rapidly. When Curtis arrived in Boston, radical abolitionism was rife. Slavery was unlawful in Massachusetts and most other northern states. But constant legal friction existed over the status of slaves who had become domiciled by their slave owners in free states or who had escaped from slave states. Did they remain slaves? Or were they free?

Slavery Law

Before independence, the American colonies followed English common law. In *Somerset v. Stewart*, Lofft 1, 98 Eng. Rep. 499 (K.B. 1772), Lord Mansfield created a common law precedent. A slave owner took his slave, Somerset, from Virginia to England, where he fled but was caught and consigned to a ship's captain for sale in Jamaica. Somerset was ordered released because nothing "in the positive law of the realm" authorized his imprisonment aboard the departing ship. Lord Mansfield ruled:

> The power of a master over his slave has been extremely difficult, in different countries. . . . It's so odious, that nothing can be suffered to support it but positive law. Whatever inconveniences, therefore, may follow from a decision, I cannot say this case is allowed or approved by the law of England; and therefore the black must be discharged.

Id.

Somerset had a bold impact on American slavery law, but its impact on American slavery's interstate problems was limited. It did not settle the question whether Somerset would remain free if he returned to Virginia. It did not consider comity (courtesy between states) between equal sovereignties. Instead, it dealt with relations between Britain and its colonies. It did not state that every slave brought into Britain became free. Abolitionists extolled *Somerset*, arguing that slavery violated natural law and was not legal outside the boundaries of any state that authorized it by positive law.

Yet *Somerset* also supported sectional accommodation. Most Southerners accepted the freedom of slaves when domiciled by their slave owners on free soil. Southern courts consistently ruled that a slave taken to live permanently in a free state or territory was emancipated. They embraced the principle of "once free, forever free." Northerners usually agreed that this freedom should not apply to situations of transit, sojourn, or temporary residence. However, some northern states began to apply *Somerset* in an extreme version by withdrawing the slave owner's right of sojourn and transit with slaves in a free state. D.E. Fehrenbacher, *Dred Scott Case* (1978).

By the mid-1830s, U.S. Supreme Court Justice Joseph Story had published his famous *Conflict of Laws*. Story's belief was that sovereign states had total control over the laws that should be enforced within their boundaries. Foreign law was applied only as a matter of comity—no nation need enforce an external law that was "incompatible with its own safety, or happiness, or conscientious regard to justice and duty." In the United States, Story's doctrine strengthened the Northern resolve not to extend comity to Southern slave owners.

In 1836 Curtis represented a slave owner in *Commonwealth v. Aves*, 18 Pick. 210 (Mass. 1836), before Judge Lemuel Shaw. Boston's Female Anti-Slavery Society claimed that Med, a six-year-old black slave child, had been emancipated when she was brought into the free state of Massachusetts by her slave owner mistress for a visit. Curtis argued for comity between free and slave states, claiming that slave owners who were temporarily in Massachusetts could take their slaves back to their slave state domiciles.

Curtis lost. Massachusetts's supreme judicial court decided that slaves became free when they entered a free state or territory. But the *Aves* case gained Curtis, now a junior partner, a reputation as one of Boston's most brilliant young lawyers.

Sectional slavery tension heightened dramatically. Slaves escaped to free states and were caught. Slave owners took them to free states, and they refused to return to slave states. Court rulings were inconsistent. In *Prigg v. Pennsylvania*, 16 Pet. 611 (1842), the

U.S. Supreme Court became involved. In 1832, Margaret Morgan, a slave, fled Maryland (a slave state) to Pennsylvania (free). Five years later, Edward Prigg, Morgan's slave owner's agent, found and seized Morgan in Pennsylvania, forcibly took her back to Maryland, and returned her to her owner. Prigg did this without obtaining a certificate required under Pennsylvania law so that he could "sell and dispose of the said Margaret Morgan, as and for a slave and servant for life." After Prigg returned to Pennsylvania, he was convicted of kidnapping Morgan.

Justice Story decreed that Margaret Morgan could not have been kidnapped because, as a slave, she was a "species of property." Edward Prigg was once again a free white man. Margaret Morgan was now once again, a slave. Fehrenbacher, *supra*.

Prigg led to *Strader v. Graham*, 10 How. 82 (1850). Slave musicians were taken briefly from Kentucky to Ohio by their slave owner. They escaped to Canada and freedom. The slave owner sued for damages those who had assisted in the escape. Kentucky's appellate court agreed with the slave owner. The Supreme Court agreed with the Kentucky appellate court. Justice Taney claimed no federal jurisdiction existed because Ohio (free) was a state and no longer under federal authority as part of the Northwest Territory. If slaves entered a free state and became free under its law, then returned to a slave state, they became slaves again under that state's law.

Taney said the issue hinged on whether slaves who traveled with the permission of their slave owners from Kentucky to Ohio acquired a right to freedom in Ohio that they retained after returning to Kentucky. It did not matter whether the slaves went to Ohio and became permanently domiciled there or went only as temporary sojourners; Kentucky decided the status of blacks domiciled in Kentucky. When they returned to Kentucky, slavery reattached. The Court rejected the argument that a slave automatically became free when she became a resident of a free state, and the state court's decision concerning the slavery status of blacks in the state was final. These cases foreshadowed *Dred Scott*. G.E. White, *American Judicial Tradition* (1988).

The Missouri Compromise of 1820 had prohibited slavery in the American territories north of 36 degrees 30 minutes north latitude. The Compromise strengthened the Fugitive Slave Act of 1793. In fact the Compromise was repealed in 1854 by the Kansas Nebraska Act, in which the choice of slavery was left to settlers in those two territories. After 1848, the American West was vastly increased as a result of war with Mexico. Slavery became an explosive issue. Could Congress outlaw slavery in the new territories? The truce between North and South was tenuous. As part of the Compromise of 1850, California was admitted as a free state. Ambiguous phrases concerning the New Mexico and Utah territories were intended to allow the territorial legislatures to exclude slavery. So far, Taney had been cautious.

Curtis's Life

Meanwhile, Curtis was the model of the prosperous and proper citizen. In 1843 he became politically active, joining the Whig Society and becoming a member of the exclusive Boston Athenaeum. In 1844, he published a treatise supporting Daniel Webster's claim that states could not repudiate public debts. Webster became a major force in Curtis's life.

Curtis disapproved of slavery. He recognized that runaway slaves had natural rights, but he warned that helping them in free states by refusing comity to Southern slave owners could lead to a civil war. He argued that an arrest warrant was valid in the case of Thomas Sims, a fugitive slave seized in Boston. He questioned the wisdom of a political agreement that put ardent anti-slavery advocate Charles Sumner in the U.S. Senate. But he never supported the spread of slavery. When Eliza Maria died in 1844, Curtis was left a widower with five children. Two years later, he married his partner's daughter, Anna Wroe Curtis, and had three children with her. Curtis entered politics as a Whig and served in the Massachusetts legislature. His reputation continued to grow when he succeeded Justice Story, who had been one of his law professors, on the Harvard Corporation, the college's governing board. He worked long hours to support his large family.

The Fugitive Slave Act of 1850 galvanized powerful opinions in Massachusetts. Abolitionists violently criticized it for its lack of due process. Federal commissioners were empowered to enforce it by taking runaway slaves into custody and returning them to their Southern slave owners. Senator Daniel Webster was under attack for supporting the act as part of the Compromise of 1850. Curtis was alarmed by the abolitionists who swore they would not allow a fugitive slave to be taken from Massachusetts, "Constitution or no Constitution, law or no law."

In an address at Faneuil Hall, Curtis said the founders knew the Union could not be formed unless the Constitution contained Article IV, Section 2, stating that a person held to service in one state who escapes into another shall be delivered up on claim of the party to whom such service shall be due. He claimed,

> If anyone in this age expects to live in peace, side by side with the slaveholding states without some effectual stipulation as to the restoration of fugitives, he must either be so wise to foresee events in no way connected with human experience or so foolish as to reject experience and probabilities as guides of action.

Curtis believed that Massachusetts should not be involved with fugitives' rights. "Whatever natural rights they have, and I admit those natural rights to their fullest extent, this is not the soil on which to vindicate them." Like Lincoln, who later carried a copy of Curtis's *Dred Scott* dissent in his pocket, the Union's preservation was Curtis's first priority. A.H. Kelly & W.A. Harbison, *American Constitution* (1955).

Supreme Court Appointment

In 1851, Justice Levi Woodbury of the U.S. Supreme Court died. President Millard Fillmore, the last Whig president, sought the guidance of Secretary of State Daniel Webster in finding a "worthy young Whig to fill the vacancy." Fillmore wrote, "I have . . . formed a very high opinion of Mr. B.R. Curtis. What do you say of him? What is his age? Constitution? & legal attainments? Does he fill the measure of my wishes?" J.A. Garraty & M.C. Carnes, *American National Biography* (1999).

Curtis never sought a judicial appointment. As were Justices Marshall and Story, he was a strong believer in Federalism. Curtis was a skilled advocate, "the first lawyer of America" according to the *Massachusetts Law Quarterly*; H.J. Abraham, *Justices, Presidents and Senators* (1992).

Webster's praise put Curtis on the U.S. Supreme Court. But his confirmation proceeding was delayed by Senate abolitionists for more than two months. His tenure lasted from 1851 to 1857. Curtis wrote 53 majority opinions and 13 dissents. He was the first Supreme Court Justice who had graduated from law school.

Curtis became an abolitionist target as soon as he was confirmed. As a Supreme Court justice riding circuit, he presided with District Judge Peleg Sprague in *United States v. Morris*, 26

Fed. Cas. 1323 (case no. 15,815; C.C.D. Mass. 1851). In 1850 Shadrach, a slave, escaped from Norfolk, Virginia, and fled to Boston. He changed his name to Frederick Jenkins and worked as a waiter in a coffeehouse. His slave-owner's agent found him in 1851.

The Fugitive Slave Act of 1850 expedited the return of slaves to their owners without the necessity of jury trials because Northern jurors were unsympathetic to slavery laws. Jenkins was taken before a federal magistrate for an order allowing him to be returned to Virginia. The act required slave owners to present only "satisfactory proof" of ownership in an ex parte summary proceeding before federal magistrates in order to receive a certificate permitting them to take slaves back to their slave states. Slaves could neither testify nor have anyone testify on their behalf. S. Campbell, *Slave Catchers* (1970); J. Abramson, *We, the Jury* (1994).

Jenkins's hearing was underway when a boisterous crowd burst into the courtroom and "invited Shadrach to accompany them . . . [They] hurried him through the square into Court Street, where he found the use of his feet, and they went off toward Cambridge, . . . the crowd driving along with them and cheering as they went." Jenkins fled to Canada and freedom. Eight people were charged with "aiding, abetting, and assisting" Jenkins's escape, a violation of the Fugitive Slave Act of 1850. Abramson, *id.*

In May 1851, a jury trial began for three defendants. Rather than argue the doctrine of jury nullification, Jenkins's lawyer in his summation told the jury they could decide first whether the Fugitive Slave Act was constitutional; if they decided that it was not, they could use the same right of judicial review claimed by the court to acquit the defendants.

Curtis stopped him. He told the jurors that they "have not the right to decide any question of law . . . [it was] their duty and their oath . . . to apply to the facts, as they may find them, the law given to them by the court." Curtis told the jurors they were not the judges of the law: "They are to take the law from the court and apply it to the facts which they may find from the evidence, and thus frame their general verdict of guilty or not guilty." Abramson, *id.*

In his opinion Curtis wrote that juries were not

the final judge of the existence, construction, and effect of every law which may be material in the trial of any criminal case. . . . To enforce popular laws is easy. But when an unpopular case is a just cause, when the law, unpopular in some locality, is to be enforced there, then comes the strain upon the administration of justice; and few unprejudiced men would hesitate as to where that strain would be most firmly borne.

Curtis's warning was ignored. The defendants were acquitted. No charges were pursued against the others. Because of the *Morris* decision and similar cases where runaway slaves were faced with a return to their Southern masters, Curtis became very unpopular in Massachusetts. Curtis's *Circuit Court Reports*, vol. I; Abramson, *supra*; L. Menand, *The Metaphysical Club* (2001); Curtis, ed., *Memoir, supra*.

Then came the *Dred Scott* case.

Dred Scott Appeal

The following Statement of Facts was signed by the parties and submitted to the Court as part of the *Scott v. Sandford* record that reached the U.S. Supreme Court:

In 1834, Dred Scott was a negroe slave belonging to Dr. Emerson, a surgeon in the army of the United States. In that year, Dr. Emerson took the plaintiff from the State of Missouri to the military post at Rock Island, in the State of Illinois, and held him there as a slave until 1836. Dr. Emerson then removed the plaintiff to the military post at Fort Snelling, in the territory of the United States 36 degrees 30 minutes, and north of the State of Missouri, where he held the plaintiff as a slave until 1838.

In 1835, Harriett, who was the negroe slave of Major Taliaferro, an officer of the army, was taken by her master to Fort Snelling, where she was held as a slave until 1836, when she was sold to Dr. Emerson, who held her as a slave at Fort Snelling until 1838. In 1836, the plaintiff and Harriett, with the consent of Dr. Emerson, intermarried at Fort Snelling. Eliza and Lizzie are children of that marriage. Eliza was born on board a steamboat, on the river Mississippi, north of the north line of the State of Missouri; Lizzie was born in the State of Missouri, at Jefferson Barracks, a military post. In 1838, Dr. Emerson removed the plaintiff and his wife and children to the State of Missouri, where they have ever since resided. Before the commencement of this, Dr. Emerson sold and conveyed the plaintiff and his wife and children to the defendant, as slaves, and the defendant has ever since claimed to hold them, and each of them, as slaves. It is agreed that Dred Scott brought suit for his freedom in the Circuit Court of St. Louis County; that there was a verdict and judgment in his favor; that on a writ of error to the Supreme Court [of the state], the judgment below was reversed, and the same remanded to the Circuit Court [of the state], where it has been continued to await the decision in this case [in the Circuit Court of the United States].

At the trial, the jury, under an instruction from the court that upon the facts of the case the law was with the defendant, found a verdict that the plaintiff, his wife, and children, were "negroe slaves, the lawful property of the defendant." Upon this verdict, the court gave judgment for the defendant, and the plaintiff filed exceptions to the instructions of the court, and upon these exceptions the case came up, by writ of error, to the Supreme Court of the United States.

The defendant's name, "Sanford," is misspelled as Sandford in the official record.

Seven of the U.S. Supreme Court justices were Democrats, including Chief Justice Roger Taney from Maryland, James M. Wayne from Georgia, John Catron from Tennessee, Peter V. Daniel from Virginia, John A. Campbell from Alabama, Samuel Nelson from New York, and Robert C. Grier from Pennsylvania. Curtis was the Court's only Whig. John McLean of Ohio was a Democrat who became a Republican before the decision.

In February 1856 the Supreme Court heard 12 hours of oral arguments over three days. Justice Nelson, concerned that a major split on the Court might be used at the upcoming presidential election, wanted the case argued again after the election. On May 12, Taney ordered rearguments at the next term, and the lawyers spoke again for three days in December. On February 11, 1857, the justices first met to consider the *Scott* case in conference.

The Court appeared ready to rule 7–2 against Scott based on the reattachment doctrine in *Strader v. Graham*. Scott had returned to the slave state of Missouri. Nelson wrote a 5,000-word draft opinion in which Scott remained a slave and Nelson's decision would stop any discussion about slavery in the territories. Nelson wrote, "The law of the State [Missouri] is supreme over the subject of slavery within its jurisdiction." Illinois law granting Scott freedom had no jurisdiction in Missouri.

Nelson, by using the pronoun "we," obviously thought his draft opinion would be the Court's opinion. K.L. Hall, *The Supreme Court and Judicial Review in American History* (1985); Kelly & Harbison, *supra*.

Then Curtis and McLean went in a different direction. Wayne, disturbed, urged Taney to write an opinion covering all the questions in the case. Wayne looked for a broad decision that would quell agitation between North and South. Taney agreed. Curtis (ed.), *supra*; Fehrenbacher, *supra*.

Politics now added an unusual twist. James Buchanan was elected president in November 1856, and his term began in March 1857. President-elect Buchanan wrote Catron to find out how the Court would rule. Catron told him a decision was imminent, but Grier was undecided about the issue of excluding slavery from the territories. Buchanan, desperate to settle the slavery dispute with a strong, decisive opinion, talked to Grier, persuading him, a fellow Pennsylvanian, to support Taney's opinion. Grier, who initially had wanted to exercise judicial restraint by not deciding either the citizenship or the constitutionality issues, changed his position and joined the Taney majority. Fehrenbacher, *supra*.

In his inauguration speech on March 4, President James Buchanan referred to the judicial decision that would resolve the territorial slavery issue. Abraham Lincoln and his Republican colleagues were livid.

Scott Decision

On March 6, 1857, the *Scott v. Sandford* decision was delivered. Chief Justice Taney first read the majority opinion, about not only Scott's slave status issue but also the crucial issue of whether Congress had the constitutional right to forbid slavery in the territories. In ruling that Scott could not bring his suit because he was not a citizen under the Constitution, Taney said:

> It is difficult at this day . . . to realize the state of public opinion in relation to that unfortunate race, which prevailed in the civilized and enlightened portions of the world at the time of the Declaration of Independence, and when the Constitution of the United States was framed and adopted. . . . They had more than a century before been regarded as beings of an inferior order, and altogether unfit to associate with the white race, either in social or political relations; and

so far inferior, that they had no rights which the white man was bound to respect; and that the negroe might justly and lawfully be reduced to slavery for his benefit. He was bought and sold, and treated as an ordinary article of merchandise and traffic, whenever a profit could be made by it. This opinion was at that time fixed and universal in the civilized portion of the white race.

Taney concluded:

The Scotts were black. They were slaves. But even if they were free, they could never be citizens of the United States because of their long recognized servile status. Slave codes and their cultural subservience convinced [Taney] that in 1787, when the Constitution was signed, blacks would always be excluded from citizenship. Therefore, blacks, whether slave or free, were not citizens under the Constitution and never could be.

But Taney was not done. In the first major exercise of judicial review since *Marbury v. Madison* in 1803, he ruled that the Missouri Compromise of 1820 was unconstitutional. He cited the due process clause of the Fifth Amendment, claiming slaves, as Story had ruled in *Prigg*, were "property." Not people. Slave owners had the right to take their ruled "property" wherever they wished. And this status would never change. Freeing a slave would deprive the slave owner of his "property" without "just compensation." The Bill of Rights protected the "property" of the slave owners. It was not written to protect slaves.

Nelson and Catron followed, with brief opinions. Curtis and McLean read their dissents the following day. The other opinions were filed. Only Wayne completely concurred with Taney, but the result was clear. Scott had lost. Fehrenbacher, *supra*.

George Curtis had joined Scott's lawyer, Montgomery Blair, in arguing that Congress had power over the territories. He wrote that once Taney refused Scott's legal standing to sue, Taney's further remarks denying the constitutionality of the Missouri Compromise were extra-judicial. Nelson's opinion correctly avoided the issue. Curtis and McLean, the dissenters, having accepted Scott's constitutional "standing" to sue, could correctly continue and determine the constitutionality of the Missouri Compromise.

Curtis and McLean were blamed for widening the issue. Others criticized Taney for being a strict constructionist. Taney claimed,

"No one supposes that any change in public opinion . . . should induce the court to give to the words of the Constitution a more liberal construction . . . than they were intended to bear when the instrument was framed." Taney refused to interpret the Constitution in the context of changing American values. Some writers insist he advanced the modern doctrine of liberal judicial review. Most historians agree he made a political decision.

Curtis's Dissent

Curtis rejected Taney's opinion. First, he refuted Taney's claim that because Scott was black, he could not be a citizen. Free blacks were citizens in several northern states in 1787 at the time of the Constitutional Convention. States could confer citizenship because there was no federal citizenship clause in the Constitution except that relating to the naturalization of foreigners. Therefore, state citizenship was primary, and citizens of the states were automatically citizens of the United States.

Curtis stated:

Of this there can be no doubt. At the time of the ratification of the Articles of Confederation, all free native-born inhabitants of the States of New Hampshire, Massachusetts, New York, New Jersey, and North Carolina, though descended from African slaves, who were not only citizens of those States, but such of them as had the other necessary qualifications, possessed the franchise of electors, on equal terms with other citizens.

Next, Curtis said that Scott's residence in the free state of Illinois and the free Territory of Wisconsin made him a free man. He cited law that distinguished temporary sojourners in free northern states and territories from those who became domiciled. Scott had been domiciled in both the free state of Illinois and the free Wisconsin Territory for many years. Comity and the Constitution required the Missouri court to give Scott his freedom.

Then Curtis struck at Taney's opinion that the Missouri Compromise was unconstitutional. He cited *American Insurance Company v. Canter*, 1 Pet. 511 (1828). Chief Justice John Marshall's interpretation was that federal power over the territories was derived from the Constitution in addition to its power to acquire territory. Curtis listed 14 instances since 1789 when Congress had legislated about slavery in the territories. He concluded that the

Missouri Compromise was constitutional. Therefore, Scott's residence in a free state and a free territory made him a free man.

Taney v. Curtis: The Letters

Taney's opinion was withheld from the public for several weeks after he read it in court. Speculation became rampant that Taney was making major revisions. Curtis was concerned because his opinion had focused on some of Taney's points.

On April 2, Curtis sought a copy of Taney's opinion from the Court clerk. The clerk refused, saying he had received an order from Taney with the concurrence of Wayne and Daniel that the opinion would not be available until it had been published officially in Howard's Reports. On April 6, Taney's written confirmation included the comment, "I have observed that the opinion of the Court has been greatly misunderstood and grossly misrepresented in the publications in the newspapers." Fehrenbacher, *supra*.

Curtis, believing the order did not apply to Court members, sent a second request to the clerk for a copy. The clerk replied that it did apply. Curtis then wrote to Taney, asking for a copy. Taney, clearly enraged, replied:

> It would seem from your letter to me that you suppose you are entitled to demand it as a right, being one of the members of the tribunal. This would undoubtedly be the case if you wished it to aid you in the discharge of your official duties. But I understand you as not desiring or intending it for that purpose. On the contrary, you announced from the Bench that you regarded this opinion as extrajudicial—and not binding upon you or anyone else.

Curtis hotly responded. On May 13, he wrote that it was a violation of the court rules to withhold an opinion and he had a right to it. On June 11, Taney finally answered, acerbically, stating he did not want to continue the "unpleasant correspondence that Curtis had begun." In reply to the charge that the opinion of the Court was materially altered after it was delivered from the bench, Taney continued:

> There is not one historical fact, nor one principle of constitutional law, or common law, or chancery law, or statute in the printed opinion which was not distinctly announced and

maintained from the Bench; nor is there any one historical fact, or principle, or point of law, which was affirmed in the opinion from the Bench, omitted or modified, or in any degree altered, in the printed opinion.

But he conceded that "proofs and authorities to support principles asserted" in his opinion had been added.

In Curtis's memoir, George reveals that Curtis filed the letters with his private papers and summed up the correspondence in his own handwriting. After detailing his efforts to obtain the majority opinion, Curtis observed that Taney did not conform to the Court's rules, which required, "All opinions delivered by the court shall, immediately upon the delivery thereof, be delivered over to the clerk to be recorded." Supreme Court Rules of Practice, Rule 25.

Instead, Curtis wrote the following:

> The opinion delivered by the Chief Justice was retained, and many material additions were made to it. I have marked in the margin of my copy the passages which I believe have been thus inserted. I have no doubt of the correctness of my memory on this subject. I heard the opinion read twice: once in conference, and once from the bench. I listened to it with attention, and believe I know where and in what it was changed. These additions amount to upwards of *eighteen* pages. No one can read them without perceiving that they are in *reply* to my opinion.

In his final paragraph, Curtis added: "My purpose in the above correspondence was to place before Judge Taney the true character of his act, not to enter an embittered controversy with him. I believe I have accomplished this purpose, and that he knows it."

Resignation

On September 30, 1857, Curtis resigned. Although his official reason was that he could not support his family on his salary, in a letter to his uncle, George Ticknor, he wrote, "I say to you *in confidence* I cannot again feel that confidence in the court, and that willingness to cooperate with them, which are essential to a satisfactory discharge of my duties as a member of that body; and I do not expect its condition to be improved." Curtis, ed., *supra.*

Abraham Lincoln adamantly refused to accept Taney's assertion that neither the Declaration of Independence nor the Constitution was ever intended to include blacks. He protested that Taney was doing "obvious violence to the plain unmistakable language of the Declaration. . . . [the Declaration] is assailed, and sneered at, and construed, and hawked at, and torn, till, if its framers could rise from their graves, they could not at all recognize it."

In a speech, Lincoln declared:

We think the *Dred Scott* decision is erroneous. We know the court that made it, has often over-ruled its own decisions, and we shall do what we can to have it to over-rule this. We offer no resistance to it. . . . All the powers of earth seem rapidly combining against him [the slave] . . . They have him in his prison house; they have searched his person, and left no prying instrument with him. One after another they have closed the heavy doors upon him and now they have him as it were, bolted in with a lock of a hundred keys, which can never be unlocked without the concurrence of every key; the keys in the hands of a hundred different men, and they scattered to a hundred different and distant places; and they stand musing as to what invention, in all the dominions of mind and matter, can be produced to make the impossibility of his escape more complete than it is.

D.H. Herbert, *Lincoln* (1995).

Almost three years later, President Buchanan told the American people the *Dred Scott* decision was the solution to the slavery issue:

The right has been established of every citizen to take his property of any kind, including slaves, into the common Territory belonging equally to all the States of the Confederacy, and to have it protected there under the Federal Constitution. Neither Congress nor a Territorial legislature nor any human power has any authority to annul or impair this vested right. . . . Thus has the status of a Territory during the intermediate period from its full settlement until it shall become a State been irrevocably fixed by the final decision of the Supreme Court. Fortunate has this been for the prosperity of the Territories, as well as the tranquility of the States.

Fehrenbacher, *supra*.

G.E. White wrote of Taney:

> Under the pressure of events, he departed from his usual practice and sought a ringing affirmation of overriding principles, in the Marshall tradition. But the first principles had vanished; available in their place were only opposing sets of deeply held values. His choice between those sets of values exacerbated tensions in his own time and has left him vulnerable to the moral censure of later generations.

White, *supra.*

Afterword

After resigning from the Court, Curtis returned to a successful law practice in Boston. He argued 22 cases before the U.S. Supreme Court and 12 before the Supreme Judicial Court of Massachusetts. Curtis taught at the Harvard Law School and was a prolific writer, publishing books on the exercise of executive power and decisions by the U.S. Supreme Court.

His happy second marriage ended with Anna's death on April 4, 1860. Curtis was married a third time on August 20, 1861, to Maria Malleville Allen, with whom he had three children. She was a resident of Pittsfield, Massachusetts, where the Curtises maintained a country estate. Five of Curtis's 12 children survived him.

During the Civil War, Curtis supported President Abraham Lincoln "so long and so far, and by all ways and means possible to a good citizen." But Curtis believed Lincoln exceeded his constitutional authority by suspending the writ of habeas corpus and issuing a preliminary Emancipation Proclamation.

In 1868 Curtis represented President Andrew Johnson in his impeachment trial. Curtis convinced a Senate majority that the Founders did not envision political disagreements as the constitutional test for impeachment. It was a trial of, not a vote of confidence in, the president.

The defendant in *Scott v. Sandford,* John Sanford, died in an asylum two months after Taney's opinion.

Dred Scott and his family were freed by their new owner, Taylor Blow, in May 1857. Dred and Harriet Scott posted a $1,000 bond, with Blow acting as security for good behavior, a legal requirement for the Scotts to continue living in Missouri. After 16 months of freedom, Dred Scott died of tuberculosis. In 1957, at a centennial observance, a granite marker provided by Blow's granddaughter was placed on Scott's grave at Calvary Cemetery in St. Louis. It carries this inscription:

> Dred Scott Born About 1799 Died Sept. 17, 1858. Dred Scott Subject Of The Decision Of The Supreme Court Of The United States In 1857 Which Denied Citizenship To The Negro, Voided The Missouri Compromise Act, Became One Of The Events That Resulted In The Civil War

Justice Nelson wrote to Curtis in 1860, stating, "The Republican leaders are unyielding, and I think there is no hope for an adjustment through them . . . If the Union be saved, it must be by the masses of the people."

After the Civil War, the 13th and 14th Amendments to the Constitution overturned the *Dred Scott* decision.

Justice John A. Campbell of Alabama resigned from the Supreme Court on April 26, 1861. He was appointed assistant secretary of war for the Confederacy. When Campbell was imprisoned after the war, Curtis and Nelson interceded with President Andrew Johnson and persuaded him to release Campbell.

Chief Justice Roger Taney remained a Unionist during the Civil War. He died on October 12, 1864, at the age of 87. In an interview shortly after the *Scott v. Sandford* decision, Taney said: "I am not a slaveholder. More than thirty years ago I manumitted every slave I ever owned except two who were too old when they became my property to provide for themselves. These two I supported in comfort as long as they lived." Abraham, *supra.*

On October 15, 1864, Curtis eulogized Taney at a meeting of the Boston Bar Association: "The great powers intrusted to the court by the Constitution and laws of his country he steadily and firmly upheld and administered. . . ." A.F. Westin, *An Autobiography of the Supreme Court* (1963).

In June 1874, Curtis rented a villa at Newport, Rhode Island, so his family could spend the summer months together. He died there on September 15, 1874. Curtis is buried at Mount Auburn Cemetery in Cambridge, Massachusetts.

6

The Long, Strange Case of Dr. Samuel Mudd

The Lincoln Assassination

At 10:20 PM on Good Friday, April 14, 1865, the celebrated actor John Wilkes Booth entered the presidential box at Ford's Theatre in Washington, D.C., and shot President Abraham Lincoln, mortally wounding him. Booth broke his left leg while escaping. Several hours later, he and co-conspirator David Herold arrived at the farm of Dr. Samuel Mudd, five miles from Bryantown, Maryland. The doctor responded to their call for help.

The tragedy of Lincoln's death led to controversy. Did Booth act alone? Was Dr. Mudd a simple country doctor who provided medical attention to a stranger in distress, or was he a co-conspirator in Lincoln's death? What did Mudd know? When did Mudd know it? Should Mudd's name be "mud"? On one side were Mudd and, later, his grandson, who successively pursued a 138-year legal battle and public relations campaign to clear the family name. On the other were historians who reject Mudd's claim of innocence.

This was Dr. Mudd's account: He had been awakened on Saturday, April 15, at 4:00 AM by a young man who explained that his friend's leg had been hurt when his horse fell and landed on him.

Mudd sent the men to an upstairs bedroom. When he cut off the injured man's boot, Mudd found a straight break about two inches above the instep. He improvised a splint. Mudd insisted that the stranger had kept his lower face concealed by a shawl, although the doctor noticed he had a mustache and whiskers. Mudd paid John Best, a handyman, $25 to make a pair of rough crutches. The stranger requested a razor to shave his mustache. When the young man asked the shortest way to Parson Wilmer's house, Mudd pointed out the route through nearby Zekiah Swamp.

While the injured man rested, Mudd rode toward Bryantown, attempting unsuccessfully to find a carriage. There, he heard rumors of the attack in Washington. On the way back, he stopped at a neighbor's house and told him the terrible news that the president and the secretary of state had been assassinated.

The strangers were leaving Mudd's farm when he returned in the evening. Mudd's wife later told him that the man's whiskers were askew as he came downstairs. Mudd reported the suspicious visit to his cousin the next morning and asked him to tell the authorities.

As Booth and Herold zig-zagged through southern Maryland and across the Potomac River to Virginia, they received help from Confederate sympathizers who were never charged with aiding the fugitives. On April 26, Booth and Herold were surrounded by Federal soldiers in a barn near Bowling Green, Virginia. Herold surrendered. The barn was set afire. Sergeant Boston Corbett shot Booth to death. According to Corbett, Booth's last words were, "Tell my mother I die for my country." Booth's diary was handed to Lafayette Baker, who gave it to Secretary of War Edwin M. Stanton. It was not presented at the subsequent trial.

Booth's alleged co-conspirators were rounded up and tried, including Dr. Mudd. Splinting Booth's leg forever linked Mudd to the conspiracy to assassinate Lincoln. Trial witnesses testified that Mudd had twice met with Booth several months before Lincoln's assassination. Mudd was convicted.

But this was only the beginning of the saga. Mudd's grandson, Richard Mudd of Saginaw, Michigan, spent his long life fighting the conviction and defending Samuel Mudd's name. In his self-published book, Richard Mudd wrote about his grandfather. Sam Mudd was born on December 20, 1833, and raised on the family plantation, Oak Hill, in Maryland, about 30 miles from Washington, D.C. He graduated from Baltimore Medical College and married his childhood sweetheart, Sarah Frances "Frank" Dyer. At the time of the assassination, Sam lived with his wife and four young children and farmed a 218-acre tract of his father's land.

When the Civil War broke out, Maryland seemed likely to join the Confederacy. After it was occupied by Federal troops, it became a border state. Sam Mudd, with his labor-intensive tobacco crops, was a slaveholder. Like many of his Charles County neighbors, he was a Southern sympathizer. But Richard Mudd claimed it was his grandfather's acts of courtesy and hospitality toward Booth that "came close to costing the young physician his life." R. Mudd, *Samuel Alexander Mudd and His Descendants* (1982).

Background

If Samuel Mudd was involved with Booth, it is likely that he knew only of Booth's original plot, which was to kidnap Lincoln and take him to Richmond, Virginia, as a hostage. Booth fantasized this would bring about a prisoner exchange and gain the South time to regroup. In August 1864, recruiting conspirators for his abduction plan, Booth contacted boyhood friends Michael O'Laughlin and Samuel Arnold.

Next, Booth secured a letter of introduction from a man named Patrick Martin in Montreal to William Queen and Sam Mudd. Queen's son-in-law introduced Mudd to Booth at St. Mary's Church at Bryantown on November 11, 1864. Mudd claimed that Booth said he was interested in buying land and purchasing a horse. Booth stayed overnight with Mudd and purchased a one-eyed horse from Mudd's neighbor.

On December 23 in Washington, D.C., Mudd introduced Booth to John Surratt Jr., the youngest child of Mary Surratt, who ran a boarding house. They talked in Booth's room at the National Hotel. John Surratt was a Confederate courier whose contact in Richmond was Confederate Secretary of State Judah P. Benjamin. The Surratt Tavern, previously owned by the family, was a "safe house" on the route between Richmond and Washington. Also at the meeting was Louis Weichmann, Surratt's roommate, a Federal government employee who, like the Woody Allen character Zelig, was present at significant moments without participating in Booth's meetings. He became a star witness for the prosecution. There is no credible evidence that Mudd met with Booth after this time.

Surratt contacted George Atzerodt, who ran a ferry service in Port Tobacco, Maryland, and also recruited David Herold, a 22-year-old employee at the Navy Yard pharmacy. An avid bird hunter, Herold knew the back roads of southern Maryland. The last to join was Lewis Powell, aka Lewis Payne.

As John Surratt later explained, Booth's plot to abduct Lincoln failed. He first considered snatching Lincoln from Ford's Theatre. Then, Booth learned that on March 17, 1865, the president would visit the Seventh Street Hospital to join wounded soldiers watching the play *Still Waters Run Deep*. The conspirators—Arnold, O'Laughlin, Powell, Atzerodt, Herold, Surratt, and Booth—would seize Lincoln's carriage and drive directly to southern Maryland.

But Lincoln did not appear. Instead, he was meeting with the Indiana governor at the National Hotel, ironically the same hotel where Booth was living. Surratt said, "It was our last attempt." Arnold ended his affiliation with Booth. O'Laughlin took no further part. E. Steers Jr., *Blood on the Moon* (2001).

Murder

Booth devised a different plan. Both Lincoln and Booth admired Shakespeare's tragedies. Booth decided to become Brutus to Lincoln's Julius Caesar. His hatred of Lincoln increased with his knowledge of plans for reconstruction, including an elective franchise for the "colored" man.

Booth called for a dramatic, three-pronged strike. Atzerodt, Powell, and Herold were given supporting roles. Mary Surratt played a cameo in which she later was alleged to have delivered a package of binoculars and a message to the drunken innkeeper at the Surrattsville tavern, telling him to have the weapon and whisky ready. On April 14, Atzerodt arrived at the Kirkwood Hotel, where Vice President Andrew Johnson was staying. Atzerodt's assignment was to kill Johnson, but he lost his nerve. That evening, Herold led Powell to Secretary of State William H. Seward's house. Powell attacked Seward, his family, and servants. Seward and his son suffered severe injuries, but all survived. Powell rode and then abandoned the one-eyed horse.

Booth kept the starring role for himself. He brought his horse to the alley of Ford's Theatre and found Edward (Edman/Ned) Spangler, a stagehand who had worked on the Booth estate, and asked him to watch his horse. Spangler, busy moving scenery, passed the task to a vendor, Joseph Burroughs, known as "John Peanuts." Booth, familiar with the building, went to Lincoln's box where the president, first lady, and two guests were watching the play *Our American Cousin*. General Ulysses S. Grant and his wife had been invited to attend, but they had declined, preferring to visit their children. Booth quietly opened the door of the box and fired his derringer directly at Lincoln's head. As he leaped to the stage, Booth's spur caught in the Treasury Guard flag decorating the presidential box. Booth shouted *Sic semper tyrannis*, hobbled through the rear door, mounted his horse, and fled.

Word of the tragedy spread through the capital, and Secretary Stanton moved rapidly. He summoned Lafayette Baker, head of the National Detective Police, to capture the conspirators. Eight suspects were arrested, and Stanton insisted that they be tried by a military commission so the government could control the proceedings. Some cabinet members protested, but Attorney General James Speed and Army Advocate General Joseph Holt agreed with Stanton. On May 1, 1865, President Andrew Johnson created the nine-man Hunter Commission, made up of seven generals and two colonels, to conduct the non-jury trial.

Speed justified the military commission by calling the defendants "enemy belligerents" who planned to disrupt the Federal government and its military objectives. Killing the commander-in-chief was considered a military crime and an offense against the laws of war. The government was adamant that the Lincoln death plot was backed by the Confederate government, although Jefferson Davis and his cabinet had left Richmond before the city was surrendered on April 3 and before General Robert E. Lee surrendered the Army of Northern Virginia at Appomattox on April 9, 1865. Civil courts were open and functioning in Washington, D.C. E. Steers Jr., ed., *The Trial* (2003).

Benn Pitman, the brother of Isaac Pitman who created shorthand, was the official recorder to the Hunter Commission. His spelling of the names O'Laughlin, Weichmann, and Payne has been used in the following excerpts.

Trial

On trial were Atzerodt, Herold, Payne (Powell), Mary Surratt, Mudd, Arnold, O'Laughlin, and the stage hand Spangler. All were charged with "maliciously, unlawfully and traitorously . . . conspiring . . . to kill and murder [Abraham Lincoln, Andrew Johnson, and William H. Seward] and lying in wait with intent . . . to kill and murder [Andrew Johnson and Ulysses S. Grant]." Each pleaded not guilty. Tried as unindicted co-conspirators were Confederate President Jefferson

Davis and his Canadian-based operatives. The government's case against them was based on the testimony of three witnesses whose credibility quickly collapsed.

Steers, *The Trial, supra.*

The specific charge against Mudd was that "on various days between March 6 and April 20, 1865, he did advise, encourage, receive, entertain, harbor, and conceal, aid and assist" John Wilkes Booth, the Surratts, and the other defendants, "with knowledge of the murderous and traitorous conspiracy aforesaid, and with the intent to aid and assist them in the execution thereof and in escaping from justice after the murder of the said Abraham Lincoln." B. Aymat & E. Sagarin, *A Pictorial History of the World's Great Trials* (1983).

Mudd, told he could retain counsel, hired Frederick Stone, Charles County's leading lawyer. Mudd's wife retained Thomas Ewing Jr., as the principal lawyer to defend her husband. Ewing, a former chief justice of the Kansas Supreme Court and brother-in-law of General William Tecumseh Sherman, had just resigned his commission as a brigadier general in the Union Army. S. Carter, *The Riddle of Dr. Mudd* (1974); Steers, *The Trial, supra.*

Ewing protested to Special Judge Advocate John Bingham that it was unconstitutional for civilians to be tried by a military commission when civilian courts were available. Ewing claimed the military commission was illegal as it was not created by Congress, and it violated the Fifth Amendment to the Constitution, which provided for a grand jury indictment in a case involving capital punishment, and the Sixth Amendment, which called for a "speedy and public trial by an impartial jury." Steers, *Id.*

Speedy it was. The commission first met on May 10, 1865. The trial began three days later, and 366 witnesses testified. As in most civilian courts at that time, criminal defendants were not permitted to testify on their own behalf.

The prosecution began its case against Mudd with the testimony of Lieutenant Alexander Lovett, who had investigated Mudd's role in Booth's escape. Lovett arrived at the Mudd farm on Tuesday, April 18, 1865, and asked Mudd about Booth. Mudd replied that he had not recognized Booth. Lovett said when he returned three days later to search the house, Mudd's wife brought a riding boot downstairs. Inside the boot, Lovett read the name "J. Wilkes." Lovett said he asked Mudd about this, and Mudd denied noticing it. Lovett said Mudd later admitted having met Booth once to discuss a horse sale on a Sunday in November 1864 at St. Mary's Church near Bryantown.

Louis Weichmann contradicted Mudd's story when he testified that he and John Surratt Jr. met Booth and Mudd on a D.C. street. Booth invited them to his hotel room for a drink. Although Weichmann said he met Mudd in Washington in January 1865, it was the December 23, 1864, meeting at the National Hotel to which he was referring.

> *Weichmann:* [Mudd] and John Wilkes Booth were walking together. Mudd introduced Booth to both of us . . . Booth invited us to his room at the National Hotel. When we arrived there, he told us to be seated, and ordered cigars and wine for four. Dr. Mudd then went out into a passage and called Booth out, and had a private conversation with him. When they returned. Booth called Surratt, and all three went out together and had a private conversation, leaving me alone.
>
> *Judge Advocate:* Can you state the nature of their conversation?
>
> *Weichmann:* I did not hear the conversation; I was seated on a lounge near the window. On returning to the room the last time, Dr. Mudd apologized to me for his private conversation, and stated that Booth and he had some private business; that Booth wished to purchase his farm, but that he did not care about selling it, as Booth was not willing to give him enough. Booth also apologized, and stated to me that he wished to purchase Dr. Mudd's farm. Afterward they were seated round the center table, when Booth took out an envelope, and on the back of it made marks with a pencil.

Weichmann testified about Booth's conversation: "He hoped the war would soon come to an end, and spoke like a Union man." He added: "I had never seen Dr. Mudd before that day. I had heard the name of Mudd mentioned in Mrs. Surratt's house, but whether it was Dr. Samuel Mudd I cannot say." Carter, *supra.*

Ewing held Weichmann to the January date and provided witnesses to show that Mudd did not travel to Washington in January 1865. In his summation, Ewing said: "It will be observed that the only men spoken of as having seen the accused on this occasion are Booth, who is dead, and Surratt, who is a fugitive from the country. So there is no one who can be called to confirm or refute his statements."

Ewing tried to convince the commission that Mudd cooperated with the authorities by reporting the visit to his farm by the two strangers. He brought in George Mudd, Sam's cousin, who described how Sam met him after church on Easter Sunday and told him about the events of Saturday morning. Sam asked George, a well-known Union man, to inform the authorities. George spoke with Lieutenant David Dana on Monday morning, but Sam was not interviewed until Tuesday, and again on Friday. Ewing pointed out that the government agents waited longer than Mudd to pursue the lead.

Ewing also defused testimony by former slaves who said Sam Mudd had earlier sheltered Confederates including John Surratt and had mistreated a slave. He attacked the credibility of a witness who said Sam Mudd had predicted Lincoln's death. Samuel Knapp Chester, a fellow actor and friend of Booth, gave the only testimony about the plot to capture Lincoln, which he mentioned while explaining that Booth had access to large sums of money. However, Edward Steers Jr., a historian critical of Mudd, claims that admitting involvement in the unsuccessful abduction plot, not the murder, would not have been a defense because the conspirators were guilty of a shifting conspiracy, the kidnapping plot having evolved into the assassination. Steers, *Blood on the Moon*, *supra*.

Ewing argued on Mudd's behalf:

> I will show, first, that Dr. Mudd is not, and cannot be, guilty of any offense known to the law. Not of treason. The overt act attempted to be alleged is the murder of the President. The proof is conclusive, that at the time the tragedy was enacted Dr. Mudd was at his residence in the country, thirty miles from the place of the crime. Those who committed it are shown to have acted for themselves, not as instruments of Dr. Mudd. He, therefore, cannot be charged, according to law, and upon the evidence, with the commission of this overt act. There are not two witnesses to prove that he did commit it, but abundant evidence to show negatively that he did not. . . .
>
> If a man receives, harbors, or otherwise assists to elude justice, one whom he knows to be guilty of felony, he becomes thereby an accessory after the fact in the felony. . . . Now, let us apply the facts to the law, and see whether Dr. Mudd falls

within the rule. On the morning after the assassination about daybreak, Booth arrived at his house. He did not find the Doctor on watch for him, as a guilty accomplice, expecting his arrival, would have been, but he and all his household were in profound sleep. . . . The Doctor rose from his bed, assisted Booth into the house, laid him on a sofa, took him upstairs to a bed, set the fractured bone. . . . But he did not know, and had no reason to suspect that his patient was a fugitive murderer.

E.W. Knappman, *Great American Trials* (1994).

Ewing quoted *Wharton's American Law*: "If a person supply a felon with food, or other necessaries for his sustenance, or professionally attend him sick or wounded, though he know him to be a felon, these acts will not be sufficient to make a party an accessory after the fact." He conceded that showing Booth's companion the route to Wilmer's could have implicated Mudd if he had known the crime and the criminal, but Ewing insisted that Mudd did not know the crime until he went to Bryantown and did not have the least suspicion of the criminal until after Booth had gone.

Conviction

On June 30, 1865, all eight defendants were convicted. George Atzerodt, David Herold, Lewis Powell aka Payne, and Mary Surratt were sentenced to death by hanging. Everyone expected Mary Surratt to be spared, including five members of the commission, who sent a clemency plea to President Johnson. Holt claimed the plea was attached to the court's findings and presented to the president; Johnson later said he did not receive the commutation petition but that he would have signed it.

On July 7, 1865, a steamy afternoon, Mary Surratt was hanged at Washington Penitentiary along with Powell, Atzerodt, and Herold. Mary Surratt was the first woman executed by the U.S. government. Mudd, Arnold, and O'Laughlin were given life sentences. Spangler was sentenced to six years. The vote against Mudd was five to four, one vote short of death. He was found guilty of all charges with the exception of "receiving, entertaining, and harboring and concealing" the defendants, except Booth and Herold, and of "combining, confederating, and conspiring with Spangler." E.S. Trindal, *Mary Surratt: An American Tragedy* (1996).

Booth, of course, was dead. The remaining co-conspirator sought by the detectives had escaped. John Surratt, who had been in Elmira, New York, on the night of the assassination, had fled to Canada and then to Rome, where he became a papal Zouave (guard) at the Vatican. He was recognized by a tourist but escaped by jumping into a deep ravine. Captured in Alexandria, Egypt, he was returned and tried in the Criminal Court for the District of Columbia, where he was charged in a plot to kidnap, not a plot to kill, Lincoln. Weichmann, called to testify, said the abduction plans collapsed about three weeks before the assassination. On August 10, 1867, Surratt's trial ended with a hung jury, and the prosecution did not seek another trial. Passions had subsided. By 1868, Surratt was a free man. E.C. Weckesser, *His Name Was Mudd* (1991).

Meanwhile, Mudd, Arnold, O'Laughlin, and Spangler had been sent to the New York Penitentiary in Albany. Stanton transferred the convicted conspirators to Fort Jefferson on Dry Tortugas, a string of islands 70 miles from Key West. The fort was stark and isolated. Conditions were debilitating. Mudd tried unsuccessfully to escape.

While Mudd was in prison, the decision in *Ex parte Milligan*, 71 U.S. 2 (1866), was announced. Lambdin P. Milligan, a Confederate sympathizer who was indicted for conspiracy and tried by a military commission in Indiana, was found guilty in December 1864 and sentenced to be executed. His lawyers filed for a writ of habeas corpus. The case was heard by the U.S. Supreme Court in April 1866. Chief Justice Salmon P. Chase concurred in the court's decision that a trial before a military commission violated Milligan's rights under the Constitution. Milligan, a private citizen, was neither the resident of a seceded state nor a prisoner of war. No fighting was going on in Indiana, and the civil courts were open. Milligan's status resembled Mudd's. It was a vindication of Ewing's argument. Carter, *supra*.

In 1867, yellow fever struck Fort Jefferson. When the prison doctor died, Mudd volunteered to treat the remaining convicts and guards even though he was suffering from the fever. O'Laughlin died, but Mudd persevered and saved lives.

The next year, because of the decision in *Milligan*, Baltimore lawyer Andrew Sterrett Ridgely filed a petition for a writ of habeas corpus for Mudd with Chief Justice Chase, who returned the petition with a note to file it in the district where Mudd was imprisoned. Accordingly, *Ex parte Mudd* came before the U.S. District Court for the Southern District of Florida, claiming Mudd, Arnold, and Spangler had been entitled to a jury trial in a civilian court. But Judge Thomas Jefferson Boynton denied the petition, ruling that Lincoln's assassination was the murder of the commander-in-chief in time of war while in a "fortified city" within the war zone.

Mudd appealed. However, President Johnson gave Mudd an unconditional pardon on March 19, 1869, because of his lifesaving efforts; as a result, Mudd's appeal became moot. His name was removed from the appellate file. The case was argued before the U.S. Supreme Court, but before the opinion could be written, Johnson pardoned the remaining co-defendants, Arnold and Spangler. The appeal was dismissed.

Mudd, released from Fort Jefferson on March 8, 1869, returned to his home. He practiced medicine and farmed. Spangler, who had become Mudd's close companion in prison, went to live on Mudd's farm. Mudd died on January 10, 1883. He is buried at St. Mary's Roman Catholic Church Cemetery—the church where Mudd first met Booth 19 years earlier. Mudd's wife, "Frank," died on December 29, 1911, and was buried next to her husband.

Richard Mudd

Mudd's grandson, Richard Mudd, was not satisfied with his grandfather's pardon. An industrial physician and surgeon for General Motors, Richard Mudd never gave up trying to exonerate his grandfather. The popular saying "His name is mud" threatened the reputation of the well-researched family tree. Waging a militant campaign, he lectured and appealed to state legislatures, beseeching them to pass resolutions publicly declaring his grandfather's innocence.

His attack was twofold: a public relations barrage and a political/legal crusade. Books written by family members—including Nettie Mudd Monroe, Sam's ninth and youngest child, and John McHale Jr., an ex-FBI agent who married Sam's great-granddaughter—created the image of an innocent country doctor:

Mudd recorded the publicity in chapter XXII of Nettie's book. One entry reads: "Widespread attention of the public to the fate of Dr. Mudd resulted from a fine article in the *Saturday Evening Post* of October 2, 1926, by George Allan England. To encourage the *Post* to accept this article, the author (Mudd) obtained signatures of persons at Henry Ford Hospital, Detroit, where he was an intern urging the *Post* to accept the article." N. Mudd, *The Life of Samuel A. Mudd* (1975).

A 1936 Paramount Pictures movie, *The Prisoner of Shark Island*, directed by John Ford and starring Warner Baxter, portrayed Sam Mudd as a folk hero. In the film, Mudd was an innocent victim falsely accused of Lincoln's murder and subjected to cruel punishment.

Louise Arehart, youngest of Sam's 33 grandchildren, convinced her brother to sell the family farmhouse and surrounding land to the Maryland Historical Trust in 1968. The Samuel A. Mudd House Museum is open to the public.

Richard Mudd petitioned successive presidents, with some success. In October 1959, President Dwight Eisenhower had a plaque erected at Fort Jefferson memorializing Mudd's heroic efforts during the yellow fever outbreak. Mudd appealed to President Jimmy Carter as well. On July 24, 1979, Carter wrote that the Hunter Commission's finding of Samuel Mudd's guilt and his sentence were binding and conclusive judgments and that there was "no authority under law by which I, as President, could set aside his conviction. All legal authority vested in the President to act in this case was exercised when President Andrew Johnson granted Dr. Mudd a full and unconditional pardon on February 8, 1869." But he sympathized with the Mudds.

Mudd next appealed to President Ronald Reagan, who sent a letter stating, "I came to believe as you do that Dr. Samuel Mudd was indeed innocent of any wrongdoing." J.E. McHale Jr., *Doctor Samuel A. Mudd and the Lincoln Assassination* (1995).

In June 1992, Representatives Steny Hoyer of Maryland and Thomas Ewing of Illinois introduced House Bill 1885 to set aside Mudd's conviction, but the bill died in committee.

By this time, Mudd had found a new outlet. In October 1990, he filed a petition with the Army Board for Correction of Military Records (ABCMR), a civilian body responsible for making recommendations regarding errors and injustices in military records. The ABCMR considered not guilt but jurisdiction. Mudd requested that the board set aside his grandfather's conviction and have it expunged from the National Archives.

The hearing featured famous names from the nineteenth century. Chairing the board was Charles A. Chase, a great-grandnephew of former Supreme Court Chief Justice Salmon

P. Chase. After an opening statement by Richard Mudd, two lawyers discussed the legality of bringing civilian defendants before a military commission during peacetime. One of the lawyers was Candida Ewing Steele, the great-great-granddaughter of Samuel Mudd's lawyer, General Thomas Ewing.

Laura Chappelle, Mudd's great-great-granddaughter and an appellate lawyer from Michigan, testified about the legal restraints faced by Mudd and Ewing in providing a defense. Author J.E. McHale testified, as did Richard Mudd's son, Thomas Boarman Mudd, who told "a touching story of his great-grandmother." The closing speech was by Richard Mudd, two days short of his 91st birthday. As he reached advanced age, Richard Mudd became quotable. In January 1992, the board agreed and recommended that Mudd's petition be implemented. Mudd, *supra*; McHale, *supra*.

The ABCMR concluded that it "had the advantage of hindsight and looked at the facts of the case with more detachment than was possible in the emotionally charged atmosphere after the Civil War." It considered *Ex parte Milligan*, which was decided after Mudd's trial, and found Mudd's case so analogous that it used the same rationale. Moreover, it disputed the attorney general's opinion in 1865 that the crimes were "uniquely military" and noted that none of the individuals with whom Mudd was alleged to have conspired was a member of, or closely involved with, the military.

The board observed that General Lee had surrendered a month before the trial began: "There is no evidence that the capital was under siege or that any Confederate forces had invaded or were likely to invade the District of Columbia in the spring of 1865." Finally, it found

> no good reason why Dr. Mudd should not have been tried by a civilian court. It, therefore, unanimously concludes that the military commission did not have jurisdiction to try him, and that in so doing denied him his due process rights, particularly his right to trial by a jury of his peers. This denial constituted such a gross infringement of his Constitutionally protected rights, that his conviction should be set aside. To fail to do so would be unjust.

In July 1992, Acting Assistant Secretary of the Army William D. Clark refused to accept the ABCMR's recommendations, saying the board was not in the business of settling historical disputes.

Mudd continued his campaign. In August 1992, he petitioned the secretary of the Army, seeking a reversal of Clark's decision. Assistant Secretary of the Army Sara E. Lister declined his request for reconsideration and reversal of Clark's decision.

That December, Mudd filed an action in the U.S. District Court for the District of Columbia to have Lister's decision reviewed, and for a writ of mandamus directing the secretary of the Army to adopt the ABCMR's recommendations. He asked for a declaratory judgment that Samuel Mudd had been wrongfully convicted.

While they awaited further legal action, the family won a public relations victory when, in a University of Richmond moot court trial with Candida Ewing Steele and F. Lee Bailey on the defense team, Mudd's conviction was overturned.

In October 1998, Judge Paul L. Friedman of the D.C. District Court dismissed Mudd's petitions. But he ruled that the secretary of the Army's decision rejecting the ABCMR's recommendations was reached in an "arbitrary and capricious" manner. He ordered the Army to reconsider its recommendation. Mudd's quest still had life.

On March 6, 2000, the Office of the Secretary of the Army rejected this request to throw out Mudd's conviction by a military commission, stating the decision was based on a narrow question: whether a military commission had jurisdiction to try Samuel Mudd. It cited *Ex parte Quirin*, 317 U.S. 1 (1942), which held that enemy belligerents who engage in hostilities in the United States, even if American citizens, can be tried by military commissions. The defendants in *Ex parte Quirin* were trained as saboteurs. During World War II, they crept ashore at night on Long Island from a German submarine, changed from military uniforms into civilian clothes, and dispersed throughout the country with a plan to damage the American war industry. Two of the saboteurs, Ernest Peter Burger and Herbert Haupt, were American citizens. L. Fisher, *Nazi Saboteurs on Trial* (2003).

A year later, Judge Friedman ruled that the Army had properly evaluated the ABCMR's recommendations. In his final decision, Judge Friedman upheld the legal jurisdiction of the military commission, affirming Boynton's 1868 decision ruling that *Ex Parte Milligan* was not applicable in Mudd's case.

Richard Mudd died at the age of 101 in 2002, but his son continued to pursue the case. On November 8, 2002, in the U.S. Court of Appeals for the District of Columbia Circuit, Thomas B. Mudd's appeal in *Mudd v. White* was denied. This time, the court ruled that Samuel Mudd lacked proper standing to sue because he was not a member of the military. The Mudd heirs' final step was an appeal to the U.S. Supreme Court.

In February 2003, the Court refused to hear the appeal of the 138-year-old conviction of Mudd for complicity in Lincoln's assassination because the deadline for filing had been missed. The long legal battle ended, not with a bang but a whimper.

Surratt Society member Richard Willing, legal correspondent for *USA Today*, wrote in the *Surratt Courier*:

> The error by the Mudd's Washington, D.C. lawyer . . . snuffs out the last hope of Mudd's descendants to overturn the conviction. "It's heartbreaking to lose this way," said Thomas B. Mudd of Saginaw, Michigan. "We never held out great hope that the Supreme Court would do justice for Dr. Mudd. But not to even get the case in front of them after all this time, that's really hard to take." The lawyer acknowledged that he just blew it, missing a deadline for filing a petition for certiorari.

"Getting the appeal was a long shot," Willing wrote. The court receives about 8,000 appeal requests each year and usually accepts fewer than 90. At least four of the nine justices must agree that an appeal should be heard. Chief Justice William Rehnquist, in *All the Laws but One*, which he wrote in 1998, criticized the revival of the Mudd case as a misuse of judicial power. *Surratt Courier* (April 2003).

The Mudd family might take consolation from the fact that the expression "His name is mud" does not derive from their forefather. Instead, it dates back to the 1820s, according to Eric Partridge, who cites an 1823 quotation, "And his name is Mud!" T. Burnam, *More Misinformation*, available at Mudd Miscellany, wesclark.com/jw/mudd.html (2007).

But the Mudd saga may not be over. On April 16, 2004, two days after the 139th anniversary of the assassination of Abraham Lincoln, Thomas B. Mudd, a retired history teacher, stated in the *Holland Michigan Sentinel*, "I'm still going to fight for my great-grandfather's innocence."

7

The Unusual Judah
P. Benjamin

Abraham Lincoln called him the "smartest" person in the Confederate government. Jefferson Davis proclaimed him a "master of law." At a gathering of barristers in the Inner Temple, Sir Henry James, England's Attorney General, said, "We found a place for him in our foremost rank."

He was Judah P. Benjamin. Successful lawyer and Senator in the United States. Cabinet officer in the Confederate States. Queen's Counsel in England. Lauded on two continents. How did this happen? At the age of 55, Judah P. Benjamin underwent a major mid-career crisis. When the Confederacy lost the Civil War, Benjamin abandoned law and politics in America and fled to England and a new life. This time he would become a British barrister.

Judah P. Benjamin's American career was more than the usual Horatio Alger success story of a poor boy who worked hard to achieve success. Benjamin's ascent, in which he survived a scandal at Yale and an unconventional marriage, was more remarkable in the nineteenth century because he was a Jew.

His work history resonates today when we are constantly warned that no career is safe; never stop networking; as soon as you land a job start looking for the next. Although Benjamin's career path resulted more from national insurgency than job restructuring, the results are similar. He never stopped learning, spoke several languages, worked hard, and adapted to changing circumstances.

This strange odyssey began on the Caribbean island of Saint Croix, where Benjamin was born in 1811 of parents who had migrated from England. It continued in Charleston, New Haven, New Orleans, Washington, D.C., Richmond, London, and Paris. His was a life filled with fresh beginnings.

Judah P. Benjamin was raised in rooms behind his parents' store in Charleston, South Carolina. After attending Fayetteville Academy with financial help, he entered Yale at just 14 years old, only to leave college two years later in 1827.

Retreating south to New Orleans, Benjamin found work clerking in a law office. To earn extra money, he gave English lessons to the children of wealthy, French-speaking Creoles. One of his students was Natalie St. Martin, a belle with dark hair and eyes, little education, extravagant tastes, and a love of pleasure. He was 21 and she only 16 when they met, and they married in 1833.

Benjamin was now a practicing lawyer with few clients. Using his law examination notes, he wrote a book with Thomas Sliddell: *Digest of the Reported Decisions of the Superior Court of the Late Territory of New Orleans and the Supreme Court of the State of Louisiana.* The title was long. Its success immediate. Lawyers clamored for copies. Benjamin had taken his first step toward success. E. Evans, *Judah P. Benjamin* (1988).

As his star rose in New Orleans, his fame spread beyond Louisiana and the South. He was retained to represent clients in California, Mexico, Ecuador, and the Galapagos Islands. By 1839, he was busy, urbane, and very wealthy.

Benjamin purchased a partnership in Bellechasse, a sugar plantation with 140 slaves near New Orleans. Gossip claimed that he installed his wife there to keep her from sharing her charms with other men. As his career flourished, his marriage floundered. In 1845, Natalie took their two-year-old daughter, Ninette, to live in Paris. Benjamin accepted this decision and planned yearly visits.

Meanwhile, he appeared in cases of national significance. He won a reversal for several insurance companies in the landmark case of *McCargo v. New Orleans Insurance Company* & *Lockett v. Merchants' Insurance Company*, 10 Robs. La. Rpts. 202, 339 (1842). A shipload of slaves loaded in Virginia for transport to Louisiana had been lost when 19 slaves mutinied. They murdered the captain and forced the crew to change course to the Bahamas. There, the mutineers were taken into custody. The slaves not involved in mutiny or murder were permitted to land in Nassau, which was British and, therefore, free territory. The question: Were the slaves now free because they entered free soil with the permission of a British officer? The company that claimed ownership of the slaves and intended to sell them in Louisiana argued that this was foreign intervention. The reason—they were insured against such a loss.

Benjamin and the carriers he represented insisted that the issue was not foreign intervention. He claimed the British officer's reaction was normal and natural, the act of a free man who values freedom for others. Benjamin contended that the insurance companies' policies did not protect them against a loss by an act of human decency. Concluding his argument, Benjamin said:

> It is obvious that the only criterion by which they can be governed is that which is insisted upon by the American government, viz: if the blacks reach there under the control of the whites and as their slaves, so consider them; but if the blacks reach there uncontrolled *by* any master and apparently released from any restraint on the part of whites, to consider them as free. These are the principles on which by the law of nations Great Britain has the right to regulate her conduct.

Benjamin won. The Louisiana Supreme Court ruled in favor of the insurance companies. He could now name his own price for a retainer. No one mentioned that a slaveholder had made this plea for liberty.

However, Benjamin's eyesight was now affected by his long hours of work and, forced to stop practicing law, he decided to become a full-time sugar planter. After Natalie left Bellechasse, Benjamin invited his mother and sister to live there. He built a grand, new three-story plantation mansion. Enthusiastic as ever, Judah Benjamin plunged into the study of sugar production and, with his partner, pioneered new methods. By 1847, he had recovered his health and returned to law in New Orleans. Five years later, a disastrous flood hit the plantation. Soon after, he sold his interest in Bellechasse.

Benjamin had entered politics in 1844 when he was elected to the Louisiana Legislature and to two state constitutional conventions as a Whig. In 1852, he was elected Senator from Louisiana to the United States Congress.

President Millard Fillmore nominated Benjamin at the age of just 41 to be a justice of the United States Supreme Court, the first Jew to be nominated. Benjamin declined. It would be another 66 years before Louis Brandeis would become the first Jewish Supreme Court Justice.

In 1858, after Benjamin began his second Senate term, President James Buchanan offered him an appointment as Minister to Spain. Again, Benjamin declined.

Benjamin changed his allegiance to the Democratic Party when the Whigs passed into historical oblivion. He became the South's spokesman for secession. In one of his Senatorial orations, recorded in the *Congressional Globe* (34th Cong., 1st and 2d sess., pp. 1092-98), Benjamin defined the philosophy of secession, stating that the Constitution was a compact among equal, sovereign states but "convert it into a bond of distrust, of suspicion, or of hate; and the entire fabric which is held together by that cement will crumble to the earth, and the rest scattered in dishonest fragments upon the ground."

He tried to disarm the Abolitionists with his rhetoric. He wanted the Supreme Court to decide the Kansas-Nebraska Act. He said "strange, strange, sir" that the South wanted to do that, but the North resisted. He said "the calm, cold, quiet, calculating North, always obeying the law, always subservient to the behest of the Constitution, whenever the question of slavery arises—in this alone—appeals to Sharpe's rifles instead of courts of justice." Benjamin's sense that slaveowners would do well with the high court proved correct. *Dred Scott v. Sandford*, 60 U.S. (19 How) 393 (1857), was decided a year later, saying Congress could not outlaw slavery in any territory. The Supreme Court was pro-slavery. Evans, *supra*.

While in Washington, Benjamin pursued a personal dream. In August 1857, he made a voyage on the steamer Texas to Mexico to revive interest in a risky but potentially profitable project. He was helping to organize a railroad from New Orleans through Mexico across the Isthmus of Tehuantepec to the Pacific Ocean. Benjamin succeeded in obtaining from President Juárez a right of transit for 60 years and an option for an additional 25 years. He also obtained 500,000 acres of right of way on the banks of rivers. In Washington, he arranged for the Postmaster General to deliver California mail across the Tehuantepec route for one year. The project was derailed by the Civil War. Benjamin's black box containing bonds and company stock was later seized by General Benjamin Butler's Union troops when they occupied New Orleans in 1862. These remnants of his lost hopes now reside in the National Archives in Washington, D.C.

Another hope was also dashed in Washington. He persuaded Natalie to join him after his reelection in 1858. In his enthusiasm, he decorated the elegant, three-story Decatur House with extravagant European opulence. It was the former home of Martin Van Buren and Henry Clay. With equal enthusiasm, the congressional ladies gossiped about Natalie's foreign affairs. Varina Davis wrote: "His life in his family must have been gruesome, but he always spoke of himself as the happiest of men." Natalie sailed for Paris in 1859, a few months after she arrived. She did not return to America. V.H. Davis, letter (1898).

Back to work. One of Benjamin's most important cases was *United States v. Castillero*, USDC (ND-Cal), No. 420, which involved the title to the rich New Almaden silver mine in California. Castillero was a Mexican officer who had received his land title from the Governor of Mexico in 1845. Once California became a state in 1849, the government tried to declare his claim invalid. He had leased his mine to wealthy English mining interests, who could afford to battle the claim. Litigation continued for ten years. In Benjamin's opening argument, he charged the government with "spoliation and oppression" and with violation of its treaties with Mexico. "We acquired from Mexico nothing but what Mexico owned, and she did not own this mine when she ceded this territory to the United States," he argued. "It belonged to one of her citizens. She did not claim it—did not pretend it was hers. Whence then the right of the Government of the United States?" R.D. Meade, *Judah P. Benjamin* (1943, reprinted 1975); Evans, *supra*.

When the case reached the United States Supreme Court in 1863, Benjamin was Secretary of State for the Confederacy, which made it impossible for him to argue before the Court. His brief was filed by lawyers for the company. Although three judges dissented, Benjamin's clients lost the case.

Lincoln was elected in 1860 and, following the lead of South Carolina, Louisiana seceded. So, on February 4, 1861, Senator Benjamin resigned from the United States Congress and returned home to serve the South.

The war years were, for Benjamin, the dark years. On February 25, 1861, he became President Jefferson Davis's first Attorney General. The Confederacy lacked a functioning Supreme Court at the time, a historical oddity in this newly forged country whose political structure so closely replicated the United States. His tenure was short.

Benjamin's next post was Secretary of War. Here, he endured criticism and anti-Semitic comments for the Confederate losses at Fort Henry, Fort Donelson, Roanoke Island, and the failure of Confederate agents in Europe to corner the munitions trade. Southern newspapers attacked him. His career reached its nadir when the Confederate Congress passed a resolution stating that Benjamin's retirement was "a high military necessity." (*Journal of Confederate Congress*, Feb.-Mar. 1862). Letters published in two newspapers in the North, claiming that Benjamin had been suspended from Yale for stealing other students' possessions in 1827, added to the furor. Throughout this period, Davis was his shield.

Confederate Diplomat

On March 17, 1862, Davis appointed Benjamin as Secretary of State. His European connections and his fluency in French and Spanish were assets. Recognition by England and France was vital to Confederate success. Benjamin strove to attain it. He failed.

In the sunset of the war as Southern hopes faded, Benjamin sent an envoy, Duncan Kenner, to England and France with an offer to emancipate the slaves in return for recognition of the Confederacy. Southern armies needed recruits. English and French recognition was impossible without victories. It was too late, too long. On March 14, 1865, Lord Palmerston refused.

Benjamin's relationship with Davis had begun in a near-duel in 1858 over a minor issue when Davis was United States Secretary of War and Benjamin a United States Senator. Benjamin challenged; Davis apologized. But the Civil War years brought the two men together, as Benjamin became an intimate advisor. Varina Davis, Jefferson's intelligent and devoted wife, became a friend. Now, it was time to say farewell.

After Lee surrendered at Appomattox, Benjamin fled to England via Florida, Bimini, Havana, and Nassau. It had been unclear what the future would hold for him in America. Life looked bleak for a Jewish Confederate cabinet minister and a confidant of the now vilified Jefferson Davis. Davis himself was imprisoned for two years before his indictment for treason was dismissed. Davis and Benjamin were even suspected by some of complicity in the Lincoln assassination. The Confederate Secretary of State was an inviting target. Perhaps confirming his apprehension, Benjamin was indicted for treason with Robert E. Lee, Jefferson Davis, and John C. Breckenridge in 1866. Benjamin risked arrest if he was found in the United States. He never returned.

On August 30, 1865, Benjamin arrived in London, where James Mason was closing the Confederate consulate. He traveled to Paris to see Natalie and Ninette, whom he had not seen for five years. Friends sought to keep him there. But London was it. A lawyer he was. A barrister he would be.

His arrival in London was not without warmth. He was treated with "great kindness and distinction." Benjamin Disraeli arranged a dinner so Judah Benjamin could meet William Gladstone and his favorite poet, Alfred Lord Tennyson.

At the age of 55, a man once nominated for the highest court in the United States started law school all over again, ironically at Lincoln's Inn. The Inn had a three-year requirement for admission to the bar and was reluctant to change the rules for an exiled Southerner. He apprenticed under Charles Pollack, who had a mercantile practice. Pollack tells about one of the first cases he assigned to his prize pupil. It was a search-and-seizure issue: the right of police to search suspects in custody. Pollack said, "The only fault to be found was that the learning was too great for the occasion, going back to first principles on each point. Many years after, I was told that the opinion was held in high respect and often referred to by the police and at the Home office." C. Pollack, "Reminiscences of Judah Philip Benjamin," *Fortnightly Review*, LXIX (1898).

He studied and dined for six months with young law students before Lincoln's Inn agreed to waive its three-year requirement. In 1866, Benjamin, the Southern expatriate, became a barrister, 34 years after he began his American career as a lawyer. His English admission petition lists him as a "political exile." So began his second career.

But he was a barrister with few clients. It was time once again to write a book. In 1868, he wrote his second legal best seller. The English version, officially titled *Treatise on the Law of Sale of Personal Property, with References to the American Decisions, to the French Code and Civil Code*, remains authoritative as "Benjamin on

Sales." There were three editions. It was New Orleans revisited. Again, the title was long. Again, it was an immediate success. Retainers rolled in.

In 1869, in his first major case in London, he once more represented a Southerner, a former Confederate agent. *United States v. McRae*, Law Rep 8 Eg 69, concerned a suit by the United States for money and cotton held by the agent, Colin McRae. The question: Should the relief sought include loans from English and French nationals? Benjamin argued the appeal.

Before a stunned court, Benjamin said, "[I]f you will only listen to me—if you will only listen to me—if you will only listen to me—I pledge myself you will dismiss the suit with costs." They listened. The court held that there was "not a tittle of evidence" to show that any money or goods of the plaintiffs in their own right ever reached the hands of the defendant. A fellow barrister said of Benjamin's skills, "He makes you see the very bale of cotton that he is describing as it lies upon the wharf."

Charles Pollack recounted a cross-examination by Benjamin at the Assizes in a Liverpool court. An expert testified that the collapse of a warehouse causing damage to cotton stored there was not the fault of the warehouse owner. Benjamin, seeking to discredit the expert, asked:

> Q: I think, sir, you said you had great experience in the building of warehouses?
>
> A: Yes.
>
> Q: And you have carefully considered the causes which lead to their weakness?
>
> A. Certainly.
>
> Q: And you have applied those considerations to the present case?
>
> A. I have done so.
>
> Q. Then will you kindly answer me one more question. Why did that warehouse fall?

Benjamin sat down with a laugh. The expert vainly tried to reply to Benjamin's question. Benjamin's final response was, "Thank you. I have no more questions with which to trouble you." Benjamin won. Pollack, *supra*.

In 1872, Benjamin was made Queen's Counsel, a barrister's ultimate honor. An American who had been practicing in England for six years! He had reached the top. He was famous. So sought after that he limited his practice to the Court of Appeals, the Privy Council; and the House of Lords. Herbert Asquith, future Prime Minister, was associated with him on an appeal to the Supreme Court of South Australia. Replicating the international practice he had developed in New Orleans, he argued briefs in cases from Scotland, Ireland, New Zealand, Canada, Malta, the British Supreme Consular Court of Constantinople, the Supreme Court at Shanghai, and the Supreme Court of South Australia.

Perhaps his most famous English case was *Queen v. Keyn*, the *Franconia* case. Ferdinand Keyn was the captain of a German vessel that ran down an English steamer in the Channel within three miles of Dover, sinking the ship and causing the death of a passenger. Although Keyn was found guilty of manslaughter when tried at the Old Bailey, the presiding judge was not certain that the court had jurisdiction. On appeal before a special court of 14 judges, Benjamin defended the captain. The case was considered of great importance as it affected the lives of English subjects and the security of the English coast.

The Times of London stated that the question was whether foreign seamen in such offenses were liable to criminal jurisdiction at all because "relatives of those of our subjects whose deaths are thus caused are not likely to undertake the task of following the foreigners into their own country, with their witnesses, and prosecuting them there." Benjamin argued that this was not a question of municipal law, but a question of maritime law.

It was a "talking court." He had to face severe questioning not only by opposing lawyers but also by the judges. The *Times* devoted whole columns to the contest. Once more, Benjamin's argument prevailed. The judges by a 7 to 6 vote freed Keyn on the ground that the English courts lacked jurisdiction. Subsequently, Parliament passed the Territorial Waters Act to deal with such cases. The ex-American was the talk of the town.

Benjamin was unique—a leading British barrister who had received all of his previous training and legal experience in American courts. Word reached the United States. "He must be regarded as the most famous advocate at the English Bar at the present moment," wrote Moncure Conway in his "London Letter" to the *Cincinnati Commercial*. Benjamin had been an American lawyer who argued cases before the United States Supreme Court. Now, as a British barrister, he argued cases before the House of Lords and the Privy Council.

The last American known to have called on Benjamin was Gustavus Wald of Cincinnati. He watched Benjamin in the courtroom. Here is what he saw:

> English lawyers are much less emphatic and vehement in argument before a court than are American lawyers. But no lawyer I heard in England was so absolutely impersonal as Benjamin. On both occasions that I heard him he seemed not to represent his client, but abstract justice, the law. . . . Never raising his voice above the conversational tone, making no gestures, apparently having no personal interest in the event of the matter in hand, he stated his views upon the subject under discussion so easily and so quietly that no one not interested in it would have been moved to pay any attention. But anyone following him while he spoke would be ready at once to declare that the traditional belief that the law is difficult, obscure, or uncertain is false. As he spoke all uncertainty seemed to vanish; there appeared to be but one view which could in reason be accepted, and that view was presented so simply and clearly that it seemed that any boy of ten could not fail to grasp it.

Benjamin told Wald that financially, in spite of an absence of the large fees he had enjoyed in America, he did quite well. He added that "The most delightful thing about a practice here is that I never have to talk to, or even see, a client. My terms are known . . . and there is no such thing as bargaining about fees." But he also said that the separation of the English legal profession into barristers and solicitors was "a real public mischief."

That he had done quite well was evident in the large, three-story mansion he built on the Avenue D'Iena near the Arc de Triomphe in the most fashionable section of Paris. Natalie and daughter Ninette, who had married a well-born French army officer, selected the furnishings. Benjamin was longing for retirement, stating that he wanted to "spend, to lend, and to give when once I shuffle off my wig and gown." But his expenses were heavy. He sent money to family members in America as well as to tradesmen in France.

He retired after a severe heart attack in 1882. On June 30, 1883, a dinner was given for him at the Inner Temple. The British Bar came en masse for this tribute. The Lord Chief Justice, the Solicitor General, the Lord Advocate for Scotland, the Attorney General for Ireland, and more than 200 judges, Queen's Counsel, and other barristers arrived. The Attorney General summed up the life achievement of Judah Benjamin:

> You know how Mr. Benjamin came among us and how we received him . . . we grudged him not the leadership which he so easily gained—we were proud of his success, for we knew the strength of the stranger among us and the bar is ever generous even in its rivalry that is based on merit. And the merit must have been there, for who is the man save this one of whom it can be said he held conspicuous leadership at the bar of two countries? To him, the change of citizenship and transition in his profession seemed easy enough. From the first days of coming he was one of us . . . The years are few since Mr. Benjamin was a stranger to us all, and in those few years he has accomplished more than most men can ever hope in a lifetime to achieve.

Benjamin then made his final public statement:

> From the bar of England I never, so far as I am aware, received anything but warm and kindly welcome. I never had occasion to feel that any one regarded me as an intruder. I never felt a touch of professional jealousy. I never received an unkindness. On the contrary, from all quarters I received a warm and cordial welcome to which, as a stranger, I had no title, except that I was a political exile, seeking by honorable labor to retrieve shattered fortunes, wrecked in the ruin of a lost cause. P. Butler, *Judah P. Benjamin* (1907, reprinted 1980); Evans, *supra*.

Judah Benjamin died in Paris on May 6, 1884. He could not be buried in consecrated ground as a Jew because of his marriage. But Natalie, a Catholic, now argued for him. She persuaded the authorities that Benjamin had become a Catholic convert. His presence in the family tomb at the Père-Lachaise Cemetery was long unmarked, but in 1938, the Paris chapter of the Daughters of the Confederacy provided this inscription which describes his unusual career:

UNITED STATES SENATOR FROM LOUISIANA, ATTOR-
NEY GENERAL, SECRETARY OF WAR AND SECRETARY
OF STATE OF THE CONFEDERATE STATES OF AMERICA,
QUEEN'S COUNSEL, LONDON.

Natalie remained in France. Her letters have been destroyed.
One sentence survives in a reply to her husband. "Don't talk to me
about economy," she wrote. "It is so fatiguing." Her long life
ended in 1891. B.J. Hendrick, *Statesmen of the Lost Cause* (1939).

Judah Benjamin's biography discloses that he is pictured on the
Confederate $2.00 bill, but in a final twist, his name is associated
with another war.

The SS *Judah P. Benjamin* (0007) was one of 2,751 EC2 type Liberty ships built in the United States during World War II to replace
cargo ships torpedoed by U-boats. Liberty ships were named after
prominent deceased Americans. Launched in 1942, the SS *Judah P.
Benjamin* survived the war and was scrapped in 1961. "SS *Judah P.
Benjamin*," www.usmm.org/libertyships.html (2007); F. Brummett, *Oral Statement* (2007).

SECTION III

Passion and Murder in America

The sedate East preferred quiet deaths—a pretty girl drowned in a well or a wise old man poisoned. The wild West engaged in gunfire.

8

The Life and Death of George Wythe

"I Am Murdered"

George Wythe's name has disappeared from the fame surrounding the Founding Fathers, but in an era of great men, he was celebrated for his honesty, his patriotism, his work revising the laws of Virginia, and, most of all, his teaching. Eighty-one-year-old George Wythe had

> a regular habit of bathing, winter and summer, at sunrise. He would put on his morning wrapper, go down with his bucket to the well in the yard, which was sixty feet deep and the water very cold, and draw for himself what was necessary. He would then indulge in a potent shower-bath, which he considered the most inspiring luxury. With nerves all braced, he would pick up the morning Richmond *Enquirer* and seating himself in his armchair, would ring a little silver bell for his frugal breakfast.

> This was brought in immediately by his servant woman, Lydia Broadnax, who understood his wants and ways. She was a servant of the olden time, respected and trusted by her master, and devotedly attached to him and his—one of those

whom he had liberated, but who lived with him from affection.

This is the setting in George Wythe Munford's *The Two Parsons*, describing Wythe's murder. Munford's book, published in 1884, tells of events that occurred in 1806, but the account is largely accurate. The author's father, William Munford, was a clerk of the court at the time of Wythe's death. He lived with George Wythe for three years studying law and said Wythe was the best friend he ever had and one of the most remarkable men he ever knew. J.P. Boyd, *The Murder of George Wythe* (1949); G.W. Munford, *The Two Parsons* (1884).

George Wythe Sweeney, grandson of Wythe's sister Anne, was part of Wythe's household in Richmond, Virginia, along with Lydia, a free black woman who had been Wythe's cook for several decades, and a 15-year-old freed mulatto boy named Michael Brown, to whom Wythe was teaching classical languages. They lived in a yellow wooden house with a large garden. Thomas Jefferson, who considered Wythe his second father, believed the old man to be without an enemy in the world.

But on Sunday morning May 25, 1806, this Edenic existence ended. Sweeney was in debt. Lawyer William Wirt wrote to James Monroe that the young man "had been in the habit of robbing his uncle with a false-key, had sold three trunks of his most valuable books, and had forged his checks on the bank to a considerable amount. . . ." I.E. Brown, *American Aristides* (1981).

Sweeney, afraid his forgeries would be discovered, knew that he and Michael Brown were beneficiaries under Wythe's will and that if Brown predeceased him, Sweeney would inherit Brown's share as well as his own. Sweeney was anxious for Wythe's death.

Munford describes Sweeney's activities on that fatal morning as told by the housekeeper, Lydia. Sweeney went into the kitchen unusually early before breakfast was ready and said, "Aunt Lydia, I want you to give me a cup of coffee and some bread, because I won't have time to stay for breakfast." Lydia replied, "Mars George, breakfast is nearly ready . . . I have only got to poach a few eggs and make some toast for the old master; you had better stay and eat with him." "No," he said, "I'll just take a cup of that coffee now, and you can toast me a slice of bread."

While Lydia toasted the bread, Sweeney took the coffeepot to the table. Lydia continued, "I saw him throw a little white wrapper in the fire. He then drank the coffee he had poured for himself, and ate the toast with some fresh butter. He told me goodbye and went about his business. I didn't think there was anything wrong then. In a little while I heard the old master's bell."

Lydia carried Wythe's breakfast to him. He drank a cup of coffee and ate his toast and eggs while reading his newspaper. Lydia returned to the kitchen. "I gave Michael as much coffee as he wanted and then I drank a cup myself. After that, with the hot water in the kettle I washed the plates, emptied the coffee grounds out and scrubbed the coffee-pot bright."

Wythe became sick three hours later. He told Lydia to send for a doctor. Although Munford's story indicates that Lydia and Michael became ill immediately, it was actually a day or two later. Michael died on June 1. Lydia concluded, "All these things make me think Mars George must have put something in the coffeepot. I didn't see him, but it looks monstrous strange." On June 8, George Wythe died.

Sweeney was arrested, but because of her race, Lydia could not testify at his trial. Blacks could not testify against whites. The legal proceedings charging Sweeney with the murders of Wythe and Michael Brown and with two charges of forgery began, but all that occurred after the end of Wythe's eventful life.

Life

Born in 1726, Wythe grew up without the benefits of the education he provided for such luminaries as Thomas Jefferson, John Marshall, Edmund Randolph, and Henry Clay. Wythe's father died when George was three. His Chesterfield plantation went to George's older brother. After learning Latin and Greek and developing a love of classical philosophy from his mother, George apprenticed in the law with an uncle. Two years of dull office work were followed by independent study, and at 20, George Wythe was admitted to the Virginia bar. He joined the practice of Zachary Lewis in Spotsylvania County and the next year married Lewis's daughter, Ann. She died eight months later.

Wythe began again in Williamsburg, where he became a clerk of the House of Burgesses and built a law practice. Famous for his integrity, he was compared to the sixth-century BC Athenian Aristides, "the Just." He was the very model of an honest lawyer. Trying only those cases he believed in, Wythe dropped any case in which the client had lied to him, and returned the fee. George Washington was his most illustrious client.

Wythe had a nemesis, Edmund Pendleton, who shadowed him throughout his life. From their early days as lawyers until Pendleton's death in 1803, they were opponents and staunch enemies. Wythe had the worst time because although he was the most prepared and learned, Pendleton was more handsome, glib, and successful. Brown, *supra*.

Wythe's older brother died, and Wythe inherited the estate, but he remained in Williamsburg. Seven years after Ann died, George married Elizabeth Taliaferro. The couple moved into an attractive house provided by her father.

Then, Wythe, childless, began his career as a teacher. He met the perfect student. Thomas Jefferson, like Wythe, was ravenous for knowledge, exploring the classics, science, philosophy, mathematics—almost every field of endeavor. Wythe was a tough tutor. Before eight each morning, Jefferson read ethics, religion, and philosophy. Then, until noon, he studied Coke, Hume, Locke, Blackstone, Montesquieu, and English constitutional law. The afternoon was devoted to government and history. In the evening, "he relaxed with literature and the arts." Brown, *supra*.

Wythe trained Jefferson in legal office work, courtroom observation, reading, and briefing. In 1767, he "introduced Jefferson to the General Court." Although Jefferson practiced for only seven years, he used his legal skills throughout his life. Biographer Richard B. Morris noted: "The imprint of his legal training is found in all his state papers. The Declaration of Independence is really a bill of indictment." Brown, *supra*; J. Blackburn, *George Wythe of Williamsburg* (1975).

Wythe led an active, patriotic political life. He became a member of the Continental Congress in 1775, signed the Declaration of Independence in 1776, and attended the Constitutional Convention in 1787, leaving early because his wife was dying.

In 1777, Wythe, Jefferson, Pendleton, Thomas Lee, and George Mason were appointed to revise the laws of Virginia from the Glorious Revolution of 1688 in England to the Declaration of Independence in 1776. Lee and Mason were unable to continue because of health problems. Jefferson and Wythe worked for two years. Their greatest concerns were providing freedom of religion and broad public education. They wanted to end primogeniture. Pendleton opposed this reform, but it passed—a rare victory for Wythe over his opponent. Slavery was not addressed here, so ironically the ban on African-Americans being able to testify against whites remained and later helped Wythe's murderer escape justice. However, any change would doubtless have been declined by the legislature.

In 1779, with Jefferson's backing, Wythe was appointed to the first chair of law in the United States, at the College of William and Mary, two decades after Blackstone became the first professor of law at Oxford. For the next 12 years, he trained many of the nation's leaders. Jefferson observed: "Wythe's school is numerous. They hold weekly [moot] courts and assemblies in the capitol. The professors join in it; and the young men dispute with elegance, method and learning." W. Clarkin, *Serene Patriot: A Life of George Wythe* (1970).

During his time as law professor, Wythe also served as a judge on Virginia's high court of chancery. There, in 1782, he applied the doctrine of judicial review in *Commonwealth v. Caton*, 4 Call 5, stating:

> Nay more, if the whole legislature, an event to be deprecated, should attempt to overleap the bounds prescribed to them by the people, I, in administering the public justice of the country, will meet their united powers at my seat in this tribunal; and pointing to the Constitution, will say to them, "here is the limit of your authority; and hither shall you go but no further."

Wythe's decision foreshadowed by 21 years his former student Chief Justice John Marshall's momentous decision in *Marbury v. Madison*, 1 Cranch 137 (1803); College of William & Mary, Commemoration Ceremonies, 1954; B. Schwartz, *A History of the Supreme Court* (1993).

In 1788, the Virginia House of Burgesses created a separate court of appeals. Edmund Pendleton, elected as one of the five judges, became chief justice. Wythe was left as the sole chancellor on the state high court of chancery. This suited Wythe until he realized his decisions were consistently overturned.

Henry Clay, who learned law while serving as Wythe's secretary in Richmond for two years, later wrote a letter for Benjamin Minor's 1852 memoir of Wythe. Clay told of hearing Wythe declare to a friend that he was so exasperated with Pendleton that he planned to "quit the bar, go home, take orders and enter the pulpit." His friend replied, "If you do, Mr. Pendleton will go home, take orders, enter the pulpit, and beat you there."

Fiercely attacking the appellate reversals, Wythe wrote a book explaining his version of the cases. The title tells the tale: *Decisions of Cases in Virginia by the High Court of Chancery, with Remarks upon the Decrees by the Court of Appeals Reversing Some of Those Decisions.*

Wythe's writings were replete with classical allusions: Aeschylus, Euripides, Xenophon, Horace, Homer, Justinian, Milton, Herodotus, and Cicero often appeared. Late in life, he studied Hebrew.

In their final confrontation, Pendleton, who was near death, came to Richmond ready to overturn a Wythe decision. He died before he could act. The court split. Wythe was upheld.

Wythe expressed his views on slavery in *Hudgins v. Wright*, which he decided the year of his death. He wrote that when a person claims to hold another in slavery, the burden of proof lies on the claimant, and he declared the slaves free. But Wythe also went beyond this. In the most significant part of his ruling, he stated that slaves were entitled to their freedom "on the ground that freedom is the birthright of every article of our political catechism, the bill of rights." Wythe's decision was upheld by the appeals court, but on different grounds. Brown, *supra.*

The Duval–Jefferson Letters

Wythe was dying. William Duval, executor of Wythe's estate, was a close friend of both Wythe and Jefferson. During Wythe's two weeks of agony, Duval repeatedly wrote to Jefferson to relate the events.

The Duval–Jefferson letters are in the Library of Congress but remain unpublished. They are identified and included in "Notes for the Biography of George Wythe" (Manuscript Collection, Library of Congress) and the Jefferson Papers, 1751–1826 (Manuscript Collection, Library of Congress).

In his first letter to Jefferson on June 4, 1806, Duval wrote, "Worthy Sir, Geo W. Sweeney who lived with Mr. Wythe was committed to Gaol on the 27th of May last for forging Six checks on the Bank of Virginia." As to Wythe's condition, he described that Wythe "never suffered more in his Life . . . , that he ate his Breakfast as usual, that about Nine O'Clock in the morning he was attacked in the most violent manner."

Duval called in three doctors [James McClurg, James Currie, and James Drew McCaw] to examine Wythe. Duval's letter continued, "They pronounce his death to be certain in a day or two.

They say that his Constitution was remarkably strong for a person of his age." Explaining that Lydia Broadnax and Michael Brown had been afflicted with the same malady shortly after Wythe, he commented, "We had no idea that Sweeney had poisoned the whole Family." Describing the forged checks, Duval noted: "Yellow Arsenic was found in Sweeney's Room & many other strong Circumstances concurred to induce a believe [sic] he had poisoned the whole Family."

Duval continued, stating that "by the hand of a Youth to whom he was kinder than a Father is about to be taken from us the most virtuous and illustrious of our citizens—one among the best of men—whom even Death can't terrify or alarm." He added: "On Sunday Morning June the first [at] last Michael the Mulatto Boy Died . . . As a Magistrate I requested four eminent Physicians to open the body of the Boy. They did so; from the Inflammation in the Stomach & Bowels, they said that it was the kind of Inflammation induced by Poison."

In his letter to Jefferson, he described Wythe's reaction to Michael's death: "He drew a long breath, and pathetically said 'Poor Boy.'" Duval observed, "The Boy was humble and good. . . . He had caught the Sauvity of his Master's Manners." Wythe, evidently realizing that he was a victim of poisoning, asked for his will so he could add a codicil excluding Sweeney as a beneficiary. On June 5, he exclaimed, "I am murdered!" Duval wrote that Wythe's last words were said to have been, "Let me Die righteous [sic]."

On June 8, Duval sent the last of the letters to Jefferson:

Our venerable, great, and pious Friend departed this Life about half an Hour after Nine of the Clock this morning. Doctors Foushee, Murrie, Greenhow, McClurg, and McCaw opened his chest and bowels. There was considerable inflammation in his Stomach. It is strongly suspected that he & Michael Brown were poisoned with Yellow Arsenic by George W. Sweeney.

Jefferson responded:

. . . the last announcing the death of the venerable Mr. Wythe, than whom a purer character has never lived. His advanced years had left us little hope of retaining him much longer, and had his been brought on by ordinary decays of

109

time and nature, altho' always a subject of regret, it would not have been aggravated by the horror of his falling by the hand of a parricide . . . I thank you for the attention you have been so kind as to show in communicating to me the incidents of a case so interesting to my affections.

He was my antient [*sic*] master, my earliest & best friend; and to him I am indebted for first impressions which have had the most salutary influence on the course of my life. I had reserved with fondness, for the day of my retirement, the hope of inducing him to pass much of his time with me. It would have been a great pleasure to recollect with him first opinions on the new state of things which arose so soon after my acquaintance with him; to pass in review the long period which has elapsed since that time, and to see how far those opinions had been affected by experience & reflection, or confirmed and acted on with self-approbation.

Boyd, *supra*; A.T. Dill, *George Wythe, Teacher of Liberty* (1979); "Notes for the Biography of George Wythe," *supra*; Jefferson Papers, 1751–1826, *supra*.

Court of Examination

The deaths of Wythe and Brown led to murder charges against Sweeney. He was ordered to appear at a hearing on June 18, before the mayor and two magistrates in the Richmond hustings court. Based on the substantial evidence of guilt, they concluded that Sweeney be jailed and remanded to appear on June 23 before a special court of examination. At the court, witnesses were questioned for nearly five hours. This transcript still exists.

Tarlton Webb, the first witness, testified that Sweeney purchased rat poison known as ratsbane from him between May 7 and May 13. Sweeney told him he planned to commit suicide. Then, Webb said, Sweeney went to him the day before being arrested for forgery and showed Webb a paper envelope containing ratsbane. Sweeney said he was going to kill himself and offered Webb some of his ratsbane if he wanted to join him in suicide. Boyd, *supra*; Clarkin, *supra*.

William Rose, the Richmond City jail warden, testified that Sweeney was not searched when he was arrested for forgery on May 27, but shortly after he was confined, Rose's servant found a packet of arsenic in the garden outside the prison wall. Rose then remembered that he had noticed earlier a thick packet of paper in Sweeney's pocket. Webb identified the packet as the same one containing ratsbane. Boyd, *supra*; Clarkin, *supra*.

William Claiborne told of his suspicion that Sweeney had poisoned the whole family. This was based on Wythe's change in his will, disinheriting Sweeney, and his wish that Sweeney's room be searched. Claiborne testified that he visited Wythe the day after Sweeney was jailed for forgery (May 28). Wythe told him that he had been "as well as usual" on the Sunday morning (May 25). After eating breakfast, he became violently ill with diarrhea. Broadnax became ill the following day (May 26), and Brown the day after that (May 27). Clarkin, *supra*.

Samuel McCraw, Wythe's friend, testified that when he visited Wythe, who was on his deathbed, on June 1 to attest to the new will, Wythe told him to search Sweeney's room. McCraw and others did. There, they found a "squire of blotting paper" that was identical to the paper envelope later found in the garden outside the prison wall, several strawberries sprinkled with what appeared to be arsenic, and a glass container containing a compound of arsenic and sulphur. Clarkin, *supra*; E.W. Knappman, ed., *Great American Trials* (1994).

The court of examination found Sweeney guilty. He was ordered to remain in jail and held for trial in the district court on September 1. Sweeney's lawyers were two of Virginia's finest, William Wirt and Edmund Randolph. Boyd, *supra*.

Trial

Sweeney appeared for trial on two counts of murder and four counts of forging Wythe's name. The trial transcript was destroyed during the Civil War when Richmond was under siege, but newspaper accounts from the Richmond *Enquirer* remain. Dill, *supra*.

The jury heard that Wythe had amended his will to exclude Sweeney from his inheritance. On June 1, Wythe had dictated and executed a codicil to his will that revoked

> said will and codicils in all the devises and legacies in them or either of them, contained, relating to, or in any manner concerning George Wythe Sweeney, the grandson of my sister: but I confirm the said will and codicils in all other parts except as to the devise and bequest to Michael Brown . . . who, I am told, died this morning.

In a blow to the prosecution, the physicians who cut open Wythe's body had reached inconclusive results. The examination was unscientific. None would declare for certain that arsenic had killed Wythe.

Lydia Broadnax never had the chance to tell the jury her story about what happened on the morning of May 25 due to the Virginia statute that prohibited African-Americans, whether slaves or free, from testifying against whites.

The Richmond *Enquirer* summarized Sweeney's trial: ". . . on the charge of administering arsenic to his great Uncle, the venerable George Wythe. After an able and eloquent discussion, the jury retired, and in a few minutes, brought in the verdict of not guilty." The newspaper further stated that Sweeney was acquitted because "some of the strongest testimony . . . was kept from the petit jury, . . . it was gleaned from the evidence of negroes, which is not permitted by our laws to go against a white man." Richmond *Enquirer, supra*; R.B. Kirtland, *George Wythe* (1986).

A similar indictment against Sweeney for poisoning Michael, the mulatto boy, was quashed without a trial. In the end, Sweeney was convicted of forging his uncle's name to checks drawn upon the Virginia Bank. Richmond *Enquirer, supra*; Boyd, *supra*.

The inept autopsy and exclusion of Lydia Broadnax's testimony insured Sweeney's acquittal. Sweeney was found not guilty of the murder counts on September 8, 1806; he was, however, sentenced on the forgery counts to six months in jail and an hour on the pillory in the market house in Richmond. But because the statute did not list the newly established state banks as potential victims, the court ordered a new trial on the forgery convictions. As a result, the prosecuting attorney entered a *nolle prosequi*, dismissing the forgery counts. Sweeney was free. Dill, *supra*.

Memorial

Wythe was given a state funeral, at which William Munford spoke: "The venerable George Wythe needs no other monument than the services rendered to his country, and the universal sorrow which our country sheds over his grave." Richmond *Enquirer, supra*. Virginians agreed. No monument marks Wythe's grave.

Wythe, in his will, had asked Jefferson to take care of Michael Brown. Wythe and young Michael were the subject of a letter

112

written by President Jefferson on June 22, reflecting his regard for his friend:

> I sincerely regret the loss of [Michael] not only for the afflic-
> tion it must have cost Mr. Wythe in his last moments, but also
> it has deprived me of an object for attentions which would
> have gratified me unceasingly with the constant recollection
> and execution of the wishes of my friend.

Boyd, *supra*.

Afterword

The Virginia forgery statute was amended shortly after the Sweeney trial to include banks, but the prohibition against testimony by African-Americans was not repealed until 1867. Boyd, *supra*.

President George Washington appointed Edmund Randolph as the first attorney general of the United States in 1789, and in 1794 Washington appointed him secretary of state to succeed Jefferson. Randolph continued his career as an outstanding trial lawyer after successfully defending Sweeney.

William Wirt, appointed attorney general in 1817 by President James Monroe, held that position for 12 years, longer than any other attorney general. Wirt argued 174 cases before the U.S. Supreme Court, and he represented Callender in the sedition trial.

Henry Clay became a major figure in the Whig party, serving as speaker of the House of Representatives, senator from Kentucky, and secretary of state under President John Quincy Adams. He was the principal author and sponsor of the Missouri Compromise.

George Wythe Sweeney left Richmond after his acquittal. He reportedly reappeared in Tennessee, where he was convicted and imprisoned for stealing horses. After serving his term, he disappeared in the West.

In 1920, the College of William and Mary created the Marshall-Wythe School of Government and Citizenship. The school was named in honor of

> John Marshall who, as Chief Justice of the Supreme Court
> of the United States, was the great expounder of the Consti-
> tution, and of George Wythe, who, as the teacher of both
> Marshall and Jefferson and a host of others only slightly
> less prominent, had made an invaluable contribution to the

establishment of our system of representative constitutional government and the sound principles of law which implement it and make it effective.

O.L. Shewmake, *The Honorable George Wythe* (1950).

In 1922, the Sons of the Revolution, Sons of the American Revolution, Virginia Bar Association, and Association for the Preservation of Virginia Antiquities dedicated a grave marker, a tablet with the Great Seal of Virginia, designed by Wythe in 1776, at the top and the following inscription:

This tablet is dedicated to mark the site where lie the mortal remains of George Wythe, born 1726–died 1806, jurist and statesman, teacher of Randolph, Jefferson, and Marshall, first professor of law in the United States, first Virginia signer of the Declaration of Independence.

9

The Trial of Levi Weeks
Hamilton and Burr for the Defense

What a trial! A dead 22-year-old woman. A celebrity defense team starring political enemies Aaron Burr and Alexander Hamilton. A young, charismatic defendant. A prosecutor so fatigued after a marathon presentation during which he had not slept for 44 hours that he was unable to give a closing argument. The judge's charge to the jury, assuring the outcome. A jury that deliberated and returned in five minutes with a verdict. Who killed Gulielma Sands? Thanks to Court Clerk William Coleman's transcript, the first American verbatim report of a criminal trial, the Levi Weeks trial of 1800 still commands our attention.

Once past the quaint phrasing of the indictment and the free-flowing testimony, the trial seems strikingly contemporary. The prosecutor builds his case on circumstantial evidence but is toppled by his own witness. The defense team is formidable. All-stars Burr and Hamilton are joined by prominent lawyer Henry Brock-holst Livingston. Constructing their defense, they stomp across the reputation of anyone in their way. Expert witnesses testify. Newspapers feed the clamor. Missing are jury accommodations, advanced medical science and CNN.

New York City: 1799

Gulielma Sands, known as Elma, lived in the New York City boarding house of Catherine and Elias Ring. In June 1799, Levi Weeks arrived as a boarder. Levi spread his attentions among the three young women in the household. In late August, frightened by a yellow fever epidemic, the women except for Elma left the city. Alone in the house with Elias and some paying guests, Elma and Levi began an affair.

Levi enjoyed the fling. For Elma, it was an opportunity. Levi would be quite a catch. Lurking in the background was an unsavory roomer, Richard Croucher. The women returned in September. Sadness filled the city on December 14 when George Washington died, but Elma looked forward to a happier occasion. On the evening of Sunday, December 22, Catherine helped Elma dress for a secret wedding to Levi. She heard the pair leave the house. Twelve days later, on January 2, 1800, Elma's body was found in the water at the bottom of Manhattan Well. The crowds that came to see her body were so large that the open coffin was moved to the street. Levi Weeks was arrested and charged with murder.

From 1784 to 1800, Jeffersonian Republican Aaron Burr and Federalist Alexander Hamilton, together or in opposition, appeared in almost every major case. Levi Weeks was employed as a carpenter by his brother Ezra, a prosperous builder. Ezra had worked with architect John McComb Jr. to construct The Grange, Hamilton's country house. Ezra had provided supplies for the Manhattan Company water system, Burr's business venture. The Manhattan Company owned Manhattan Well. J. Parton, *Life and Times of Aaron Burr* (1858).

The Trial: March 31, 1800

On March 31, 1800, at 10 AM, the trial began at the Court of Oyer and Terminer in the City Hall. Chief Justice of the New York Supreme Court John Lansing presided, joined by Mayor Richard Varick, City Recorder Richard Harrison, and Alderman Robert Lenox.

The jury: dock builder, ship's chandler, six merchants, grocer, baker, measurer, and a Quaker who did not ask to be excused. Quakers routinely refused to participate as jurors in death penalty cases.

The Clerk read the indictment which began: "... Levi Weeks, late of the seventh ward, of the city of New York, in the county of

New-York, labourer, not having the fear of God before his eyes, but being moved and seduced by the instigation of the devil, on the 22d day of December, in the year of our Lord 1799. . . ." Levi Weeks pleaded "not guilty" to this indictment for attacking Elma and throwing her into the well to drown, or killing her first and tossing her body into the well.

The prosecutor, 31-year-old Assistant Attorney General Cadwallader Colden, gave his opening statement:

> In a cause which appears so greatly to have excited the public mind, in which the prisoner has thought it necessary for his defence, to employ so many advocates distinguished for their eloquence and abilities, so vastly my superiors in learning, experience and professional rank; it is not wonderful that I should rise to address you under the weight of embarrassments which such circumstances actually excite. But gentlemen, although the abilities enlisted on the respective sides of this cause are very unequal, I find consolation in the reflection that our tasks are so, also.
>
> Levi Weeks, the prisoner at the bar, is indicted for the murder of Gulielma Sands. He is a young man of reputable connections, and for ought we know, till he was charged with this crime, of irreplaceable character, nay of amiable and engaging manners, insomuch that he had gained the affections of those who are now to appear against him as witnesses on this trial for his life. . . . The deceased was a young girl, who till her fatal acquaintance with the prisoner, was virtuous and modest, and it will be material for you to remark, always of a cheerful disposition, and lively manners, though of a delicate constitution. We expect to prove to you that the prisoner won her affections, and that her virtue fell a sacrifice to his assiduity; that after a long period of criminal intercourse between them, he deluded her from the house of her protector under a pretense of marrying her, and carried her away to a Well in the suburbs of this city, and there murdered her. No wonder, gentlemen, that my mind shudders at the picture here drawn, and requires a moment to recollect myself. . . .
>
> I will not say, gentlemen, what may be your verdict as to the prisoner, but I will venture to assert, that not one of you or any man who hears this cause, shall doubt that the unfortunate

117

young creature who was found dead in the Manhattan Well, was most barbarously murdered.

Elias Ring, and Catherine his wife, keep a boarding-house in the upper part of Greenwich-street; the deceased was a distant relation of theirs who lived with them. Hope Sands, a sister of Mrs. Ring, and Margaret Clark, lived in the same house. In July last, the prisoner was received into the house as a boarder. Upon his first coming, for about a month, he showed some attention to Margaret Clark, but soon after was observed to attach himself in a very particular manner to the deceased. Their conduct soon led to suspicions in the family, that there was an improper intercourse between them.

In the month of September, Mrs. Ring fled from the fever, leaving the care of her house to her husband, and the deceased; and leaving in it also the prisoner and some other boarders. Mrs. Ring remained out of town about six weeks, and in that time it is certain that the prisoner and the deceased lived together in the most intimate manner. On the first of December last, the deceased disclosed to Hope Sands, that on the next Sunday she was to be married to the prisoner, but at this time, and whenever afterwards she spoke on the subject, enjoined on Hope the strictest secrecy, forbidding her to tell even Mrs. Ring, saying that Levi meant to keep their marriage a secret, even from her and therefore that no one should go with them to see the ceremony performed.

Between this time and the time of her departure from the house, it will be seen, she frequently spoke of her approaching marriage, and always with cheerfulness and a lively pleasure. On Saturday, the 21st of December, the day before the fatal accident—Hope disclosed the secret to Mrs. Ring, informing her that Elma was to be married the next evening. On the Sunday about dinner time, Mrs. Ring discovered to the deceased that she knew her intentions. The deceased, you will find, then confessed that she was to be married, and that the prisoner was to come for her that night at 8 o'clock. Mrs. Ring pressed the deceased to be of the party. She said Levi would not consent, as he meant to keep his marriage a perfect secret from all. In the evening you will see, the deceased began to dress herself, in which Mrs. Ring assisted her; the deceased appeared perfectly

118

cheerful all this time, she put on her hat and shawl, and went to a neighbor's and borrowed a muff, which she promised to return in a little time. She also took up a pocket-handkerchief belonging to one of the boarders, saying she should not make use of it, and would return it before it was missed.

You will have evidence that the prisoner had left the house of Mr. Ring, about five o'clock in the afternoon, and that about eight o'clock in the evening the deceased stood leaning over the front [Dutch] door, looking out—that Mrs. Ring desired her to come in, saying she did not believe Levi would come, to which she answered, she did not fear, it was not yet eight, but she left the door and went in with Mrs. Ring, and in a little time the prisoner returned and came into the room where was Elias Ring, Mrs. Ring, the deceased, and two boarders by the names of Lacey and Russel. Mrs. Ring set with them about five minutes, when she got up and went to the street door, and leaned over it till Lacey and Russel went upstairs to bed. She then left the street door, and as she does perfectly remember, shut it after her; she went into the room again, and was hardly seated when the deceased went upstairs; Mrs. Ring immediately followed her, found her in her room above, pinned on the shawl for her, and after being with her not more than two minutes, left her in the room opposite the stairs, just on the point of coming down.

Mrs. Ring returned to the room below where the prisoner was; in about a minute he took up his hat, and as he opened the room door to go out, Mrs. Ring heard somebody come lightly down the stairs, and as she supposes, meet him at the bottom; she then heard two voices whispering at the foot of the stairs for about a minute, she then heard the street door open and immediately shut; she took a candle and went to the door to look after them but it was dark and so many people passing, that she could not distinguish any one. The street door you will find, opens with a great and remarkable noise, in consequence of its being out of order. Gentlemen, it will be necessary for you to pay particular attention to this part of the evidence, for if you do believe that the prisoner, at this time, went out of the house with the deceased—I do not see how he can be acquitted.

After Mrs. Ring shut the door, it was not again opened till the time when she supposes the prisoner and the deceased went out. We shall show you that there were no other persons in the house till ten or eleven o'clock but Elias Ring, who remained in the common sitting room, and the two lodgers, Lacey and Russel, who we shall prove to you lodged together, and were not out of their lodging-room from the time they went upstairs. From this time the deceased was never after seen till her corps [sic] was found in the Manhattan Well. She had the marks of great violence upon her, and great part of her cloaths [sic] were torn off.

We shall produce a number of witnesses, who, between the hours of 8 & 9 of the evening of the 22d of December, heard, from about the place of the Well, the voice of a female crying murder, and entreating for mercy. It will be shown to you, gentlemen, that there was the track of a single horse sleigh, which we shall prove that at some time between the Saturday night before, and Monday morning succeeding, must have come out of Greenwich-street, and passed in a very extraordinary manner near the brink of the Well; that the snow round the edge of the Well was much trodden, and that the sleigh after having made a curious turn or stop near the Well, must have passed on to the Broadway road, and, in coming into that, turned towards town.

We shall proceed to show you, that on the evening after the 22d of December, soon after the deceased left her house, she was met a few hundred yards from her house in the way towards the road that leads to the Well, in company with two men. That a few hundred yards further on and about the same time, a single horse sleigh was seen with two men and a woman in it; the horse of a dark colour and without bells, passing on towards the road or street which leads from Greenwich-street to the Well.

Our next testimony will be, to prove to you, that a number of young gentlemen riding for pleasure on the same evening, as they were coming into town, between 8 and 9 o'clock, on the Broadway road, when they were some distance nearer to the town than the place where the track of the one horse sleigh was discovered to have turned into the Broadway road, they were overtaken by a single horse sleigh, which passed them with the horse on a full gallop, and without bells; there were

120

two men in it and the horse was dark coloured. We shall then show you that Mr. Ezra Weeks, the brother of the prisoner, was the owner of a single sleigh, and a dark horse, and that the prisoner had access to it when he chose, and we shall produce to you such testimony, as we suppose will satisfy you that this horse and sleigh was taken out of the yard of Ezra Weeks, about 8 o'clock in the evening of the 22d of December, and was returned again into the yard in less than half an hour.

You will see, gentlemen of the jury, that we have only circumstantial evidence to offer to you in this case, and you must also perceive that from its nature it admits of no other. I shall, however, reserve my remarks upon this subject, for a future stage in the cause; and shall, without delaying you longer, proceed to call the witnesses.

Seventy-five witnesses appeared, but most were fringe players. Several prosecution witnesses attested to Elma's cheerful personality. Defense witnesses spoke of Levi's kindness and good character. Weeks's lawyers were rarely identified, although when the defense requested permission to take the deposition of Elizabeth Watkins, the transcript states that Colden, Hamilton, and Judge Lansing went to her house.

Catherine Ring was Colden's star witness. A Quaker, she was not sworn in but "affirmed." Quakers did not take oaths because their religion required them to tell the truth. They were respected because they took this requirement seriously. E.F. Kleiger, *The Trial of Levi Weeks* (1989).

Catherine corroborated Colden's opening statement. She said that on December 22, Elma was happily preparing for a secret marriage to Levi, and shortly after 8 PM, Levi entered the house and Elma went upstairs. She detailed their movements and her conviction that they left the house together. Levi returned alone about 10 PM.

When Catherine began to relate a remark made by Elma, the defense objected. Colden claimed "such testimony was proper to show the disposition of mind in the deceased when she left the house" . . . Burr replied that hearsay was only admissible in "cases *in extremis*, after the fatal blow was struck." The court sustained Burr's objection.

Catherine testified that after Elma's disappearance, her friendship with Levi turned to suspicion. Levi denied any marriage plans and tried to convince Catherine that Elma was suicidal. He said that he would never marry without his brother's approval. Catherine stated when Levi said, "Mrs. Ring, you are not so much my friend as you have been," she replied, "Indeed, Levi, I shudder to think I ever indulged a favorable thought of thee."

Catherine explained that Elma was not a Quaker although she was Catherine's relative. Elma was allowed to spend time alone with Levi because they appeared close to marriage.

The defense established that Elma's bedroom had a common wall with that of their next door neighbor, Mr. Watkins. This was important to the later testimony of Watkins, who became a defense witness.

Hope Sands, Catherine's sister, was Colden's next witness. She said that after Elma's body was found, Levi pressured Catherine and Hope to sign a paper stating that Levi paid no special attention to Elma and that nothing passed between them concerning courtship or marriage. They refused to sign.

Cross-examination was brief. Hope said that Levi was well liked and that Elma and Levi once had locked themselves away for an hour. Although Hope had met Levi's brother, Elma had not. The only time she knew Levi went out with Elma was when Elma, Hope, and Levi went to a museum.

Colden called Elias Ring, who added that in September, while Catherine was in the country, Levi and Elma were constantly together in private. Elias assumed they would be married.

Colden: Did you see anything improper or immodest in the behavior of Elma until she was acquainted with the prisoner?
Ring: No. Never.

Weeks's lawyers used the cross-examination to prepare a theory of Elma's death, picturing her as a loose woman. Suicide was the other possibility. Ring was asked about the partition between his and Watkins's houses.

Defense: What material is the partition made of between Watkins's house and yours?
Ring: It is a flank partition, lathed and plastered.
Defense: Could you hear the noise of children through?
Ring: No; not as I can recollect.
Defense: Is Mr. Watkins a clever man and a good neighbor?
Ring: Yes, he is.

Ring would later doubt Watkins's qualifications as a good neighbor.

Margaret Clark testified next. She said she went to the country in late August and returned to the Ring house about November 12. After that, she noticed that Levi and Elma appeared more intimate.

Defense: Did not Levi pay as much attention to Hope Sands as he did to Elma?

Clark: Yes, I think he did, and more, too.

Isaac Hatfield had boarded at the Rings' while the women were away. Hatfield saw "a great intimacy between the prisoner and the deceased, such as to induce me to suppose he was paying his addresses to her with a view to marry."

Richard David Croucher, a lodger, was the next prosecution witness. Croucher said there was a warm courtship between Levi and Elma, and he saw them in a very intimate situation. Weeks's lawyers had their own plans for Croucher. They questioned his activities the evening of December 22.

Croucher: I supped that night at Mrs. Ashmore's, but that's not her real name—it is 884 Bowery Lane—It was the birthday of her son—she has had a good deal of my money, and I thought I would go and sup with her . . . In the course of the evening . . . I crossed twice or three times from Greenwich-street to Broadway and was once at the coffee house. I went out to the Bowery and returned to Mrs. Ring's.

Defense: What time did you return home that night?

Croucher: It was my agreement with Mrs. Ring to be home at 10 o'clock a'nights but on this occasion I stayed out till eleven or half-past eleven.

Defense: Have you ever had a quarrel with the prisoner at the bar?

Croucher: I bear him no malice.

Defense: But have you never had any words with him?

Croucher: Once I had. . . .

Defense: Were you ever upon any other than friendly terms with Elma?

Croucher: After I offended the prisoner at the bar, who she thought was an Adonis, I never spoke to her again.

Levi's apprentice and roommate, William Anderson, said Levi was "not more particular in his attentions to Elma than to Margaret and Hope." Anderson testified: "One day Levi said, 'You must not think it strange of my keeping Elma's company—it is not for courtship or dishonor, but only for conversation.'" But then Anderson continued: "One night I pretended to be asleep, and the prisoner undressed himself, and came with a candle and looked to see if I was asleep or not. Supposing I was, he went downstairs in his shirt, and did not come back until morning." Anderson added that Elma was cheerful, but less so the Sunday she disappeared.

Colden's case was proceeding smoothly. Catherine Ring sent Elma and Levi out the door together. The next step was to convince the jury that Levi took Elma to the well in Ezra's sleigh. But the vital link connecting Elma to the sleigh disintegrated when Susanna Broad, an "aged and very infirm woman," testified: "I live opposite Ezra Weeks's lumber yard, and on the night the deceased was lost, I heard the gate open and a sleigh or carriage come out of the yard about 8:00. It made a rumbling noise, but had no bells on it, and that it was not long gone before it returned again." Colden asked no questions. The defense lawyer cross-examined Mrs. Broad and destroyed her credibility. She insisted she saw the sleigh in January. But January was the wrong month.

Weeks's suicide theory was not without problems because witnesses reported they heard calls for help from the vicinity of the well between 8 and 9 PM. Catherine Lyon testified that a half hour or less after she saw Elma in Greenwich Street shortly after 8 PM, she heard a woman cry "Murder! Murder! Oh, save me!"

Sleigh sightings were abundant. Margaret Freeman saw a one-horse sleigh on Greenwich Street "with two men and a woman in it, all talking and laughing, very lively, particularly the woman." William Lewis claimed he discovered the track of a one-horse sleigh only three hundred feet from the Manhattan Well. Others saw the sleigh. Two people confirmed hearing the cries. Colden called Andrew Blanck, whose son said he found Elma's borrowed muff in the well on Christmas Eve. On Christmas Day, Blanck saw a one-horse sleigh track within 10 feet of the well, and men's tracks nearby.

The trial had been underway for 15 hours. At 1:30 AM, the jurors, falling asleep, requested an adjournment. The court reluctantly agreed to adjourn until 10 AM. Constables were sworn to keep the jury together "in some private and convenient place, and two more were sent to wait upon them and bring them refreshments."

In a time of one-day trials, there were no provisions for sequestering juries. Finally, "the picture room" in the City Hall was selected. The jurors retired, uncomfortable, but surrounded by portraits of famous people. Kleiger, *supra*.

The Trial: Day Two

At 10 AM on Tuesday, April 1, Colden called his final witnesses. Dr. Skinner, a dentist with an interest in surgery, saw the corpse in the coffin. He thought compression marks on the neck might have been made by hand but admitted under cross-examination that he was incapable of judging how they occurred.

James W. Lent, who helped lift Elma's body from the well, described her injuries. When he said she appeared as if she had been murdered, the defense interjected, "You are to tell what you saw, not what conclusion you made. That is for the jury." Lent told of going to the police and then with an officer to find the prisoner. After Lent offered sympathy for Levi's situation, Levi said, "Is it the Manhattan Well she was found in?" "I said I knew not what well she was found in—I did not then know the Manhattan Well—This was about half past three in the afternoon. . . ."

Juror: Was there any mention made of the Manhattan Well in the presence of the prisoner before he asked the question?
Lent: I did not hear any. I don't believe there was.

Lent was not cross-examined. Weeks's team had a new problem.

Colden's next witness, Dr. James Snedecher, thought that Elma's left collarbone had been broken. The most respected physician called was David Hosack. An eminent diagnostician and botanist, Hosack was a founder of Bellevue Hospital and Hamilton's personal physician. After seeing the body in the coffin, he noticed livid spots on the neck that he said were the result of violent pressure. Asked by Colden whether any person could have committed such an act of violence on his own person to have produced such effects, Dr. Hosack replied, "I do not think it could be done." The defense did not cross-examine. Kleiger, *supra*; L. Baker, "The Defense of Levi Weeks," *A.B.A. J.* 63, June 1977.

Elizabeth Osborne, who lent Elma her muff, said she understood it was found in the well. The defense established that the muff was found several days before the body was discovered.

Colden's final witnesses, three men, explained that Ezra Weeks's horse could make the round trip from the Rings' to Manhattan Well and back to Weeks's stable in 15 or 16 minutes. Colden closed his case by reading from *Essays: The Laws of Evidence*, by John Morgan, explaining the acceptability of circumstantial evidence to substantiate a charge of murder.

The defense began its case with an address to the jury. In *Aaron Burr*, Milton Lomask writes that while Hamilton was florid and emotional, Burr appealed not only to the heart but to the head. He claims this is a "rare" example of Burr's style. But Ron Chernow in *Alexander Hamilton* claims that "we can make some educated guesses, for instance, the grandiloquent lawyer who opened the defense case spoke in a florid style reminiscent of Hamilton rather than the more succinct Burr." But Hamilton's grandson and biographer Allan McLane Hamilton has the final say: "Burr made the opening speech, and Hamilton interrogated most of the witnesses." M. Lomask, *Aaron Burr* (1979); R. Chernow, *Alexander Hamilton* (2004); A.M. Hamilton, *The Intimate Life of Alexander Hamilton* (1910).

After lashing out at the rumors that threatened an impartial trial, Burr said:

> Notwithstanding there may be testimony of an intimacy having subsisted between the prisoner and the deceased, we shall show you that there was nothing like a real courtship, or such a course of conduct as ought to induce impartial people to entertain a belief that marriage was intended; for it will be seen that she manifested equal partiality for other persons as for Mr. Weeks. It will be shown that she was in the habit of being out of evenings, and could give no good account of herself; that she had at sometimes asserted that she had passed the evening at houses where it afterwards appeared she had not been. We shall show you that if suspicions may attach anywhere, there are those on whom they may be fastened with more appearance of truth than on the prisoner at the bar. Certainly you are not in this place to condemn others, yet it will relieve your minds of a burden.

> There will be two modes of giving a solution—first, that the deceased sometimes appeared melancholy, that she was a dependent upon this family, and that a gloomy sense of her situation might have led her to destroy herself. As to the incident of the sleigh, we shall account for his whole time during that evening, except about 15 minutes, which was employed in walking from one house to another; and we shall show you that the whole of his conduct has been such as to totally repeal the ideas of guilt. It will appear that at 10 o'clock the same evening,

he supped at his brother's, perfectly tranquil. The story you will see, is broken, disconnected, and utterly impossible. We shall show you that the sleigh of Ezra Weeks was not out that evening, indeed the testimony of the good old woman was such as could not gain the least belief, especially when you see that in matter of date and time she was totally lost. . . .

Burr's speech ended with praise for Levi's character and stories of men falsely charged and later found innocent. As to Levi's question about whether the body was found in Manhattan Well, the defense would prove "that he had been previously informed that the muff had been found there and it was therefore natural to inquire if the body was not found there also."

The first defense witness was Demas Meed, Ezra's apprentice. He explained how difficult it would be for someone to use the horse without his knowledge. Meed was vague about the time but certain it was "a little before nine when he saw Levi sitting in Ezra's parlor."

Lorena Forrest, Ring's neighbor, testified with mixed results. At 1 PM on January 2, the day the body was found, she told Levi that Catherine had mentioned that the muff and handkerchief had been found in a drain by Bayard's Lane.

> *Juror:* Was the Manhattan Well mentioned?
> *Forrest:* There was nothing said about the Manhattan Well.
> This refuted the defense explanation, but the questioning quickly turned to possible suspects.
> *Defense:* Did you not hear Mr. Croucher say that he came near the Well the evening when she was missing?
> *Forrest:* Yes, he told me he did and said he generally came that way.

Joseph Watkins, the next witness, suggested that Elma entertained other men, including Catherine Ring's husband.

> *Watkins:* '[B]out the middle of September, Mrs. Ring being in the country, I imagined one night I heard a shaking of a bed and considerable noise there, in the second story, where Elma's bed stood. . . . I heard a man's voice and a woman's. I am very positive that the voice was not Levi's.

Watkins added, "I said to my wife, 'It is Ring's voice' and I told my wife, 'That girl will be ruined next.' "

Watkins claimed he heard the bedroom noise 8 to 14 times while Catherine was away. He also aided the defense by stating that Catherine believed Elma was staying at the Watkinses' house one night when she was not. Not only did Watkins suggest that Elma was generous with her sexual favors, but he then jabbed at Croucher, saying, "I don't know but I once said to Croucher that I believed he had a hand in it." Watkins testified that Croucher spread suspicion against Levi.

Three physicians testified in Weeks's defense. Dr. Prince attended the coroner's jury and said that nothing in Elma's appearance would discount her drowning herself. Dr. McIntosh eliminated a murder motive. He examined the body and decided Elma was not pregnant. Colden did not cross-examine. It is not possible to determine the accuracy of McIntosh's examination. And, of course, Elma could have falsely told Levi she was pregnant. Dr. McIntosh did not see "marks of violence sufficient to cause her death." Dr. Romayne, the third physician, never saw the body but claimed the appearance of marks may be affected by death. However, the coroner's jury's verdict was "murder by some person or persons yet unknown." Kleiger, *supra*.

The defense team tried to cast suspicion upon Croucher, but the testimony dealt only with Croucher's gossip. The highlight, literally, came during the testimony of William Dustan when he said that Croucher entered his store and announced, "Levi Weeks is taken up by the High Sheriff and there is fresh evidence against him from Hackensack." Coleman writes: "One of the prisoner's counsel held a candle close to Croucher's face, who stood among the crowd, and asked the witness if it was he and he said it was." Both Burr and Hamilton claimed credit for this dramatic flourish, and the story grew over the years.

Witness Hugh McDougall reinforced the effect of Croucher as a villain, which after the trial he proved to be. McDougall: "I had been acquainted with Mr. Croucher for some time, but I never liked his looks. On the second of January . . . he was extremely busy among the crowd to spread improper insinuations and prejudices against the prisoner."

Next, Timothy Crane, a lodger for two weeks at the Rings' when Elma disappeared, observed that Elma was sick nearly half the time. One night, a doctor was present, and she asked him for laudanum, which he dropped into her mouth. He claimed Levi seemed unchanged at work after Elma's disappearance.

John McComb, the architect, said that he and his wife walked from Ezra's house to Henry Clements's, stayed for about 20 minutes, and saw Levi when they returned a little after nine. Ezra's wife Elizabeth's deposition was read. She testified that McComb left the house about 8:20 or 8:25 PM and that shortly after, Levi came in, cheerful as usual. Clements was also a friend of the Rings.

Ezra Weeks agreed with his wife and explained why Levi blurted out the name of Manhattan Well: "About 2 PM on January 2, Levi came in and told me that Mrs. Forrest had told him the muff and handkerchief were found in a well near Bayard's Lane. I told him it must be the Manhattan Well." But Mrs. Forrest had actually mentioned a drain near Bayard's Lane. Colden asked Ezra why he thought of Manhattan Well, and he replied that he had furnished the wood and he rode past it almost daily.

Witness Frederick Rhinelander said he timed the walk to Manhattan Well. It took 20 minutes to go and 15 to return. Ezra Weeks, recalled, was asked if he knew his horse and sleigh had been used Sunday evening. He referred the question to his apprentice. Four character witnesses for Levi ended Weeks's defense. Colden called three character witnesses for Elias Ring, including Henry Clements, who also testified that when McComb arrived at his house, he remarked that it was about 9 PM, "rather late to visit a neighbor." The final significant witness, Ann Ashmore, corroborated Croucher's alibi.

The prosecution's case ended at 2:25 AM, Wednesday, April 2. Burr read from *Hale's Pleas of the Crown* concerning presumptive evidence, and Hamilton proposed the case be submitted without further argument. Colden, "sinking under his fatigue," asked for an overnight adjournment. He wanted the jury to hear his closing argument. The court refused. Coleman gives this account:

At the end of the regular trial, the chief justice charged the jury after admitting he had thought closing arguments of counsel would have given him "time to adjust the mass of evidence." He advised the jury that minute detail was not essential to determine the case. It was their duty to "find the prisoner guilty if in their consciences they believed him so from the evidence—to acquit him if they thought him innocent." They could find him guilty only if the circumstantial evidence was so established and connected as to produce a rational conviction he was the perpetrator of the crime.

Then Justice Lansing evaluated the evidence: That it was doubtful whether Gulielma Sands left the house of Elias Ring in company with the accused "so as to cause him to account for her." That if the testimony of Susanna Broad did not satisfy the jury, the testimony about the sleigh and the cries of distress could have no application to the prisoner, and that Mrs. Broad's testimony was confused and indistinct. He said the prisoner appeared to have a fair character, that it was difficult to "discover what inducement could have activated him" to commit the crime, that declarations made when he became a suspect did not appear inconsistent with innocence. Lansing claimed the prisoner's time was accounted for that night "except a few minutes" and it was doubtful that the victim "had been exposed to any other violence than that occasioned by the drowning." He said that even if the credibility of some witnesses was questioned, "the court were unanimously of the opinion that the proof was insufficient to warrant a verdict against him, and that with this general charge they committed the prisoner's case to their consideration." The jury deliberated for five minutes and returned with a verdict of not guilty.

Afterword

Estelle Foy Kleiger relates that Ezra Weeks offered Court Clerk William Coleman $500 to alter or omit his note in the preface of his transcription that he would make no remark upon the guilt or innocence of Levi Weeks. Coleman refused Weeks's money and his subsequent offer to buy Coleman's entire edition for $1,500. This bribery attempt led Kleiger to suggest that money may have bought the shocking testimony of neighbor Joseph Watkins. Kleiger, *supra*.

The Dream Team appeared again in court within a week, but on opposite sides. On April 7, in the U. S. Circuit Court for the District of New York, they argued the case of *Jouet v. Jones*. An equity case with Burr for the complainant and Livingston and Hamilton for the defendants, who included Livingston, it was dismissed with costs. Hamilton's Cash Book includes an entry of $500 charged as his fee. J. Goebel Jr. & J.H. Smith, eds., *The Law Practice of Alexander Hamilton*, vol. 5 (1981).

Levi Weeks left New York and returned to Massachusetts. He finally settled in Natchez, Mississippi, where he became a well-known architect, the designer of Auburn, a mansion designated as a national historic landmark. He married Ann Greenleaf and had four children.

Richard Croucher was convicted on July 8, 1800, of raping a 13-year-old servant girl sent by Croucher's new wife, Mrs. Stackhaver, to clean Croucher's room at the Ring house. Again, Colden was the prosecutor. Livingston defended Croucher, suggesting his unhappy bride may have framed him. Croucher was sentenced to life imprisonment. Pardoned and later convicted of fraud in Virginia, he returned to England where it was reported that he was executed for committing "a heinous crime." Kleiger, *supra*; J. C. Hamilton, *History of the Republic in the Writings of Alexander Hamilton* (1864); H. C. Lodge, *Alexander Hamilton* (1898).

Aaron Burr shot Alexander Hamilton in a duel at Weehawken, New Jersey, on July 11, 1804. Hamilton died the next day. While continuing to serve as vice president of the United States, Burr was indicted in New York for challenging Hamilton and in New Jersey for murder. No action was taken, but his reputation was destroyed. In 1807, Burr was tried and acquitted of treason by Chief Justice John Marshall for an alleged attempt to invade Spanish-controlled Mexico and encourage western American states to secede and join Burr's new nation. Burr died on September 14, 1836.

On November 10, 1806, President Thomas Jefferson appointed Henry Brockholst Livingston as an associate justice of the U.S. Supreme Court. He died on March 18, 1823.

In 1810, Cadwallader David Colden was elected mayor of New York City. He was later elected to Congress.

On December 12, 1829, Justice John Lansing was in New York City on business. He left his hotel room to post a letter and was never seen again.

Burr used the legal language of the law that created the Manhattan Water Company to start a Jeffersonian Republican-friendly bank. It rivaled the two Federalist banks organized by Hamilton. The Manhattan Bank later merged and is now Chase Manhattan Bank.

In 1802, architects John McComb Jr. and J.F. Mangin won the design competition for the new New York city hall, the seat of government since 1812.

Manhattan Well still exists in New York City, under an alley on Greene Street with wooden water towers on nearby Soho rooftops. The spring runs beneath Spring Street and empties into the Hudson River. D. Lane, "The Original 'Dream Team,'" *Crime Magazine* (1998).

10

Wild Bill Hickok
The Two Trials of Jack McCall

Wild Bill Hickok, America's last great gunfighter, was shot in the back of the head while playing poker in the gold mining town of Deadwood, Dakota Territory. Legend has it that when he was shot, his cards, which were strewn on the floor, were the Ace of Spades, the Ace of Clubs, the Eight of Clubs, the Eight of Spades, and the Jack of Diamonds—forever known as the Dead Man's Hand. The story of Wild Bill and how he met his death lives on in the popular imagination. But for lawyers, the story of what happened afterwards may be even more fascinating.

Wild Bill Hickok

James Butler Hickok was born in Troy Grove, Illinois, in 1837 and moved to Kansas in 1855. Drifting from job to job, he served as lawman, army scout, and professional gambler. Some claim he killed 100 men along the way. He was once acquitted of manslaughter. His marksmanship was legendary. He could simultaneously pull a pistol in each hand, fire them both, and strike objects on opposite sides at the same time.

Hickok roomed with a succession of prostitutes, and he drank too much. In *The West: An Illustrated History*, Geoffrey Ward quotes a reporter for the *St. Joseph Union*: "If the enthusiastic admirers of this . . . 'plainsman' could see him in one of his periodic drunks, they would have considerable romance knocked out of them."

Wild Bill became a famous lawman by cleaning up the notorious cow town of Abilene. When Hickok accidentally killed a special deputy during a gunfight, however, the town council decided not to renew his contract. Ward describes Hickok's decline. After an unsuccessful tour in 1873 with Buffalo Bill in a melodrama and a failed attempt at gold mining, Hickok spent his time drinking and playing poker.

Yet Wild Bill remained a celebrity, the first of the "fast guns." In Abilene, there had been several efforts to kill him in order to collect a rumored reward of $10,000 that a Texas family was said to have pledged to avenge the death of their son. In *The American Cowboy in Life and Legend* (1972) by Bart McDowell, this explanation is given for Wild Bill's murder:

> This same rumor followed Hickok north to Deadwood, South Dakota, five years later. "My father rode into town with Wild Bill," Mrs. N.A. Erickson told me outside her mobile home there. ". . . You know what happened on August 2. That was the day reward-hungry Jack McCall shot Wild Bill from behind, killing him instantly. My father heard those shots. He was just across the street."

Shortly before the fatal poker game, Wild Bill had a premonition of his fate. According to the *Virginia Evening Chronicle*, August 4, 1877, Wild Bill wrote a letter to his wife on the day before his death:

> Dead Wood Black Hills Dacota [*sic*]
> August 1st 1876
>
> AGNES DARLING, if such should be we never meet again, while firing my last shot, I will gently breathe the name of my wife—Agnes—and with wishes even for my enemies I will make the plunge and try to swim to the other shore.
>
> JB HICKOK
> WILD BILL

The Shooting

On the afternoon of August 2, 1876, Wild Bill was wearing a Prince Albert frock coat when he sat down at a table at Nuttall and Mann's No. 10 Saloon in Deadwood. His custom was to hold his drink in his left hand so that his right—his "shooting" hand—would be free. And he liked to sit with his back to the wall. On that day, however, the empty chair at the poker table faced the wall. Wild Bill twice asked to change his seat, but the other three players assured him that he had nothing to fear.

Suddenly, a drifter named Jack McCall entered history. He slipped through the rear door of the saloon and stood at the bar. Without warning, he pointed his pistol and, shouting "Take that," shot Wild Bill. The bullet exploded from Wild Bill's head and lodged in the wrist of Captain Massie, one of the card players.

Wild Bill died instantly. McCall raced from the saloon. He jumped on a horse, but the saddle slipped. He fell to the ground, and after a quick chase by the town's citizens, he was arrested.

Instead of a lynching, one of America's strangest legal episodes followed. The Deadwood civic leaders immediately organized a jury trial. In a unanimous verdict, the jury found McCall not guilty. But the federal government decreed that the trial was illegal. A second jury was empaneled, this one under federal law. They found McCall guilty. Jack McCall is thus one of the few defendants who was not only tried twice for the same offense but who was acquitted in the first trial and convicted in the second.

McCall's First Trial: August 1876, Deadwood

McDaniel's Theater was the courtroom for McCall's first trial. Judge W.L. Kuyendall was appointed President of the Court. He had resigned his position as Secretary of the Wyoming Stock Growers' Association to join the gold rush. In *They Called Him Wild Bill* (1964) by Joseph Rosa, Kuyendall describes how he organized the trial.

> To observe the proper formalities, I was selected to act as chairman. After stating the object of the meeting to be the organization of a second miners' court to try the case the next day, I stated that if any man present were not in harmony with the movement then was the time for him to leave. All remained.
>
> It was decided the jury should be selected by making out a list of twenty names of miners from each of the three mining

135

districts, the name of each to be written on a separate piece of paper and well shaken in a hat, the twelve drawn therefrom to be the jury, lists to be made by a committee to be selected by the meeting when court convened next morning. On motion I was elected judge, Isaac Brown, sheriff, John Swift, clerk, Colonel May, Prosecuting Attorney, and Judge Miller, attorney for the prisoner. Both were able lawyers at that time, although without clients, for there was no law in force then or for months afterwards.

While willing to assume the responsibility, I refused to serve unless all those present agreed to be present with their revolvers when the court convened to see that a proper jury committee was selected and to remain through the trial and see the proceedings through to the end. I told them that if any of them would not do this, to retire immediately. Again all remained and by a rising unanimous vote pledged themselves. When the court convened the committee and jury were selected and sworn according to program.

Three men were sent to tell the miners in Deadwood Gulch and Whitewood Creek about the trial, which began the day after the shooting—at 9 AM, August 3, 1876. Kuyendall observes the scene:

> The prisoner . . . entered a plea of "Not Guilty," the trial proceeding under all forms of law. Evidence of the killing by the prisoner developed an absolutely cold-blooded, cowardly assassination without any warning or extenuating circumstances whatever.

Several witnesses testified about details of the shooting. Others testified about McCall's good character. McCall testified on his own behalf. He forcefully claimed that his brother was killed by Wild Bill a week before. The jury was hung 11–1 for acquittal, but the final holdout eventually agreed to join the majority. McCall was acquitted. The verdict was not popular.

The chronology of the day before the shooting does not substantiate McCall's claim. Hickok was playing cards at Nuttall and Mann's No. 10 Saloon when a bystander dropped into the game. It was Jack McCall. After McCall lost consistently, Wild Bill offered him money for a meal. McCall refused. This event calls into question the motive of revenge for a brother's murder and opens the possibility of self-pity and a drunken belief by McCall that Wild Bill cheated him at cards.

There was talk in Deadwood that McCall was a killer hired by the lawless elements in town who feared that Hickok would become marshal. In *Deadwood, the Golden Years* (1981), Weston Parker takes this theory to an extreme:

> At least one member of the jury was later killed while attempting to rob a stage, and it may well be that the "jury" was packed by those criminals who may have conspired to have Bill killed.

Interlude: Wyoming Territory

Shortly afterwards, Wild Bill's best friend, California Joe, arrived in Deadwood and threatened McCall. Frightened, McCall left town and headed for the Wyoming Territory. There, he told strangers how he killed Wild Bill and even boasted about it.

But McCall's prosecutor in the Deadwood trial, Colonel May, was relentless. On August 29, 1876, Colonel May convinced United States Marshal Balcombe that the Deadwood trial was illegal because Deadwood was an "outlaw" town. He claimed that its inhabitants had no right to be there because the Black Hills were part of an Indian reservation where the United States government had sole jurisdiction. Marshal Balcombe agreed that the United States District Court, not the hastily improvised Deadwood court, was the proper forum. The Deadwood trial was therefore not recognized by the United States courts.

Colonel May and Marshal Balcombe found McCall in Laramie, and Balcombe arrested him. McCall was charged a second time for the same killing. He was arraigned in Yankton on October 18, 1876.

McCall's Second Trial: December 1876, Yankton

McCall's second trial began on December 4, 1876 in Yankton. His lawyers were Oliver Shannon and General W.H.H. Beadle. Witnesses testified for the prosecution, but McCall's counsel did not produce any defense witnesses. McCall did not testify. Double jeopardy was not raised.

The jury did not hear McCall's claim of revenge for his brother's death. The defense evidently relied on the prosecution's failure to prove guilt beyond a reasonable doubt. This obviously was a dangerous strategy, not only because there were several eye-witnesses but also because McCall admitted the killing in the first trial and countless times thereafter.

Given the eyewitness testimony and McCall's admission that he had shot Wild Bill, the defense also raised McCall's diminished capacity based on his drunken condition. In fact, his drunkenness was stressed in the clemency petition and was referred to as a defense considered by the jury in an opposition brief.

Before the jury deliberated, a motion for a new trial and arrest of judgment was made. The court denied the motion, stating:

> As to the objection that the defendant should have been indicted and tried on the other side of this court, it is well settled that a trial for homicide, committed in an Indian reserve, must be had on the Federal side of a Territorial court, and is governed by U.S. Statutes and the rules of the common law. . . . It is therefore considered and adjudged that the motions for a new trial, and in arrest of judgment be, and they are hereby overruled.

By the Court,
P.C. Shannon, Judge.
[United States v. John McCall,
Opinion of the Court]

The jury deliberated from 7 PM to 10:15 PM on December 6, 1876. The foreman then handed the court clerk the written verdict: "Guilty as charged in the Indictment."

McCall was sentenced on January 3, 1877. Although he made an impassioned plea, the court was unmoved and sentenced McCall to death.

Mary McCall's Letter

After McCall's conviction, his sister, Mary McCall, mailed a letter to the United States Marshal of Yankton.

Dear Sir,

> I saw in the morning papers a piece about the sentence of the murderer of Wild Bill, Jack McCall. There was a young man of the name John McCall left here about six years ago, who has not been heard from here in Louisville,

who [se family] were very uneasy about him since they heard about the murder of Wild Bill. If you can send us any information about him, we would be very thankful to you.

This John McCall is about twenty-three years old, has light hair, inclined to curl, and one eye crossed. I cannot say about his height, as he was not grown when he left here. Please write as soon as convenient, as we are very anxious to hear from you.

Very respectfully,
Mary McCall

The letter was never answered by the Marshal. Presumably, Mary McCall could have informed the authorities whether Jack McCall had a brother. That would have helped to substantiate or refute McCall's claim in the first trial that Wild Bill had murdered his brother. This letter was shown to McCall shortly before his execution. He admitted that it was from his sister, and he sent a reply.

Writ of Error and Application for Pardon or Commutation

A Writ of Error was filed with the Supreme Court of the Dakota Territory. The Second Judicial Court denied the Writ and upheld the verdict on January 20, 1877. *Yankton Press and Dakotian*, Jan. 20, 1877.

A Petition for Pardon or Commutation was filed four days later. The spearpoint of the petition was McCall's diminished capacity because of his substantial alcoholic consumption. It was signed by John Pennington, Governor of the Dakota Territory, and endorsed by William Dewey, a prosecution witness. It stated:

> . . . McCall in his defense had claimed that he was drunk at the time the alleged murder took place and in fact had fallen down three times when crossing the street to the saloon. It was also alleged that while there was unquestionable proof of the killing, grave doubts existed when the history of the case showed a total absence of motive for the act of vengeance, money, or anything else traceable to a natural cause.

The governor went on to allege that McCall's first knowledge of the killing "was whilst sitting on a log in the outskirts of the village, with five or six men around him, and when returning to consciousness was told that he had 'got into a bad scrape,' and when asked what it was, was told by them that he had killed 'Wild Bill.' "

The governor's petition was supported by one drawn up by Beadle and Shannon [McCall's lawyers]. It was signed by a number of local businessmen, among whom was D.C. Neagle, speaker of the House of Representatives. That petition claimed that McCall was born in New Orleans, that his occupation was hunter and miner, and that he had never been convicted of any crime.

The petition consisted of a five-point declaration, pointing out that no logical reason had been found for the murder—"that he killed the deceased we have no doubt, but that he murdered him we do not believe." The petition suggested that perhaps McCall was suffering from delirium tremens.

The petition also referred to McCall's lack of friends and to the fact that the witnesses he wanted to testify on his behalf could not be found in time as they had gone gold-prospecting. As for the victim, the petition mused:

"We have no word to utter about the deceased. We knew him only from reputation as 'Wild Bill' and propose that the grass that grows over his grave may be as green and beautiful as that of any other spot."

In conclusion, it was suggested that it was the state of society in Deadwood that contributed largely to McCall's downfall. File No. F-307, Records Group No. 204; Rosa, *supra*.

On February 7, 1877, an Opposition Brief was filed, stating:

I have never known a case where the interests of a prisoner were more carefully guarded by the Court than this one. Witnesses were sent for at the expense of the Government, where there were grave doubts as to their materiality, and the trial postponed nearly two months, and it was only after the Marshall made his return, and it was evident that no such witnesses as he desired could be obtained, that the trial proceeded.

The prosecution pointed out that the district court's judgment had been unanimously affirmed by the entire bench and that McCall's "alleged drunken state" had been considered by the jury but no "mitigating circumstances" were found.

The prosecution then struck back at McCall's contention that Wild Bill was a blackguard, stating:

140

[McCall's] counsel find it convenient to refer to the deceased as a "notorious character," and as one whose real name was only disclosed by the evidence. A reference to the indictment will show that both his real name and the alias of "Wild Bill" were used in it. But the name "Wild Bill" had been given to him and fastened upon him so that he was really better known by that than by any other, and without any discredit to himself.

It is a part of history of the war, that this man, by reason of his fearless, and efficient service as a Union Scout among the guerrillas of Missouri, Arkansas and Eastern Kansas, and by his contests with these same guerrillas even after the war closed, when they so persistently pursued him, won this name of "Wild Bill," and he certainly had no reason, during his life to be ashamed of it. The same policy pursued him even to the Black Hills, his old enemies giving him a bad name whenever and wherever they dared do it.

Although the evidence was clearly inadmissible in a case like this, where the prisoner sought the deceased, and while in no danger, shot him from behind, I do not object to, and the court permitted testimony as to the character of the deceased for violence. One witness, for some years a passenger conductor on the Kansas Pacific Railway, who knew him there, ten years or more ago, and who had known him since at Cheyenne and in the Black Hills, said he was not a quarrelsome man and never quarreled unless forced into it. Other witnesses gave him the same character and no one gave him a different one.

How many *aliases* the prisoner has, it would be difficult to tell. Although declaring upon his arraignment that his true name was John McCall, he asserted immediately before sentence was passed upon him that it was not his true name. He seems to be a person of a depraved and wicked heart, without regard for human life, as was shown by a murderous attack upon the keeper of the jail here, in an attempt to escape, a short time before his trial. Coming, as it is now asserted from the south, he had conceived for some cause, or without cause, an especial hatred for "Wild Bill."

The prosecutor then outlined the shooting and its aftermath. Surprisingly, he concluded:

[I do not seek the life] . . . of this unfortunate man, and if I should consult my own feelings and inclinations, I should

141

prefer a substitution of imprisonment for life to the death penalty as a punishment for murder. The law of the United States recognizes the latter, however, and not the former, and upon my conscience I am utterly unable to see any extenuating circumstances in this case.

U.S. Marshal J.H. Burdick was unsettled. If there was to be an execution, he needed to have a scaffold built. He sought guidance, writing:

Dear Judge:

I wish you would do me the favor to call at the office of the Atty Gen at as early an hour as will suit your convenience after the receipt of this, and learn if you can whether McCall's sentence will be commuted by the President or not. Should you learn that it will be, please suggest to the Atty Gen the propriety of his telegraphing me to that effect, as I must commence preparations as soon as one week from tomorrow, and don't want to incur any expenses to the Government unless there is a necessity for it. . . .

Very respectfully,

J.H. Burdick
U.S. Marshall

Marshal Burdick received the death warrant on February 14, 1877. He still delayed erecting the scaffold, however, because he did not have official confirmation from Washington. Finally, on February 19, 1877, Burdick received an unambiguous directive from Attorney General Alphonso Taft, father of future President William Howard Taft.

DEPARTMENT OF JUSTICE, WASHINGTON, Feb. 19 1877
To J.H. Burdick, U.S. Marshall, Yankton, Dakota Terr'y: The Attorney General directs me to say to you that he has considered the application made on behalf of John McCall, convicted of Murder and declines to interfere with the sentence pronounced by the Court.

A.R. Dutton, Chief Clerk.

File No. F-307, Records Group No. 204.

Burdick then began to have a scaffold built on the school section north of the Catholic cemetery in Yankton, Dakota Territory.

If Deadwood had been a legitimate town, McCall would have remained free. If the Dakota Territory had been a state when Hickok was killed, the governor could have commuted the sentence or pardoned McCall. Instead, McCall would be executed in a public hanging.

On January 22, 1877, a newspaper correspondent wrote that the governor was opposed to the re-arrest of persons tried and acquitted in the Black Hills and believed persons tried under these laws should not have their lives the second time put in jeopardy for the same offense.

Execution: March 1877

The execution—the first legal hanging in Yankton—was scheduled for March 1, 1877. A large crowd of spectators followed the death wagon. At 9 AM, Marshal Burdick and two assistants entered McCall's cell and the death warrant was read to him. Several carriages waited outside the jail.

At 9:30 AM, Marshal Burdick and his deputy entered the first carriage. McCall, along with a Catholic priest and a newspaperman, entered the second carriage. The cortege then proceeded to the scaffold, passing McCall's open grave on the way. Hundreds of spectators followed in carriages, on horseback, and on foot.

When the cortege reached the gallows, McCall was assisted up the steps. The crowd gathered below. McCall placed himself over the trap. His hands and feet were bound, and he knelt to pray. He then stood up, and a black cap was placed over his head. Marshal Burdick adjusted the noose around his neck. McCall requested another moment to pray. He then asked that the noose be tightened.

"Oh God" were McCall's last words when the trap door was sprung at 10:15 PM. Two doctors pronounced him dead twelve minutes later. *Yankton Press and Dakotian*, Mar. 1 1877; June 23, 1881.

The reason for McCall's killing of Wild Bill remains unknown. His claim that Hickok killed his brother is unsubstantiated. Rumors that lawless elements of Deadwood hired him as an assassin or that he was a reward hunter remain rumors. Drunkenness, self-pity, or envy may have been his only motive. Like many killers of famous people, he attained notoriety by association.

Afterword

So, the American West's most controversial and colorful character was killed by an unknown drifter named Jack McCall, and the saga of the Wild West came to an end. Joseph Rosa concludes:

> Few of the thousands of tourists who visit Deadwood each year and stand around the grave of Wild Bill really appreciate the part that he and his contemporaries played in the winning of the West. Overplayed by the false West of the dime novel, screen, and television, the real contribution of these men has long been lost. But each in his own way contributed something to the expansion of the United States.
>
> It might be said that Wild Bill's death was destiny fulfilled, that McCall's pistol [he claimed to have had only one live round in it] was an instrument of fate, or that the last game of poker was the culmination of a chain of events predestined to end the career of the Old West's most colorful and controversial figure. It might also be said, with truth, that Wild Bill had outlived his time and had to die.
>
> His era was dying anyway; times were changing. Soon the day of the quick-triggered individual who held citizens in awe or terror, meting out his own justice [or injustice] to keep or break the peace, would be over, and the two-gun man a memory. For a nation was virtually being born around them, and there was growing a society that would frown on him and his kind, with no understanding of what made him or why. . . .
>
> The real Wild Bill Hickok remains an enigma, a controversial character who will always to some extent baffle those who seek the man behind the legend. In an age when the ability to handle a gun meant the difference between life and death, he emerged the victor in all such encounters. Where others were coarse, harsh, and unwashed, he appeared clean, gentlemanly, well dressed, and well mannered. Yet his recklessness, zest for excitement, and amazing ability to find trouble—even without seeking it—made him truly a product of his time—a time that was short, both for him and for America.

Rosa, *supra*.

In *The Last West* (1974), Russell McKee marks the brief period from 1860 to 1890, the span of one generation, as one of the richest times in our national history. All the best-known town marshalls and six-shooter bad men from that era provide a virtual Who's

Who of American Folklore—names such as Wild Bill Hickok burned forever into our hero cult. By government announcement, the frontier was declared officially closed in 1890.

Since 1928, the town of Deadwood, South Dakota has been the site of a reenactment of the *Trial of Jack McCall*. Tourists have been empaneled as jurists to determine whether Jack McCall was guilty.

On August 29, 1930, a bronze tablet was dedicated to Wild Bill in the New State Park in Troy Grove, Illinois, with this inscription:

JAMES BUTLER
"WILD BILL" HICKOK,
PIONEER OF THE GREAT PLAINS, BORN HERE MAY 27, 1837, WAS ASSASSINATED AT DEADWOOD AUGUST 2, 1876. SERVED HIS COUNTRY AS A SCOUT AND SPY IN THE WESTERN STATES TO PRESERVE THE UNION IN THE CIVIL WAR. EQUALLY GREAT WERE HIS SERVICES ON THE FRONTIER AS EXPRESS MESSENGER AND UP-HOLDER OF LAW AND ORDER. HE CONTRIBUTED LARGELY IN MAKING THE WEST A SAFE PLACE FOR WOMEN AND CHILDREN. HIS STERLING COURAGE WAS ALWAYS AT THE SERVICE OF RIGHT AND JUSTICE. TO PERPETUATE HIS MEMORY THIS MONUMENT IS ERECTED BY THE STATE OF ILLINOIS.
A.D. 1929

11

Justice Stephen Field, Justice David Terry, and Sarah Althea Hill

U.S. Supreme Court Justice Stephen J. Field was traveling by train from Los Angeles to San Francisco on August 13, 1889, with a bodyguard, David Neagle. Unaware of Field's presence, former California Supreme Court Justice David S. Terry and his wife, Sarah Althea Hill Terry, boarded the train that evening near Fresno. Terry had represented Sarah in a federal case in the U.S. District Court and Field's judgment against her had provoked a wild scene. This time, their accidental meeting would end with Terry's death.

Neagle urged Field to have breakfast on the train the next morning, but Field insisted on eating in the Lathrop Station dining room. The Terrys entered. After Sarah left the room, Terry approached Field and struck his face. Neagle fired two shots at Terry, killing him.

California's gold rush had attracted men like Field and Terry. Self-made men with money, weapons, strong opinions, and political connections came to dominate the state. Sarah Althea Hill's lawsuit was an amusing diversion. In the opening skirmish in 1883, the multimillionaire builder of the Virginia & Truckee Railroad and creator of the Bank of California's Comstock Lode monopoly, former

U.S. Senator William Sharon, was arrested for adultery. *Nevada Online Encyclopedia,* www.onlinenevada.org/william_sharon (2007).

After his wife died, Sharon enjoyed a succession of female salaried companions. Newspaperman William Neilson claimed that Sharon had fathered a child with another woman while he was married to Sarah Althea Hill. He claimed that Sarah had a marriage contract signed by the senator. The adultery charge was a device to publicize Sarah's marriage claim and to prepare for a profitable divorce. Shock waves rippled through San Francisco. R.H. Kroninger, *Sarah and the Senator* (1964).

In October 1883, Sharon countered by suing Sarah in the U.S. District Court in San Francisco. He alleged that he was never married to Sarah, that the marriage contract was a forgery, and that the court should prohibit any use of it. Sharon decided that a federal venue would be more receptive to his claim. The adultery case was dismissed, but the timing of the federal suit, filed a month before Sarah's divorce case, later became significant. *Sharon v. Hill,* 26 Fed. 337 (1885).

Sarah and Sharon's tumultuous battle in both state and federal courts created a complex maze of litigation lasting from 1883 to 1890. Neagle's role in Terry's death brought about a significant U.S. Supreme Court case, *In re Neagle,* expanding the limits of executive power. *In re Neagle,* 135 U.S. 1 (1890).

California Divorce Trial

Pretty Sarah, whose fashionable dress was admired daily by the newspapers, entered the clerk's office of the San Francisco Superior Court in November 1883, filing the state court case of *Sharon v. Sharon.* Sarah clutched the piece of paper that proved her claim. Throughout the subsequent proceedings, she protected this marriage contract as her key to a life of wealth and happiness. Handwritten on both sides of the paper were these statements:

> I, Sarah Althea Hill, of the City and County of San Francisco, State of California, age 27 years, do here, in the presence of Almighty God, take Senator William Sharon, of the State of Nevada, to be my lawful and wedded husband, and do here acknowledge and declare myself to be the wife of Senator William Sharon, of the State of Nevada.
> (Signed) Sarah Althea Hill, August 25th, 1880,
> San Francisco, Cal.

I agree not to make known the contents of this paper or its existence for two years unless Mr. Sharon himself see fit to make it known.

(Signed) S.A. Hill.

I, Senator William Sharon, of the State of Nevada, age 60 years, do here, in the presence of Almighty God, take Sarah Althea Hill, of the City of San Francisco, Cal., to be my lawful and wedded wife & do here acknowledge myself to be the husband of Sarah Althea Hill.

(Signed) Wm. Sharon, Nevada, Aug. 25. 1880.

On March 10, 1884, when the trial began, Sarah was described by the *San Francisco Chronicle* as "looking as demure, innocent and sweet as the arts of the toilet could make her. Her costume was black silk over which she wore a brocaded velvet dolman faced with black fur around a throat which, if the truth be told, is no longer as round and full as it no doubt was not many years ago. The face is shapely and oval. The features are regular." The *Chronicle* noted that Sharon was "small in stature but erect in carriage . . . he is apparently the least remarkable man in the courtroom." Sarah's lead lawyer was the flamboyant George Washington Tyler, assisted by his son, W.B. Tyler. David S. Terry joined Sarah's team. General William Barnes was Sharon's chief lawyer. Superior Court Judge J.F. Sullivan presided. Kroninger, *Sarah*; O. Lewis & C.D. Hall, *Bonanza Inn* (1939).

Sarah told the following story. She came to San Francisco from Cape Girardeau, Missouri, in 1871. Sarah was introduced to Senator Sharon at the Belmont train station. In 1880, when she visited his office to give him $7,500 to invest for her, he offered her $1,000 a month and his daughter Flora's white horse if she would let him "love her." She rebuffed him. He said he was teasing, that he wanted to marry her, but he wanted secrecy because of his legal problems with "a girl" who claimed her baby was his child. Several weeks later, Sarah returned to his office, where Sharon read from law books to convince her that a private marriage was legal.

Sarah said that Sharon dictated the contract to her. They signed the paper, and Sarah was provided with an apartment in Sharon's Grand Hotel, which was connected by a passageway to his Palace Hotel. Sharon sent Sarah letters from Nevada beginning, "My Dear Wife." Sarah claimed that she acted as hostess at Sharon's Belmont mansion near San Francisco. Their relationship cooled in

149

the fall of 1881. Sharon demanded that Sarah sign a paper confessing she had no claim and that she was receiving $500 a month as his mistress. She refused. He arranged to pay her the $7,500 invested with him and ordered her to leave her apartment. To enforce Sarah's eviction, Sharon had the carpets torn up and the doors removed.

After several attempts at reconciliation, including one amorous encounter witnessed by a young neighbor named Nellie Brackett, Sarah decided to vindicate her name in court. At the conclusion of Tyler's case, Sarah was confident of success in establishing the marriage and receiving a divorce. She looked forward to generous alimony payments and a share of the community property acquired after the marriage. Kroninger, *Sarah, supra*; A.R. Buchanan, *David S. Terry of California* (1956).

Experts

The defense attack was three-pronged: They intended to prove that Sarah did not act as a married woman, disprove Sarah's testimony, and, most important, provide testimony of handwriting experts refuting the legitimacy of the marriage contract and "Dear Wife" letters. Barnes was able to show that some witnesses gave false testimony, and accounts of Sarah's belief in fortune-tellers and love potions were colorful, but these points were peripheral. Henry Hyde, a Sharon lawyer, became a handwriting expert. He had "some facility at distinguishing handwriting" and was a member of the San Francisco Microscopical Society. Kroninger, *Sarah, supra*; Lewis & Hall, *supra*.

When Hyde was asked whether there had been an erasure on the "Dear Wife" letters, he peered through microscopes and magnifying glasses for ten days. Barnes suggested that the documents be subjected to chemical analysis, but Tyler countered that in the pending USDC case, Sarah's papers must be intact. Tyler challenged Hyde's statements. Barnes introduced a second expert, George C. Hickox, who said the word "wife" in the letters was not Sharon's handwriting. He insisted that the signature on the contract was genuine but that Sharon had signed a blank piece of paper. Tyler disdainfully declined cross-examination.

Sharon, the last witness, gave this version. In August 1880, a young woman arrived unannounced at his office. She asked about stocks, but he gave no advice. She invited him "to come up and see her." He did, and when she accepted an invitation to dine in his Palace Hotel apartment, he proposed to pay her $500 a month to sleep with him. She declined. But Sarah finally climbed into his bed, sealing the offer. Sharon insisted that the word "wife" in the letters was a forgery. As to the contract, his signature was possibly genuine, along with "Nevada" and the date, but he never signed the contract. He first saw it in 1883.

When the trial resumed on July 15, Judge Sullivan, with Sarah watching, refused to allow chemical analysis of the documents. Barnes rested. Tyler, in rebuttal, qualified an obviously unqualified "expert" who claimed that the handwriting was genuine.

Next came Max Gumpel. His testimony proved to be a bombshell. Hired by Barnes as a handwriting expert, Gumpel had examined the written documents, but he told Barnes that his conclusions made it impossible to testify for Sharon. Gumpel felt it was improper to testify for Sarah, but the judge ordered him to testify since Barnes had stipulated that Gumpel was an expert. Tyler happily proceeded with Gumpel as Sarah's witness. Gumpel testified that the handwriting was genuine. Sarah was jubilant. Kroninger, *Sarah, supra.*

In the summation, Terry entered the case. Hickox had criticized the contract, saying that words were printed, retouched, and written over each other, and at the close, the writing was smaller and the lines were closer together. But Terry said of Hickox: "Every peculiarity which he points out as a badge of fraud is found in his own manuscript." Lewis & Hall, *supra.*

In December 1884, Judge Sullivan gave his opinion. Sullivan castigated the perjury of several witnesses. But the judge ruled that the contract and the "Dear Wife" letters were genuine and that the parties had conducted themselves as married persons. Sharon had signed the contract because he was "a man of unbounded wealth possessed of strong animal passions that, from excessive indulgence, had become unaccustomed to restraint."

The divorce was granted. The *San Francisco Morning Call* noted that Sarah, wearing a "shrimp wrapper of a very elegant pattern," announced to the press: "I am so happy. I feel just like a young kitten that has been brought into the house and set before the fire."

The superior court in San Francisco had not received official notice of the USDC case and, therefore, treated it as though it did not exist. It was a time of rejoicing, but Barnes would seek a new trial. More important, the USDC had not yet rendered a decision in Sharon's case against Sarah. Buchanan, *supra.*

151

Federal Trial

Sharon v. Hill, the USDC trial in Sharon's 1883 suit to enjoin Sarah from using the marriage contract, now began before Judges Matthew Deady and Lorenzo Sawyer, who were joined by U.S. Supreme Court Justice Stephen J. Field. The two cases, which ran successively, brought opposite results. The USDC trial replicated the witnesses and exhibits; but it introduced a new handwriting expert, R.W. Piper of Chicago.

Sarah was determined to protect the documents again. She spent a night in jail rather than submit them for tests. Sarah protested a witness's statement, saying, "I will shoot him yet; that very man sitting . . . I can hit a four-bit piece nine times out of ten." When Sharon's lawyer, O.P. Evans, examined a witness, Sarah pulled out a pistol. Evans said, "Do you want to shoot me?" Sarah replied, "I am not going to shoot you just now unless you would like to be shot and think you deserve it." Evans protested, "No, I would rather not be." Evans insisted that Sarah give him the weapon. Field ordered that Sarah be disarmed before each court session. Another major principal in the impending tragedy had entered the scene.

Stephen J. Field

Stephen J. Field, born in Connecticut in 1819, grew up in Stockbridge, Massachusetts. He attended Williams College and studied law with his brother David in Albany. Touring Europe in 1848, he disapproved of the revolutionary fervor. After returning home, he joined the 1849 California gold rush. Field opened a San Francisco law office, but clients were scarce. Taking a boat downriver to a tent town near Sacramento, he purchased 65 lots on credit. Townspeople assumed he was wealthy and bought his lots. He campaigned for a town government and became the alcalde (judge). He had been in Marysville for three days. At the end of six months, Field boasted that he was worth more than $100,000. S. Field, *Personal Reminiscences of Early Days in California* (1877).

California became a state and adopted a constitution. In 1850, Field's office of alcalde was abolished. He was succeeded by a state judge, William Turner, a hot-tempered Texan. They clashed, and Field became the first lawyer in California held in contempt of court. The California Supreme Court set aside the contempt ruling, saying it "should be used with great prudence and caution."

152

Later, as a state legislator, Field managed to send Turner to a district where there were "only grizzly bears and Indians." Field always punished his enemies. C.B. Swisher, *Stephen J. Field: Craftsman of the Law* (1930); Kroninger, *Sarah, supra*.

Field was appointed to the California Supreme Court in 1857. David S. Terry had become chief justice two years earlier. In 1859, Terry resigned to fight a duel with U.S. Senator David Broderick, who had insulted his honor. Terry killed him. Field then became chief justice. Earlier, Broderick had protected Field when Turner challenged him to a duel. Field's admiration for Broderick was equaled only by his subsequent animosity toward Terry. R.H. Kroninger, *The Justice and the Lady* (1977).

In 1863, President Abraham Lincoln appointed Field an associate justice of the U.S. Supreme Court. Many of Field's friends were railroad magnates, and he protected business interests. Terry, in opposition, voiced the need of farmers and merchants for railroad regulation. A.H. Kelly & W.A. Harbison, *The American Constitution* (1955).

During Sarah's trial, Field unsuccessfully sought the Democratic Party presidential nomination. Terry did not attend the California convention, but he was a powerful force. Field blamed Terry for his defeat in the primary, and he never forgot it. Buchanan, *supra*; Kroninger, *Sarah, supra*.

Field served on the court for 34 years. Beginning with his dissent in the *Slaughter-House Cases*, 83 U.S. 36 (1873), he interpreted the Fourteenth Amendment's due process clause to shield businesses from state legislation. His use of economic substantive due process came to fruition in *Allegeyer v. Louisiana*, 165 U.S. 578 (1897). After his death, Field's judicial philosophy continued to prevail until *Nebbia v. New York*, 291 U.S. 502 (1934) and *West Coast Hotel Co. v. Parrish*, 300 U.S. 379 (1937). B.F. Wright, *The Growth of American Constitutional Law* (1942); W. Lockhart, Y. Kamisar, J. Choper & S. Shiffrin, *Constitutional Law* (1986).

Federal Verdict

When Sharon's USDC case against Sarah ended, the transcript was given to Judges Sawyer and Deady. Piper, the new handwriting expert, claimed that Sharon's signature had been forged. This conflicted with Sharon's testimony at Sarah's divorce trial. Moreover, Piper declared, it was forged by Max Gumpel. The "Dear Wife" letter in ink was a tracing, as was the word "wife" in two other letters.

153

Sharon died in November 1885. He had assigned his estate in trust for his children and expressly excluded Sarah. Under California's community property law, Sharon could only dispose of his half of the community property, so if Sarah won, she would inherit her share.

The USDC case was decided in December 1885, a year and two days after the superior court decision in California. Judges Deady and Sawyer wrote separate opinions. Deady said that "the sin of incontinence in a man is compatible with the virtue of veracity and does not usually imply the moral degradation and insensibility that it does in a woman." Deady went on: "It must be remembered that the plaintiff is a person of long standing and commanding position in this community, of large fortune and manifold business and social relations, and is therefore by all that these imply specially bound to tell the truth." Deady dismissed Gumpel's expertise but believed Piper: "He appeared from his own account to be an expert of celebrity."

After declaring that the authenticity of the documents was the only issue, Deady condemned Sarah's morals and attacked the state of California for allowing "the integrity of the family, the cornerstone of society" to be based on "furtive intercourse befitting a brothel." Judge Sawyer agreed. So ended 1885. A year earlier, Sarah had been happily divorced in the San Francisco Superior Court. Now, in the USDC, she was denounced as a harlot and she was denied use of the marriage contract. The new year began with happier news. Sarah married David Terry. However, this pairing would prove to be deadly. When Tyler was disbarred because of his conduct in an unrelated case, Terry became Sarah's lawyer.

David S. Terry

Born in Kentucky in 1823, the six-foot-three, 250-pound Terry was a capable lawyer and a tough fighter. A former Texas Ranger who arrived during the gold rush, Terry was prickly about honor. He carried a bowie knife and used it. Early in his career, Terry stabbed a litigant in court. The year he won a California Supreme Court seat, he thrust his knife into an abolitionist leader's shoulder during a street fight. After his duel with Broderick, Terry resumed his Stockton law practice. In 1863, he left California and fought for the Confederacy. By 1878, Terry's legal stature had been restored. A. Quinn, *The Rivals* (1994); Buchanan, *supra*.

Terry enjoyed life with his wife Cornelia at his Stockton home and Fresno ranch. Three sons had died in infancy, and another (David) died while cleaning a revolver. But his son Sam had been admitted to the bar, and his youngest son Clinton worked as an engineer. In December 1884, Cornelia died. A few months later, after surgery, Sam died. When Sharon's death set Sarah free to marry, Terry was available. C. Rasmussen, "One 19th Century Jurist Lacked Prudence," *Los Angeles Times* (February 15, 2004); Kroninger, *Sarah, supra.*

Decisions

In January 1888, Sharon's heirs lost their appeal from the divorce decree when the California Supreme Court based its decision on the statutory definition of marriage. Sarah celebrated, but her elation did not last. Kroninger, *Sarah, supra.*

Barnes, representing the heirs, needed to reopen the USDC judgment. He tried to force Sarah to turn over the contract. Sarah was threatened with imprisonment for contempt of court if she failed to obey the order. In August, Sarah's uninhibited behavior caused a minor sensation. As she passed Judge Sawyer on a train, Sarah grabbed his hair and said: "I will give him a taste of what he will get by and by. Let him render this decision if he dare." *In re Neagle, supra*; Buchanan, *supra.*

In September 1888, Barnes's petition to revive (reopen) was granted. Field acknowledged that Terry had attempted to appeal and that Barnes had deliberately delayed substituting the Sharon estate as a party in the USDC case. Field read the decision. Sarah was ordered to turn over the contract she had guarded for so long.

Sarah jumped to her feet and pointed a finger at Field.

Sarah: Are you going to take it upon yourself to order me to give up that contract?
Field: Sit down, Madame.
Sarah: I will . . . .
Field: Marshal, put that woman out.
Sarah: Judge Field, how much have you been paid for that decision? . . . .
Field: Marshal, put that woman out.
Terry: Don't put a finger on my wife. Get a written order.

Terry said he would take her out himself. When the marshal tried to pass by with Sarah, Terry leaped to his feet and struck him. Bystanders threw Terry to the floor and pinned his arms. Sarah fought to help him but was overcome and led away.

Terry: Let me go. I only want to accompany my wife and I'll go quietly.

During the melee, Field continued reading. Terry tried to join Sarah in the marshal's room but was barred. Terry drew a knife. A deputy put a gun to Terry's head, but Terry ignored him.

Terry: Stand back. I'm going to my wife and no man shall stop me.

While Terry was fighting several deputies, the order came to arrest both Terry and Sarah. Terry, disgruntled, said: "Tell that old bald-headed son of a bitch, Field, that I want to go to lunch." Terry spoke softly to Sarah: "My Dear, why did you bring on all this trouble?" Sarah was sentenced to thirty days in the Alameda County Jail.

Terry: I'll go with you.
Reporter: You have been sentenced to six months.
Terry: What! Damn them! What am I to be in prison for?
Sarah: (laughing) Yes. It was as hard to get in here as it now is hard to get out.

Sarah had dropped her satchel in the uproar and demanded it be returned. A deputy searched the bag and found a loaded pistol. Kroninger, *Sarah, supra;* Swisher, *supra; In re Neagle, supra.*

Field ruled that Terry's conduct "had been an insult to the emblem of the nation's majesty" and his claim that he meant no harm was an appeal to "childish incredulity." Field said that Terry was under "great excitement and unless he cools down before his term of imprisonment is finished, he may attempt to wreak bodily vengeance upon the judges and officers of the court." On the way to jail, Sarah said she would "kill Sawyer and Field." Terry's lawyer said that Terry told him he intended to humiliate Field: "I do not intend to kill him, but I shall insult him by slapping his face, knowing that he will not resent it as he is a coward." Buchanan, *supra; In re Neagle, supra.*

Field made certain that Terry served the six months. When he was released, Terry was ordered to surrender to a grand jury indictment initiated by Field. He was charged with assault, and Sarah was charged with impeding an officer during the courtroom fracas. They posted bail and were released. *In re Neagle, supra*; Kroninger, *Sarah, supra*; Buchanan, *supra*.

Sarah's case continued on a downward spiral. Appeals were denied. The California Supreme Court had changed justices during the year. It now cited the two-year secrecy clause in the contract as a reason to overturn Judge Sullivan's decision. The case had to be retried. Sarah was defeated. Terry filed for a rehearing, citing the inconsistency with the court's ruling the previous year. The California Supreme Court would consider whether to grant a rehearing within thirty days. By then, Terry would be dead. Kroninger, *Sarah, supra*.

Endgame

David Neagle, a bystander who helped disarm Terry during the courtroom fracas, was hired as a deputy to serve as Field's bodyguard in 1889 when Field insisted on riding the Ninth Circuit. Neagle had tried a variety of jobs. When Field and Neagle took the Southern Pacific train to San Francisco and, by coincidence, the Terrys boarded a day coach near Fresno, the fatal encounter was imminent. *In re Neagle, supra*; Kroninger, *Sarah, supra*.

The restaurant manager at Lathrop, near Stockton, described the scene. Terry and Sarah left the train and entered the dining room where Field and Neagle were seated. Sarah returned to the train in great haste. "Well, you better go and watch her," Terry cautioned the manager when he saw Field. Terry sat down and then rose and walked to Field's table. The manager watched from the door as Terry struck Field twice on the cheek with the back of his hand. Neagle stood, drew a revolver, aimed it at Terry's chest, and fired. As Terry collapsed, Neagle fired again at his head. Sarah rushed in, cradled Terry, kissed him, and lamented that she could not live without him. She pleaded with strangers for revenge and ran to the train where she banged on Field and Neagle's locked door. Kroninger, *Sarah, supra*; Buchanan, *supra*; *In re Neagle, supra*.

Neagle was arrested and taken to jail in Stockton. Field took the train to San Francisco. The San Joaquin County district attorney insisted that Field should be arrested. The next day, Sarah signed arrest warrants charging Neagle with murder and Field as his accomplice. Sheriff Cunningham of San Joaquin County took the train to San Francisco to serve Field's arrest warrant. Field accepted service of the warrant in his hotel room and agreed to meet the sheriff at court the following afternoon. Field said, "I am glad to see you, sir, and wish you to perform your duty. Because I may be a judge, . . . I am not excused from the proper processes of law." However, Field had already contacted Sawyer's clerk. Kroninger, *Sarah, supra.*

When Field and the sheriff arrived in Judge Sawyer's court, the clerk handed Field a previously prepared writ of habeas corpus. Sawyer ordered Field to appear before the USDC in San Francisco. Field posted a $5,000 bond to preclude returning to Stockton before the preliminary hearing. The USDC hearing on the writ for habeas corpus was expedited so that it was heard before the Stockton date, and Field was absolved of any complicity in Terry's death. The Stockton hearing never took place. State proceedings against Field were dropped.

Sheriff Cunningham returned to Stockton without Field but with a writ of habeas corpus to remove Neagle to San Francisco. Judge Sawyer presided at Neagle's habeas corpus hearing in the USDC. Field testified that Terry's fist was about to land a third blow when Neagle shouted, "Stop! Stop! I am an officer! Stop!" "Instantly," Field said, "two shots followed." Field insisted that if Neagle had delayed two more seconds, both Field and Neagle would have been Terry's victims. However, the next day, Neagle said that he had jumped between Field and Terry as Terry was reaching for his bowie knife to attack Field. There was no cross-examination. No knife was found. Terry was unarmed.

Judge Sawyer read his decision. If the killing was "an act done in pursuance of a law of the United States, or an order of a court thereof, it was a federal case." Since Field could have performed judicial functions in the dining room, Neagle had the duty to defend him there, just as in court. Were Neagle's actions excessive? It was not for the state to decide. Sawyer concluded that Neagle's killing of Terry was "commendable. Let him be discharged." Field presented Neagle with a gold watch inscribed, "with appreciation, in great peril." Kroninger, *Sarah, supra;* Buchanan, *supra;* Lewis & Hall, *supra.*

In re Neagle

The U.S. Supreme Court upheld Judge Sawyer's USDC decision. Justice Samuel Miller wrote:

We cannot doubt the power of the president to take measures for the protection of a judge of one of the courts of the United

States who, while in the discharge of the duties of his office, is threatened with a personal attack which may probably result in his death. . . . There is positive law investing the marshals and their deputies which not only justify what Marshal Neagle did in this matter, but which imposed it upon him as a duty. . . . He was acting under the authority of the law of the United States, and was justified in so doing; and he is not liable to answer in the courts of California on account of his part in that transaction.

Field did not participate. In *The Supreme Court in United States History*, Charles Warren called the sanction given to Neagle's action "the broadest interpretation yet given to implied powers of the national government under the Constitution." *In re Neagle, supra.*

Popular sentiment had been against Field's arrest, but people believed Neagle should be tried in a California court. U.S. Senator (1893–1899) Stephen M. White wrote:

That Terry-Field episode was a most unfortunate affair. I think it is a grave mistake to assert federal control of the case. The U.S. judges are personally bitterly hostile to the Terry side and I believe they will take jurisdiction and discharge Neagle without a trial. The case is practically being tried by Field, though he is behind the scenes. When Field "hates," he hates "for keeps" and will do anything to win.

Swisher, *supra.*

Sarah Alone

The retrial of the divorce case was set for July 1890. The superior court decided that because the USDC case was filed first, it must prevail. Timing, finally, was everything. Sarah, haggard and disheveled, appeared alone. Judge Shafter told her the contract was inadmissible because of the USDC ruling. Sarah did not react. The contract had been destroyed in a fire at Terry's ranch the year before. Judge Shafter ruled against Sarah. She carried on, preparing an appeal. At the deadline, she raced through the city, completed the paperwork, and arrived at the county clerk's office too late. Kroninger, *Sarah, supra.*

It was over. Sarah was inconsolable. On February 14, 1892, newspaper headlines described her as hopelessly insane. She never recovered. Sarah died in the State Hospital for the Insane in Stockton,

California, on February 15, 1937. Sarah Althea Hill lost her case, her husband, and her mind.

Afterword

Stephen Field and his wife, Sue Virginia, were childless. Sue's young niece, Charlotte Anita Whitney, was their surrogate daughter. But unlike Field, Whitney became a political radical, organizing the Communist Labor Party of California. In 1919, she was convicted under California's Criminal Syndicalism Act. Her conviction was upheld by the U.S. Supreme Court in *Whitney v. California*, 274 U.S. 357 (1927). Justice Louis Brandeis questioned whether Whitney's membership in the Communist Labor Party presented a clear and present danger. Brandeis foreshadowed *Brandenburg v. Ohio*, 395 U.S. 444 (1969), in which the court ruled that "the contrary teaching of *Whitney* cannot be supported."

In *Make No Law* (1991), Anthony Lewis wrote: "Brandeis's words were for the ages, but they also helped Anita Whitney. A month after the Supreme Court turned down her appeal, the governor of California, C.C. Young, pardoned her. In his message he quoted the Brandeis opinion." J.W. Johnson, ed., *Historic U.S. Court Cases* (1992).

In 1866, Field's younger brother, Cyrus, was credited with laying the first successful transatlantic telegraph cable. His brother David Dudley Field created the Field Code in New York, the first systematic codification of New York law.

12

Mountain Meadows Massacre

Just as Marcel Proust's famous madeleine brought forth volumes of memories, a gift from our friends, Maryellen and Roy Halpern, of a small jar of elderberry jelly from Colorado City, Arizona, caused us to recall the recent hunt for a local polygamist leader. Then came remembrance of a darker past—the Mountain Meadows massacre of 1857 in southern Utah Territory, when travelers were met not with jams and jellies, but with death.

Our personal experience in the beehive state has been positive. We came upon St. George, Utah, on a summer evening in the 1960s and discovered a square dance in full swing at a park bandstand. In those days, coffee cups in cafes were set upside down so that a small defiance of local approval was needed to turn them over and drink the brew. Acquaintances in the oil industry insisted wryly that it was possible to abstain from alcohol, go to bed early, and still have a good time in Salt Lake City. In Spanish Fork, we visited a sweet lady, Alberta Aitken, who had telephoned and inquired whether we had a common ancestor. No such connection appeared, but on our trip she gave us a bagful of peaches and a transcript of her family's dangerous journey by covered wagon to the Mormon settlement.

Not long ago, we booked a room in St. George's Seven Wives Inn. Polygamy was presented to tourists as a quaint tradition. The city was booming with new residents ranging from retirees to New Agers. Upscale restaurants shared the town center with the historic winter house of Brigham Young.

But in 1857, Utah's residents were in a less hospitable mood. The Mormons had been termed mutinous, and President Buchanan ordered the army to the Utah Territory to put down the "rebellion." Many of the faithful were determined to defy any incursion into their land. The Mormon sect had originated with prophet Joseph Smith in New York and was organized in 1830 into the Church of Jesus Christ of Latter-Day Saints (LDS). Smith led his growing flock to Ohio, Missouri, and Nauvoo, Illinois. After 11 years of strife, Joseph Smith and his brother Hyrum were arrested. A mob stormed the prison cell and killed them. Seeking freedom from persecution, the Mormons followed their new leader, Brigham Young, to the Great Salt Lake basin. Now, again, they felt threatened. J. Brooks, *The Mountain Meadows Massacre* (1962).

The same year, a group of about 140 settlers left Arkansas. Their leader, 43-year-old Alexander Fancher was en route to his ranch in Visalia, California, bringing his wife Eliza and their nine children, along with household goods and a large herd of cattle. He shared command with "Captain Jack" Baker, the herd boss. The wagon train reached Salt Lake City on August 3 and then headed for the grazing lands of Mountain Meadows, 35 miles beyond Cedar City. They passed Jacob Hamblin's summer cabin a few miles before reaching their campsite. S. Denton, *American Massacre* (2003).

War fever flourished in the territory. The Reformation the year before had heightened fanaticism. Brigham Young was prepared to evacuate Salt Lake City. He conferred with the Indians, whom the Mormons believed shared with them the blood of Israel. Young told them that unless they stood by the Mormons, both groups would be killed by the federal government. Rumors swirled that the emigrants had poisoned the Indians' springwater and meat. George A. Smith was sent to the southern towns to give military orders to each commander. The Mormons were told not to sell grain to outsiders. Tensions increased. W. Bagley, *Blood of the Prophets* (1950).

Before the Fancher party reached Utah, one of the original Mormon apostles, Parley Pratt, was stabbed to death in Arkansas by an angry husband, a Gentile whose wife had entered a polygamous marriage with Pratt. The Mormons recounted their past suffering. Stories spread that the emigrants had insulted the Mormons. In Cedar City, Isaac C. Haight, the highest religious authority and town military commander, called a meeting of the Stake High Council to decide whether to kill the Fancher party and avenge the blood of the prophets. They sent for direction from Brigham Young but did not wait for a reply. They dispatched a messenger to "Indian Farmer" John D. Lee at Harmony to take charge of the Indians, "the battle-ax of the Lord." The crime was set in motion. Brooks, *supra*; T. Alexander, *Utah, the Right Place* (1995).

Mountain Meadows: September 7–11, 1857

The horror began on Monday, September 7, with an Indian attack. A child remembered the scene. "Our party was just sitting down to a breakfast of quail and cottontail rabbits when a shot rang out from a nearby gully, and one of the children toppled over, hit by the bullet." Several emigrants were killed before the men fired back. An Indian was killed, and the knees of Paiute war chiefs Moquetus and Big Bill were shattered. The attack was not successful. The emigrants strong defense made it obvious, Lee later said, "that the Indians could not do the work." Bagley, *supra*.

The Fancher party circled their wagons and endured a siege. On Wednesday, young William Aiden rode with two companions to get help. They approached the campfire of three Mormons—William Stewart, Benjamin Arthur, and Joel White. Stewart shot Aiden dead. The other two men escaped but were followed and killed.

Thursday night, Haight and Major John Higbee rode from Cedar City to confer with their military superior, Colonel William H. Dame, president of the Parowan Stake. According to Higbee, Dame's orders were to compromise with the Indians if possible, letting them take the stock if they would leave the company alone. On no condition should they precipitate a war with Indians while there was an army marching against the people. Dame said they should try to restrain the Indians and save the company. If that was not possible, they should save the women and children. Higbee carried the orders to Major Lee. A second detachment of the Iron County militia that arrived under Higbee's command included Private Philip Klingonsmith and Nephi Johnson, an Indian interpreter. Bagley, *supra*; Alexander, *supra*; Denton, *supra*.

On Friday, September 11, William Bateman, carrying a white

flag, joined Lee, and they approached the besieged camp. Lee told the party's leaders that the Mormons would protect the emigrants by escorting them from the meadow. One wagon was loaded with young children and another with a woman and a few wounded men. Women and older children followed them. After they were given a head start, each man, unarmed, walked single file with an armed Mormon guard beside him. Major Higbee was in command. Lee was ahead near the wagons. The command was given: "Halt! Do your duty!" Suddenly, the men were shot by their guards. Those who escaped when protesting Mormons refused to shoot were gunned down by other Mormons or Indians. The women and older children were killed by Mormons in disguise and Indians with knives and hatchets. The wounded in the wagon were shot at close range. Shrieks and screams gave way to silence.

Even before the attackers stripped the corpses, distributed the loot, and rounded up the herd, a story was fabricated to blame the Indians for the mass murder. Klingonsmith, the only man to publicly admit killing an emigrant, left the church and swore in an 1871 affidavit that the affair was a military operation. He stated that Lieutenant Colonel Haight told him that headquarters ordered for all but the little children to be killed. Klingonsmith said that after he shot the emigrant man next to him, he left to gather the children, who were taken to Hamblin's cabin and then placed in Mormon homes. He claimed that Haight and Dame quarreled that evening, and Haight told Colonel Dame that if Dame was going to report the massacre, he should not have ordered it. Dame appeared shocked at the bloodshed and directed that the Indians, who were given some goods and cattle, be calmed and kept from the trail.

Haight and Lee discussed how to inform Brigham Young. In Lee's *Life and Confessions of John Lee*, he wrote that "Haight then told me that it was the orders of the Council that I should go to Salt Lake City and lay the whole matter before Brigham Young." Haight refused to write a report, saying: "You can report it better than I can write it. You are like a member of Brigham's family, and can talk to him privately and confidentially." Lee's account described the emigrants' bad conduct and blamed the Indians. The settlers, of course, were unable to tell their story, although several children recalled chilling details. Brooks, *supra*.

The approaching war was a more immediate concern for the leaders in Salt Lake City. Plans were made to evacuate the city. A Mormon army was in place. Only the onset of extremely cold weather prevented a war. The U.S. Army retreated to winter quarters. The following spring, after mediation by Buchanan's friend, Thomas L. Kane, President Buchanan issued a pardon to the LDS leadership and installed civilian administrators in the Utah Territory. Governor Cummings, who replaced Young, was sympathetic to the church, but Judge Cradlebaugh, associate justice for the territory's southern district, was determined to investigate the massacre.

In 1859, the 17 surviving children of the Fancher party were turned over to federal officials to be reunited with relatives. The government received bills from the Mormon families for their keep. In April, Judge Cradlebaugh and his military escort attempted to capture and try the leaders involved in the massacre. Haight, Higbee, and others took off, fleeing to the mountains. Even Jacob Hamblin, who had become a federal official, would not help. Haight resigned from his post. Dame remained a bishop.

With Abraham Lincoln's election as president in 1860, new federal appointments were made, but the Civil War captured the nation's attention. In 1870, as non-Mormons began arriving on the transcontinental railroad, Young began distancing himself from Lee. In September, on an expedition with explorer John Wesley Powell looking for a Colorado River crossing, Young advised Lee, his second adopted son, to move into Arizona to avoid an arrest warrant. Other leaders were in hiding. Klingonsmith changed his name to P.K. Smith and lived in Nevada. Dame went on a mission to England. Haight and his son-in-law Higbee had left for Arizona. In October, Haight and Lee were excommunicated. Haight was restored four years later after shifting responsibility to Lee and those at the scene. Denton, *supra*.

In 1871, at Young's command, Lee began a new life. He sold his prosperous farms. In December, with two wives, Rachel and Emma, and 13 children, he began his exile in a barren wilderness with sandstone walls where the Colorado and Paria Rivers joined. Lee remained devout. He had been present in Missouri in 1838 when Governor Boggs issued "extermination orders" and 17 Mormon men and boys were murdered at Hauns Mill. He had guarded Joseph Smith's home. Lee was not aware that Philip Klingonsmith's affidavit earlier that year detailed the actions of the Mormons at Mountain Meadows. The Indians could no longer be accused of the slaughter. Brooks, *supra*; Denton, *supra*.

Lee constructed the first ferryboat to cross the Colorado River.

It was 26 feet long. "Lees Ferry" remained the only crossing for Mormon settlers between Utah and Arizona until 1928. Lee built a profitable business and provided hospitality to well-known figures. Artist F.S. Dellenbaugh described the scene. Lee was reserved at first. Rachel Lee kept watch. She left after dark for the cabin at Jacob's Pool. Emma Lee was a stout, happy young woman with two small children. Lee talked of the massacre, claiming he tried to stop the carnage. He insisted that Brigham Young was innocent. Waiting for Powell on his second expedition, Powell's men traded chores for cooked meals and found Lee "genial, courteous and generous." Denton, *supra*; Bagley, *supra*; D. Worster, *A River Running West* (2001).

The Poland Bill in 1874 redefined Utah court jurisdiction. It installed a U.S. attorney and marshal and extended juries to non-Mormons. The first grand jury under the new law indicted Lee, Dame, Higbee, Klingonsmith, Stewart, and three others. In November, the federal marshal sent his deputy, William Stokes, to arrest Lee. Stokes found him hiding in a chicken coop at the Panguitch home of one of his wives. Lee surrendered, and Rachel Lee accompanied him to jail at Beaver. Dame was arrested and placed in the territorial penitentiary. The national press, certain that Lee would implicate Young, converged on Beaver.

First Trial

Judge Jacob Boreman presided over the jury selection of eight Mormons, one lapsed Mormon, and three Gentiles. The church hired lawyers Jabez Sutherland and George Bates, while W.W. Bishop and Wells Spicer were determined to defend Lee. U.S. Attorney William Carey led the prosecution, assisted by Robert Baskin. Carey agreed to drop charges against Lee if his confession was complete. When Lee provided additional evidence against Haight and Higbee but exonerated Young and George Smith, Carey withdrew his early version of a plea bargain.

Lee's trial began on July 23, 1875, and with an overflow crowd, the court was moved to a nearby saloon. Klingonsmith, who had turned state's evidence, was the prosecution's star witness, describing the scene he had outlined in his affidavit and adding the presence of Indians. He failed to testify that Lee had killed anyone. Other witnesses were called, but none testified to seeing Lee commit murder. Before the defense case began, Sutherland told the judge he wanted to show that the "red man" compelled the whites to take part. Baskin countered that duress could not justify such a killing.

Spicer opened Lee's defense, blaming the Arkansans' hostile actions and the Mormons' fear of the Indians. He claimed that Lee acted under orders. The press called his morning argument "Spicer's boomerang," as it rebounded against Lee. But he had scored. There was no evidence that Lee was a murderer. The witnesses Robert Keys and Asahel Bennett saw bodies weeks after the slaughter. Elisha Hoops and Philo Farnsworth told a version of the poison story. Annie Elizabeth Hoag testified. Sutherland insisted that the Mormons had not murdered the emigrants but had rushed to their aid. In closing, Bishop spoke for five hours. Prosecutor Baskin charged that the Mormons had done nothing to bring justice to the emigrants' deaths. Most of the property was "appropriated by the men who murdered the parents of those little orphan children." He insisted that Brigham Young was an accessory, as no Mormon would act without his sanction. Baskin said he did not expect a guilty verdict.

The Transcript

We decided to look at the transcripts, so we drove to Cedar City and asked a friendly clerk for the trial records of *People v. Lee et al.* What had Bishop talked about for five hours? Suddenly, we were immersed in the nineteenth century, where letters copied at Brigham Young's office in 1857 were models of beautiful penmanship. By the 1870s, the court reporter was using a typewriter. Other documents were still handwritten, ink blots visible. We could read the lawyers' words and follow Bishop's argument:

> "They start with Robert Keys. Well he is perhaps a pure, good and upright man, but unfortunately for the prosecution, he does not know anything about the case. He returned from California some months after the transaction, passed the meadow on his way and saw some bones there. . . . If Robert had lived in the days of Shakespeare and been acquainted with that wonderful writer, what an improvement could have been made in his tragedies. We can only conjecture from the style and manner of this Robert as he with guttural sounds described the place where according to his unreasonable version the young lady lay—the one that he tells us was then undecayed—that the destroyers, death and time, had not

marred her fair features or robbed nature of its loveliness. That she lay there with a smile on her countenance, a magic but still silent witness, of one of man's most unnatural crimes. Incredible statement! Bearing no semblance of truth.

"Next comes Asahel Bennett, . . . one that is naturally honest and intends to be fair." But, Bishop said, "He thought he was at the scene for two hours looking upon the mass of human remains, when in fact he was there for but two minutes. So much for that. He was there—was greatly excited while there . . . and is now greatly prejudiced against the defendant and the whole Mormon people and that he is now an unfortunate old man whose judgment and reason have been dissipated by age and association cannot be questioned."

Klingonsmith came under a savage attack: "The next witness is a peculiar pet of the U.S. Attorney; the monster self-accused murderer, who comes here to aid the government—a miscreant called Klingonsmith." Bishop challenged Klingonsmith's actions: "He did not even raise his voice to prevent the massacre, but contented himself with asking the question 'What will be the result if the emigrants are all killed?' . . . After this, he settled back in his seat with a look of satisfaction beaming on his stolid features and said, 'I concluded to let it all go, it was useless to oppose the will of those in authority!'" Bishop outlined Klingonsmith's participation and concluded:

> Such is the fiend in human shape that asks you to believe his statements which have been made with his traitorous tongue. . . . Klingonsmith, with murder in his heart, blood on his hands, perjury on his tongue and misery in his soul returns to testify in this case . . . Klingonsmith stands here a confessed liar, coward and murderer. Hence, you are justified in disregarding all that he has said as a witness before you.

Bishop shredded all the witnesses, but Annie Elizabeth Hoag was singled out. "Next comes that unreliable witness—that raving crazed old woman—tongue tied in the middle and working at both ends. The vibrating of this female capon so long has it been vibrating, has injured her sense of hearing. Yet to her this must be a blessing judging from the effect of her talk upon others, for being deaf, she is freed from the torture of listening to her own wild and meaningless ravings."

Bishop told the jury that they were asked to convict Lee because he was near the massacre. They were asked to believe a man who had proven himself to be one of the vilest criminals of the age. They were asked to convict John D. Lee because all the people were watching and the defendant was old. Judge Boreman instructed the jury that even if the Arkansans had provoked the Indians, it did not justify murder, and there was no evidence that white men had been compelled to participate. If Lee had conspired, he was guilty even if he had not killed an emigrant. The case went to the jury on August 5, 1875. The jury was deadlocked. The Mormons and the lapsed Mormon voted to acquit Lee. The three non-Mormons voted that he was guilty. The public was outraged. Lee and Dame waited in the penitentiary for Lee's next trial.

Second Trial

On September 11, 1876, the nineteenth anniversary of the massacre, Lee returned to Beaver and Judge Boreman for his second trial. Juanita Brooks wrote, "The whole tone had changed." Baskin and other non-Mormons believed the LDS leaders had entered into an agreement with District Attorney Sumner Howard that Lee might be convicted if the charges against the other men were withdrawn. Brooks, *supra*.

The jury was composed entirely of Mormons. The indictment against Dame was quashed. Sutherland and Bates resigned, but Spicer and Bishop returned to defend Lee. Depositions by Brigham Young and George Smith were read. Men who had participated and kept quiet now came forward. Their memories were selective. They remembered only Klingonsmith and Lee at the scene. Samuel Knight said he arrived "on an errand of mercy" and was told of the plan to kill the Fancher party. Samuel McMurdy admitted he was there on Higbee's orders and said he saw Lee "kill some." Asked if he had killed any of the emigrants, McMurdy replied, "I believe I am not on trial here." Brooks, *supra*.

Nephi Johnson, who said his orders came from Haight, helped Lee make arrangements with the Indians. He observed the massacre from a distance and claimed that Lee fired at a woman. He saw the woman fall. Jacob Hamblin, who had been away marrying a new wife, testified that Lee told him Dame ordered the killings. Hamblin said that Lee described a scene in which two young women who had escaped the killing were found in the bushes by

169

an Indian. Hamblin also said Lee told him that the Indian shot one, and Lee cut the other woman's throat. Lee realized that he had been abandoned and allowed no defense. In his summation, Bishop argued that Lee had simply followed orders. Bagley, *supra*.

Although Lee had provided most of the emigrants' goods and cattle for Mormon use, Sumner Howard decided to blame the crime on Lee's greed. In Howard's address to the jury, he began by calling the massacre "a great bugbear ever since this occurrence by which you have been characterized as a people unworthy of political power." Howard reminded them that "somebody must be responsible for this murder." Then he pounced. "I say now, and I will prove to you . . . that the reasonable motive . . . is the motive that I attribute to John D. Lee, and that to plunder and nothing else." Claiming that the documents provided by Young and Smith "clear the skirts of the church," Howard turned to Bishop: "I say the church don't need defending; but where are you in this matter, Brother Bishop?" Bishop replied, "Couldn't you have called out the authorities at Cedar City?" Howard insisted there was no evidence that Lee was ordered to commit this crime.

Howard reminded the jury that Lee was the first white man to appear with the Indians. What was Lee doing there? He said Lee told Knight that the Indians needed leadership: "I ran a very narrow chance. I got a bullet through my hat and one through my hickory shirt and they [the Indians] were repulsed." Describing the massacre, Howard repeated the question, "Was that an act of mercy?" Howard reached his conclusion: "A diabolical deed was committed . . . not a question was asked and an answer given by which you can infer that he did it under any motive than that of avarice, than that of gain. . . . The only evidence you have after he ordered Nephi Johnson to watch it [the loot] is . . . it was traced into John D. Lee's possession." Howard vindicated the church and demanded Lee's conviction.

On September 20, the jury deliberated for three and a half hours and brought in a verdict. Convicted of murder in the first degree, Lee was sentenced to die on October 10 and was given his choice of execution. Beheading was associated with atonement. Lee said, "I prefer to be shot."

At the sentencing, Judge Boreman stated that Lee's trials revealed that high LDS authorities had "inaugurated and decided upon the wholesale slaughter of the emigrants." He observed that they had been "a persistent and determined opposition to an investigation of the massacre." Howard later emphasized the importance of obtaining more convictions, but no one else was prosecuted. Unsuccessful appeals extended Lee's execution date. He was embittered at becoming a scapegoat, but he was resigned. On March 23, 1877, at Mountain Meadows, Marshal Nelson read the death warrant and blindfolded Lee. Sitting on the end of his coffin, Lee raised his hands and instructed the firing squad, "Center my heart, boys." They fired, and he fell into his coffin and died without a struggle. Bagley, *supra*.

Afterword

Brigham Young died six months after Lee. Klingonsmith disappeared. Haight died alone in Arizona in 1886. The church denounced polygamy in 1890, and in 1896 Utah became a state. Higbee's indictment was finally dismissed. Statehood had made the territorial charges invalid, and there was no longer enough evidence for a trial. Judge Higgins in Beaver said it was "the last indictment pending, except for that of William Stewart who is dead." Bagley, *supra*.

Plaques marking Mountain Meadows and Lonely Dell do not mention Lee's execution. At Mountain Meadows, the Mormon church erected a sign on U.S. Forest Service land. It reads: "In the early morning hours of September 7 [1857], a party of local Mormon settlers and Indians attacked and laid siege to the encampment. For reasons not fully understood, a contingent of territorial militia joined the attackers. The Iron County militia consisted of local Latter-Day Saints acting on orders from their local religious leaders and military commander, headquartered thirty-five miles to the northeast in Cedar City."

At the Lonely Dell Ranch, Glen Canyon National Recreation Area, a National Park Service sign ignores Rachel Lee and omits the massacre. It states:

"Oh, what a lonely dell" was Emma Lee's first reaction to the isolated, barren, desert valley that became her new home in 1871. The name stuck over the years for the many different families that tried to make a living here. As the first permanent residents of the area, John Doyle Lee, his wife, Emma, and their family were sent here by the Mormon church to establish a ferry service across the Colorado River. Many pioneers, coming from southern Utah, needed the service to reach northern

Arizona. The Lees built two log cabins, planted shade trees and dammed and diverted the tiny Paria river for irrigation. Warren Johnson and his family replaced the Lees in 1875, completing the ranch and operating the ferry for the next 20 years. For travelers along the long desert road between Utah and Arizona, the ranch was a welcome oasis. John D. Lee, a leading colonizer of southern Utah, he was aggressive, industrious and loyal to his church. Emma Batchelor Lee, the 17th of Lee's 19 wives, she was known for her stamina and firm character.

SECTION IV

Defending
Irish Rebels

The Irish struggled down a longer road to independence from England. Rebellion had severe consequences. In court, barristers used their skills to transform a punctuation mark or a misspelled word into the defendant's freedom.

13

A Punctuation Mark

Rex v. Casement

O But we talked at large before
The sixteen men were shot,
But who can talk of give and take
What should be and what not
While those dead men
are loitering there
To stir the boiling pot?
                              "Sixteen Dead Men," W.B. Yeats

Fifteen Irish Nationalists were shot for taking part in the Easter
Monday uprising in Dublin on April 24, 1916. Yeats's sixteenth
Irish patriot met a different death.

Tall, gaunt, bearded Sir Roger Casement was a retired British
Consul official who had been knighted by the Crown for revealing
the abuse of native workers in Peru and the Congo. However, in
1916, he was tried and convicted in London under the Treason Act
of 1351, an obscure law written in Norman French.

Casement became the first Knight of the Realm since Sir Walter
Raleigh in 1603 to be prosecuted under this law, enacted during

the reign of Edward III. While the Crown summoned the jury's patriotism, the defense stressed the Act's lack of punctuation. Outside the courtroom, scandal erupted over the contents of Casement's "Black Diaries." Yet, his fate may have depended, in part, upon a different revelation.

What did Casement do to merit such punishment? His story is woven into the fabric of Ireland's struggle for independence.

Casement's Role

Casement's involvement began in London in 1913. In England, Home Rule for Ireland suddenly seemed feasible. After failing twice, a Home Rule bill finally was passed by Parliament in April 1913.

There was instant rancor. In the north, Protestants who wanted to remain part of the United Kingdom threatened an armed insurrection. An Ulster Volunteer Force was organized. It was soon countered by an Irish Volunteer Force in the south. Although raised in the north as a Protestant, Casement participated in organizing the southern force in November 1913. Both sides bought arms from Germany.

As tensions between England and Germany mounted and Europe was threatened by war, the Home Rule Act was shelved for the duration.

Casement and his revolutionary cohorts were cynical of the promise of Home Rule. Casement considered it an English hoax to encourage Irishmen to join the British Army to fight Germany. He joined a disparate faction of Irish revolutionaries to plot an insurrection. Casement's role was to find foreign support. As with Spain in 1601 and with France in 1798, Ireland would attempt to force freedom from England with the help of England's enemy. This time, the enemy was Germany.

In December 1914, Casement arrived in Germany with a dual objective. Talking to British prisoners of war, he would solicit Irish soldiers for an Irish Brigade. If the Germans won a sea victory, the Brigade would be landed in Ireland. They would not fight for Germany against England in World War I but for Irish independence. Casement also wanted German arms. The Germans grew cooler as Casement's success with prospective Irish recruits proved unproductive. P. De Rosa, *The Rebels: The Irish Rising of 1916* (1990); R. Kee, *The Green Flag: A History of Irish Nationalism* (1972).

176

The Arrest: April 21, 1916

A German agreement to aid the planned Easter Rising by sending arms and returning Casement to Ireland came to a calamitous end. After dark on Easter Friday, April 21, 1916, Casement pushed off in a rubber raft from German U-boat 19 and landed on Banna Strand in County Kerry. He was arrested the following day. To prevent its capture, the German ship carrying the weapons, the *Aud*, was scuttled.

Casement's mission to deliver 20,000 rifles, 10 machine guns and 5 million rounds of ammunition to Irish nationalists had been foiled. As he rode through Dublin on a train en route to prison in London, Casement was powerless to convince the Irish leaders that, if the Rising depended on his delivery of German arms, plans should be halted.

Casement's arrest ignited an unfortunate series of events. He was in custody when Padraic Pearse declared Ireland's independence on the steps of the General Post Office in Dublin on Easter Monday, April 24. The Rising, as Casement feared, was doomed. Pearse was one of the 15 leaders court-martialed and shot. The death sentences of others, including Eamon de Valera and Countess Constance Markiewicz, were commuted. Michael Collins was among 1,867 revolutionaries interned in Wales.

Meanwhile, Casement's capture made explosive news in England. Headlines on the front page of the *London Daily Express* on April 25 shouted "INVASION OF IRELAND," "NOTORIOUS IRISH TRAITOR," "RENEGADE'S LIFE STORY," "BRITISH PENSION," and "GERMAN GOLD."

The Trial

Initially, Casement, like the other Irish insurgents, was set to be court-martialed, but a political decision was made to try Casement under the Treason Act of 1351. The Treason Act of 1543, which governed procedure, determined that a jury trial with three judges take place in the Lord Chief Justice's Court in the Royal Courts of Justice in London. The judges were the Lord Chief Justice of England, Viscount Reading; Mr. Justice Avory; and Mr. Justice Horridge. Speaking for the Crown was the brilliant Attorney General Sir Frederick Edwin Smith, K.C. Smith, a militant Orangeman who had been involved in the shipment of German weapons to the Ulster Volunteer Force in 1913, opposed Home Rule.

Sergeant Sullivan, T. Artemus Jones, and John Morgan were Casement's barristers. Sergeant Sullivan practiced in Dublin. He retained the honorary title Sergeant, prevalent in the twelfth century, but long since disregarded in England. John Morgan was a constitutional scholar.

Casement's team also included two solicitors; Gavan Duffy, an Irish Nationalist who would later gain prominence in Irish politics, and Michael Doyle, an American lawyer who supported Irish causes and had won a libel case for Casement in New York. Not only was this the only jury trial involving a leader of the Rising, it was held in England with English jurors and judges. The defendant was Irish. The defendant was arrested in Ireland. Casement protested that this was unfair. The trial lasted four days.

Day One: June 26, 1916

During voir dire, the defense selected lower middle-class jurors. The Crown challenged Irishmen, and doing so, accidentally dismissed one vehement Orangeman.

The Indictment. Oyez. The indictment was read by the King's Coroner. Sir Roger Casement, Knight of the Realm, was charged with:

> High treason by adhering to the King's enemies, elsewhere than in the King's realm, to wit, in the Empire of Germany, contrary to the Treason Act of 1351.

25 Edward III St. 5. C.2

The principal overt acts involved soliciting disaffected prisoners of war to forsake allegiance to the King. An additional charge of landing arms was dismissed, and Casement pleaded "Not guilty" to the remaining counts.

Sullivan moved for dismissal of the charges on legal grounds. This argument would be heard when the prosecution rested. The meaning of the Treason Act of 1351 would be the cynosure of the defense.

Smith's Opening Statement. At midday, Attorney General F.E. Smith began with subtle invective, spearing Casement as a turncoat.

> May it please your Lordships, gentlemen of the jury, the charge upon which the prisoner is arraigned is a very grave one. The law knows none graver. The prisoner was an able

and cultivated man, versed in affairs and experienced in political matters . . . not as you will hear, a lifelong rebel against England and all that England stands for, as others well known in Irish history have been . . . (he had) a considerable career of public usefulness.

Smith read aloud Casement's letter to Sir Edward Grey, the Foreign Secretary, expressing gratitude for his knighthood. It began:

I find it very hard to choose the words in which to make acknowledgment of the honour done me by the King. I am much moved at the proof of confidence and appreciation of my service on the Putumayo conveyed to me by your letter, wherein you tell me that the King had been graciously pleased upon your recommendation to confer upon me the honour of knighthood. I am, indeed, grateful to you for this signal assurance of your personal esteem and support. I am very deeply sensible of the honour done to me by His Majesty.

Smith laid the letter down and proceeded:

Gentlemen, I read that letter because you ought to remember that those were the feelings on the 19th June, 1911, towards the country which he had served for so long, and towards the Sovereign of that country, of a man of mature years—he was, I think, forty-seven years old at the time that letter was written, a man who had nineteen years' experience of the methods of government of this country, in which indeed he had, and not without credit, borne a part.

Such a man writes in terms of gratitude, a little unusual, perhaps, in their warmth and in the language almost of a courtier, to express his pleasure at the title with which his Sovereign had rewarded his career. . . . And this was in 1911.

Smith commented on Casement's longstanding awareness of the problems between England and Ireland.

The history of the relations of England and Ireland up to that date were as well known as they are today. The controversies, bitter and protracted, often tragic, springing from those relations were either the commonplaces of contemporary politics, or they filled the better known pages of elementary

179

histories. And well understanding these controversies, fully versed in the wrongs of which Irishmen were fruitful in complaint, knowing England's ideals of government well—for at the outposts of the Empire he had carried them out—he sends his humble duty to his Sovereign.

Smith charged Casement with opportunistic loyalty.

What occurred between 1911 and 1914 to affect and corrupt the prisoner's mind I cannot tell you, for I do not know. I only know of one difference. The Sovereign of the country to whom his humble duty was sent in 1911 was in that year the ruler of a great and wealthy nation, unequaled in resources, living at peace, unassailed, and it almost seemed unassailable.

In 1914 this same nation was struggling for its possessions, for its honor, for its very existence in the most prodigious war which has ever tested human fortitude. To the Sovereign of that country in its hour of unchallenged greatness he sends his humble duty. It will be my task now to acquaint you with the method in which he carried out his humble duty in times dark enough to test the value of the unsolicited professions he was so forward in making.

Forming an Irish Brigade

Smith recounted the early months of World War I before revealing Casement's role.

Between the months of September and December, 1914, the fortunes of the struggle in France were such that a large number of British soldiers were taken captive by the enemy, and amongst those prisoners were many brave Irish soldiers.

At that time, the prisoner was in Germany moving with freedom about the country, apparently an honored guest of the German nation. The full story of the circumstances under which he went to Germany it is not in my power to tell. But it is evident that the part he was to play was that of a man willing, and it was hoped able, to seduce from their allegiance to the King, their Sovereign and his, the Irish prisoners of war who, after fighting valiantly for the Empire, had been captured in this war. We may perhaps surmise . . . that they were

180

simple, unlettered men, unlikely, it may have been thought, to resist a specious appeal.

These men were collected by the Germans for the purpose of listening to addresses or lectures on Irish history and other matters from the prisoner, who, like themselves, had embraced the service and eaten the bread of this country.

Smith painted a vivid picture of an ungrateful subject luring Irish soldiers to treason.

Whether it entered his head that he was exposing poor men, his inferiors in education, age and knowledge of the world, to the penalties of high treason, I cannot tell you, for I do not know . . . but I shall be in a position to call before you evidence which will show that between the middle of December, 1914, and 19th February, 1915, the prisoner repeatedly addressed these prisoners of war. I do not think it likely that he dwelt upon his own connection with the country which had afforded him a career, which had decorated him with a title, and from which he had accepted a pension. I suspect he did not inform them that three years before he had sent his humble duty to the Sovereign whose soldiers—while their hearts were heavy with captivity—he was attempting to seduce and to corrupt.

Smith stirred and roused English patriotism.

He stated that he was forming an Irish Brigade, and he invited all the Irish prisoners of war to join it. He pointed out repeatedly, and with emphasis, that in his opinion everything was to be gained for Ireland by Germany winning the war; and that the Irish soldiers . . . had the best opportunity they ever had of striking a blow for Ireland by entering the service of the enemies of this country.

Smith listed Casement's promises, but described the Brigade as "defending" Ireland.

He said that those who joined the Irish Brigade would be sent to Berlin, they would become the guests of the German Government, and in the event of Germany winning a sea battle, (he) would land a brigade in Ireland to defend the country against the enemy, England. And that in the event of

Germany losing the war, either he or the Imperial German Government would give each man in the brigade a bonus of 10 to 20 pounds, with a free passage to America.

Such were the temptations unfolded to his simple listeners . . . in the straits, the bewilderment, and perhaps the despair in which these prisoners then were.

He contrasted the soldiers' conduct to Casement's disloyalty.

Gentlemen: to the honour of Ireland, let it be recorded that the vast majority of the Irish prisoners treated the rhetoric, and the persuasions, and the corruptions of the prisoner with contempt. He was received with hisses, and was on at least one occasion driven from the camp. The Munster Fusiliers were particularly prominent in their loyal resentment of the treacherous proposals made to them. One private in that regiment actually struck, so it is recorded, the prisoner, who was saved from further violence by the intervention of an escort of Prussian Guards, who had been assigned to him for his protection by a nation which thinks of everything.

Two men, Robinson and O'Brien, who will be called before you, and who refused to join the Irish Brigade, were transferred to another camp for punishment, and were then put upon short rations. The few men who were seduced from their allegiance by the arguments addressed to them by the prisoner were rewarded by being given a green uniform with a harp and shamrock worked upon it, with unusually liberal rations . . . and . . . greater leisure and liberty. . . .

Smith charged Casement with treason, an interpretation of the law which will be attacked by Sullivan.

The inference will probably be drawn by you, that it was intended then that such men as could be seduced from their allegiance should form the first fruits of a body which should be actually used for the purpose of raising armed insurrection in Ireland against the forces of the Crown, and of acting as a trained and instructed nucleus round which the disaffected section of the population might rally and grow.

The treason which is charged against the prisoner is the treason which consists of adherence to the King's enemies in

182

the enemy country, and in relation to that treason, evidence will be given to you of many overt acts; of the attempt to seduce, and in some cases of the actual seduction of His Majesty's soldiers from loyal allegiance to His Majesty; the plotting and contriving to effect a hostile landing, with stores and arms, and with armed men in His Majesty's Dominions.

Smith twisted Irish nationalism into "unhappy" Ireland, a victim of conspiracies.

Gentlemen, I have said as much as is necessary at this stage to inform you of the treasonable activities of the prisoner in Germany. We must now pass to that unhappy country which has been the victim in its history of so many cruel and cynical conspiracies, but surely never of a conspiracy more cruel and more cynical than this.

After describing the scuttling of the *Aud* and Casement's arrest, Smith climaxed his oration with a crushing and powerful challenge by asking the defense to explain why Casement went to Germany. He concluded with clever grace.

I have, I hope, outlined these facts without heat and without feeling. Neither in my position would be proper, and fortunately none is required. Rhetoric would be misplaced, for the proved facts are more eloquent than words. The prisoner, blinded by a hatred to this country, as malignant in quality as it was sudden in origin, has played a desperate hazard. He has played it and he has lost it. Today, the forfeit is claimed.

The Crown's witnesses described Casement's career in the Foreign Service and his pension. Former prisoners-of-war testified about Casement's efforts at Limburg to recruit them.

The first day ended with the testimony of a Kerry laborer. He had seen a red light at sea at 9:30 PM, April 20, the night before Casement was arrested. This was the clandestine German submarine. The Crown had started to tighten the noose.

Day Two: June 27, 1916

The second day began with John McCarthy, an Irish farmer, who testified that while walking along Banna Strand at 4:00 AM on Good Friday, he found an abandoned boat, a dagger, and revolvers. Next, young Mary Gorman identified Casement. She saw him at

4:30 AM on Good Friday. She was followed by police who narrated Casement's discovery, arrest, detention and transfer to London. Constable Riley testified that he obtained a code from a small boy, Martin Collins, who saw Casement tearing it up. Evidence of a railway sleeper ticket found in Casement's overcoat pocket and a diary page were introduced.

A copy of the *London Gazette*, dated August 5, 1914, with the declaration of war with Germany, and a prisoner-of-war camp poster became exhibits. The Crown rested.

The Defense's Motion to Quash. Sergeant Sullivan rose. He argued that the indictment should be quashed because the alleged treason as charged "by adhering to the King's enemies elsewhere than in the King's realm, to wit, in the Empire of Germany, contrary to the Treason Act of 1351" was not the correct interpretation of the Act.

The age of the Act was both striking and troubling. It provided not only the death penalty for treason with which Casement was charged, but also for anyone (1) who imagined the King's death, (2) who violated the King's wife, (3) who violated the King's eldest unmarried daughter, (4) who violated the wife of the King's eldest son, (5) who counterfeited the King's seal, (6) who counterfeited the King's money, or (7) who committed religious heresy.

Sullivan declared that Casement's actions were not an offense within the language of this 1351 Act written by a long-forgotten scrivener. This treason was defined:

> ou soit aherdant as enemys nostre seigneur le Roi en le roialme donant a eux eid ou confort en son roialme ou par aillours.

It was translated as "levying war against the King or being adherent to the King's enemies in his realm giving them aid and comfort in the realm or elsewhere." Because there was no punctuation, the meaning was unclear. It could be interpreted in two very different ways.

If there were commas setting off "giving them aid and comfort in the realm" and they were words of apposition, treason could be understood as being adherent to the King's enemies in his realm or elsewhere, as the Crown claimed. However, the statute without commas could mean being adherent to the King's enemies in his realm and giving them aid and comfort in the realm or elsewhere, as Sullivan insisted. H.M. Hyde, *Famous Trials 9: Roger Casement* (1964).

184

Sullivan's contention was that Casement must remain in the King's realm to be guilty under the Treason Act of 1351, even while committing acts which might have given Germany aid and comfort outside the realm. Casement was not in the United Kingdom or its Dominions when he endeavored to coax Irish soldiers from their allegiance. Therefore, he was not guilty under the Act.

Day Three: June 28, 1916

The third day began with Sergeant Sullivan resuming his argument to quash the indictment. Professor Morgan fortified it, insisting that until the reign of Henry VIII, there was no such offense as treason outside the realm known to the law, because no means had been found to try it. Morgan said, "The authorities on the point are overwhelming, and no medieval lawyer would come to any other conclusion."

The judges did not welcome this view. They held that a treasonable offense committed by a British subject abroad was always triable at common law in England and was unlikely to have been limited by this Act to a person who was within the realm at the time he committed the treason. The Lord Chief Justice denied the motion, stating:

> Now from the year 1351 until the thirty-fifth year of the reign of King Henry VIII, there is little to assist us; but in the reign of Henry VIII, a statute was passed which in my view is important in this connection. The statute is entitled "An Acte Concerninge the triall of Treasons comytted out of the King's Majesties domynions." It recites that doubts and questions had arisen as to the trial of treasons . . . committed abroad. It is worth noting that the doubts had not arisen as to whether the act, if committed abroad, would amount to treason, but only as to the trial. Then the statute proceeds: "Be it enacted by authority of this present Parliament that all manner of offences . . . declared . . . by any of the laws and statutes of this realm to be treasons, they shall be tried by the King's Justices," that is, the King's Bench.

The Lord Chief Justice proceeded:

> At all events it makes it clear that after that date, any treason committed out of the realm may be tried, as this one is being tried, by His Majesty's Judges in the King's Bench.

185

Sullivan introduced no defense witnesses. He would rely on his summation. But first, he told the court that Casement wished to speak.

Casement was permitted under English law to make a statement in his defense. The jury was cautioned that Casement was not under oath and, therefore, would not be exposed to cross-examination.

Casement's Statement. Casement read from a paper he took from his waistcoat pocket. He said:

My lords and gentlemen of the jury, I desire to say a few words only with reference to some of the statements made by the prosecution. As to my person and the honour of knighthood conferred upon me, I will say one word only. The pension I had earned by services rendered, and it was assigned by law. The knighthood it was not in my power to refuse.

Casement protested four misstatements.

First, I never at any time advised Irishmen to fight the Turks against Russians, nor to fight with Germans on the western Front. Secondly, I never asked an Irishman to fight for Germany. I have always claimed that he has no right to fight for any land but Ireland. Thirdly, the horrible insinuation that I got my own people's rations reduced to starvation point because they did not join the Irish Brigade is an abominable falsehood. Fourthly, there is a widespread imputation of German gold. . . . I have never sold myself to any man or to any Government, and have never allowed any Government to use me. From the first moment I landed on the Continent until I came home again to Ireland, I never asked for nor accepted a single penny of foreign money. . . . I left Germany a poorer man than I entered it.

He expressed his gratitude to English and American sympathizers and then criticized Smith's "veiled allusion" to the Easter Week rebellion, adding:

. . . Since the Rising has been mentioned, however, I must state categorically that the Rebellion was not made in Germany and that not one penny of German gold went to finance it.

He challenged these charges, he said, because they reflected on his honor and tarnished his cause.

Sullivan's Summation. Sullivan rose. He spoke for the first time to an English jury. He appealed to English fair play. He discredited Private Neill, who had testified that Casement asked Irishmen to fight for Germany. Sullivan claimed Casement was interested only in using the Irish Brigade in Ireland, allied with the Irish Volunteer Force, after World War I. He said this was justified because the Ulster Volunteer Force had armed themselves, partly with German aid. Sullivan tailored his summation to the English jury. His eloquence was noted by the *Times* of London. He began:

> Gentlemen of the jury, it is indeed a matter of congratulations that such a trial as this at such a time is taking place here in the capital city of your nation in open court according to the ordinary process of law regulating the lives of the civil subjects of His Majesty. . . . The trial is the trial for the life of a man. It is more than that. You represent your country. . . . The prisoner is not a countryman of yours. He is a stranger within your gates. He comes from another country where people, though they use the same words, perhaps, speak differently; they think differently; they act differently. It is your duty to demonstrate in the face of the world, whose attention is challenged, by this brave proceeding of open trial in such a case, that old virtue for which you have achieved a reputation the world over—the virtue of the accordance of fair play between man and man. . . .

Did the prisoner adhere to the King's enemies in Germany? Sullivan urged that Casement's purpose was solely Irish Independence. Never to help Germany with her war with England.

> I would most respectfully subscribe to the doctrine that no Irishman has a right to take up views or risk his life for any cause that is not in the service of Ireland . . . now the intention of the prisoner is the whole substance of the offence of treason. It is his view of his own acts which must justify him or condemn him. Unless he (Casement) intends treachery to the King, the fact that others may use with advantage that which he does, against his intention, perhaps to the public detriment of the realm, does not make him guilty of treason.

Sullivan continued to cleave a wider wedge between Casement and Germany's aims.

Oh, says the Attorney-General, the German Government were interested in his succeeding. What cared he? He was not a German. It was nothing to him what were the calculations of any German as to what would be the result of anything he did . . . because, if what he stated again and again with variations to every man who was called as a witness about his speeches was truly in his mind, I will show you, I confidently hope, that represented no form of treason. . . .

He argued that Casement's recruitment of an Irish Brigade was only in opposition to the northern Ulster Volunteers who had been recruited to defy Home Rule and who had received German help "to resist the King and Commons and to blow the statute off the book with powder."

Sullivan's explanation of Casement's actions was that if the Crown could not protect the constitutional freedom of the majority, the final resort of any man was to stand with weapons in his hands. When he expanded beyond the evidence, he was interrupted by the Lord Chief Justice and Smith. Sullivan apologized. He foundered. He was helpless. He could not continue. The Court recessed.

Day Four: June 29, 1916

Sullivan could not proceed. Later, he said his collapse was caused by three days of "worrying." Artemus Jones completed Casement's argument, answering Smith's charge. Why did Casement go to Germany?

Not for the purpose of helping Germany to fight England, but for the purpose of forming an Irish Brigade to strive for something they had a right to strive for, the protection of their countrymen if they were coerced or tyrannized by armed forces in Ireland which were not controlled by the Executive Government.

Jones said the illegal importation of arms was an offense against the Defence of the Realm Act. Casement should have been proceeded against under that Act as a rebel, not under the Treason Act of 1351. He sought to recount inflammatory speeches by Ulster leaders, but he was interrupted because they were not in evidence. When he tried to interpret "aid and comfort," he was told that the phrase was a matter of law. It was not for the jury. Jones continued:

The ancient and valiant race from which this man springs does not produce the type of man who shrinks from death for the sake of his country.

The history of Ireland contains many melancholy and sad chapters, and not the least sad is the chapter which tells . . . so eloquently of so many mistaken sons of that unfortunate country who have gone to the scaffold, as they think, for the sake of their native land. If the Crown have made out their case, it is our duty as lawful citizens to return a verdict of guilty; but I claim this, that the law requires that the Crown should prove their case and prove it to the hilt, and you must with sure judgement and clean consciousness consider if you be satisfied upon that point.

And if you do that, if you approach the case in that spirit and apply that test to it, dark and heavy as the case may be as far as the defence is concerned, I do suggest to you that there is a way open to you to return a verdict which would be none the less just because it is humane.

Smith's Summation. Smith could speak or abstain. Feeling he needed the final word, he stood and attacked the defense. Instead of looking toward future strife, Smith contended that all effort should be deployed in the defense of England against Germany.

Had the acts for which the prisoner stands arraigned been committed before the war took place . . . at the time when the acts which he alleges on the part of the Ulster Volunteers were taking place, these words might have been a good defence or a bad defence, but they would at least have had great relevance . . . but I remind you of this, that there had intervened one circumstance which had altered the whole phase of Irish politics.

It was that the greatest military power which the world had ever known was trying to destroy this country and trying to make an end of this Empire. Since these controversies arose, what honest citizen was thinking or talking of whether or not there might at some future day be resistance to the Home Rule Bill? From the moment that Germany made her tiger spring at the throat of Europe, I say from that moment, the past was the past in the eyes of every man who wished well for England.

Smith echoed the question he had posed in his opening statement when he quietly inquired why Casement had gone to Germany.

> The question that I asked, as I then said deliberately and pointedly, has never been answered. Why has it never been answered?

Smith explained why there was no acceptable answer.

> I can tell you. It has never been answered because no answer to that question could be given which is consistent with the integrity of the prisoner. Why did he go to Germany? His case ... is that he went there to make sure there would be some men who would be strong enough to balance the Volunteers in the North of Ireland after the war.
>
> Where do you think would be the place in which his efforts might be most fruitful ... ? Do you not think that if that really was his object, he might possibly have stayed in Ireland where he would have still been in the King's realm?
>
> Why go to Germany? Why go and corrupt other men, to make them in breach of their duty incur grave penalties? Gentlemen, you can sweep away all these belated afterthoughts and sophistries about old Irish politics and the Volunteers in the north of Ireland.
>
> They were never in his mind when he made those speeches, they never inspired the appeals he made, they had no relation to it, and, as I have said, they are afterthoughts when it is necessary to attempt to exhume some defence, however remote, from the facts in which the prisoner finds himself.

Smith discussed Neill's unsupported testimony. Then, he used his ace: the typewritten code which had been discarded by Casement upon his arrival in Ireland.

> The fact that this code was available for communication with the Aud would not prevent it from being available for communication with other people in Germany; but the mere fact that such a suggestion should be possible shows really that there is no doubt in the mind of anybody that there was a connection between the Aud and the landing of the prisoner in Ireland.
>
> If the prisoner did not come in the Aud ... then it is obvious, I think, that, coming from Germany as we know he did,

at least we must draw an irresistible inference; we have the railway ticket from Berlin to Wilhelmshaven, dated 12 April, a few days before the date of landing—he came in some other German vessel, or some neutral vessel arranged for by the Germans.

I cannot tell you what the vessel was. But you will remember that the witness Hussey saw a red light out at sea on Thursday evening, which may have been connected with the actual landing of Casement.

Smith was reminded by an associate that not only had a German railroad ticket been found in Casement's pocket, a diary page confirmed his movements.

One of my learned friends reminds me that in the diary . . . on 12 April, the very date of the ticket from Berlin to Wilhelmshaven, this entry appears, "Left Wicklow in Willie's yacht." False names are used for places which will satisfy you, I think, as to the meaning of what that entry is. The entry is on 12 April, the day when the ticket was issued in Germany.

The Court cautioned the jury that no evidence linked the diary to Casement. Smith continued:

This code . . . shows that the prisoner Casement . . . had agreed with the Germans to send them messages arranging for a landing, asking for another ship, and asking for explosives, for cannons, and for ammunition.

Smith closed:

Gentlemen, if you can reconcile those facts with the submissions which have been made to you on behalf of the defence, do so. If those facts taken together, his journey to Germany, his speeches when in Germany, the inducements he held out to these soldiers, the freedom which he there enjoyed, the cause which he pursued in Ireland, the messages which he contemplated as likely to take place between himself and the Germans, satisfy you of his guilt, you must give expression to that view in your verdict.

Now came Casement's greatest setback. A jury instruction defining treason made it legally impossible for acquittal. H.W.

Nevinson, a war correspondent who covered the trial, said, "No chance of escape was given, and indeed there was none." The Court told the jury:

> You have to determine whether the prisoner was contriving and intending to aid and assist the enemy. If what he did was calculated to aid and assist the enemy, and he knew it was so calculated, then, although he had another or ulterior purpose in view, he was contriving and intending to assist the enemy.
>
> It is necessary that you should pay particular attention to this direction, which is a direction of law to you. The questions of fact upon it, of course, you will determine for yourselves, but it is necessary that you should understand that . . . if he knew or believed that the Irish Brigade was to be sent to Ireland during the war with a view to securing the national freedom of Ireland, that is, to engage in a civil war which would necessarily weaken and embarrass this country, then he was contriving and intending to assist the enemy.

Verdict

The jury retired at 2:53 PM. They deliberated for 55 minutes. The King's Coroner announced the verdict:

Sir Roger David Casement, you stand convicted of high treason. What have you to say for yourself why the Court should not pass sentence and judgment upon you to die according to law?

Casement's Speech from the Dock. Casement gave this final oration:

> There is an objection, possibly not good in law, but surely good on moral grounds, against the application to me here of this old English statute, 565 years old, that seeks to deprive an Irishman today of life and honour, not for "adhering to the King's enemies" but for adhering to his own people.
>
> When this statute was passed in 1351, what was the state of men's minds of the question of a far higher allegiance— that of a man to God and His Kingdom? The law of that day did not permit a man to forsake his church or deny his God save with his life. The heretic then had the same doom as the traitor.
>
> Today a man may forswear God and His heavenly kingdom without fear or penalty, all earlier statutes having gone the way of Nero's edicts against the Christians, but that Con-

stitutional phantom, The King, can still dig up from the dungeons and torture chambers of the Dark Ages a law that takes a man's life and limb for an exercise of conscience.

If true religion rests on love, it is equally true that loyalty rests on love. The law I am charged under has no parentage in love and claims the allegiance of today on the ignorance and blindness of the past.

Casement angrily hurled the angst of 700 years of English rule at the Court.

I am being tried, in truth, not by my peers of the life present, but by the peers of the dead past; not by the civilization of the twentieth century, but by the brutality of the fourteenth; not even by a statute framed in the language of an enemy land—so antiquated is the law that must be sought today to slay an Irishman, whose offense is that he puts Ireland first.

Edward III was King not only of the Realm of England, but also of the Realm of France, and he was not King of Ireland. Yet his dead hand today may pull the noose around the Irishman's neck whose Sovereign he was not, but it cannot strand round the Frenchmen's neck whose Sovereign he was.

Casement attacked his conviction by an English jury.

And what is the fundamental charter of an Englishman's liberty, that he shall he tried by his peers. With all respect I assert this Court is to me, an Irishman, not a jury of my peers to try me in this vital issue, for it is patent to every man of conscience that I have a right, an indefensible right, if tried at all, under this statute of high treason, to be tried in Ireland before an Irish Court and an Irish jury.

This Court, this jury, the public opinion of this country, England, cannot but be prejudiced in varying degree against me, most of all in time of war. . . . Place me before a jury of my own countrymen, be it Protestant or Catholic, Unionist or Nationalist, Sinn Feiners or Orangemen, and I shall accept the verdict and bow to all its penalties.

Blaming Conservatives for procuring arms from Germany, and so, forcing Irish Nationalists to secure arms as well, he defended his cause.

193

If small nationalities were to be the pawns in this game of embattled giants, I saw no reason why Ireland should shed blood in any cause but her own. . . . Home Rule when it comes, if come it does, will find an Ireland drained of all that is vital to its very existence. . . . We are told that if Irishmen go by the thousands to die, not for Ireland, but for Flanders, for Belgium, for a patch of sand on the deserts of Mesopotamia, or a rocky trench on the heights of Gallipoli, they are winning self government for Ireland. But if they dare to lay down their lives in their native soil, if they dare to dream even that freedom can be won only at home by men resolved to fight for it there, then they are traitors to their country. . . . But history is not so recorded in other lands.

Casement justified Ireland's independence:

Self government is our right, a thing born in us at birth; a thing no more to be doled out to us or withheld from us by another people than the right to feel the sun or smell the flowers, or to love our kind.

Casement ended. He thanked the jury and, once more, asserted his right to a jury of his peers, "a right to be tried in . . . Ireland, my own country. . . ."

Clerks placed squares of black velvet on the wigs of the judges. The Lord Chief Justice quietly delivered the sentence:

And it is that you be taken hence to a lawful prison, and thence to a place of execution, and that you be there hanged by the neck until you are dead . . . and may the Lord have mercy on your soul.

Mr. Justice Avery intoned, "Amen." P. Singleton-Gates and M. Girodias, *The Black Diaries of Roger Casement* (1959); The Public Records Office, London; Hyde, supra.

The next day, the *London Gazette* printed an announcement that the King had removed Roger David Casement from the Order of Knights Bachelor.

The Appeal: July 17, 1916

Again, the issue was the interpretation of the Treason Act of 1351. Sullivan powerfully reargued his point that Casement had committed no treasonable offense within the language of the Act which, he claimed, required Casement's presence "in the realm." Casement had not been "in the realm," but in Germany. Sullivan conceded that Lord Coke [1552-1634] had disagreed with his view, but he explained Coke's opinion was not binding. He argued that cases Coke relied on involved military commanders who were always within the jurisdiction of the King's Marshal.

He cited *Rex v. Lynch*, 1 K.B. 444 (1903). Colonel Arthur Lynch had commanded an Irish Brigade fighting against England in the Boer War. Elected to Parliament from Galway during his absence, Lynch was arrested and tried for treason upon his return to England. He was found guilty and sentenced to death. However, Lynch's sentence was commuted to life imprisonment. Within a few months, he was released and later pardoned.

Sullivan argued that from 1351 to 1903, when Lynch was convicted of treason, there had been no decision about the Act concerning "adhering" outside the realm. He insisted that the Lynch case was incorrectly decided and not a decision upon the statute.

Cited on Casement's behalf was *Rex v. Keyn*, 2 Ex. D 63 (1876), the *Franconia* case, in which Judah Benjamin, Q.C., the former American lawyer and Confederate cabinet minister, won fame as an English barrister. It held that English law did not apply to the German captain of a foreign ship that sank a British ship near the English shore.

Checking punctuation, Justices Darling and Atkin had examined the Treason Act of 1351 in the Parliamentary and Statute Rolls. If, in lieu of commas, the scribe used "breaks" in the form of transverse lines in the parchment paper, the Crown's interpretation might be bolstered. After looking at the Statute Role under a magnifying glass, Justice Darling decided that a break after the second "realm" was not written in pen, but was the result of folding during six centuries.

On the second day, the Judges announced that the Attorney General need not reply. An ominous sign for Casement.

The decision was delivered by Mr. Justice Darling, who stated:

The main point raised in the exceedingly able argument of counsel for the appellant was that this statute had neither created nor declared the offense of being adherent to the King's

195

enemies beyond the realm of the King; and that the giving of aid and comfort, "par aillours"—that is, outside the realm—did not constitute a treason which could be tried in this country unless the person . . . was in the realm at the time. . . . This argument was founded on the difficulties which must arise owing to the doctrine of venue. . . . It was said this must be so or a case could be found where a man had, altogether outside the realm, given aid and comfort to the King's enemies, and had been indicted within the realm and tried for it. Such a case would be difficult to find. . . . First, if a man did those things . . . it is highly improbable that he would put himself in peril by returning. . . .

Darling declined to read the statute as if for the first time. Instead, the Court affirmed the opinions of legal authorities including Coke. Darling claimed the court did not rely on *Rex v. Lynch* because there was "ample authority in the decisions and opinions of the great lawyers referred to in giving the judgment of this court. It only remains to say that the appeal is dismissed."

Casement's Last Chance

Now only two hopes remained; an appeal to the House of Lords or a reprieve by the Home Secretary. No appeal to the House of Lords could be made without the consent of the Attorney General. Smith was not only the prosecutor, he was the Attorney General. He refused.

A reprieve by the Home Secretary was Casement's last hope. A clemency effort was launched. A petition, signed by celebrities including George Bernard Shaw, Arnold Bennett, G.K. Chesterton and John Galsworthy was submitted to Prime Minister Herbert Asquith by Sir Arthur Conan Doyle. The petitioners referred to the merciful treatment of Confederate leaders in America after the Civil War. Shaw said the way to make Casement a hero was to hang him.

However, Casement's diaries, which the Crown had retrieved from his 45 Ebury Street address, were leaked to the press. Controversy erupted over whether the diaries were forged or whether Casement was a homosexual who had recorded his sexual activities. The "Black Diaries" were used to dishonor him and alienate public sympathy. The Archbishop of Canterbury, the Bishop of Durham and Irish leader John Redmond refused to sign petitions for Casement because of the scandal.

In America, Irish fervor was intense. On July 29, the American Senate passed a resolution requesting clemency, but it was not given to the British Foreign Secretary until August 2. After diary passages were shown to President Woodrow Wilson, he refused to intercede.

Casement's execution was scheduled for August 3. The Cabinet was anxious. A certificate of Casement's insanity was considered, but rejected. Sir Earnley Blackwell, Legal Advisor to the Home Office, provided this advice:

> So far as I can judge, it would be far wiser from every point of view to allow the law to take its course, and by judicious means to use these diaries to prevent Casement attaining martyrdom.

Singleton-Gates and Girodias, *supra*.

This memorandum was circulated. The undecided ministers agreed.

The pendulum then swung toward Casement. Eva Gore-Booth, sister of Easter Rising leader Countess Markiewicz, circulated a letter protesting that Casement had returned to Ireland to halt the rebellion. Then, the clock stopped.

In a deadly oversight, Casement had left a file in the courtroom. It contained a copy of an Agreement of December 1914 which stated that if the Germans were unable, through lack of naval superiority, to transport the Irish Brigade to Ireland, the Brigade might be used in Egypt against British forces. The papers were returned unread to Casement in prison. He sealed them in a package to be sent to his solicitor. Instead, the prison governor gave them to the Home Office "to censor." Attached to the papers was a note in Casement's handwriting: "There is enough in these papers to hang me ten times over. . . ."

There was no reprieve.

At 9:15 AM on August 3, 1916, Casement was hanged at Pentonville Gaol in London. His relatives asked that his body be interred in County Antrim. The request was rejected. John Quinn, Casement's friend, wrote this lead paragraph in an article about Casement:

> Roger Casement is dead. Tried in an English court upon the charge of treason, convicted by an English jury, sentenced by English judges, judgment affirmed by an English court of

appeal, hanged in accordance with English law, his body buried in quicklime and in a nameless grave, his case is now transferred from the English courts and English public to the court of history and to the judgment of the world.

New York Times Magazine (August 13, 1916).

Afterword

Ireland, except for the counties of Antrim, Derry, Down, Fermanaugh, Armagh and Tyrone, achieved independence in January 1922 as a result of the Anglo-Irish Treaty. These six Ulster counties, now known as Northern Ireland, remain in the United Kingdom to this day. Casement was born in County Antrim.

Attorney General F.E. Smith was knighted. He and Michael Collins became friends in 1921 when both were members of delegations negotiating the Anglo-Irish Treaty.

Sergeant Sullivan continued to practice as a Barrister in Dublin and was brought to the English Bar by F.E. Smith.

T. Artemus Jones qualified for a place in legal history as a plaintiff. The Paris correspondent of an English newspaper, depicting high life at fashionable French resorts, wrote, "Why, there is Artemus Jones with a woman who is not his wife. . . . Who would suppose . . . he was a churchwarden at Peckham?" Barrister Thomas Artemus Jones—not a churchwarden at Peckham—sued and won 1,750 pounds [in] damages. A judge remarked that if the writer had stuck to Tom Jones, he would have been safe. J. Dean, *Hatred, Ridicule or Contempt* (1953).

Thousands of Mourners

Michael Doyle practiced as an international lawyer in Philadelphia. He became a member of the Permanent Court of International Arbitration at the Hague. In 1922, he participated in writing the Constitution of the Irish Free State.

Colonel Arthur Lynch, whose treason case was cited by Sullivan, remained in Parliament for 16 years until 1918. As a colonel in the British Army, he conducted a recruiting program in Ireland.

In Peru, the Putumayo Indians rebelled a few days after Casement's execution, killing Europeans. According to the local missionary, they had been goaded to desperation by ill treatment "though the wholesale crimes of former times had disappeared; the shootings, tortures and all the villainy Casement exposed."

198

Roger Casement's body was returned to Arbour Hill in Dublin on February 23, 1965. Thousands of mourners passed by. The next day he was buried in Glasnevin Cemetery.

The interpretation of the Treason Act of 1351 in *Rex v. Casement*, 1 K.B. 98 (1917) has not changed. The same law was applied in the trial and death sentence of William Joyce, who was convicted of making Nazi propaganda broadcasts on German radio during World War II under the name of Lord Haw Haw. *Joyce v. D.P.P.*, 1 All.E.R. 186 (1946).

I say that Roger Casement
Did what he had to do.
He died upon the gallows,
But that is nothing new.

"Roger Casement," W.B. Yeats

14

The Spelling Game
Russell's Cross-Examination of Pigott

Lower down, please, leaving spaces, write the word "hesitancy."
With a small "h."

———Sir Charles Russell

Two savaged bodies were found in Phoenix Park in Dublin at 7:00 PM on May 6, 1882. Members of the ruling government of the United Kingdom, Lord Frederick Cavendish, chief secretary for Ireland, and Thomas H. Burke, undersecretary, on their first day in Ireland to begin their new roles, had been mutilated with 12-inch-long surgical knives by assassins of the Irish National Invincibles. This secret society was an offshoot of the Irish Republican Brotherhood (IRB), whose comment was that the assassins "deserve well of their country." R. Kee, *The Green Flag: A History of Irish Nationalism* (1972).

On February 3, 1883, eight men convicted of the murders were executed at Kilmainham Prison. J.B. Hall, *Random Records of a Reporter* (1930). The murders cast a sinister shadow on the negotiations for home rule that were ongoing between Charles Parnell, the Irish Parliamentary Party's leader, and British Prime Minister William Gladstone.

There had been a long struggle for Irish freedom. Now there was a clash between Parnell's nonviolent approach and the terror tactics of the IRB. Parnell wanted England to recognize Ireland as a separate entity within the United Kingdom. The IRB's program was to fight for full independence. They seized the opportunity of the Phoenix Park murders to sabotage Home Rule efforts.

No evidence existed that Parnell had any involvement with the IRB. But if the IRB could link Parnell in some way to the Phoenix Park murders, his integrity would be destroyed. Parnell's quest for Home Rule for Ireland within the United Kingdom would end.

Parnell had another enemy eager to destroy his reputation and the Home Rule movement. On March 7, 1887, the conservative *Times of London* began publishing a series of articles entitled "Parnellism and Crime," suggesting that Parnell's Home Rule movement "was a revolutionary movement, stained by crime, and designed to overthrow British authority in Ireland." R.B. O'Brien, *The Life of Lord Russell of Killowen* (1901).

In April 1887, the *Times of London* published the following letter, signed by Parnell:

Dear Sir,

I am not surprised at your friend's anger, but he and you should know that to denounce the murders was the only course open to us. To do that promptly was plainly our best policy. But you can tell him, and all others concerned, that, though I regret the accident of Lord F. Cavendish's death, I cannot refuse to admit that Burke got no more than his deserts. You are at liberty to show him this, and others whom you can trust also, but let not my address be known. He can write to the House of Commons.

Yours very truly,
Charles S. Parnell

Parnell's alleged comment that "Burke got no more than his deserts" caused an immediate sensation with Parliament and the public. Parnell, outraged, rose in the House of Commons, denounced the letter as a "villainous and bare-faced forgery," and demanded the appointment of a Select Committee to investigate the letter's origins. Initially, Parnell's request was denied. Later, however, on August 13, 1888, pursuant to an Act of Parliament, a special commission was created with three judges who were appointed to investigate the *Times*'s claim that Parnell was the author of this incriminating letter and others the *Times* had obtained. J. McCarthy, *A History of Our Own Times from 1880 to the Diamond Jubilee* (1897).

Sir Charles Russell

Parnell now turned to Sir Charles Russell for guidance. Russell, a northern Irishman from Newry in County Down, was educated at St. Vincent's College, Trinity College in Dublin, and Lincoln's Inn in London. He began his legal career in Belfast and moved to London, where he won renown as a barrister. He gladly accepted Parnell as a client after first giving up his general retainer to represent the *Times*.

On October 22, 1888, Russell appeared before the special commission as lead counsel for Parnell. Attorney General Sir Richard Webster represented the *Times*. The commissioners were Justices Hannen, Day, and Smith. Before the hearings ended, 340 witnesses, including Parnell, testified during 63 sittings. But the outcome hinged on the credibility of Richard Pigott.

The *Times*'s charges were: Parnell wrote the letter the *Times* had published, and 65 named Irish Members of Parliament (which really meant the entire Irish Parliamentary Party) belonged to "a lawless, violent, rebellious, and even a murderous organization whose aim was the plunder of landlords and the overthrow of English rule." O'Brien, *supra.*

The *Times* had purchased the incriminating letters from Mr. Houston, the Secretary of the Irish Loyal and Patriotic Union. Houston had bought them from Richard Pigott. But who was Pigott? Where had Pigott obtained the letters?

On February 20, 1889, Pigott, former editor of the *Ulsterman* newspaper, took the witness stand. Pigott testified that he was hired by the Irish Loyal and Patriotic Union to search for any writing that would incriminate Parnell. His peregrinations led him to Paris, where he met an agent of the *Clan-na-Gael*, who allegedly told Pigott he had no hesitation in destroying Parnell's reputation. Pigott said he bought letters by Parnell, including the letters published in the *Times*. His testimony lasted until noon of his second day. He solved the puzzle of who gave him the letters, where he received them, and what he did with them. Pigott was the man of the hour.

Spellcheck

Now it was Russell's turn. After Pigott's explanation, there was seemingly little to add. The special commission's intense focus was to determine whether the first Parnell letter the *Times* published in April 1887 was signed by Parnell. Or was it a forgery? Russell counterattacked with a one-two punch.

To begin, Russell focused on the second Parnell letter published in the *Times*. This letter, allegedly signed by Parnell in 1882 before the Phoenix Park murders, contained a fatal flaw. R. Kee, *Ireland* (1982). It read as follows:

> What are these people waiting for? This inaction is inexcuseable. Our best men are in prison and nothing is being done. Let there be an end to this hesitency. Prompt action is called for. You promised to make it hot for old Forster and Co. Let us have evidence of your power to do so. . . .
>
> Yours very truly,
> Chas. S. Parnell

Two words, "inexcusable" and "hesistancy," were misspelled. Russell learned that Pigott had a habit of mispelling "hesitancy." Seizing on "hesitency," Russell sought to prove that Pigott, not Parnell, had authored the letters. Clearly, this required the greatest delicacy.

To demonstrate Pigott's inaccurate spelling of "hesitancy," Russell designed a series of questions to keep Pigott unaware of the spelling trap. R. Parry O'Brien, an intimate friend of Parnell and a barrister-at-law of the Middle Temple, assisted Russell in Parnell's defense. Appearing before the special commission, he sat at the counsel table with Russell and wrote comments about the cross-examination. O'Brien, *supra*; F. L. Wellman, *The Art of Cross-Examination* (1962).

It was now Russell's turn to challenge Pigott's testimony. (O'Brien's comments are included here as well, in italic text within brackets.)

Russell: Mr. Pigott, would you be good enough, with my Lord's permission, to write some words on that sheet of paper for me? Perhaps you will sit down in order to do so? (A sheet of paper was then handed to the witness.) Would you like to sit down?

Pigott: Oh, no, thanks.

President: Well, but I think it is better that you should sit down. Here is a table upon which you can write in the ordinary way—the course you always pursue. (Pigott sat down.)

Russell: Will you write the word "livelihood?

Pigott: (Wrote.)

Russell: Just leave a space. Will you write the word "likelihood"?

Pigott: (Wrote.)

Russell: Will you write your own name? Will you write the word "proselytism," and finally—I think I will not trouble you at present with any more—"Patrick Egan" and "P. Egan"?

Pigott: (Wrote.)

Russell: There is one word I had forgotten. Lower down, please, leaving spaces, write the word "hesitancy." With a small "h."

Pigott: (Wrote.)

Russell: Will you kindly give me the sheet.

[Pigott took blotting paper to lay on the sheet.]

Russell: Don't blot it, please.

Attorney General: My Lords, I suggest that had better be photographed, if your Lordships see no objection.

Russell: Do not interrupt my cross-examination with that request.

Russell had succeeded. Pigott spelled the word "hesitancy" as "hesitency." This misspelling's significance escaped Pigott and the Attorney General. Powerful evidence was now in the record that Pigott and not Parnell had authored at least the letter containing the word "hesitency."

[O'Brien: *Little did the Attorney General at that moment know that, in the ten minutes or quarter of an hour which it had taken to ask these questions, Russell had gained a decisive advantage. Pigott had in one of his letters to Pat Egan spelt "hesitancy" thus: "hesitency." In one of the incriminatory letters "hesitancy" was so spelt; and in the sheet now handed back to Russell, Pigott had written "hesitency" too.*

In fact, it was Pigott's spelling of this word that had put the Irish members on his scent. Pat Egan, seeing it spelt with an "e" in one of the incriminatory letters, had written to Parnell saying in effect Pigott is the forger: "In the letter ascribed to you, 'hesitancy' is spelt 'hesitency.' That is the way Pigott always spells the word."

These things were not dreamt of in the philosophy of the Attorney General when he interrupted Russell's cross-examination with the request that the sheet "had better be photographed." So closed the first round of the combat. Russell went on in his former courteous manner, and Pigott, who had now completely recovered confidence, looked to stand to his guns.]

The Archbishop's Letter

A surprise awaited Pigott. [O'Brien: *Before the trial, O'Brien said, "I know that you have got materials from Archbishop Walsh." Russell replied "How important it is to keep everything secret relating to Pigott. You know how much depends on his cross-examination." Russell intended to show that Pigott was a liar.*]

This was Russell's second punch. Pigott was evidently working both sides. He made money on the forgery of the letters, but then he wrote letters to the Archbishop of Dublin warning him of the impending harm to Parnell and the Irish Parliamentary party with the revelation of the same letters. Pigott seems to have been seeking a reward. Russell caught him on inconsistencies.

> *Russell:* The first publication of the articles "Parnellism and Crime" was on the 7th March 1887?
>
> *Pigott:* I do not know.
>
> *Russell:* Well you may assume that is the date.
>
> *Pigott:* I suppose so.
>
> *Russell:* And you were aware of the intended publication of the correspondence, the incriminatory letters?
>
> *Pigott:* No, I was not aware of it.
>
> *Russell:* What?
>
> *Pigott:* No, certainly not.
>
> *Russell:* Were you not aware that there were grave charges to be made against Mr. Parnell and the leading members of the Land League?
>
> *Pigott:* I was not aware of it until they actually commenced.
>
> *Russell:* What?
>
> *Pigott:* I was not aware of it until the publication actually commenced.
>
> *Russell:* Do you swear that?
>
> *Pigott:* I do.
>
> *Russell:* Very good, there is no mistake about that.

[O'Brien: *Then there was a pause; Russell placed his hands beneath the shelf in front of him, and drew from it some papers—Pigott, the Attorney General, the judges, every one in Court looking intently at him the while. There was not a breath, not a movement. I think it was the most dramatic scene in the whole cross-examination, abounding as it did in dramatic scenes.*] Then, handing Pigott a letter, Russell said calmly:

Russell: Do not trouble to read it all; tell me if it is your letter?

Pigott: [*Took the letter and held it close to his eyes as if reading it*]

Russell: Do not trouble to read it.

Pigott: Yes, I think it is.

Russell: Have you any doubt of it.

Pigott: No.

Russell: My Lords, it is from Anderton's hotel, and it is addressed by the witness to Archbishop Walsh. The date, my Lords, is the 4th of March, three days before the first appearance of the first of the articles, "Parnellism and Crime."

Russell (reading): "Private and confidential. My Lord—The importance of the matter about which I write will doubtless excuse this intrusion on your Grace's attention. Briefly, I wish to say that I have been made aware of the details of certain proceedings that are in preparation with the object of destroying the influence of the Parnellite party in Parliament."

Russell: What were the certain proceedings that were in preparation?

Pigott: I do not recollect.

Russell: Turn to my Lords and repeat the answer.

Pigott: I do not recollect.

Russell: You swear that—writing on the 4th of March, less than two years ago?

Pigott: Yes.

Russell: You do not know what that referred to?

Pigott: I do not really.

Rusell: May I suggest to you?

Pigott: Yes, you may.

Russell: Did it refer to the incriminatory letters among other things?

Pigott: Oh, at that date? No, the letters had not been obtained, I think, at that date, had they, two years ago?

Russell: I do not want to confuse you at all, Mr. Pigott.

Pigott: Would you mind giving me the date of that letter?

Russell: The 4th of March.

Pigott: The 4th of March.

Russell: Is it your impression that the letters had not been obtained at that date?

Pigott: Oh, yes, some of the letters had been obtained before that date.

Russell: Then, reminding you that some of the letters had been obtained before that date, did that passage that I have read to you in that letter refer to these letters among other things?

Pigott: No, I rather fancy they had reference to the forthcoming articles in the *Times*.

Russell: I thought you told us you did not know anything about the forthcoming articles.

Pigott: Yes, I did. I find now I am mistaken—that I must have heard something about them.

Russell: Then try not to make the same mistake again, Mr. Pigott.

Russell: "Now," you go on (continuing to read), "I cannot enter more fully into details than to state that the proceedings referred to consist in the publication of certain statements purporting to prove the complicity of Mr. Parnell himself, and some of his supporters, with murders and outrages in Ireland. . . ."

Russell: Who told you that?

Pigott: I have no idea.

Russell: But that refers among other things, to the incriminatory letters.

Pigott: I do not recollect that it did.

Russell: Do you swear that it did not?

Pigott: I will not swear that it did not.

Russell: Do you think it did?

Pigott: No, I do not think it did.

Russell: Do you think that these letters, if genuine, would prove or would not prove Parnell's complicity in crime?

Pigott: I thought they would be very likely to prove it.

Russell: Now, reminding you of that opinion, I ask you whether you did not intend to refer—not solely, I suggest, but among other things—to the letters as being the matter which would prove complicity or purport to prove complicity?

Pigott: Yes, I may have had that in my mind.

Russell: You could have had hardly any doubt that you had?

Pigott: I suppose so.

Russell: You suppose you may have had?

Pigott: Yes.

Russell: This is the letter and the statement (*reading*), "Your Grace may be assured that I speak with full knowledge, and am in a position to prove, beyond all doubt and question, the truth of what I say." Was that true?

Pigott: It could hardly be true.

Russell: Then did you write that which was false?

Pigott: I suppose it was to give strength to what I said. I do not think it was warranted by what I knew.

Russell: You added the untrue statement in order to add strength to what you said?

Pigott: Yes.

Russell: You believe these letters to be genuine?

Pigott: I do.

Russell: And did at this time?

Pigott: Yes.

Russell: (*reading*) "And I will further assure your Grace that I am also able to point out how these designs may be successfully combated and finally defeated."

How if these documents were genuine documents, and you believed them to be such, how were you able to assure his Grace that you were able to point out how the design might be successfully combated and finally defeated?

Pigott: Well, as I say, I had not the letters actually in my mind at that time. So far as I can gather, I do not recollect the letter [to the Archbishop Walsh] at all. My memory is really a blank on the circumstance.

Russell: You told me a moment ago, after great deliberation and consideration, you had both [the incriminatory letters and the letter to Archbishop Walsh] in your mind.

Pigott: I said it was probable I did; but I say the thing has completely faded out of my mind.

Russell: I must press you. Assuming the letters to be genuine, what were the means by which you were able to assure his Grace that you could point out how the design might be successfully combated and finally defeated?

Pigott: I cannot conceive really.

Russell: Oh! try, You must really try.

Pigott: I cannot.

Russell: Try.

Pigott: I cannot.

Russell: Try.

Pigott: It is no use.

Russell: May I take it, then, your answer to my Lords is that you cannot give any explanation?

Pigott: I really cannot absolutely.

Russell: (*reading*) "I assure your Grace that I have no other motive except to respectfully suggest that your Grace would communicate the substance to some one or other of the parties concerned, to whom I could furnish details, exhibit proofs, and suggest how the coming blow may be effectually met." What do you say to that, Mr. Pigott?

Pigott: I have nothing to say except that I do not recollect anything about it absolutely.

Russell: What was the coming blow?

Pigott: I suppose the coming publication.

Russell: How was it to be effectively met?

Pigott: I have not the slightest idea.

Russell: Assuming the letters to be genuine, does it not even now occur to your mind how it could be effectively met?

Pigott: No.

[O'Brien: *Pigott now looked like a man, after the sixth round in a prize fight, who had been knocked down in every round. But Russell showed him no mercy.*] Here is the final extract:

Russell: (*reading from another letter by Pigott to Archbishop Walsh*) "I was somewhat disappointed in not having a line from your Grace, as I ventured to expect I might have been so far honored. I can assure your Grace that I have no other motive in writing save to assert, if possible, a great danger to people with whom your Grace is known to be in strong sympathy."

Pigott: Yes.

Russell: What do you say to that?

Pigott: That it appears to you clearly that I had not the letters in my mind.

Russell: Then it appears to you clearly that you had not the letters in your mind, what had you in your mind?

Pigott: It must have been something far more serious.

Russell: What was it?

Pigott: I cannot tell you. I have no idea.

Russell: It must have been something far more serious than the letters?

Pigott: Far more serious.

Russell: Can you give my Lords any clue of the most indirect kind to what it was?

Pigott: I cannot.

Russell: Or from whom you heard it?

Pigott: No.
Russell: Or when you heard it?
Pigott: Or when I heard it.
Russell: Or where you heard it?
Pigott: Or where I heard it.
Russell: Have you ever mentioned this fearful matter—whatever it is—to anybody?
Pigott: No.
Russell: Still locked up, hermetically sealed in your own bosom?
Pigott: No, because it has gone away out of my bosom, whatever it was.

[O'Brien: *On receiving this answer Russell smiled, looked at the Bench, and sat down. A ripple of derisive laughter broke over the Court, and a buzz of many voices followed. The people standing around me looked at each other and said, "Splendid." The judges arose, the great crowd melted away, and an Irishman who mingled in the throng expressed, I think, the general sentiment in a single word, "Smashed."*

The cross-examination had commenced at about twenty minutes past two; it was over for the day at about twenty minutes to four, when Pigott left the box a broken man . . . It was the most exciting time I ever spent. In the end we came simply astonished that a fellow creature could be such a liar as Pigott. It was very funny too; but I could not help thinking of Becky Sharp's "It's so easy to be virtuous on 5,000 pounds a year," and to see the old man standing there with everybody's hand against him, driven into a corner at last, after all his turns and twists, was something pathetic. Of course, it is a tremendous triumph for the Home Rulers. On Friday, Feb. 22, the Court adjourned until Tuesday, 26th.]
On that morning Pigott was again called, but there was no answer.

President: Where is the witness?
Attorney General: My Lords, as far as I know, I have no knowledge whatever of the witness; but I am informed that Mr. Soames has been sent to his hotel, and he has not been there since eleven last night.
Russell: If there is any delay in his appearance I ask your Lordship to issue a warrant for his apprehension and to issue it immediately.

[O'Brien: *It was decided, however, that no steps should be taken until next day. Next day the Attorney General informed the Court that a document in Pigott's handwriting had been received from Paris. A closed envelope, addressed to one of the* Times *agents, was then handed to Mr. Cunynghame, Secretary to the Commission. The envelope contained a confession of guilt taken down by Mr. Labouchere, M.P., in the presence of Mr. G.A. Sala, and signed by Pigott on February 23 at Mr. Labouchere's house. I shall quote one passage from the confession:*]

> The circumstances connected with the obtaining of the letters as I gave in evidence are not true. No one save myself was concerned in the transaction. I told Mr. Houston that I had discovered the letters in Paris, but I grieve to have to confess that I simply fabricated them using genuine letters of Messrs. Parnell and Egan in copying certain words, phrases, and general character of the handwriting. I traced some words and phrases by putting the genuine letters against the window and placing the sheets on which I wrote over it. These genuine letters were the letters from Mr. Parnell, copies of which have been read in Court, and four or five letters from Mr. Egan which were also read in Court.
>
> I destroyed these letters after using them. Some of the signatures I traced in this manner, and some I wrote. I then wrote to Mr. Houston, telling him to come to Paris for the documents. I told him that they had been placed in a black bag with some old accounts, scraps of paper, and old newspapers. On his arrival I produced to him the letters, accounts, and scraps of paper. After a brief inspection he handed me a cheque in Court for 500 pounds, the price I had told him I had agreed to pay for them. At the same time he gave me 105 pounds in bank notes as my own commission.

[*In the face of this confession the* Times *of course withdrew the facsimile letter, and the Commission found that it was a "forgery." The last scene in this squalid drama was enacted on March 5th. A warrant had been issued for Pigott's arrest on the charge of perjury. The police tracked him to an hotel in Madrid. "Wait," he said to the officers who showed him the warrant, "until I go to my room for some things I want." The officers waited; the report of a pistol was heard; there was a rush to Pigott's room; and the wretched man was found on the floor with a bullet through his brain. He had died by his own hand.*]

Pigott's confession was read to the special commission. *New York Times* (1890). In the special commission's report submitted to Queen Victoria, paragraph IX (b) read:

[Charge] That Mr. Parnell was intimate with the leading Invincibles, that he probably learned from them what they were about . . . and that he recognized the Phoenix Park murders as their handiwork.

[Finding] We find that there is no foundation for this charge.

When Parnell entered Parliament after the Report's issuance, he was greeted with an ovation. "The moment he appeared, the whole Liberal party, including the occupants of the front Opposition bench, rose to their feet, and standing, cheered him again and again. Some even among the Tory ranks joined in the demonstration. . . . Not often has such a scene been witnessed in the House of Commons. . . . That scene was the zenith of Mr. Parnell's Parliamentary career." McCarthy, *supra*.

Afterword

Parnell's vindication united Irish nationalists around him as their leader. But in December 1889 he was named as a co-respondent in a divorce petition involving his married lover, Katherine O'Shea. As a result, he lost his position as leader of the Irish Parliamentary Party and his political career ended. Parnell married Katherine O'Shea in June 1891. He died that October.

Gladstone's Home Rule bill was defeated in Parliament in 1886, by a vote of 341-311. His second Home Rule bill was defeated in 1893. In March 1894, Gladstone resigned. He died in 1898.

In 1914 a third Home Rule bill was enacted and suspended until 1918 when World War I ended. By then the Easter Rebellion in 1916 had led to the formation of Sinn Fein and an Irish demand for independence. A period of terrorism from 1919 to 1921 culminated in a peace treaty.

Archbishop Walsh died in 1921, the same year Ireland achieved its independence. Civil war broke out, and Republican Michael Collins's funeral was held the following year in Dublin's St. Mary's Pro-Cathedral.

Sir Charles Russell became Lord Chief Justice of England in 1894. He addressed the American Bar Association in Saratoga, New York, in August 1896. Russell died in 1900.

The *New York Times* ran a headline in 1910 about the author of the stories on "Parnellism and Crime," which contained the forged letter: "Author of Parnell Articles Revealed At Last; Sir Robert

Anderson, Formerly of Scotland Yard, Casually Admits That He Wrote Them and Ends Years of Speculation about Their Origin."

James Joyce gave both Pigott and his misspelled word "hesitency" literary immortality in *Finnegans Wake*: "Unhesitent in his unionism but a piggoted [*sic*] nationalist." And Joyce also invented the word "piggotry."

Pigott's final ignominy may have been as a subject in a poem by William Topaz McGonagall, poet of Dundee, born in 1877 and often considered the worst poet in the English language. McGonagall's poem begins:

> *Richard Pigott, the forger, was a very bad man,*
> *And to gainsay it there's nobody can,*
> *Because for fifty years he pursued a career of deceit.*
> *And as a forger few men with him could compete.*

SECTION V

Fighting
Nazi Injustice

Hans Frank was a constitutional lawyer who created
Nazi law. The horrors of World War II followed. Finally,
punishment resulted at the war crimes trials.

15

Hans Frank
Hitler's Lawyer

I have no conscience; Adolf Hitler is my conscience.
————Hans Frank, 1935

This is the story of Hans Frank. He created the legal system for the Third Reich. Although Frank tried to protect procedural legal rights for ethnic Germans, he made Adolf Hitler's will the ultimate source of German law. As Governor General of Poland during World War II, Frank supplied slave labor to Germany and collaborated in the extermination of Jews. Then, as a scholar, he returned to Germany and lectured about the importance of the rule of law. In 1946, Frank was found guilty of war crimes by the International Military Tribunal at Nürnberg.

1900–1933

Who was Hans Frank? Born in Karlsruhe, Germany, on May 23, 1900, son of a lawyer, Frank studied political economy and law at Munich University and the University of Kiel. In 1919, during the political turmoil in Bavaria after World War I, Frank joined the Epps Freikorp, a militant anti-Communist group. In 1923, Frank joined the Nazi Party. He received a Doctorate of Laws degree in 1924.

Disillusioned with the Nazi Party's policy concerning territorial claims in Austria's southern Tyrol, he left the party in 1926 and spent a year traveling in Italy learning the language. In 1927, he returned to Germany, rejoined the party, and became an Assistant Professor at Munich University, where he taught constitutional law. Frank, a cultured German, recited Heinrich Heine's poetry and performed piano pieces by Chopin and Beethoven.

Frank's strange odyssey began in 1927 when he read an advertisement in the Nazi Party newspaper, *Volkischer Beobachter*. Storm troopers had been arrested after rampaging through a Berlin restaurant where a Jewish family was having dinner. The Nazi Party wanted an aggressive lawyer to represent these "poor party members without means." W.L. Shirer, *The Rise & Fall of the Third Reich* (1960); J. Persico, *Nuremberg* (1995). Frank answered the advertisement, offering his services pro bono. He bought a third-class ticket to Berlin and was successful in obtaining lenient sentences for the Nazi defendants.

Frank's next stop was Nazi Party headquarters, where he met Adolf Hitler. Hitler, impressed, invited him to "come and work for the party." Frank's career possibilities were now unlimited. Political turmoil was rife. The Nazis continually incited violence. The Nazi roar to power was fueled by street terror. Assault, battery, attempted murder, murder, libel, and slander were handy political tools. Disregard for the Weimar legal system was routine. Legal cases piled up. The Weimar Republic was overwhelmed by 40,000 cases involving Nazis between 1927 and 1930. Frank, at the request of Hitler, was personally involved in 2,400 of them. In 1928, Frank formed the Union of Nazi Lawyers and became their leader. He became Hitler's personal lawyer. He was on his way.

Then came Frank's signature case. As leader of the Nazi Party's Legal Division, he represented three German Army lieutenants, Hans Ludin, Richard Scheringer, and Hans Friedrich, all charged with "preparing to commit high treason." Fired with Nazi propaganda, they tried to persuade their fellow officers not to combat the Nazis if they launched an armed revolt.

This landmark case became known as the Leipzig Reichswahr trial. It began in Germany's Supreme Court in Leipzig on September 30, 1930. The Nazis had just made stunning gains in national elections. The Nazi Party was now Germany's second largest political party.

Frank called Hitler, himself, to testify. As a witness for Frank's clients, Hitler had an international forum. He reassured the world that the Nazis would never try to seize power by force. If the young officers thought otherwise, they were mistaken. Hitler assured the court: "Our movement has no need of force. The time will come when the German nation will get to know of our ideas; then 35 million Germans will stand behind me. . . . When we do possess constitutional rights, then we will form the State in the manner which we consider to be the right one." The President of the Court asked, "This too, by constitutional means?" Hitler's response, "Yes."

Hitler was asked if he repudiated a statement he made in 1923 that "heads would roll." Hitler's classic answer: "I can assure you that when the National Socialist movement is victorious in this struggle, then there will be a National Socialist Court of Justice, too. Then the November 1918 revolution will be avenged and heads will roll." *Frankfurter Zeitung*, September 1930; Shirer, *supra*.

When the trial ended on October 4, the defendants were found guilty. But they received mild sentences. Hitler's testimony made world headlines. The Nazis were jubilant. Three years later, Hitler ruled Germany.

Frank regarded this case as his finest hour and his greatest service to the Nazi Party. Hitler encouraged him to enter politics. In 1930, he was elected to the Reichstag, one of its youngest members.

1933–1939

When Hitler became Germany's chancellor, on January 30, 1933, Frank's career soared. His résumé now included such prestigious appointments as Bavarian Minister of Justice; Commissioner of Justice; Reich Law Leader; Reich Minister of Justice without Portfolio; founder and President of the Academy of German Law; and member of the Faculty of Law at Munich University. These elite positions gave Frank control of both the legal profession and the judicial system. He would use these offices to promote Hitler's will as the core of German law. His goal: create a Nazi legal system; legitimize the Nazi Party.

As a constitutional scholar, Frank recognized that Hitler's "will alone was not yet law." J. Noakes & G. Pridham, *Documents on Nazism* (1975). Yet, he knew Hitler ". . . was hypersensitive towards any attempt to impose the slightest . . . legal restriction upon his authority, which had to be completely untrammelled, theoretically absolute and contained within his own person." I. Kershaw, *The Nazi Dictatorship* (2000). Noakes and Pridham observe that, "at an early stage, Hitler made it clear that he was not prepared to let legal niceties stand in his way."

On February 27, a month after Hitler took power, a mysterious fire destroyed the Reichstag, the country's legislative headquarters. Marinus Van der Lubbe, a Dutch communist, was convicted of arson and sentenced to prison. Hitler was outraged and demanded a death penalty. At a Cabinet meeting, the Reich Minister of the Interior said that it must be possible to impose, with retroactive effect, a sentence of death by hanging. The constitutional principle prohibiting ex post facto laws would not apply. A law mandating the death penalty for arson was passed. The same month as the fire, Hitler spoke to the Reichstag, exhorting them that "the law cannot be allowed to lead to the granting of equality. . . ." Noakes & Pridham, *supra.*

Against this background, Frank began radically to reshape German law so Hitler would have absolute legal power. Scrapping Roman law underpinnings, Frank cited the Nazi Party's Article 19, which was included in the Nazi Party Program in Munich on February 24, 1920. It stated: "We demand that Roman Law, which serves a materialistic World Order, be replaced by German Law." S. Piotrowski, *Hans Frank Diary* (1961).

Frank extolled Article 19 as Germany's "Magna Carta." German lawyers were implored to "fight" for Frank's interpretation. Hitler was to be the undisputed authority of German law. Lawyers and judges were now agents of the new Nazi state, enforcing Hitler's will.

Frank wrote nothing to implement Article 19. Instead, he modified, changed, and ignored any Weimar Republic law that impeded Nazi power. The judiciary would no longer interpret written law. Under Frank's interpretation of Article 19, cases would be decided on what the judge thought Hitler would do if he, himself, was deciding the case.

Frank, eager in his new role, moved quickly. First came the legal profession. Germany's lawyers no longer owed their primary allegiance to their clients. Instead, "lawyers were to be regarded as servants of the movement, guided by its objectives and its conception of the needs of the German people." Shirer, *supra.* German lawyers were then, "dragooned into party-controlled 'fronts' and 'academies' established for their indoctrination and were forced to be responsive to the directives of . . . Hans Frank. . . ." K. Bracher, *The German Dictatorship* (1970).

Beginning in June 1933, Frank created legal associations including the German Legal Front; the Federation of Lawyers, Judges, and Prosecutors; the Academy of German Law to Implement Article 19; the National Congress of Lawyers; and the National Association of Lawyers. Frank exhorted these groups to promote "through National Socialism a German Law for the German Nation."

In December 1933, Frank "as the leader of all Reich lawyers . . . proclaimed a German legal estate." Finally, in 1935, Frank stated, "For the first time in the history of the nation, affection for the Führer has become a legal concept." Shirer, *supra*. Article 19 was now implemented. It was Germany's law and remained so for the duration of the Third Reich.

Germany had no place for Jewish lawyers. They were excluded from the National Association of Lawyers and no longer listed in its annual directory. As Bavarian Justice Minister, Frank had Jews banned from practicing law in Bavaria. Finally, in September 1938, legislation against Jews entering the legal profession in Germany was adopted by the Reich Justice Ministry. Hitler approved it. I. Kershaw, *Hitler*, (1998); S. Friedlander, *Nazi Germany and the Jews*, vol. 1 (1998).

Next came the judiciary. Nominees were politically and racially screened. Judicial appointments were made only if the candidate accepted Nazi "ideological orthodoxy." But finally even that was not enough. In June 1934, Hitler declared himself "supreme judge." He would remove judges if he thought their sentences were too lenient or disloyal to the party goals. G. Craig, *Germany 1866–1934* (1978).

In 1936, Frank announced: "The National Socialist ideology is the foundation of all basic laws, especially as explained in the party program and in the speeches of the Führer. There is no independence of law under National Socialism." He told judges how to apply Nazi justice. "Say to yourselves at every decision which you make: 'How would the Führer decide in my place?' In every decision ask yourselves, 'Is this decision compatible with the National Socialist conscience of the German people?' " Shirer, *supra*.

Judges were strongly encouraged to convict defendants even though they had not violated a written law if they had committed

221

any act which the judge found socially or politically unacceptable. German judges must look beyond written law.

Hitler's Justice

Frank encouraged judges to differentiate between law and justice in applying Nazi law:

> National Socialism substitutes for the conception of formal wrong the idea of factual wrong: it considers every attack on the welfare of the national community, every violation of the requirement of the life of a nation as wrong. In future, therefore, wrong may be committed in Germany even in cases where there is nothing (no written law) against what is being done. Even without the threat of punishment, every violation of the goals towards which the community is striving is wrong per se. As a result, the law gives up all claim to be the sole source for determining right and wrong. What is right may be learned not only from the law but also from the concept of justice which lies behind the law and may not have found perfect expression in the law.

Noakes & Pridham, *supra*.

In May 1936, as Frank's power increased, he announced: "There is in Germany today only one authority, and that is the authority of the Führer." Shirer, *supra*. Thereafter, every judge had to join the League of National Socialist German Jurists. Strict judicial adherence to Nazi principles was maintained under a Civil Service law passed in 1937. Any judge could be dismissed for "political unreliability."

Frank then took an even bolder step. Germany's lawyers were inculcated with Nazi legal philosophy. The Lawyer's Union became the Union of Guardians of Law. Frank elevated his own title from Leader of Reich Lawyers to Leader of Reich Law. Appearing before the Annual Congress of Lawyers, Frank declared: "Our Führer has redeemed the German Reich, the German nation and German law. Apart from the authority of the state, no legal authority exists." Piotrowski, *supra*.

In 1938, Frank defined Hitler's power under Article 19:

> "Even if no further decisions or legal formulations were added to the present laws of the Third Reich governing its legal structure, as a result of five years' government by the Führer there can be no juridical doubts about the following absolutely clear principles of the Reich.

At the head of the Reich stands the leader of the Nazi Party as leader of the German Reich for life. He is, on the strength of his being leader of the Nazi Party, leader and Chancellor of the Reich. As such he embodies simultaneously, as Head of State, supreme State power and, as chief of the Government, the central functions of the whole Reich administration. The Führer and Reich Chancellor is the constituent delegate of the German people, who without regard for formal preconditions decides the outward form of the Reich, its structure and general policy.

Frank declared:

The Führer is supreme judge of the nation . . . There is no position in the area of constitutional law in the Third Reich independent of this elemental will of the Führer. The real characteristic of constitutional law in the Third Reich is that it does not represent a system of competencies but the relation of the whole German people to a personality who is engaged in shaping history. We are in a judicial period founded on the Führer's name, and shaped by him.

Shirer, *supra*.

Frank's legal theory placed Hitler above the principles in written constitutions or laws. He stated:

The Führer is not backed by constitutional clauses, but by outstanding achievements which are based on the combination of a calling and of his devotion to the people. The Führer does not put into effect a constitution according to legal guidelines laid before him but by historic achievements which serve the future of his people. Through this, German Constitutional Law has produced the highest organic viewpoint which legal history has to offer . . . Whether the Führer governs according to a formal written constitution is not a legal question of the first importance. The legal question is only whether through his activity the Führer guarantees the existence of his people.

Noakes & Pridham, *supra*.

Addressing German jurists, Frank claimed Hitler's authority was based on divine right: "Formerly we were in the habit of saying: 'This is right or wrong.' Today we must ask the question: 'What would the Führer say?' We are under the great obligation of recognizing as a holy work of our Folk Spirit the laws signed by Adolf Hitler. Hitler has received his authority from God." R. E. Conot, *Justice at Nuremberg* (1984).

Frank continued to separate substantive law from procedural rights. In 1934, Hitler cracked down violently on a perceived plot by Ernst Röhm, Chief of Staff of the SA Storm Troopers, to overthrow him. Frank objected when SA members were hunted down and killed without a trial. As a result, Hitler grudgingly granted some of the Storm Troopers the procedural rights to an arraignment and trial.

In May 1939 in Leipzig, Frank gave the closing address at the first National Guardians of Law Day, stating: "No one can be sentenced without having had the chance of defending himself. No one can be deprived of his dignity, freedom, life or income unless sentenced by a court of law. A defendant must have the chance of choosing his counsel. No one should be considered an enemy of society at large without proof of his guilt." Piotrowski, *supra.* As the Third Reich's leading legal authority, Frank's prestige continued to soar throughout Europe. He now received honorary doctor of law degrees from both the University of Bologna in Italy and the University of Bucharest in Romania.

The actual functioning of the new German legal system is exemplified in the Mark Luftgas case. His court record is in the German Judicial Archives. The Luftgas case is unusual because it contains the actual written record of Hitler personally intervening after the case had already been decided, and Luftgas had begun to serve his sentence.

This is how his case progressed. Luftgas, who was Jewish, had collected more eggs than the law allowed. He was tried and convicted of hoarding and sentenced to 2-1/2 years in prison. While Luftgas was serving his sentence, Hitler happened to read a newspaper article about the case. Hitler had never met Luftgas. He neither read the file nor discussed the case with the prosecutor or the sentencing judge. Hitler did not ask the prosecuting authorities to seek a new sentencing hearing. His involvement was a "command" that Luftgas should die. And Hitler's "command" was law. It was consistent with Frank's concept that Hitler's will was Nazi law. The Luftgas court record contains the following messages:

Reich Minister and Head of the Reich Chancellery [Dr. Lammers] to State Secretary Schlegelberger, Acting Minister of Justice . . . The Führer has been shown the enclosed press cutting concerning the sentencing of the Jew, Mark Luftgas, to 2-1/2 years' imprisonment by the Special Court at Bielitz. The Führer desires that Luftgas should be sentenced to death. I would be obliged if you would make the necessary arrangements as soon as possible and report to the Führer through me on the measures you have taken.

Lammers to SS Gruppenführer Julius Schaub: On receiving your letter . . . I contacted the Reich Minister of Justice and requested him to make the necessary arrangements. Schlegelberger to Lammers. . . . On receiving the Führer's command passed on to me by the Minister of State and Head of the Chancellery I handed over the Jew, Markus Luftgas, who was sentenced by the Special Court at Kattowitz to 2-1/2 years' imprisonment, to the Secret State Police for execution.

Noakes & Pridham, *supra*.

Hilter's "command" that Luftgas's sentence of 2-1/2 years of incarceration be changed to death was completed. Hitler's "command" was legal.

1939–1945

Germany conquered Poland in September 1939. Poland was quickly dismembered. Hitler annexed a large portion of western Poland to Germany. The eastern portion was annexed by the Soviet Union. The central portion, which remained under German rule as an occupied territory, was named the Government General of Poland with Krakow as its capital. Poland as a country ceased to exist.

Hitler made Frank the Governor General of Poland. Frank envisioned himself as a Teutonic Knight. He would lead Germany's crusade in the *Drang nach Osten*, the March to the East, The Third Reich's Eastern European destiny. But Hitler regarded Frank as the Government General's caretaker. He regarded the Polish Territories as Germany's cesspool. And ultimately the killing ground for Europe's Jewry.

Frank's new post began as darkness descended on Poland. His role: destroy the Polish economy, send forced labor to Germany, and liquidate the Polish intelligentsia. He had reached the apex of his career.

Frank poured out his invective toward Jews and Polish intellectuals in his diary, which he would later describe as an "historic document," and which, as we shall see, was to play a significant role in the Nürnberg trials. On March 2, 1940, Frank recorded that he told a meeting of the Reich Defense Committee: "I am responsible for what has happened since 11 October 1939, no matter what happened, how it happened or by whom it was done. I bear the responsibility and I am not passing it on to anybody. And because of this I also want to stress that this responsibility can be borne. If there were here and there events which were, let us say, regrettable from the point of view of humanity in general, we must accept the responsibility all the more."

In an entry on May 30, 1940, Frank encouraged the liquidation of Polish intellectuals in Poland: "I pray you gentlemen, to take the most rigorous measures possible to help us in this task. The men capable of leadership in Poland must be liquidated. Those following them . . . must be eliminated in their turn. There is no need to burden the Reich with this . . . no need to send these elements to Reich concentration camps. . . . They would be put out of the way . . . right here in Poland." Frank, impressed with the results, praised an SS officer who was responsible for killing 3,500 Polish intellectuals: "What you, Brigade-führer Streckenbach, and your people have done in the Government General must not be forgotten; and you need not be ashamed of it." Conot, *supra;* S. Wiesenthal, *Justice Not Vengeance* (1989).

Frank reveled in his new role. Jubilant balls and feasts were held in Krakow's gothic Wawel Castle, ancient seat of Polish kings. Even Reichsmarshall Hermann Goering, whose greedy ostentatiousness was considered unrivaled, called Frank "King Stanislaus." C. Zentner & F. Bedurftig, *The Encyclopedia of the Third Reich* (1991).

An SS report describes Frank's life as Governor General of Poland: "His day consists of running around from castle to castle in a magnificent carriage with guards of honor, books, music, plays, and banquets . . . . There is nothing natural, no simplicity, all is pose and playacting and serves to satisfy his intoxication, brought about by ambition and lust for power, and at the same time his likeness to Mussolini, of which he is convinced by his flatterers, is interpreted as fate and destiny."

As ruler, Frank did not talk about legal rights. Frank had a different legal concept. While hosting lavish dinners, he boasted in his diary that: "Poland shall be treated like a colony. The Poles will become the slaves of the Greater German Empire. If I put up a poster for every seven Poles shot, the forests of Poland would not be sufficient to manufacture the paper for such posters." L. Snyder, *The Encyclopedia of the Holocaust* (1976).

Frank was excited about deporting 1.3 million Poles to Germany as forced laborers. But Germany's leading jurist disclosed that his Polish program would not include the "rule of law," writing:

We will hold on to the Government General and will never give it up again. . . . I admit, quite openly, that this will cost the lives of several thousand Poles, primarily from the intellectual upper class. . . . We liquidate things in this country. We will do so in the manner which proves simplest. . . . Our primary object here in this area is to fulfil National-Socialism's great mission in the East. It cannot, therefore, be our object to set up here a State based on the rule of law. . . . Anyone suspected by us should be liquidated forthwith.

But Frank had even more draconian plans for the Jews. On October 7, 1940, he recalled a speech as he wrote in his diary: "At the current level of permitted rations some 1,200,000 Jews had been expected to die of hunger. We must obliterate the Jews. We cannot kill them with poison. But some way or other we will achieve their extermination. My dear comrades! . . . I could not eliminate all lice and Jews in only one year. ["Public amused," he notes in his diary]. But in the course of time, and if you help me, this end will be attained."

Frank established ghettos, concentrating Jews in tightly guarded areas. On October 15, 1941, Frank issued a decree making it a crime for any Jew to escape from a ghetto. Special courts were created where Jews would be summarily tried. The penalty was death. Poland Ministerstwo Spraw Zagraniczych, *Polish White Book: German Occupation of Poland* (1942).

German manpower soon proved inadequate to capture and return escaped Jews. The judicial procedures of the Special Courts were cumbersome and time consuming. Frank's solution: all judicial procedures would be dispensed with. Jews found outside the ghettos would be "shot on the spot." The Deputy to the Governor of the Warsaw District was relieved and pleased at Frank's Executive Order, stating, "gratefully one had welcomed the shooting order . . . whereby Jews encountered in the countryside could be shot."

Frank's edict became known as "the shooting order." C. Browning, *Ordinary Men* (1992).

Germany invaded the Soviet Union on June 22, 1941. Hitler's plans for a rapid victory were thwarted when the German Army was stopped by the Red Army in December 1941 before reaching Moscow. That December, Frank did not mention legal rights when he told a cabinet session at his headquarters in Krakow: "As far as the Jews are concerned, I want to tell you quite frankly that they must be done away with in one way or another . . . Gentlemen, I must ask you to rid yourself of all feeling of pity. We must annihilate the Jews." *Nürnberger Dokumente*, CA, IV; *Nürnberger Dokumente*, 2233-C-PS; Shirer, *supra*.

But the irony of Nazi insistence on obedience to party and military regulations caught up with Frank. Despite his enthusiastic efforts to subjugate Poland, Frank and his wife, Brigette, sent a vast variety of plundered goods to their Schliersee home in southern Germany, making him open to charges of official misconduct. The list included: a moleskin jacket; a beaver coat; a musquash coat; an ermine coat; two broadtail coats; an ermine jacket; a silver fox cape; a blue fox cape; furs; rings; gold bracelets; gold fountain pens; tinned food; picnic hampers; coffee machines; dried fruit; sheets; blankets; furniture; 50 lbs of beef; 50 lbs of pork; 20 geese; 50 chickens; 25 lbs of salami; 30 lbs of ham sausage; 25 lbs of ham; 175 lbs of butter; 110 lbs of cooking oil; 30 lbs of sugar; sculptures; icons from Polish churches; a painting by Rembrandt; Leonardo da Vinci's *Lady with an Ermine*; and 200,000 eggs, far more than the number for which poor Luftgas had forfeited his life. Shirer, *supra*.

On December 1, 1941, this inventory was sent to SS Chief Heinrich Himmler with a report condemning Frank: "This affair constitutes a case of corruption of the basest sort, all the more deplorable in that it shows that Germans are misusing their positions as senior political leaders of the Reich to enrich themselves personally by exploiting the circumstances arising from the war." H. Hohne, *The Order of the Death's Head* (1970).

While this matter was pending, Frank tended to his duties. According to his diary, on December 16, 1941, Frank said: "We shall have pity only for the German people and for no one else in the world. The others did not have any pity for us either. And I must say, as an old National Socialist: should the Jewish brotherhood in Europe survive the war, whereas we had sacrificed our best blood to save Europe, this war would only be a partial success." "My attitude towards the Jews will therefore be based only on the expectation that they should disappear. They must go. I have entered into negotiations for their deportation to the East. A big conference on this question is taking place in Berlin in January, to which I shall send Secretary of State Dr. Bühler. This conference is to be held in the Reich Security HQ with SS Obergruppenführer Heydrich. At any rate, a great Jewish migration will begin."

The "big conference" Frank was referring to was the Wannsee Conference, which convened at Am Grossen Wannsee in Berlin on January 20, 1942. SS Obergruppenführer Reinhard Heydrich presided over 15 bureaucrats representing Germany's most important state agencies. Dr. Bühler attended as Frank's emissary. The conference was convened to implement a Führerprinzip (Executive Order) mandating the legal extermination of Europe's Jewry. Heydrich announced, "I have just come from the Reichsführer: the Führer has now ordered the physical annihilation of the Jews." Together they planned how it would be done. The use of death camps at Sobibor and Treblinka in the General Government of Poland was discussed in the implementation of the "final solution of the Jewish problem." Four representatives at the Wannsee Conference were lawyers. R. Ionid, *The Holocaust in Romania* (2000); Piotrowski, *supra*; R. Hilberg, *Documents of Destruction* (1971); D. Edmonds & J. Eidinow, *Wittgenstein's Poker* (2001); I. Trunk, *Judenrat* (1972); *Nürnberger Dokumente*, NG-2886; V. P. Longerich, *Spiegel Special* (2001).

Frank could now confront Himmler's charges of his personal corruption. Frank and Himmler collided in a power struggle. On March 5, 1942, Frank, claiming his innocence, appeared before a military tribunal. His judges were Himmler, Hans Lammers, and Martin Bormann. Frank's conduct was found unlawful under Nazi law. Although he remained Governor General, Frank was reprimanded and stripped of limited procedural authority over various racial and police enforcement matters. Himmler's power in Poland increased. One result was that after April 18, 1942, Jews, Poles, Gypsies, Russians, and Ukrainians would not be prosecuted within the judicial system for any criminal offense. They would be dealt with under Himmler's Executive Orders. Noakes & Pridham, *supra*.

Frank's Due Process

During his reign in Poland, Frank was considered a frivolous dandy by Hitler's inner circle. His lavish lifestyle was tolerated, but by March 1942, their patience had waned, and his reprimand by the Himmler court-martial had undermined Frank's authority. Frank rebounded when a letter arrived from his long-ago first love, Lilli Gau. Although both were married, they began an affair. Frank made plans to marry Lilli. Then Frank decided that he would stand up for his principles and advocate for Germans a return to due process and a system of justice. Persico, *supra*.

Frank returned to Germany. As Reichminister and Governor General, he spoke on constitutional issues. According to his diary, his lectures were enthusiastically received.

At Berlin University on June 9, 1942, Frank gave a lecture entitled "The Idea of Law and the National Community," in which he insisted: "Without law—or contrary to law—no German Reich is conceivable. A people cannot be ruled by force, a community without law is unthinkable.... It is intolerable that the State should be able to deprive a member of the community of honor, liberty, life and property, declare him an outlaw and condemn him, without first giving him an opportunity to reply to the accusations made against him."

"Law and the European Revival" was the title of Frank's next lecture. On July 1, 1942, he told the Vienna Academy of Sciences:

> I shall continue to assert, with all the force at my command, that it would be bad if the Police State were to be represented as the ideal of National Socialism. Nowadays many people say that humanity is an out-of-date notion, something incompatible with the severity of this period. That is not my opinion. The principle which every State, including our own, must follow, is that its methods must be designed to meet the historical tasks which any State must fulfill but that, in no circumstances, can a State be endangered by being humane.

At Munich University on July 20, 1942, speaking about "The Law as the Basis of a National Society," he stated: "Even in wartime, a mode of life based on the rule of law is important for the development of the community. We must not give the impression that in our Reich the law is powerless. The law is the personal safeguard of the people ... force alone cannot make the State strong. Brutality is never synonymous with strength. ... I say only the man who does not fear the law is strong."

Heidelberg University on July 21, 1942, was Frank's last stop. There he thundered: "The Police State must never exist—never! I reject it. As a National Socialist and leader of the German legal profession, I therefore feel it my duty to protest against these continual disparagements of the law and its servants. I protest against a profession being attacked and slandered simply from spite or a permanent nagging desire to criticize." Persico, *supra*; Hohne, *supra*.

A month after this last lecture, Frank said: "Jews? Yes, we still have a few of them around, but we'll soon take care of that." In giving these lectures and reflecting on his role in the 1930 Leipzig Reichswahr trial, Frank stressed his importance: "Thus I was, am and shall remain the representative jurist of National Socialism's period of struggle." Piotrowski, *supra*.

Hitler, not surprisingly, was not pleased with Frank's constitutional exhortations. Hitler forbade him from giving any further speeches in Germany and removed him from all party offices. He refused Frank's plea for a divorce. Frank offered his resignation as Governor General of Poland. Hitler would not accept it. Frank left Munich and returned to his Wawel Castle on September 16, 1942. Frank claimed he submitted his resignation 14 times during the following two years.

Germany's defeat at Stalingrad in February 1943 ended any realistic hope of a German victory. Hope started to grow among the subjugated people of Eastern Europe that Hitler might be defeated. P. Burg, *Oral Statement* (2001). In his diary on February 17, 1944, Frank reflected on the history of the Nazi movement:

> Last June it was 25 years since I got to know the Führer, and I have now been with him for 25 years; during many and difficult hours we were bound to each other. I belong to the circle of the few representatives of the earliest National Socialist's development. I was present when the Party program was formulated. I know the preparations for the first party meeting in the Mathaeser Brewery. . . . I know the history of the movement right from the beginning. For me, looking back on the 25 years of this work is a retrospect of one of the most marvelous epochs of development of our people and today also of the history of the world. That the enemies we had in Germany have organized themselves internationally and have international support, we recognize from the fact that the carrying out of the Führer's program in the world historical sense leads to the same enemy front which we saw as victors over us in 1918: the Jews, the Jesuits and the Masons.

Finally, in August 1944, Frank's resignation was accepted. The Red Army stormed into Poland. The demise of the Third Reich was near. Frank's final months in Poland were spiritless. Forgotten by Hitler, Frank was now pursued by Germany's enemies. He fled to his home in Germany, where he awaited the war's end. On May 4, 1945, the American Army arrived, and he was taken into custody by the Seventh Army's 36th Regiment. Frank, jailed in Miesbach, awaited his indictment as a war criminal.

Afterword

On November 20, 1945, the International Military Tribunal in Nürnberg was created. The tribunal indicted 23 leading Nazis. Frank was among them. There were four counts: (1) the common plan or conspiracy, (2) crimes against peace, (3) war crimes, and (4) crimes against humanity. Frank was indicted on counts 1, 3, and 4.

Frank was accorded his full legal rights. These were the rights he had advocated for ethnic Germans, but which he, as Governor General of Poland, denied to Jews, Poles, Ukrainians, Gypsies, and Russians.

The indictment against Frank charged:

> The defendant Frank between 1932–1945 was a member of the Nazi Party, a General in the SS, a member of the Reichstag, Reichminister without Portfolio, Reichscommisar for the coordination of Justice, President of the International Chamber of Law and Academy of German Law, Chief of the military district of West Prussia, Poznan, Odz and Krakow and Governor General of the Occupied Polish territories.

> The defendant Frank used the foregoing positions, his personal influence, and his intimate connection with the Führer in such manner that: he promoted the accession to power of the Nazi conspirators and the consolidation of their control over Germany set forth in Count One; he authorized, directed and participated in the War Crimes set forth in Count Three and the Crimes against Humanity set forth in Count Four, including particularly the War Crimes and Crimes against Humanity involved in the administration of occupied territories.

R. Martin, M.D., *Inside Nuremberg* (2000).

Frank's 11,367-page diary consisted of 42 red and gray leather bound volumes. Frank started making entries on October 25,

1939. He left Poland for Germany "in the sunshine of a beautiful winter's day." Frank, proud of his diary, took it to Schliersee in Germany where he opened a branch office of the "Governor General of Poland." He made entries until April 3, 1945. The diary was discovered on May 4, 1945, by Lieutenant Walter Stein of the U.S. 7th Army in Frank's house in Bavaria. Persico, *supra*. Before his trial began, Frank made two unsuccessful attempts at suicide.

On November 8, 1945, Frank told American authorities that his diary was an "historic document" and that all of the entries were "correct and accurate to the best of his knowledge." Piotrowski, *supra*. In Leipzig, the diary was printed in German and Russian so it could be used by the International Military Tribunal at Frank's trial. As Exhibit SSSR-223, it became one of the few printed documents presented to the tribunal. Frank's diary remains today in the Archives of the Polish Government in Warsaw.

The diary was the prosecution's most important written exhibit. Without it, there would have been a paucity of direct evidence linking Frank and other high Nazis with committing war crimes in Poland. Robert H. Jackson, a Justice of the United States Supreme Court and the Chief American Prosecutor, in his opening statement said:

> Perhaps the deportation to slave labor was the most horrible and extensive slaving operation in history. On few other subjects is our evidence so abundant or so damaging. A speech of the defendant Frank, Governor General of Poland, was made on January 25, 1944, in which he boasted, "I have sent 1,300,000 Polish workers into the Reich." The defendant Sauckel reported that "out of the five million foreign workers who arrived in Germany not even 200,000 came voluntarily." This fact was reported to the Führer. . . .

Dr. Alfred Seidl was Frank's lawyer. His defense included claims that Frank took artworks, including Leonardo da Vinci's *Lady with an Ermine*, from Poland to Germany, to protect them from the Soviet "barbarians"; cooperated with the prosecution by making his diary available to the Americans; helped the Poles improve their lives; defended himself against Himmler's charges; gave university lectures on the rule of law; and made futile attempts to resign as Governor General of Poland.

The death camps of Belzec, Sobibor, Plaszow, Majdanek, and Treblinka were located in the Government General of Poland.

Wawel Castle, where Frank lived, was 30 miles from the death camp of Auschwitz-Birkenau. Approximately 6 million European Jews and other "undesirables" were legally killed under German law in these camps. L. Poliakov & J. Wulf, eds., *Das Dritte Reich und die Juden; Dokumente und Aufsatze* (1955); L. Poliakov, *Histoire de l' antisémitisme* (1985). Frank claimed he was unaware of the purpose of these camps, but when confronted with his diary entries, he conceded that the atrocities committed there occurred during his leadership. Persico, *supra*.

Finally on April 18, 1946, Frank testified to his participation as Governor General of Poland in the extermination of European Jewry. His lawyer, Dr. Alfred Seidl, asked him:

> *Q:* Did you ever participate in the annihilation of the Jews?
> *A:* I say, yes. And the reason I say yes is because having lived through the five months of this trial, particularly after having heard the testimony of the witness Höss, [Höss had already testified how he had planned, supervised, and engineered the murder of 2,500,000 Jews through the use of gas chambers when he had been Commander at Auschwitz], my conscience does not allow me to throw the responsibility solely on minor people.
>
> I myself have never installed an extermination camp for Jews . . . but we have fought against Jewry for years; and we have indulged in the most horrible utterances. My own diary bears witness against me. Therefore, it is my duty to answer your question with yes. A thousand years will pass and still Germany's guilt will not have been erased.

Persico, *supra*; R. Höss, *Kommandant in Auschwitz* (1958).

Frank, realizing the incriminating entries in his diary spelled his doom, renewed his faith in Catholicism. Father Sixtus O'Connor, a Catholic priest and prison chaplain, considered Frank his prize convert. Frank confessed his guilt and begged for forgiveness from God. He told the tribunal that he regarded the trial as a God-willed world court destined to examine and put an end to the terrible era of suffering under Hitler.

When Frank proudly reminded the tribunal about the university law lectures he had given in 1942, Presiding Judge Lord Justice Sir Geoffrey Lawrence, of the United Kingdom, curious, asked Frank's lawyer, "Dr. Seidl, are there any passages in these documents [constitutional law lectures] which express the opinion that the same principles ought to be applied to other than fellow Germans?" There were none. Conot, *supra*.

During his trial, Frank wrote a memoir entitled *Im Angesicht des Galgens*. H. Frank, *In the Sight of the Gallows* (1953). In it, he attacked H. and the shame and carnage he had brought upon Germany. Frank proudly refers to his diary in his memoir, stating: "I gave myself up to the Americans. Of my own will I give them my diary of the war. I do not want to hide any sin: let what is known to God be also known to mankind." Piotrowski, *supra*.

Justice Jackson described Frank's role in his summation; "The fanatical Frank, who solidified Nazi control by establishing the new order of authority without law, so that the will of the Party was the only test of legality, proceeded to export his lawlessness to Poland, which he governed with the lash of Caesar and whose population he reduced to sorrowing remnants." B. Aymar & E. Sagarin, *World's Great Trials* (1985).

On October 1, 1946, Frank was called before the Court for its verdict. It was: "Guilty on Counts 3 and 4 The Sentence: Death." *Nürnberger Dokumente*. The *New York Times* reported: "Those who will die by the noose within 15 days, unless reprieved through an appeal within 4 days to the Allied Control Commission in Berlin, are . . . Hans Frank. . . ."

The American judge, former United States Attorney General Francis Biddle, commented: "It is undoubtedly true that most of the criminal program charged against Frank was put into effect through the police [and] it therefore may well be true that some of the crimes were committed in the General Government without the knowledge of Frank, and even occasionally despite his opposition. But it is also true that Frank was a willing and knowing participant in the use of terrorism in Poland; in the economic exploitation of Poland in a way which led to the death by starvation of a large number of people; in the deportation into Germany as slave laborers of over a million Poles; and in a program involving the murder of at least three million Jews." Conot, *supra*.

The *New York Times* put it this way:

There was not sufficient evidence of his knowledge of the common plan to allow the Tribunal to convict him on Count 1. In the war crimes and humanity crimes categories, however, Frank had described intended policy in Poland as follows: Poles would become the slaves of Greater Germany; a reign of terror was instituted, there was widespread shooting of hostages and establishment of concentration camps. He told the police of the intended liquidation of thousands of Poles, including the intelligentsia, and reduced the country to starvation through the export of food and workers to Germany. He was responsible for the ghettos and the systematic brutal extermination of the Jews.

New York Times (October 2, 1946).

Frank appealed to the Four Power Commission. On October 11, Dr. Seidl told him his appeal had been denied. While awaiting execution, Frank learned from his wife, Brigette, that their homes and possessions had been confiscated. Brigette and their five children had moved to a cold water flat. The high life was over.

In his final hours, Frank reflected on his life. Moments before his execution, he wrote: "I am seized now, as I prepare to say farewell to this earth, in order to follow the Führer, by the most profound melancholy when I recall this tremendous setting out of a whole great self-confident nation that followed a strong voice as though to a celebration of the eternal Godhead himself. Why, why was it all lost, why did it all fade away, why is it all gone, destroyed? I am seized by uncomprehending horror at the senselessness of destiny." F.R. Miale & M. Selver, *The Nuremberg Mind* (1975).

As Frank himself said shortly before his execution: "Ambition had a lot to do with it. Just imagine—I was a Minister of State at thirty; rode around in a limousine, had servants." *Id.*

Niklas Frank, Hans Frank's son, wrote a vitriolic polemic about his father, *In the Shadow of the Reich* (1991), which concludes with the son's disgust that his father withdrew his earlier reference to Germany's guilt: "In your summation . . . you uttered these slimy words: 'I must still rectify one of the statements I made here earlier. In the witness stand I spoke about the one hundred years that could not erase the guilt from our nation on account of Hitler's behavior. However, . . . the gigantic mass atrocities of the most horrible kind, which[,] I have learnt, were committed against the Germans . . . and are still being committed—all this has completely canceled out, even today, any possible guilt on the part of our people and nation.' "

Hans Frank was hanged at Nürnberg in the early morning hours of October 16, 1946.

236

16

The Ardeatine Caves

March 23, 1944, a pleasant spring day, began quietly for General
Kurt Mälzer, Germany's alcoholic commander of occupied Rome,
and his superior, Field Marshal Albert Kesselring. One hundred
twenty soldiers of the German 11th Company of the Bozen SS 3rd
Battalion carried out their daily routine by marching down the Via
Rasella. Their punctuality was clocked by an Italian armed Resistance unit, GAP Central (Gruppi di Azione Patriottica), whose
members meticulously planned the soldiers' destruction. A bomb
was concealed in a rubbish cart, and at 3:15 PM, "Paolo," a partisan dressed as a street cleaner, lit the fuse as the column marched
past. The horrific blast instantly killed 32 soldiers.

As the massive explosion was heard throughout Rome, Germans at the head of the column sprayed the shops and homes on
the street with wild gunfire. Another Resistance fighter, "Elena,"
gave "Paolo" a raincoat as cover, and they escaped.

General Mälzer quickly reached the scene. Believing the street's
residents were responsible, he forced them to stand in front of
their homes and shops and loudly threatened their immediate
death. Mälzer was incoherent with rage. He wanted every Italian

on the Via Rasella shot and all the buildings destroyed, but other German officers stopped him.

The Germans were in turmoil. They thought the Via Rasella killings required a strong response. Hitler demanded a reprisal ratio of 100 to 1. Kesselring ignored Hitler and set a death ratio of 10 to 1 to occur within 24 hours. Efforts were made to seek a Vatican intercession. According to Robert Katz, an American journalist and author, there was no reply. Germany's Vatican ambassador, Friedrich Möllhausen, was unsuccessful in his attempt to suggest an alternative in which the widows and children of the deceased SS soldiers would attend the funeral and receive a payment from the Italian government. A decision was made. The 10 to 1 ratio would remain. Lieutenant Colonel Herbert Kappler, Rome's SS commander, was ordered to prepare a "worthy of death" list of 320 men. R. Katz, *Death in Rome* (1967); R. Katz, *The Battle for Rome* (2003).

Italy, led by Il Duce Benito Mussolini, had entered World War II on the side of Hitler's Germany in June 1940, but after losing its African empire to American and British Allied forces, the Italian campaign ended in May 1943. The Allies then conquered Sicily. On the Eastern Front, the Red Army won the Battle of Stalingrad in February 1943. With 200,000 Italians killed, Hitler's war had spun around. Italy was on the losing side.

When Sicily fell, Mussolini was removed by the Italian fascist government. He was arrested and replaced by Marshal Pietro Badoglio, who ostensibly continued Italy's Axis pact with Germany but began clandestine negotiations with the United States and Great Britain. Italy surrendered unconditionally. This dramatic change of alliances from Axis to Allies was revealed in September 1943, when the Italian mainland was invaded by the Allies at Salerno, approximately 160 miles south of Rome. The British landed on Italy's toe and slogged up the Adriatic coast.

Hitler was not pleased. The Germans rescued Mussolini. In the north, Mussolini created the Italian Social Republic, a puppet fascist state that remained loyal to Hitler. After the Salerno invasion, Field Marshal Kesselring, commander of German forces in the Mediterranean, agreed with Hitler that Rome was indefensible. But Kesselring's army held back the Allies, and the Germans held Rome.

In January 1944, the Allies invaded again at Anzio, only 35 miles from Rome. Kesselring stalled this landing. Rome remained under German occupation from September 8, 1943 to June 4, 1944, when Rome was liberated two days before the D-Day landings at Normandy. W.G.F. Jackson, *The Battle for Italy* (1967); R.J.B. Bosworth, *Mussolini's Italy* (2006); E. Epstein, *Oral History* (2006).

Reprisal

Meanwhile, SS Lieutenant Colonel Kappler became the most significant figure in the reprisal. Kappler, a native of Stuttgart, Germany, was assigned to Rome in 1939. Enchanted by the ancient beauty of this ageless city, he came to love its culture. He became fluent in Italian and collected Etruscan vases. The 37-year-old Kappler considered Rome his second home. He had never been accepted for front-line duty and had never actually killed anyone. Now Kappler had to decide who should die.

Kappler began with males who had already been sentenced to death in Italian courts, but he found only two death-row prisoners. Obviously he needed many more names. He sought prisoners from the German prison Regina Coeli and the Italian prison Via Tasso. There were also Jews available. Being Jewish was enough to qualify someone as an enemy of the Third Reich. The age of the victims ranged from 14 to 75. The list included 70 Jews. Suddenly, Kappler was faced with an unexpected problem. Another German SS soldier died in the hospital. Without checking with superiors, he decided to add an additional 10 names to the list to keep the 10-to-1 ratio.

He worked all night on the list and brought it at noon to General Mälzer, who also called in SS Major Hellmuth Dobbrick, the commander of the 3rd Battalion. Dobbrick had escaped injury in the Via Rasella attack. Mälzer announced that Dobbrick and the other survivors must take their revenge by executing those on the reprisal list. Dobbrick refused. He made lame excuses. Mälzer was shocked by his refusal to obey orders.

Calling the 14th Army headquarters, Mälzer spoke to Colonel Wolfgang Hauser, General Mackensen's chief of staff. A detachment of troops must be made available immediately. Hauser also refused, saying, "It was the police who were struck; it is the police who must make the expiation." Mälzer put down the phone and said, "It's up to you, Kappler." Stunned, Kappler offered to have his men follow Mälzer's command, but Mälzer was adamant. Kappler, as head of the Rome Gestapo, must set an example. Kappler must do it. Katz, *Death, supra.*

Kappler met with the 12 officers of his command and told them they must take part in the executions. He planned to kill the 330 as efficiently, rapidly, and quietly as possible. Kappler knew at least three men personally—a nobleman, an old general, and a "communist" priest. With 156 SS men available to do the work, groups of five victims were driven in meat trucks from the prisons to the Ardeatine Caves, a network of tunnels used as a sandpit next to the Via Ardeatina. They were removed from the trucks, and each group was taken to the back of the central tunnel. They were ordered to kneel. Each was shot with one bullet at an upright angle in the back of the head.

The grisly program began in an orderly fashion, but it quickly unraveled. Some victims did not die after one shot. Some had to climb on top of dead bodies because with so many corpses there was not sufficient room on the ground. Others were decapitated by the bullets. Some Germans were incapable of firing their weapons. The cave became Dantesque, seething with gun smoke, vomit, excrement, blood, and the scattered remnants of bones, brains, and facial and body tissue. There was a constant and continual roar from shooting. There were cries and screams from those who would not go quietly. Cognac flowed freely for those Germans who were repulsed by the carnage. One German, 2nd Lieutenant Günther Amonn, refused to shoot. Katz, *Battle, supra.*

The Error of the Five Extra Men

After five hours, Kappler and "Worthy of Death" list-keeper Captain Erich Priebke realized that they had erroneously brought an additional five men whose deaths would put their assignment over the limit. Kappler had to make a quick decision. These five men had seen what was happening. The decision was to kill them. This made the final count 335. The executions had begun at 3:15 PM and ended at 8:00 PM. Kappler ordered the Ardeatine Caves sealed with explosives, and engineers returned the following day to seal the caves. It was not until 1998 that another officer at the scene told the court the details of the five extra men. Katz, *Death, supra.*

1944: Piero Caruso Trial

After Rome's liberation, a team of experts exhumed the bodies from the caves and identified them. A frantic hunt began for those responsible for the massacre. Piero Caruso, Rome's chief of police, was scheduled for trial on September 20, 1944. He had added the names of 50 inmates from Via Tasso Prison to the reprisal list. Before the proceedings could begin, Donato Caretta, who had resisted the removal of the men on Caruso's list and was in the courthouse ready to testify as a prosecution witness against Caruso, was identified as the prison warden. The crowd that surrounded the Palace of Justice seized and killed Caretta. Caruso's trial occurred two days later. Found guilty the following morning and sentenced to death, he was shot to death by 20 carabinieri that afternoon.

1945: Pietro Koch Trial

Pietro Koch was tried on June 4, 1945, in a courtroom at the University of Rome before an Italian high court of justice with jurisdiction over fascist crimes. He was found guilty of high crimes against the Resistance, including torture, deportations, and "handing over numerous patriots to the German SS to be massacred in the Ardeatine Caves." He suddenly accepted Christianity and sought forgiveness from God and all those he had caused to suffer. He was shot to death by a firing squad.

1946: Generals Mackensen and Mälzer Trial

In November 1946, Generals Eberhard von Mackensen and Kurt Mälzer were returned to Rome from England to be tried before a British military court. They claimed that Kappler told them the names on the "Worthy of Death" list were men who had already been sentenced to death or prisoners who would have been liquidated by the SS. Kappler, a prosecution witness, denied this, saying that he did not have enough death-sentence prisoners, so he added persons "worthy of death." Mackensen and Mälzer's defense of following superior orders was not considered creditable after the Nuremberg judgments, nor was there any defense under the Hague Convention of 1907, which revised the laws and customs of war on land. Mackensen and Mälzer were both found guilty and sentenced to "suffer death by being shot." The sentences were reduced and finally cancelled. Mälzer died in prison. Mackensen was released in 1952 and died at age 80 in 1969.

1947: Field Marshal Albert Kesselring Trial

Field Marshal Albert B. Kesselring was tried in February 1947 by a British military court in Venice. He was charged with responsibility for the Ardeatine Caves killings and for "inciting and commanding" his forces to kill 1,078 unarmed Italians, including children, in unrelated incidents. Kesselring's defense was similar to that of the generals.

He also claimed that a second order from Hitler exonerated him because it only required him to deliver Hitler's first order. He was merely a messenger. The court held that the Ardeatine Caves killings had no basis in any law and were war crimes. Found guilty on both counts, he was sentenced to death. Through the political influence of Winston Churchill, who said his opponent fought "hard but clean," his sentence was commuted to life and then reduced again. He was released in 1952 and spent his last years unrepentantly writing his autobiography. Kesselring died in 1960. Kesselring, *Soldat zum das letzten Tag* [*Soldier to the Last Day*] (1958); C. Barnett, *Hitler's Generals* (1989); W. Wette, *The Wehrmacht* (2006).

1948: SS Lieutenant Colonel Herbert Kappler Trial

The trial of Lieutenant Colonel Kappler began in May 1948 before a Rome-based Italian military tribunal. Kappler was a co-defendant with five subordinates. A missing co-defendant was Kappler's right-hand man, Captain Erich Priebke, who had vanished from a prisoner-of-war camp in Rimini. All were charged with homicide for provoking the deaths at the Ardeatine Caves. But Kappler's culpability was considered more odious, and he was charged with aggravating the circumstances of the crime by having "promoted and organized" the massacre. He was also charged with extorting 50 kilograms of gold from the Jewish community of Rome. The gold was given to the German state by orders from Berlin. Despite the payment, Jews were sent to Auschwitz.

Kappler testified for eight days. Using the discredited "following orders" defense, he claimed that the partisan attack was illegal, but not the reprisal. Kappler outlined his actions. He had been given the assignment of: (1) deciding who should be on the "worthy of death" list of men who had to be killed within 24 hours regardless of any civil or criminal culpability; (2) getting their hands trussed behind their backs; (3) having them transported in meat trucks to the Ardeatine Caves where they would be killed; (4) forcing five of them at a time into a kneeling position so each could be shot with a bullet in the back of the neck; (5) killing the victims so the Roman public would be unaware of what was happening; (6) destroying the cave's entrance so the killings would not be discovered. OSS RG 226, CIA, doc. 7459 (October 11, 1943).

Extortion Charge

On September 26, 1943, in Rome, Kappler had told the leaders of the Jewish community, "You and your coreligionists are Italian nationals, but that is of little importance to me. We Germans regard you only as Jews, and thus our enemy. . . . And we will treat you as such. . . . [But] it is not your lives or the lives of your children that we will take—if you fulfill our demands. . . . Within thirty-six hours you will have to pay fifty kilograms of gold. If you pay, no harm will come to you. In any other event, 200 Jews will be taken and deported to Germany, where they will be sent to the Russian frontier, or otherwise rendered innocuous." Katz, *Battle, supra.*

As the Jewish delegation left, Kappler threatened, "Mind you, I have already carried out several operations of this type and they have always ended well. Only once did I fail, but that time a few hundred of your brothers paid with their lives." The Jewish delegation was fearful of Kappler's threat, but they believed his demand of gold was a small price to pay. Some of the gold was collected from wedding bands, lockets, and dental fillings. The gold was found in General Ernst Kaltenbrunner's Berlin office after the war. Kaltenbrunner was convicted at Nuremberg and hanged in 1946. Katz, *Battle, supra.*

Kappler then received this order: "It is precisely the immediate and thorough eradication of the Jews in Italy which is in the special interest of the present internal political situation and the general security in Italy." German diplomats, including Ambassador Ernst von Weizsäcker, and the Vatican secretary of state planned to issue a letter to the German foreign service suggesting that the Pope might protest the deportations. However, this plan came too late, and the policy of papal silence continued. Kappler's SS collected and deported Roman Jews, and he sent this message to Himmler in Berlin: "Action against Jews started and finished today in accordance with a plan worked out as well as possible by the office." Katz, *Battle, supra.*

Kappler was found guilty and was sentenced to life for his role in the massacre He was also sentenced to fifteen years for extorting gold from the Jewish community and having 1,023 of Rome's Jews sent to their death. The co-defendants who carried out his orders were acquitted. Kappler was imprisoned in Gaeta, between Rome and Naples. He made several unsuccessful appeals for leniency. In August 1977, while he was hospitalized for cancer treatments, his wife, probably with the assistance of others, had him taken to Stuttgart, his home, where he died the following year. His Roman adventure was over.

1996-1998: SS Captain Erich Priebke and SS Major Karl Hass Trials

SS Captain Erich Priebke, Kappler's list-reading assistant at the Ardeatine Caves massacre, escaped trial as a co-defendant with Kappler by finding refuge in a monastery in Rimini and then taking a ship from Genoa to Argentina. There, he enjoyed a quiet and uneventful life for almost 50 years as proprieter of the Vienna Delicatessen in Bariloche. He traveled with his family to New York, Paris, and Rome on a German passport. Other war criminals who found refuge in South America using the same system included Adolph Eichmann, Joseph Mengele, and Klaus Barbie. B. Murphy, *The Butcher of Lyon* (1983); A.A. Ryan, *Klaus Barbie and the U.S. Government* (1983).

Priebke was discovered by TV newsman Sam Donaldson, who approached him in Bariloche and encouraged him to relate his wartime experiences. Discussing the Ardeatine Caves massacre, Priebke said, "We did what they ordered us. It was not a crime." Priebke was extradited to Italy. In May 1996, after a three-month trial in which civil parties representing the victims appeared as plaintiffs, the Military Tribunal of Rome found Priebke "guilty but not punishable." The court ordered his immediate release because he had obeyed a superior order. Italians were outraged. Public protest included a siege of the courthouse, and the mayor turned off the lights on the city's monuments. It was a dark night in Rome. www.answers.com/topic/erich-priebke (2007).

Priebke's luck ran out. The Supreme Court of Cassation cancelled the verdict, stating that two members of the tribunal were biased. A second trial was ordered before a military tribunal. This time, SS Major Karl Hass testified. He became the prosecution's star witness. After the war, Hass worked for the Americans as a spy. He was living in Switzerland when prosecutors found him as a result of a remark Priebke made during the Donaldson telecast. Hass went to Rome to testify under a grant of immunity, but he changed his mind. He was either attempting suicide or trying to flee when he fell from his hotel balcony. He survived. Hass testified from his hospital bed but lost his immunity.

244

Hass had excellent credentials. He had been Kappler's intelligence chief, and both he and Priebke admitted killing two men each in the Ardeatine Caves. In Kappler's trial, the court had concluded that the five extra men were killed in the massacre because of a counting error. This implicated Priebke, the list-keeper. Hass told the court what happened.

"At the Ardeatine, Priebke was there with the copy of the list. He got the people down [off the trucks] and cancelled out their names. At a certain point, one of the prisoners was not on Priebke's list. At the end, in fact, there were five extra men. That's when Kappler said, "What do I do with these five? They've seen it all." I don't know if it was Kappler himself or Priebke, or who—I don't believe it was Kappler— . . . I don't know who killed these five people." Katz, *Battle, supra.*

In 1997, the Military Tribunal of Rome followed the Nuremberg trial decision in rejecting the defense of obeying superior orders. The panel defined the Ardeatine Caves massacre as both a war crime and a crime against humanity under international law, punishable by life without parole and not subject to any statute of limitations. The Court of Cassation confirmed the sentence, but a few months later, because of the defendants' advanced age, they were ordered to be held under limited house arrest. Hass returned to a retirement villa in the Swiss Alps. He died at the age of 92. As of December 2006, Priebke was 93 and under house arrest in Italy. *Los Angeles Times* (April 23, 2004); *Los Angeles Times* (December 26, 2006).

Afterword

Many Romans remain unconvinced that the Resistance's action was worth the sacrifice of lives. Some decry it as a Communist plot. "Elena" and "Paolo," the partisans on the scene at Via Rasella, were actually Carla Capponi and her future husband, Rosario Bentivegna. After the war, Capponi served in three legislatures as an MP in the Italian Communist Party. She was a friend of intellectuals, including film director Luchino Visconti. Capponi was awarded a gold medal for bravery. It was never delivered. She and Bentivegna endured death threats. During the Priebke trial, Capponi found herself under investigation when lawyers attempted to have the Via Rasella attack defined as terrorism instead of an act of war. The inquiry soon ended. Capponi defended her role as a freedom fighter in her autobiography, *With a Woman's Heart. London Independent* obituary (December 1, 2000).

When Rome was liberated, Carla Capponi told Robert Katz:

I knew what we could expect: difficult times, maybe miserable times, but now, we would face them with a certainty. The future would not be a place where you could only beat your head against a wall, not a prison of the spirit and the flesh, but a window that had been at last opened looking out on all the world; and anything you wanted was in that open space, waiting for you to begin to fly, the way a child dreams of flying, above a garden, above a cabbage patch, over roses and wisteria. Katz, *Battle, supra.*

17

Massacre at Oradour-
sur-Glane

*Listen to the roar of the German tanks moving up toward
Normandy. . . . Thanks to you, those tanks will not arrive in
time. . . . Look fighter . . . crawling out of oak maquis . . . holding
up one of the foremost armored divisions of the Hitlerian empire—
the Das Reich. . . .*

————André Malraux

On D-Day, June 6, 1944, the German Army's elite 2nd Waffen SS
Panzer Das Reich Division was ordered to move from Montauban
in southwestern France toward Normandy to help smash the Allied invasion. Railroad transport was impossible. Partisans imper-
iled train travel south of the Loire; American and British air power
destroyed rail lines to the north. The only route for this Panzer division was by provincial roads.

Fifteen thousand soldiers, 209 tanks, and 1,400 armored vehi-
cles began their 450 mile trek north. Resistance activity was intense. The SS Das Reich struck back fiercely. Their mission
included taking brutal measures to regain control of the Limousin
and Correze areas of south central France.

On Friday, June 9, 1944, the SS Das Reich struck at the town of Tulle. German soldiers hanged 99 Frenchmen from lampposts, balconies, and trees as a reprisal for killing and mutilating 40 German soldiers.

But the Tulle hangings were only a prelude to the massacre the following day at Oradour-sur-Glane in the Limousin region. This is the story of that tragedy at Oradour and its postwar consequences—an explosion of rage and animosity within France.

The SS Das Reich had a rich military history as one of the German Army's finest fighting units. It fought to the gates of Moscow, where it was involved in "anti-partisan activity"—a euphemism for destroying villages and killing resistants. General Heinz Lammerding, its commander, was decorated twice for his service on the Eastern Front.

But the Red Army decimated the SS Das Reich during vicious fighting in Russia. By March 1944, the SS Das Reich had lost 12,500 of its 15,000 soldiers. The survivors were sent to France. There, the SS Das Reich was recreated. Unlike the halcyon days of 1940 when the Division accepted only what they considered the finest specimens of Aryan perfection, however, the SS Das Reich now included 12 other nationalities. Not surprisingly, the 2,500 survivors of the Russian winter considered themselves superior to the new recruits and to the Wehrmacht garrison soldiers who were stationed in German-occupied towns in France.

Many new recruits had been drafted in Alsace, a French province annexed by Germany in 1940. They were sent to the SS Das Reich training school in East Prussia and then joined the Division at Montauban.

The French Resistance

Standing between SS Das Reich and its destination was the French Resistance. In the French Corsican dialect, the word "maquis" refers to dense scrub and woodland, a good place to hide. By June 1944, maquis had become a slang term meaning outlaw. Members of small bands of resistance fighters in the countryside were called maquisards. The Francaise Travail et Partisans [FTP] was a Communist organization within the maquis.

The resistance movement in France was not always supported by the French people, but it grew as the German offensive in Russia stalled. And the resistance fighters were filled with rekindled fire once the Allied forces landed in Normandy on D-Day, June 6, 1944.

The goal of the maquisards was to delay the German forces bound for Normandy so that the Allied invasion would be successful.

In an "Order of the Day" dated June 9, 1944, the SS Das Reich referred to these partisan bands and the tactics for combating them:

> The guerillas have occupied the area . . . which, until now, has been weakly held by German troops. The maquis who have appeared there have exclusively communistic tendencies. The small number of armée secréte are also Communists and are also to be treated as gangs [banden]. All instructions, orders, etc. should aim to incite the civilian population against these guerilla bands and make our action appear productive. The threat from these gangs can have the most far-reaching consequences if we are unable to instill it into the minds of the population that these men have no national feeling, and to impress upon them that they are nothing more than highway robbers. On the other hand, it is necessary that our own troops behave in such a way that the civilian population is convinced of our good intentions and also of the character of our division as an elite formation.

Among the special instructions, those aimed at the Resistance were:

(e) Persons whose participation in resistance is undoubted will be treated as criminals. It may be a good idea to throw them in irons in the sight of civilian population.

(f) The inhabitants of every community will be assembled together for a count, and will be treated during the process as prisoners.

(i) Executions are to be carried out on the order of regimental or other commanders by hanging, only in such places where guerilla units fight to hold up our troops or commit atrocities (shameful treatment of wounded or dead; use of dumdum bullets, etc.). As a rule, the proportion to be applied is as follows:

for every wounded soldier . . . 3 guerillas
for every dead soldier . . . 10 guerillas

(j) Executions are in no way a public spectacle, but a punitive measure. Troops must therefore be kept at a distance until the order for the execution is carried out. Orders should be given at short notice to detail men for execution squads, and a public announcement should be made. Priests may attend executions and carry out religious functions, provided these are not of a demonstrative character. (This is very important in France).

On June 7, 1944, maquisards of the FTP attacked at Tulle, France, a hilly town of 21,000 in Correze. The maquisards fought fiercely with German garrison defenders, killing more than 50 and executing at least 10 German prisoners. The French tricolor flew over the town until German reinforcements arrived. I. Ousby, *Occupation: The Ordeal of France, 1940–1944* (1988).

Early in the morning of June 9, 1944, a unit of the SS Das Reich burst into Tulle, and the maquisards fled. German soldiers rounded up 3,000 Frenchmen and brought them to the arms factory courtyard. A proclamation was posted:

CITIZENS OF TULLE!

Forty German soldiers have been murdered in the most abominable fashion by the Communist gangs. The peaceful population has submitted to terror. The military authorities wish only for order and tranquility. The loyal population wishes this equally. The appalling and cowardly fashion in which the German soldiers have been killed proves that the instruments of Communist destruction are at work. It is most regrettable that there were also policemen and French Gendarmes who, abandoning their posts, did not follow their orders and made common cause with the Communists. For the maquis and those that help them, there is only one penalty, the hangman's noose. They do not recognize open combat, they have no feelings of honor. 120 Maquis or their accomplices will be hanged. Their bodies will be thrown in the river.

As a warning, for every German soldier wounded, three maquis will in future be hanged. For every German soldier killed, ten maquis squads or an equal number of their accomplices will be hanged. I expect the loyal cooperation of the civil population in fighting the common enemy, the Communist bands.

[signed] The General Commanding the German Troops.

Private Sadi Schneid, an Alsatian, made the following comment about the killing and mutilation of his fellow German Army soldiers at Tulle:

We arranged ourselves in front of the grave, each avoiding the eye of his neighbor because we were all crying silently. Our eighteen-year-old (minus three months) hearts could not restrain the emotion welling in our throats. I don't know if my comrades were praying, but for my part, I saw myself at the bottom of that grave, and if I recited a prayer, I don't know whether it was for my comrades at my feet, or for myself.

We refused to look closely at these bloody corpses. Was it fear of death, or did we refuse to admit to ourselves that Frenchmen could do such a barbaric thing? The German soldiers had always behaved correctly to the French population—why then this fury, to massacre Germans in this fashion? Couldn't they wait for the chance to join a decent war of revenge, with prisoners protected by the Geneva Convention?

Hascha Kurz took me with him to the headquarters of the adjutant who was talking to the company NCOs. It was a matter of finding volunteers to act as hangmen. . . . Execution was to be by hanging, because it was more humiliating than a firing squad. . . . Executioners were chosen from among the pioneer company, composed principally of native Germans with the balance from men of our company who had recently joined us from the Russian front when their units were disbanded. It proved difficult to find enough volunteers. . . . But they were reminded what these Maquisards, these communists, had done to their fellow-countrymen.

M. Hastings, *Das Reich* (1981).

The SS Das Reich's reaction was swift, violent, and final. A macabre selection occurred. The Germans planned to hang 120 Frenchmen, but they had hanged only 99 when they ran out of rope. A plea for mercy by the parish priest or the lack of rope saved 21 Frenchmen from hanging.

Private Schneid saw another Alsatian named Pierre walk away in tears "saying that he could not do that." Schneid was told by a non-commissioned officer, who despised "Franzenkopfe" like himself, "that if I did not have the courage to do some hanging, I could at least act as an escort." So Schneid and 20 other soldiers took positions close to the courtyard of the arms factory.

The next day, June 10, 1944, troops from the Der Führer Regiment of the SS Das Reich Division approached Oradour-sur-Glane, a tranquil town 22 kilometers northwest of Limoges. On this Saturday, the people of Oradour were busy. Shoppers from Limoges had arrived by train to buy farm products. An afternoon distribution of the tobacco ration was scheduled, and school children were gathering for a medical checkup. It seemed the war had passed Oradour by. S. Farmer, *Martyred Village* (1999).

But it had not. In fact, the most notorious atrocity of the Occupation in France was imminent. Major Otto Weidinger of the SS Das Reich later described the events leading to the massacre:

[Major Adolf Diekmann] arrives in an excited state [in Limoges early on June 10] and reports the following: in St. Julien, two French civilians had approached him and told him that a high German official was being held by the Maquisards in Oradour. That day he was to be executed and publically burnt amidst celebrations. The whole population was working with the Maquis, and high-ranking leaders were there at that very moment. At about the same time, the Limoges [leadership] informed the regiment that according to Intelligence from their own local informers, there was a Maquis headquarters in Oradour. Sturmbannführer [Major] Dickmann (spelled Diekmann in some sources) requests permission from the regimental commander to take a company there to free the prisoner.

Major Dickmann, Commander of the 1st Battalion of Der Führer Regiment, thought that the prisoner must be 3rd Battalion Commander, Major Helmut Kämpfe, a close personal friend. Kämpfe had fought on the Russian front, where he received the Knight's Cross. An excellent athlete, he was considered the SS Das Reich's finest soldier.

The Regimental Commander immediately granted permission for the plan, with the admonition that Dickmann must try to capture the maquis leaders. If Kämpfe were not found, he intended to use prisoners to negotiate with the Resistance for Kämpfe's release.

No evidence has ever been found of a maquis headquarters at Oradour. The nearest maquis camp was seven miles away. Dickmann probably acted on incorrect information and made no effort to confirm its accuracy. Hastings, *supra*.

Major Dickmann and Captain Kahn, Commander of the 3rd Company, conferred for almost two hours before the foray into Oradour. Finally, at 1:30 PM, the convoy was ready. One hundred twenty soldiers with two half-tracks, eight trucks, a motorcycle, and Major Dickmann's Citroen 2CV approached Oradour-sur-Glane.

Soon and suddenly, the village would feel the SS Das Reich's full fury.

The *ratissage* began. Entrances were blocked. At 2 PM, 120 soldiers of the SS Das Reich encircled the village. Townspeople and neighboring farmers were rounded up and herded into the Champ de Foire, the village square. The women and children were separated from the men.

The men were forced into a complex of six barns and a coach house where they were killed by machine guns and grenades. The barns and bodies were burned.

At about 3 PM, the women and children were forced into the local church. The windows and doors were closed. Two hours later, two soldiers ran into the church and placed a box of incendiaries on the altar. They lit a long fuse and ran. The box exploded, creating an inferno. The few women and children who were able to escape the flames were shot to death by SS Das Reich soldiers waiting outside.

Yves Rob, one of only six male survivors, told of his ordeal:

> As soon as we got there the Germans made us haul away two carts that stood in the way of the door. Then they forced us at gunpoint to go inside, and four soldiers covered us at gunpoint, and four soldiers covered us with their machine gun. We reckoned this was to keep us from running away. They talked to each other and laughed as they checked their weapons. Five minutes after we had entered the coach house . . . the soldiers began howling and opened fire on us. It was now becoming impossible to breathe, but I found a gap in the wall, quite high up. I slipped through it and hid in the next door barn. There I found four friends—Broussardier, Darthout, Hebras and Borie. I crawled under a pile of straw and beans. Borie and Hebras hid behind a wood pile. Broussardier huddled in a corner. Darthout had four bullet wounds in the legs and was bleeding from all of them. He asked me if there was room for him beside me. We huddled together like brothers and lay listening carefully to every sound from outside.

Id.

By June 11, Oradour was a smoking ruin. Six hundred forty-two people were killed, including 393 from Oradour, 167 from villages and hamlets of the commune, 33 from Limoges, and 25 from other parts of the Haut-Vienne. Neighboring hamlets remained physically intact but lost their young children who had been at the school in Oradour. Mothers who went to town looking for their children died with them. Farmer, *supra*.

Of the approximately 80 residents of Oradour who survived, some were at nearby farms, 28 hid from the roundup and escaped, and 36 had left Oradour on personal errands for the day. One woman, 47-year-old Marguerite Rouffanche, survived by climbing out a church window and hiding in the garden.

Reaction to the massacre was four-pronged. First, the Oberkommando Wehrmacht—the German High Command—was not pleased. Orders were issued for Major Dickmann's court-martial. Field Marshal Erwin Rommel offered to preside over it himself. General Heinz Lammerding evidently acquiesced.

Proceedings began, but Major Dickmann was never relieved of his command as would have been normal procedure. He was killed on June 30, 1944, when he was struck by shrapnel from a British shell in Normandy. Field Marshal Rommel committed suicide in October 1944. The court-martial never took place.

The second prong of reaction to the atrocities was taken by the French government. After the war, the survivors of Oradour demanded justice. Finally, in January 1953, 21 soldiers from Major Dickmann's company were tried in Bordeaux. Six officers and a civil magistrate, le President M. Nussy Saint-Saens, presided over the military tribunal.

Because Alsace had been reclaimed by France after the war, 14 of the German soldiers were now French citizens. Two Alsatians had been in custody since the end of the war, and 12 Alsatians were arrested in 1952. Except for Sergeant Georges-René Boos, all were charged with war crimes. Boos was charged with treason because he was a volunteer.

The Alsatians claimed that they, too, were victims of the Germans. But the law of "collective responsibility" was the law of France, and they had the burden of proving themselves not guilty. The Alsatians argued that the law of collective responsibility should not apply to them and made a motion to sever their case from the prosecution of the German defendants. Theolleyre, *Proces d' après-guerre*. Their motion was denied. On the second day of the proceedings, the civil magistrate became exasperated by the legal arguments concerning the application of the law of collective responsibility, stating:

254

There we have it! That's the whole problem: they pass laws in the parliament and then it's to us, the military court, that they come to suggest ways to avoid applying them.

On January 27, 1953, the National Assembly voted 365 to 238 to exempt Frenchmen from the law of collective responsibility. The next day, the National Assembly abrogated the law entirely.

Meanwhile, trial witnesses testified that after the Germans annexed Alsace, any opposition to their commands would have been fatal to the Alsatians. Then the Alsatian defendants themselves testified.

Sergeant Georges-René Boos tried to exonerate himself by methodically recounting the horrors unleashed by his comrades.

Another Alsatian who testified was Joseph Busch. Busch had been a member of the Hitler Youth. He joined the SS Das Reich in February 1944 and deserted the unit after it arrived in Normandy in June 1944. Here is what he told the tribunal:

A: When we were one kilometer from Oradour, all the officers and NCOs were called forward to Major Dickmann and Captain Kahn, from whom they got instructions.

Q: What instructions?

A: We couldn't hear what was said. But some papers were passed to them.

Q: Then what?

A: My squad drove directly to the market place. We picked up the people we met along the way, and then we helped separate them into groups and stood guard over them. I was there when a group was led off to Descourteaux's barn. We had orders to shoot when Captain Kahn fired his pistol.

Q: And then you fired?

A: Yes, Herr President—three or four times.

Q: You obeyed orders like a machine, like a mechanism that someone else operates?

A: Yes, Herr President.

Q: Then what happened?

A: Well, people fell over.

Q: Yes, but what did you do next?

A: Well, then we threw the timber and brushwood in on top of the people.

Q: Were these people still alive?

255

A: Well, they may have been, Herr President. I didn't pay too close attention. . . . I was not especially interested.

Q: Then you started the fire?

A: Yes, sir, Herr President.

Q: All in accordance with orders?

A: Yes sir, Herr President.

Q: Then what?

A: We were ordered to go to church, where I was placed on guard duty.

Q: Did you see anything there?

A: Yes. Two women came looking for their children. We told them to get out of there, or they'd be shot. But then Sergeant Boos and a German came along. They dragged the women into a barn and shot them.

Hastings, *supra.*

Marguerite Rouffanche, the only survivor to escape from the burning church, also testified. Her courtroom appearance was described in the newspaper *Le Figaro* on February 2, 1953:

> What great writers achieve by the power of art—a stripping away, concision, the power of sober lines and density like marble—Mme. Rouffanche, a peasant of the Limousin, achieves effortlessly . . . a perfectly sober account, and in that, overwhelming, reduced to the essential facts. . . . Since the ordeal has left her very weak, the magistrates, instead of asking her to come forward, draw themselves completely around her chair. She holds herself dignified and austere, dressed in clothes of deepest mourning. . . . Her face under her black hat is white as chalk. She leans her head a little to the right. Her voice, without the least trace of easy sentiment, reaches us clear and implacable. She is Nemesis, calm and inexorable.

Her final words to the court were:

> I ask that justice be done with God's help. I came out alive from the crematory oven. I am the sacred witness from the church. I am the mother who has lost everything.

When the trial began, General Heinz Lammerding was living in the British Occupation Zone in Düsseldorf. He refused to attend. The British would not extradite him, claiming that they extradited Germans for trial in France only when the charge was murder. So

Lammerding was tried in absentia. He was found guilty and sentenced to death. During the trial, Lammerding sent a notarized affidavit exonerating Dickmann's soldiers. The German press assailed Lammerding because he did not appear personally to defend his men.

After the closing arguments on February 12, 1953, the magistrate stated he hoped that the suffering on both sides might become "an element unifying French people who suffered under the same doctrines and the same men." Bitter animosity reigned, however, between the Limousins and the Alsatians. Both thought that they were victims.

The court deliberated for 32 hours before pronouncing sentences. The two officers who gave the orders at Oradour were not present. Dickmann was dead. Kahn had disappeared. The court condemned the highest ranking German at the trial, Sergeant Lenz, to death. Another German soldier who convinced the court that he was not at Oradour on June 10, 1944, was acquitted. The remaining German soldiers were given 10 to 12 years of hard labor.

Of the Alsatian soldiers in SS Das Reich, Sergeant Georges-René Boos, who had volunteered, was sentenced to death for treason. Nine Alsatians were given sentences of five to twelve years at hard labor. Four other Alsatians received sentences of five to eight years.

The third part of the reaction to the massacre occurred after the trial in Alsace, where the bizarre, historical Alsatian zigzag had created a fractious fault line. The newspaper *Nouveau Rhin Francaise*'s headline shouted, "ALSACE DOES NOT ACCEPT THIS SHAMEFUL VERDICT." The mayors of Alsatian towns gathered in Strasbourg and filed silently past the war memorial. Signs proclaiming "WE DO NOT ACCEPT THE VERDICTS" appeared everywhere.

Alsatian reaction was so intense that the French government sought a political solution. Alsatian Deputy Pierre Pflimlin of the National Assembly requested a suspension of the Alsatians' sentences. The request was denied, but the Minister of Defense took parliamentary action to grant amnesty to the Alsatians. The government supported a *loi d'exception,* providing a full and complete amnesty for those who had been "forcibly incorporated into the German armies."

Because the government wanted the amnesty to be seen as a gesture from the entire country, eight deputies proposed it. They represented all political parties except the Communists. Cabinet President René Mayor went to the Palais-Bourbon to begin the debate and to record the vote. He told the Chamber of Deputies, "The mourning and the trials of our diverse provinces should bring us to understand each other, not to tear each other apart."

The amnesty was approved. The vote was 319 for, 211 against, and 83 abstentions. Four days later, the convicted Alsatians were released and returned immediately to Alsace. The German, Lenz, and the Alsatian, Boos—both sentenced to death—were pardoned by the President of France. All prisoners were freed by 1958.

The amnesty triggered the fourth prong of reaction to the atrocities. The sentences, commutations, and releases of the convicted defendants confounded, embittered, and crushed the residents of Oradour. The President of l'Association des Families des Martyrs d'Oradour accused the deputies in the National Assembly of condoning the massacre. In Limoges, 50,000 people marched in protest.

A new Oradour had been constructed alongside the ruins of the old. After the Bordeaux trial and the subsequent commutations, the Croix de Guerre and the Legion d'Honneur that had been given to Oradour were returned in anger to the French government.

The national monument for the victims was shunned by the survivors. Two local monuments replaced it. One listed the names of the 319 deputies who had voted for amnesty. The other documented the names and addresses of the guilty Alsatian SS soldiers. Embittered residents of Limousin did not remove them until 1966.

Afterword

Captain Kahn, who led the Oradour action, lost his right arm and left eye in Normandy. He disappeared in July 1944, but in 1985 was discovered living in Sweden. In an interview, he said that he "had a bad memory." Kahn said that it was out of the question that "anyone had ever been hurt, let alone killed, by the 2nd Waffen SS Das Reich Panzer Division."

Major Helmut Kämpfe, Dickmann's friend, whose probable capture by the maquis near Oradour may have incited the massacre, has never been found.

General Heinz Lammerding returned to Düsseldorf, where he owned an engineering firm. He later migrated to Sweden. In 1965, he sued a German journalist who had written about his participation in the 99 hangings at Tulle. In his libel case, Lammerding blamed the excessive German reaction at Tulle and Oradour on SS Das Reich Majors Kowatsch and Dickmann. In a postwar written statement to his former subordinate Colonel Weidinger, Lammerding insisted that it was necessary to provoke terror among the maquisards, but as to Dickmann leaving "several hundred women and children to burn in the church, . . . it was a crime. I recognize it." Lammerding died of cancer in 1971. Hastings, *supra.*

In 1982, 36 veterans of the SS Das Reich agreed that the 642 deaths at Oradour and the 99 deaths at Tulle were justified.

In 1983, Heinz Barth, a noncommissioned officer who had been at Oradour, was tried in East Berlin for war crimes. He was sentenced to life imprisonment in East Germany. Barth was reported to have said to his recruits, "You're going to see some blood flow today, and we'll find out what the Alsatians are made of." *Id.*

British intelligence knew the exact location of the SS Das Reich on D-Day. According to the Allies' best estimates, the SS Das Reich would arrive in Normandy by June 10, 1944, and would be poised to drive the Allied armies into the sea. But the SS Das Reich was not in Normandy on June 10, 1944.

By the third day of the Allied invasion, Field Marshal Gerd von Rundstedt, the Commanding General, desperately needed the 2nd Waffen SS Das Reich Division's heavy armor. The German High Command War Diary states:

> The Führer ordered the following units to be moved in: . . . 2 SS PZ Div which had been on clearance operations in southern France.
> —Oberkommando Wehrmacht, *War Diary*

The SS Das Reich finally arrived in Normandy on June 13, 1944. After regrouping, it joined the German defense seven days later. In July 1944, the Division was surrounded. American planes attacked it 64 times. The SS Das Reich lost two-thirds of its 15,000 soldiers.

The town of Tulle was not destroyed. SS Das Reich soldiers had hurled the bodies of the 99 hanged men into a pit near the garbage dump. An inconspicuous monument was placed there in 1950. One hundred yards away, a small sign states: "SILENCE: CHAMP DES MARTYRS."

In 1946, France proclaimed Oradour "le village martyr." Near the ruins of the old town, an exhibition tells the story of the tragedy within its historical context. The town itself remains a national memorial. Everything is left in place. You may walk the streets lined with crumbling stone walls and note the rusting remains of ordinary life: a Renault sign, a baker's pan in an empty lot, a sewing machine, a burned-out car, the remains of a baby buggy. *Oradour Centre de la Memoire* (1946).

Madame Marguerite Rouffanche, the only woman who escaped from the church at Oradour-sur-Glane, died in March 1988 at the age of 92. When she died, another survivor asked, "After us, who will remember?" Farmer, *supra*.

18

Exodus
The Trial

Dr. Hautval . . . gave a reply to Dr. Wirths which . . . would live in the jury's memories for many years—a devastating reply.
———Hon. Sir Justice Frederick Horace Lawton

Leon Uris won acclaim for *Exodus,* the novel (1958). And more acclaim for *Exodus,* the film. But the most dramatic conflict unfolded in Exodus, the trial.

At Auschwitz-Birkenau, the Nazis' extermination factory, millions were killed in accordance with Nazi racial theories. Doctors selected who would live and who would die. A program was created to perform experimental surgeries on healthy inmates. The goal was to find a method to sterilize vast numbers of Jews.

The horrors of Auschwitz were described in *Exodus,* which chronicled the creation of Israel. Throughout the work, Uris named several of the *Schutzstaffel* (SS) doctors, using close approximations of their real names. A sentence on page 155 referred to the real Dr. Wladyslaw Dering, an Auschwitz prisoner-doctor: "Here in Block X Dr. Wirthe [*sic*] used women as guinea-pigs and Dr. Schumann sterilized by castration and X-ray and Caluberg [*sic*] removed ovaries and Dr. Dehring [sic] performed seventeen thousand 'experiments' in surgery without anesthetic." In 1964, Dering sued Uris in London. *Dering v. Uris and Others*, 2 W.L.R. 1298. He denied the number of surgeries and denied they were done without anesthetic. He claimed he obeyed Nazi SS physicians' orders under threat of death. But Dr. Adelaide Hautval testified that she had refused to obey the SS doctors' orders and had survived. Dr. Hautval was the star witness for the defense.

The SS doctor in charge was Dr. Edward Wirths. Born in a village near Würzburg, Germany, in 1909, Wirths joined the Nazi party in 1933 and applied for admission to the SS a year later. He arrived at Auschwitz-Birkenau in September 1942 and remained until the evacuation of the prison camp in January 1945. R.J. Lifton, *Nazi Doctors* (1986).

SS Dr. Carl Clauberg, referred to as "Caluberg" by Uris, born in 1898, reported to Heinrich Himmler in June 1943: "The method I contrived to achieve the sterilization of the female organs without operation is as good as perfected." The women were housed in Block 10. According to Dering, Clauberg was rumored to be Mrs. Himmler's gynecologist. He said he would try to take Dering from the camp to his private hospital. M. Hill & L.N. Williams, *Auschwitz in England* (1965).

Dr. Horst Schumann, born in 1909, was an SS officer who, dressed in Luftwaffe uniform, observed Dering operating on patients in Block 21. According to Dering, Schumann was experimenting with X-raying the testicles of Jewish prisoners and wanted Dering to remove them surgically afterward so the results of the radiation could be determined.

Dering was the only prisoner-doctor named by Uris. A 61-year-old surgeon from Poland, Dering practiced in London. He sued for libel seeking a judgment to compensate him for the damage to his reputation.

When World War II began in 1939, Dering was living in Warsaw, specializing in gynecology and obstetrics. He joined the Polish resistance movement. In June 1940, he was captured by the Germans and sent to Auschwitz, where he was a prisoner-doctor from August 1940 to January 1944. After the war, he migrated to England. He was placed on the United Nations' war criminal list by Poland, France, and Czechoslovakia. He spent 19 months in Brixton Prison in England while Poland unsuccessfully sought to extradite him. Then, Dering practiced medicine in Africa with the Colonial Medical

Service for ten years. He received the Order of the British Empire (OBE) for his accomplishments. Returning to London, he worked in relative obscurity and enjoyed a comfortable life.

The Issues

Dering sued Uris, the publishers, and the printers. After they apologized and paid 500 pounds, the printers were removed from the suit. The defense admitted the elements required by English libel law to be proved by the plaintiff: that the words were published, referred to the plaintiff, and were defamatory. The defendants pleaded only one defense—"justification"—that the words were true or substantially true.

The defense then had the burden of proving the words were true subject to exceptions, and they set out Particulars of Exceptions, conceding that the paragraph in *Exodus* was wrong in alleging 17,000 "experiments" but maintaining that the doctor had performed a very large number. They did not allege the operations were performed entirely without anesthetic but did allege that they were performed under a painful spinal anesthetic that left the patient entirely conscious. They corrected the location, from Block 10 to Block 21. They stated they might use a defense under section 5 of the Defamation Act and denied any injury to Dering's reputation. Hill & Williams, *supra*.

Because the defense had the burden of going forward with the evidence, Dering could sit back and watch. But the impact on the jury of the defense presenting its story first could be dangerous, so the plaintiff's lawyer, Peter Colin Duncan, decided to put Dering on the stand. Damages must be considered.

The Trial

Justice Lawton (Sir Frederick Horace Lawton) presided over the trial in the High Court of Justice, Queen's Bench Division, between Wladyslaw Alexander Dering, plaintiff, and Leon Uris, second defendant, which began on April 13, 1964. The evidence on behalf of Dering was given by seven witnesses including Polish fellow prisoners, an expert witness, and Dering himself. The defense presented 22 witnesses. Testimony was given by eight women who had been given ovariectomies, six men whose testicles had been removed at Auschwitz, expert witnesses, and fellow prisoner-doctors including the final witness, Dr. Hautval. The defense also produced an Auschwitz Prison Hospital register, a prized possession of the

263

Polish government. In it, Dering had recorded all the surgeries performed each day. Among the entries were 130 operations for which he was listed as surgeon or assistant, which the defense would present as "experimental." Forty-six entries were in Dering's handwriting.

Duncan opened for the plaintiff. He told the jury to think of the ordinary meaning of the words describing Dering in *Exodus*—they would think Dering a monster. The defense had decreased the number of surgeries and other allegations, but Duncan claimed that it is no defense to plead that words are true and then give particulars that they are not true. He said the only question was, "What is the proper sum to award as damages?"

Dering was the first witness. In discussing the oath, he said he was a Christian and a Roman Catholic. He testified that when he was taken to Auschwitz, he worked at first as a laborer. Later, he was made a prisoner-doctor and put in charge of the operating theater. Dering said that he was punished by not being allowed to leave the camp for two weeks when he refused to administer a phenol injection. SS Dr. Schumann told him he was carrying out experiments on the sexual glands of men and women by X-ray and wanted Dering to remove the X-rayed ovaries and testicles. Dering testified his first response was, "It is not an essential indication if they are not suffering from anything, and I don't think we as doctors could do these things." Schumann replied, "Don't you think I can do with prisoners what I like?" Dering said he talked to colleagues and concluded that it would be "stupidity" to refuse because the X-rayed glands were dead or could be presumed dead and if "we did not help, not only would we not save them but we ourselves would be in danger." He claimed the spinal injections were proper to prevent pain.

Dering testified that he was removed from Auschwitz to Clauberg's hospital in January 1944 and remained a prisoner, although later he was allowed to attend church and the cinema.

Cross-Examination

Lord Gardiner, representing the defense, began the cross-examination by questioning Dering about his castration of healthy men. Dering answered that he could not refuse and that if he had not done the surgery, it would have been done by an unskilled SS corporal. When asked whether he knew that Schumann was engaged in experiments to see how people could be sterilized in large numbers, Dering replied, "It was mine and my colleagues' guess why these silly experiments were carried on." But he said he could not stop them.

After Dering defended his use of spinal injections and his removal of irradiated testicles, Gardiner inquired, "Do you remember Dr. Hautval—a Frenchwoman, a very religious Frenchwoman, not a Jew?" Dering denied knowing her. Gardiner continued, "She says, you see, that in May, . . . she asked you about the operations which SS Dr. Wirths was doing, and you said you thought they could be dangerous for the women."

Gardiner asked about Dr. Samuel, a Jewish prisoner-doctor. Dering denied knowing that Samuel had removed irradiated ovaries under a general anesthetic, but he knew Samuel had been sent to the gas chamber by the Germans. "Presumably he was arrogant and he knew too much and he started one quarrel as with doctors—" Lord Gardiner interrupted, "I suggest—and I will hand you a copy—that you wrote a letter, and the view you express in it was not that he knew too much, but that he was 'old and useless and covered with eczema.'" Dering: "That is right."

In replying to Gardiner about how many experimental surgeries he admitted performing for SS Dr. Schumann, Dering referred to the registry and then said, "As far as I can remember, checking by the entries in my handwriting, eighty-five with colleagues. How many by myself I must check again. Not more than thirty-three. We had to assist German doctors."

An English anesthetist, Dr. Christopher Hewer, testified for the plaintiff, justifying the use of a spinal anesthetic if pre-medication was given first. He was cross-examined by Gardiner, who asked him whether the failure to administer general anesthetic would show a lack of humanity if the patient saw the removal of his testicle in the reflection of the operating lamp. Hewer explained that bandaging the eyes could be a simple method of avoiding that problem. Hill & Williams, *supra*.

The Defense

Lord Gardiner addressed the jury. He said that Dering claimed that the gist or substance of the words of which he complained was untrue and that it was a case for very large damages. The defendants said the gist was true and the circumstances called for damages that would be "the smallest coin of the realm."

Gardiner acknowledged the conditions in Auschwitz and that

Dering was a prisoner-doctor under Nazi domination. He told the jury that Dering was invaluable to the Nazis. They competed for his services. He was their best surgeon and an excellent administrator.

Gardiner insisted that a murderer was a murderer if he killed only one person. The number of experimental surgeries, 17,000, was copied from another book, and the source may have been Dr. Brewda (a Jewish fellow prisoner-doctor), who misunderstood when Dering said he performed 17,000 operations. He admitted that the paragraph stating the operations were done without anesthetic was wrong. The meaning of the words was a matter for the jury. He attacked the idea that removing the irradiated testicles was necessary and said the testicle was removed so it could be determined whether it was dead.

Then there was the prison register. It contained names, so a search had been made throughout the world. The defense witnesses would include victims and prisoner-doctors: Dr. Kleinova, Dr. Brewda—and Dr. Hautval, a woman of courage and character. The jury might value her evidence because she had taken part in one or two experimental operations and then refused to take part in more. Gardiner pointed out that a big part of Dering's case was that if a prisoner-doctor refused, he would be shot or sent to the gas chamber, even though Dering also told the jury that, apart from an old man who became useless, no prisoner-doctor was sent to the gas chamber after a certain time. Hautval had refused, and she was alive. Hill & Williams, *supra*.

Evidence for the Defense

Gardiner called an impressive array of victims, including Greek Jewish girls who testified of their ordeal. Ten had their ovaries irradiated and then were moved to Block 21, where Dering removed the ovaries. They were given painful spinal injections. During the surgery, Dr. Brewda stood behind their heads, comforting them. The second woman remembered a girl, Bella, who died the night after the operation, and Marta, who had been operated on twice. Another patient, Buena, "screamed very much and was taken out of the room and I never saw her again." The women were asked whether they later had children. They did not.

Professor William Charles Wallace Nixon, an expert on anesthesia, testified. Gardiner asked him about Dering's claims that if he did not do the surgeries, someone less qualified would and that there was medical benefit from removing the testicles. Nixon explained that for research purposes, removal of a testicle or ovary would have to be done by a competent person. The operation would be more risky because of the X-ray, which would reduce the blood supply to the radiated area and increase the possibility of infection or delay in healing.

The judge asked Nixon about the moral question: What would he have done in this case? He replied that whatever the risk, it would be completely contrary to his practice to comply with orders for this procedure. He cited the Hippocratic Oath; a person who submitted to an experiment must be able to make a choice. Nixon said, "If I had to perform such a mutilating operation unnecessarily, the guilt would remain with me the rest of my life."

As to the plaintiff's assertion that radiation might cause malignant results, Nixon made a distinction between X-ray radiation and radiation inserted locally. He had never known cancer to be caused by external radiation.

Dr. Adelaide Hautval

Born New Year's Day 1906, the youngest of seven children, Adelaide Hautval was known as Heidi. Her father was a Protestant pastor in Hohwald in the Rhine basin. After graduating from medical school in Strasbourg in 1934, she began practicing in hospitals and neuropsychiatric institutes in Strasbourg and Switzerland.

When Germany defeated France in June 1940, France was divided between Vichy France, ostensibly neutral, and the northern and western parts of the country that remained under German military occupation. Hautval lived in Vichy France. Her mother lived in the German Occupation Zone. When her mother died in 1942, Hautval sought a permit from German authorities to attend the funeral; it was refused. Hautval, determined to attend, crossed the demarcation line in April and was arrested at Vierzon. She was incarcerated at Bourges. While awaiting trial, she saw Jewish prisoners being mistreated. Hautval, who spoke German, protested, "They are human beings just like we are." An SS officer, aghast, stated, "From now on, you shall be treated like the Jews. Because you defend them, you can share their lot." Hautval was ordered to sew a yellow patch on her clothing. She wore a band labeled "ami des Juifs." This was her badge of honor. Hill & Williams, supra; C. Delbo, *Convoy to Auschwitz* (1965).

Hautval was sent to prison camps in Pithiviers, Beaune-la-Rolande, Romainville, Orléans, and Compiègne. Finally, on January

24, 1943, Hautval and 229 other French women were sent by train to Auschwitz, arriving three days later. Placed in Block 10, she became number 31802. Hautval remained in Auschwitz-Birkenau until August 2, 1944, when she was moved to Ravensbruck, and was liberated on April 30, 1945. Hautval stayed on to care for patients too ill to be transported and finally was repatriated to France on June 25, 1945. Delbo, *supra.*

Hautval was the last witness. Here is her testimony:

Hautval: I also had a conversation with Dr. Eduard Wirths who said that I was to help Dr. Clauberg with his work. Dr. Wirths asked me my opinion on sterilization, and I answered that I was absolutely opposed to it.

Lord Gardiner: What did he say?

Hautval: He was surprised that a doctor practicing psychiatry could find a bad method which was a selection to preserve the race. I answered that it was arguable, and also that it necessarily brought abuse. He talked to me about the Jewish questions, and I answered that we had no right to dispose of the life and destiny of others.

Lord Gardiner: Did you ever take part in any of Clauberg's experiments?

Hautval: No.

Lord Gardiner: As a result you were shot?

Hautval: No.

Lord Gardiner: Were you punished in any way?

Hautval: No, not in any way.

After she refused to do experimental surgeries with Wirths, Dr. Samuel asked Hautval to give a general anesthetic to a 17-year-old Greek girl for an ovariectomy. She did so, and then she told him she would not give another. Samuel, a prisoner-doctor, reported Hautval to Wirths for refusing to assist in these operations. He was the old man later sent by the SS to the gas chamber. Hill & Williams, *supra.*

Lord Gardiner: What happened after you refused?

Hautval: He denounced me to Dr. Wirths. Dr. Wirths called me to ask me whether it was true that I refused. I said it was true. He asked why, and I said it was contrary to my conception as a doctor.

Lord Gardiner: What did he say to that?

Hautval: He asked me: "Cannot you see that these people are different from you?" and I answered him that there were several other people different from me, starting with him!

This answer was later described by Justice Lawton as a devastating reply that he expected "would live in the jury's memories for many years."

Lord Gardiner: I shall not ask you again whether you were shot. Did Dr. Wirths say anything further?

Hautval: He said nothing. I remained in the block until the beginning of August, looking after patients. Then I was taken back to Birkenau, where I was advised to keep myself in hiding for a few weeks.

Lord Gardiner: Were you ever in fact punished at all?

Hautval: Never.

Dering's barrister, Duncan, then began his cross-examination of Hautval. She testified that her illness at Birkenau resulted from the deplorable environment, which was often fatal. Hautval said that when Wirths gave her an opportunity to perform gynecology, she became suspicious because "in that moment when I asked him he never gave me any explanation" and she had already heard about SS Dr. Clauberg's sterilization experiments. Duncan's cross-examination continued. Hill & Williams, *supra.*

Duncan: He, of course, was an SS officer?

Hautval: Yes; he was dressed in SS uniform. I agreed to go.

Duncan: I suppose you were somewhat afraid of Wirths?

Hautval: No, I don't think so, because I could have refused.

Duncan: And that is why you hid some of those with typhus on the top floor—because you thought that if you did not, they would probably be sent to the gas chamber?

Hautval: Exactly.

Duncan: You knew, of course, that if you were found doing that, you would get into serious trouble?

Hautval: It was an attitude that we all felt in the camp, and it [was] nothing special.

Duncan: It was an everyday occurrence for people to be punished, was it not?

Hautval: Yes, it was sufficient to smoke a cigarette.

Duncan: So wholly vile was the treatment that you yourself might have been sent to the gas chambers if you had been found out?

Hautval: Everything was possible.

Duncan: Did you know that Dr. Dering had hidden patients in this way?

Hautval: I did not know.

Hautval then said Wirths knew she was a psychiatrist and not a surgeon.

Duncan: Did you know that Dr. Samuel's operation was experimental?

Hautval: Unfortunately, yes.

Duncan: And because you knew he was working under Dr. Wirths's orders you did not refuse to do it.

Hautval: It was not for that reason. It was because I could not react quickly enough, and in that moment I was a little afraid of the consequences. I had just refused to take part in the other experiments and it was difficult for me, taken so suddenly, to refuse this one too.

Duncan: When you did the first operation was the Evipan anesthetic in short supply?

Lord Gardiner: You keep saying, Mr. Duncan, that she "did" the thing. She was merely the anesthetist.

Duncan: I apologize, your Honor. Did you form the view that Dr. Samuel was old and incompetent?

Hautval: Dr. Samuel was about 70. He was a Jew and profoundly aware of the dangerous circumstances in which he found himself.

Hautval thought Samuel had been a very competent doctor. Hautval thought that the anxiety under which Samuel lived had brought on senility and upset his judgment. She knew that the SS would send him to the gas chamber.

Duncan: Unhappily, there was nothing very unusual about that, was there?

Hautval: For a doctor it was unusual.

Duncan: You were a doctor. Apart from what you have told us, were you ever punished either in Birkenau or at Auschwitz?

Hautval: No, I was never punished. I refused afterwards to carry out [experiments] for Dr. Mengele, and they said, "We cannot force her to do what she does not want to do."

270

Duncan: Who was Dr. Mengele?

Hautval: He was a doctor at Birkenau who made selections with unheard-of cruelty and carried out experiments "of the worst kind" on Jewish twins.

Hautval said that when she was sent back to Birkenau, she was told by an SS doctor to "let the grass grow." "The idea was that I should not show myself so much so that I would not arouse their fury." She did not hide, but she did not work as a doctor.

Summing Up

After the final arguments, Justice Lawton began his summation. He told the jury their first task was to decide what the words meant. (Under section 5 of the Defamation Act of 1952, in respect of words containing two or more distinct charges against the plaintiff, a defense of justification shall not fail by reason only that the truth of every charge is not proved, if the words not proved true do not materially injure the plaintiff's reputation, having regard to the truth of the remaining charges.) Each charge was regarded as a "sting."

The judge explained that Duncan said the only sting of the libel was that "Our Dr. Dering is one of the Nazi fiends, and he must be a monster." Gardiner, whose defense needed two stings in order to prevail, said the first sting related to "experiments in surgery" and the second was experiments done "without anesthetic."

Justice Lawton, after reviewing the evidence, said that Dering's reasons for performing the experimental surgeries were that he would likely suffer injury if he did not perform them, that someone less qualified would have done them, and that it was possible the irradiated ovaries and testicles might later cause injury to the patients if they were not removed. The judge told the jury that Dering's defense should be looked at factually first, and then morally.

Factually, Lord Gardiner said the Germans needed doctors to sustain the labor supply and would not have killed Dering. Dr. Lorska in Block 10 had avoided doing any operations. Justice Lawton commented on Adelaide Hautval:

> Then there was Dr. Hautval—perhaps one of the most impressive and courageous women who has ever given evidence in the courts of this country, a most outstanding and distinguished person—and they knew what happened to her. She

271

had stood up to the Nazis four times, and made it quite clear at an early stage what she was prepared to do. As a result of the stand she made, she found herself summoned by Dr. Wirths; and she gave a reply to Dr. Wirths which his Lordship expected would live in the jury's memories for many years—a devastating reply; and then she had been told by an SS doctor to "let the grass grow" and he said, "I won't punish you." Then she found herself appointed as assistant to another beastly fellow carrying out experiments on Jewish twins; and once again she refused—and this character apparently said to someone standing by, "If she won't, she won't." So the jury were asked to infer that if Dr. Dering had stood up, nothing would have happened to him. The jury must consider what an ordinary, reasonable doctor would have expected to happen in 1943.

On the moral side, Justice Lawton continued, in relation to some acts, you could say you were in fear of your life. But we had always said that fear was no excuse for murder; and probably English judges would say it was no excuse for doing really serious injury.

The judge summarized the points on both sides and told the jury it was up to them to do what was fair, just, and reasonable.

Verdict

On May 6, 1964, at 11:55 AM, the case went to the jury. At 2:30 PM, they returned with a verdict:

Associate: Are you all agreed on your verdict?
Foreman: We are.
Associate: Do you find for the plaintiff or for the defendants?
Foreman: One ha'penny.
Associate: And that is the verdict for all?
Foreman: Yes.

Although the verdict was in favor of Dering, the damages awarded were the "lowest coin of the realm."

Afterword

SS Dr. Edward Wirths surrendered to a British intelligence unit in September 1945. A British officer greeted him, saying, "Now, I've shaken hands with a man who . . . bears responsibility for the death of four million human beings." Wirths hanged himself that night. He was cut down but died three days later. Before his death

272

Wirths wrote, "I tried, according to my Christian belief, to help the sick prisoners." Danuta Czech, *Kalendarium der Ereignisse im Konzentrationslager Auschwitz-Birkenau 1939-1945*; Lifton, *supra*.

SS Dr. Horst Schumann lived in the German federal republic until after 1950 without being criminally charged and then practiced in various African countries including Ghana. He was deprived of his doctorate, but efforts to extradite him for war crimes were unsuccessful. Hill & Williams, *supra*.

SS Dr. Carl Clauberg was imprisoned by Soviet authorities in 1945. He was returned to the German Federal Republic in 1955. He died in 1957 while awaiting trial for war crimes. *Id*.

SS Dr. Josef Mengele left Auschwitz shortly before the Red Army liberated it on January 27, 1945. Mengele went to Mauthausen; when that concentration camp was liberated on May 5, he disappeared, reappearing four years later in Buenos Aires, Argentina, with the records of his experiments on twins. The West German foreign ministry issued a warrant for his arrest in 1959 and sought his extradition in 1960. Mengele escaped again and spent the rest of his life in Paraguay and Brazil. On February 7, 1979, he drowned in a lake near Embu, Brazil. The world first learned of his death in 1985. *Encyclopedia of the Holocaust*; CNN, Feb 7, 2003, broadcast; *L.A. Times*, Mar. 25, 2003.

France decorated Adelaide Hautval with the Legion of Honor in December 1945 for "her devotion to her comrades in the camps of Auschwitz and Ravensbruck." Delbo, *supra*.

In Jerusalem on May 18, 1953, the Israeli Knesset passed the Yad Vashem Law creating the Holocaust Martyrs and Heroes Remembrance Authority. The law commemorated the six million Jews killed by the Nazis. Also commemorated were those "who had risked their lives in order to save Jews." On April 17, 1965, Adelaide Hautval was honored as one of the "righteous among the nations."

19

Zigzag
The Sinking of the
USS Indianapolis

War never suffers a shortage of tragedy. The toll of lives taken by the sinking of the USS *Indianapolis* increased dramatically when the Navy failed to search for survivors. Then came the general court-martial of Captain Charles B. McVay III, filled with failure and loyalty, surprises and secrecy. At the end, there was only loss.

On July 16, 1945, the U.S. Navy heavy cruiser *Indianapolis* left San Francisco with a secret cargo. Commanded by Captain McVay and with a crew of 1,196, the *Indianapolis* sped in record time to the Pacific island of Tinian. She arrived on July 26 and delivered a canister of uranium 235 and a large crate containing integral components of "Little Boy," the first atomic bomb. World War II would end less than a month later. S. Howarth, *To Shining Sea* (1999); D. Stanton, *In Harm's Way* (2001).

By then, the *Indianapolis* had been destroyed by a Japanese submarine. Although almost 900 crew members survived, only 316 were still alive after the rescue. In "the worst sea disaster in the history of the U.S. Navy," according to Congress, the men spent "four and one-half days adrift in the open sea, the remainder having perished from battle wounds, drowning, predatory shark attacks, and lack of food and potable water." Rescue was delayed because the Navy did not know the ship was missing. *Congressional Resolution* (2000).

The *Indianapolis* had won ten battle stars, but the cruiser, commissioned in 1932, was not considered safe by Admiral Raymond A. Spruance, who remarked that "her metracentric height was less than one foot and if she ever took a clean torpedo, she would capsize in short order." After serving as Spruance's flagship in the Iwo Jima campaign, she was hit by a Kamikaze suicide plane in March 1945 during the battle for Okinawa, and underwent repairs in California. S.E. Morison, *History of U.S. Naval Operations in World War II, Victory in the Pacific* (1960); B.M. Petty, *Voices from the Pacific War: Bluejackets Remember* (2004); Spruance, *Letter to Morison* (December 25, 1959).

Captain McVay, known as "Charlie," was a handsome 1920 Naval Academy graduate and admiral's son. He became skipper of the *Indianapolis* in November 1944. McVay was considered "an amiable, popular and competent officer," and the *Indianapolis* had been a "happy" ship. Morison, *supra*.

With the Tinian mission completed, the *Indianapolis* proceeded to Guam, where McVay received routing orders. On July 28, the ship started a 1,300-mile run on Code Route Peddie to Leyte. She was scheduled to arrive at 11:00 AM, July 31. The port director at Guam informed Rear Admiral Lynde D. McCormick that the *Indianapolis* was en route to train with his unit at Leyte Gulf before joining the massive fleet gathering for the invasion of Japan. The port director also notified the commander, Philippines Sea Frontier, and the port director at Tacloban in the Philippines.

The message to McCormick was garbled after it arrived at his flagship, so when another dispatch informed him when the *Indianapolis* would arrive, McCormick did not know why. Rear Admiral Jesse B. Oldendorf, in charge of the task force, knew why the ship was coming but never saw a second dispatch from CinCPAC (Commander in Chief, Pacific Fleet Headquarters) informing him of when. R.B. Lech, *All the Drowned Sailors* (1982).

At Guam, McVay had asked about an escort but was told it was not needed. In rear areas, warships were expected to be self-sufficient. Without a destroyer's sonic gear, the cruiser depended on radar and watch crews to detect enemy submarines. Tactical orders required ships to zigzag in conditions of good visibility. California lawyer Philip H. Simon, who served as a USN lieutenant on the destroyer USS *Case* in WW II, explains that when ships zigzagged, they varied the time, duration, and length of each course deviation to confuse the enemy. McVay's instructions were to use this evasive action "at discretion." P. Simon, *Oral Statement* (2006).

On Sunday, July 29, with cloud cover hindering visibility, McVay ordered the zigzagging stopped after twilight. In the sultry tropics, the ship was not "buttoned up"—some bulkheads, hatches, and ducts remained open to provide cooler air. Around 11:00 PM, McVay went to his emergency cabin behind the bridge. Standing orders stated he was to be notified if the weather changed. "In case of doubt" there was a voice tube next to his bunk. Press Release, Dep't of Navy (Feb. 23, 1946), Lech, *supra*.

The risk of submarine attack, according to later testimony by Captain Oliver F. Naquin, surface operations officer, commander, Marianas, was reported as "very slight." This was not true. Although McVay had been told of two unconfirmed submarine sightings within 100 miles of the route, he was not informed of the sinking of the USS *Underhill*, a destroyer escort, on July 24 by a Japanese *kaiten*, a human suicide torpedo, with the loss of 112 crew members.

More important, McVay was not cautioned about data produced by a code-breaking system known as ULTRA that alerted naval intelligence to the presence of four Japanese submarines of the Tamon group, including I-58, in the area. Although this vital message was passed down the chain of command from Pearl Harbor to Captain Naquin, he did not provide the information to Lieutenant Waldron, the routing officer at Guam. Its classification as "ultra-secret" meant the source was not to be divulged, but Naquin could have alerted Waldron of the danger. ULTRA was not declassified until the 1990s. Morison, *supra*; D. Kurzman, *Fatal Voyage* (1990); R.W. Love Jr., *History of the US Navy*, vol. 2, (1992); R.F. Newcomb, *Abandon Ship!* (2001).

By chance, as McVay was going to sleep, Imperial Japanese Navy Commander Mochitsura Hashimoto woke from his sleep on submarine I-58 and ordered it to emerge. Through his binoculars, he saw "a black spot clearly visible on the horizon on the rays of the moon." He ordered the sub to dive and kept his eye "glued to the periscope" as the "black spot" became a large warship. "We've got her," he thought.

Six torpedoes were readied. Hashimoto decided to keep his *kaitens* in reserve. At 1,500 meters, he gave the order "Stand by. Fire!" and waited anxiously. "Every minute seemed an age . . . then by the after turret there rose columns of water, to be followed immediately by flashes of bright red flame." He shouted, "A hit, a hit!" M. Hashimoto, *Sunk, A History of the Imperial Japanese Navy in World War II* (1954).

At 12:14 AM, the *Indianapolis* reeled as she was struck by two torpedoes, the first of which hit starboard and blew about 65 feet of the bow into the air. The second struck near midships next to a fuel tank and a powder magazine. The ship was cut almost in half and became a fierce fireball. She tilted upright before plunging down into the water. At 12:26 AM, the *Indianapolis* disappeared. Trapped, approximately 300 crewmen burned to death. Others leaped into the oily water. Many had no life jackets. Stanton, *supra*.

At sunrise Monday, July 30, a deadly ordeal began, and each day, conditions deteriorated. Clusters of men were spread over several miles. The largest group, 300 to 400 men, did not have a raft or floater net. Swimmers without life vests paddled frantically. Lieutenant Lewis Haynes, M.D., Lieutenant Thomas Conway, the chaplain, and USMC Captain Edward Parke gave advice and provided life jackets for the living that had been removed from the dead. Conway and Parke, exhausted, died. L. Haynes, *Oral History*, http://history.navy.mil/faqs/faq30=1.htm (1995).

Swept off the ship, McVay gathered eight crewmen on rafts he found and rationed Spam, crackers, and malted milk tablets. On a distant raft, USMC Private First Class Giles McCoy and Robert Brundige, S1GM, competed to outlive each other while their companions lay unconscious. Brundige later said: "We would've rode to hell with Captain McVay." After the war, McCoy formed a survivors' organization that supported McVay's actions. Stanton, *supra*.

Sharks attacked on Tuesday. After 40 hours in the water, only about 600 men were still alive. Thirst was becoming unbearable. Those who gave in and swallowed seawater died. By Wednesday morning, some were hallucinating. Haynes's crazed swimmers began stabbing each other. In ten minutes, about 50 were killed. Mirages of hotels beneath the water tempted many to dive down for a fatal drink.

Rescue

It was not until Thursday, August 2, at 8:15 AM—after 84 hours in the water—that the survivors were accidentally discovered by Lieutenant Wilbur C. "Chuck" Gwinn. He had left the pilot seat of a Navy Ventura patrol plane to go secure a flapping whip antenna and he saw an oil slick. Assuming it came from a Japanese submarine, he prepared for a bombing run; he had not heard of any missing American ship. Suddenly, he saw heads bobbing in the water. Gwinn radioed the first report of the disaster to the search and reconnaissance headquarters at Peleliu. Survivors were drenched with oil, exhausted, parched, hungry, delirious, sun-blinded, and near death.

Gwinn saw four scattered clusters including Haynes's swimmers but missed the distant rafts of McVay and McCoy. He sent a message to Lieutenant George Atteberry, his superior officer. Knowing Gwinn's fuel was limited, Atteberry ordered a Ventura bomber from his own squadron with a crew of four to head to the site; they arrived at 2:15 PM. Suddenly another plane appeared. Lieutenant Adrian Marks, a young Indiana lawyer, had read Gwinn's message and taken off from Peleliu in an amphibious plane, a Catalina. During his flight, a call came over the radio from a destroyer escort, the USS *Cecil J. Doyle*.

When Lieutenant Commander Graham Claytor, a lawyer who had clerked for Supreme Court Justice Louis Brandeis, learned of the emergency from Marks, he turned his ship around without permission and sailed toward the survivors. Marks arrived and decided with his crew to make an open sea landing. By nightfall, they had rescued 58 men. Claytor on the *Doyle* arrived at 11:45 PM and began transferring them. Claytor sent a dispatch early on Friday, August 3, notifying the Navy of the loss of the *Indianapolis*.

Urgent messages were sent. At PSF surface operations, Captain Alfred Granum, operations officer at Tolusa, was not aware of an overdue ship. Granum called Lieutenant Stewart Gibson, port director operations office at Tacloban, 20 miles away. Gibson had misinterpreted an order and had not reported the ship's non-arrival. Stanton, *supra*; Kurzman, *supra*.

On Guam, Vice-Admiral George Murray also learned of the sinking. He ordered two destroyers to the scene. Finally alert to the magnitude of the tragedy, the Navy converged in one of the greatest sea rescues in naval history. Morison, *supra*; J. Rohwer & G. Hummelchen, *Chronology of the War at Sea, 1939–1945* (1992); Kurzman, *supra*; Press Release, Dep't of Navy, *supra*.

That afternoon, PSF commanded its port director to report all combatant ships that were five hours overdue. CinCPAC ordered: "All ships with 500 or more total personnel on board shall be provided with an escort between Ulithi and Leyte regardless of speed." Lech, *supra*.

The atomic bomb, with components delivered by the *Indianapolis*, was dropped on Hiroshima on August 6. The war ended on August 14. The next day, joyful headlines proclaimed the news. Below the front-page fold of the *New York Times* was an article, declassified at last, of the loss of the *Indianapolis*. Stanton, *supra*; S. Weintraub, *The Last Great Victory* (1995).

Inquiry

McVay faced another ordeal. Fleet Admiral Chester W. Nimitz immediately organized a three-member board of inquiry on Guam. They listened to 43 witnesses from August 13 to 20, but this inquiry was not made public for more than 30 years. The board's opinion stated that Naquin's testimony of "practically negligible" submarine activity was correct. Naquin did not disclose the ULTRA warning. The board recommended that McVay be tried by a general court-martial for culpable inefficiency and negligently endangering lives. S.E. Smith, *The United States Navy in World War II* (1966); Lech, *supra*.

Nimitz objected. On September 6, 1945, he wrote to the Judge Advocate General of the Navy:

> The Commander-in-Chief, US Pacific Fleet, does not agree with the court in its recommendation that Captain Charles B. McVay III, US Navy, be brought to trial by general court-martial. . . . His failure to order a zigzag course was an error in judgment, but not of such nature as to constitute gross negligence. Therefore, a Letter of Reprimand will be addressed to Captain McVay in lieu of a general court-martial.

The officers who should have known the *Indianapolis* had not arrived at Leyte, Temporary Commander, PSF, Commodore Norman Gillette, and Operations Officer Granum, were given Letters of Reprimand. Lieutenant Commander Jules Sancho, acting port director at Tacloban, received a Letter of Admonition. Lieutenant Gibson received a Letter of Reprimand for failing to investigate the non-arrival of the ship. Gibson's order had directed that arrival reports were not needed for combatant ships, so he believed non-arrival reports also were not necessary. Nimitz now clarified the order.

Admiral McCormick was told to reprimand his personnel for failing to ask for a repeat of the garbled message. McCormick said he "assumed" the cruiser had been delayed at Guam or diverted to another command. Hashimoto had sent a radio report to Tokyo claiming he had sunk a "destroyer" and giving the latitude and longitude. The Navy received copies. No air search was ordered. Morison, *supra*; Lech, *supra*; Stanton, *supra*.

Nimitz's superior, Chief of Naval Operations Fleet Admiral Ernest J. King, insisted on McVay's general court-martial. He wrote to secretary of the Navy James V. Forrestal on September 25:

> I cannot agree with the opinion of Commander-in-Chief, US Pacific Fleet Nimitz, that the failure of Captain McVay to order a zigzag course was an error in judgment. . . . I recommend that the Secretary of the Navy direct the following action: Captain Charles B. McVay be brought to trial by general court-martial in accordance with recommendation 1.A of the Court of Inquiry.

Forrestal faced a dilemma with his admirals. He considered another investigation but finally agreed with King. Although McVay was stoic, his father was not. Admiral McVay was a stern man who valued his family's reputation. The first Charles McVay had financially supported the Naval Academy after the Civil War. Admiral McVay had commanded the Asiatic fleet during World War I. Now, the admiral was incensed and told a grandson that years before, when King served under his command, King and other officers had sneaked a woman aboard a ship. The admiral had called for a Letter of Reprimand to be placed on King's record. On November 12, Forrestal reluctantly ordered that a general court-martial of McVay should proceed without delay. Kurzman, *supra*; Morison, *supra*; Lech, *supra*; Newcomb, *supra*.

Naval historian Samuel Eliot Morison has analogized McVay's plight to the trial and execution of Admiral John Byng, Royal Navy, who failed to defeat the French at Minorca in 1757, stimulating Voltaire to observe that in England, "It is found good, from time to time, to kill one admiral to encourage the others." Morison, *supra*; Voltaire, *Candide* (1759).

Court-Martial

McVay's general court-martial began in the Washington Navy Yard on December 3, 1945. Before a judicial panel of seven naval officers, McVay pleaded not guilty to Charge I: Through Negligence Suffering a Vessel of the Navy to be hazarded, with the

specification of failing to zigzag; and to Charge II: Culpable Inefficiency in the Performance of Duty, with the specification of failure
to order the vessel to be timely abandoned.

Captain Thomas J. Ryan Jr., a highly decorated Navy lawyer and
judge advocate, was the prosecutor. He had been McVay's Annapolis classmate. Captain John P. Cady, an Annapolis graduate and
lawyer, represented McVay. When the court convened, Cady attacked the court's jurisdiction, claiming McVay's discretionary decision not to zigzag was not an actionable offense. His objection was
overruled, and 57 witnesses began testifying the following day.

Following are excerpts concerning moonlight and zigzagging.
Lieutenant Joseph Waldron, the port director routing officer at
Guam, was the first prosecution witness.

Ryan: Was the question of zigzagging discussed with McVay?
Waldron: [It was] discussed with the navigator, and indication
was made that the ship should zigzag at the commanding officer's discretion.

The cross-examination proceeded as follows:

Cady: What was your reply to Captain McVay's request for an
escort from Captain Naquin's office?
Waldron: The reply was, "Escort not needed by the *Indianapolis.*"
Cady: Were the enemy contacts shown in the intelligence brief
as given . . . greater in number or about as usual?
Waldron: They were about normal; on the average of three or
four a week.
Cady: Did they indicate to you any excessive enemy submarine
activity?
Waldron: No, sir, they didn't.
Cady: I take it that, in your opinion, at the time of your discussion with Captain McVay, the passage from Guam to be
routed according to your instructions was a perfectly normal
and routine situation.
Waldron: At the time, it was routine.

Ryan brought in an astronomer, Gerald Clemence, who said: "If
the sky were perfectly clear, the moonlight would be approximately one-fourth that of a full moon." Ryan called Michael J. Bar-
rett, in charge of Forrestal's correspondence, to introduce a copy
of a letter dated August 12 from McVay to Forrestal, which read:

"There was intermittent moonlight, and at times the visibility was unlimited." Lieutenant Charles B. McKissick, who took the 6:00 PM watch on the *Indianapolis*, was Ryan's witness.

> *Ryan:* As officer of the deck on the night of the sinking, did you receive any orders while you were on watch?
>
> *McKissick:* Yes, sir. I received orders from the captain the latter part of my watch that at the end of evening twilight we would cease zigzagging and resume base course.

In cross-examination, Cady asked: "Did you question the orders . . . to stop zigzagging at the time they were given to you?"

> *McKissick:* No, sir. I did not question the orders . . . I didn't feel like it was anything unusual. . . . At the time I came off watch, there was no moon. The visibility was very poor. It was a very dark night. . . . At times . . . it was impossible to recognize men that were standing five to ten feet of you [but] at other times the visibility seemed to be better.
>
> *Cady:* Was it customary on the ship to cease zigzagging after evening twilight?
>
> *McKissick:* Well, yes, sir, it was customary, if the visibility was poor . . . ; we did it all during the war.
>
> *Cady:* Can you testify whether or not the standing orders contained any instructions to the officer of the deck to notify the captain in case of any change in weather conditions, visibility or not?
>
> *McKissick:* I can testify definitely that those instructions were in the standing night orders. . . . I had no hesitation . . . in notifying the captain of such events. . . . It was my practice. We received dispatches all through the war much to the same effect. When any of [the submarines] were that far away, we didn't feel unduly alarmed at such a report.

Lieutenant Richard Redmayne, chief engineer on the *Indianapolis*, had just left the bridge when the ship was attacked. He was the only surviving officer of the final bridge watches. Of the 82 officers on board, only 15 survived. Ryan started his examination: "What was the weather on the night of July 29?"

> *Redmayne:* It was intermittent moonlight, with the visibility good when the clouds weren't in front of the moon.

The cross-examination continued:

Cady: Did it appear to you that you should have been zigzag-ging?
Redmayne: No, sir.

Promoted to Lieutenant Commander, Dr. Haynes, the chief medical officer, was the next witness to be cross-examined.

Cady: What were the conditions of visibility?
Haynes: I didn't notice; I believe it was very dark . . . I would like to say that under Captain McVay's command, the *Indianapolis* was a very efficient, trim, fighting ship, and I would be honored and pleased to serve under him again.

Giles McCoy, the marine who had waged the contest of survival on his raft, was questioned about the moonlight.

Ryan: Did you ever have, during this period from the explosions and when you were going over the side, any occasion to notice the weather or visibility conditions?
McCoy: Yes, sir. When I was going over the side . . . I guess the clouds just cleared the moon, and it was bright.

Ensign Harlan Twible was on duty when the *Indianapolis* was hit.

Twible: When I had gone on watch, it was quite light, but later on in the evening it got so dark that I had to request that the gun captain inform me if there was a man on the shield looking out over the sea, and . . . when it came time for me to be relieved and my relief didn't get up there, I couldn't tell whether it was one man or two.
Cady: Did you see any moon that night on watch?
Twible: I can't recall that I did. . . . There were breaks in the clouds, because I can definitely remember seeing the moon after I got into the water, but I could say that the sky was heavily overcast.
Cady: Were you able to see the horizon?
Twible: No, sir, I wasn't.

Captain Naquin, who had not shared the ULTRA data at Guam, did not reveal it now. The naval inspector general (NIG) had conducted an investigation, quizzing everyone including Naquin. In this secret record, Naquin a few days earlier had admitted to knowing of the four submarines. McVay and Cady evidently were

284

given the transcripts, but Cady did not confront Naquin. Lech, *supra*.

Cady: Why did the *Indianapolis* sail from Guam without escort?

Ryan: Objection to this line of questioning on the ground that such testimony was incompetent, irrelevant, immaterial, and was not germane to the issues in this case.

Court: Objection sustained!

Cady: What was your estimate of the risk of enemy submarine activity along the Peddie route?

Naquin: I would say that it was a low order . . . my estimate is that the risk was very slight. . . .

The court [intervening]: Had not submarines been reported in the area?

Naquin: There were literally dozens of [reports by merchant shippers], but the actual submarine activity against us was at a very low ebb.

Cady: Was there at any time any question in your mind of diverting the *Indianapolis* after she sailed?

Naquin: There was not.

Ryan asked Captain Granum about submarine danger between Guam and Leyte Gulf. Granum replied that there was "no more than a normal hazard that could be expected in wartime."

In cross-examination, Cady pushed: "Was there ever any actual confirmation of the presence of an enemy submarine in the Philippine Sea Frontier at about this time along the Peddie route?" Granum replied, "In this area, no." Questioned a month earlier by NIG, Granum admitted knowing of the sinking of the *Underhill* and said that he was "especially concerned" with the enemy submarine presence at that time. Cady did not challenge Granum.

A public clamor erupted when it was revealed that Commander Hashimoto had been flown from Japan to testify about the American ship he had destroyed. He was Ryan's witness, but his testimony supported McVay. Hashimoto spoke in Japanese with an interpreter translating his answers. At a pretrial interview, he had told Ryan that zigzagging would not have made a difference. In cross-examination, Cady established that Hashimoto had been unable to determine whether the target was zigzagging when it was first sighted, and that he saw no significant changes in its course when he later observed it. Cady did not ask Hashimoto about the visibility, which Hashimoto had told him in the preliminary interview was poor except in the direction of the moon.

> *Cady:* Would it have made any difference to you if the target had been zigzagging on this attack?
>
> *Interpreter:* It would have involved no change in the method of firing the torpedoes, but some changes in the maneuvering.

It was an extraordinary moment. McVay's wartime enemy had testified on his behalf. Kurzman, *supra*; Newcomb, *supra*.

Cady called Captain Glynn Robert Donaho, a 1924 Annapolis graduate and recipient of four Navy Crosses, two Silver Stars, and two Bronze Stars, as an expert witness for McVay. Donaho, a submarine commander, had damaged and sunk 28 Japanese ships that totaled 200,000 tons. He testified that zigzagging would not have saved the *Indianapolis*.

> *Cady:* Based on your experience, what is your opinion of the value of zigzagging of a target as affecting the accuracy of torpedo fire?
>
> *Donaho:* With our modern submarines, fire-control equipment, high-speed torpedoes, a well-trained control party, and with torpedo spreads, I didn't think that zigzagging affected the results.
>
> *Ryan* cross-examined: Now, assuming that [a] target was making seventeen knots [and changing course by 45 degrees] and that you feel that you could not come to the surface and chase, when do you think you would have had another chance to fire at this target?
>
> *Donaho:* It takes five seconds to make an observation, and about five seconds for the integration to take effect, and I could have fired within ten seconds.
>
> *Ryan:* Now . . . we have assumed that this target makes a change of course of 45 degrees. Assuming that that had been away from you, would your spread have been as likely to hit as if it had not turned?
>
> *Donaho:* Yes, sir.
>
> *Ryan:* Is it a reasonable inference from what you have just said that zigzagging as an antisubmarine measure is of no value to surface ships?
>
> *Donaho:* On the contrary, you always expect a target to zig, and you anticipate what is going to happen on the next leg. I have

personally found that a target not zigzagging would have confused me.

McVay, over Ryan's objections, stated the situation of the *Indianapolis* and asked whether, if Donaho had contact by periscope for about 27 minutes, zigzagging would have made a difference.

Donaho: Not as long as I could see the target for 27 minutes.

Ryan showed Donaho the Navy's secret zigzag plan.

Ryan: Would that have made any difference?
Donaho: No.

Then McVay asked one more question: "Is it disconcerting to you as a submarine commander to have a ship, a target, zigzag?"

Donaho: Yes, because just before firing, a zigzag throws your calculations off, and you have to get a new setup.

McVay's question was a drastic mistake, but despite this answer, Donaho's testimony generally helped his defense. McVay took the stand on the final day of the trial.

Cady: Did you give any instructions regarding zigzagging to the officer of the deck before turning in?
McVay: I did not. The conditions were such that I did not believe that zigzagging was necessary. Visibility was poor. There was no moon. . . . I had in my standing orders the conditions under which the ship should zigzag, though I did not specifically have in there to start zigzagging when . . . the visibility was good. . . . I got no impression [in Guam] of any unusual conditions in the area. . . . I considered the supervisor and officer of the deck . . . that night competent officers, and I believe that if conditions had been such as to require them to zigzag, they would have done so and informed me.
Cady: Then your doctrine as laid out in your standing night orders had been demonstrated effective; is that correct?
McVay: That is correct.
Cady: Did you see any moonlight after the explosion?
McVay: No, sir, I did not. In fact, it was so dark on the bridge I couldn't recognize anybody.

Cady asked McVay to explain his admission in a prior inconsistent statement contained in the August 12 letter to Forrestal, introduced by Ryan, in which McVay had described "intermittent moonlight."

McVay: I submitted the letter under some duress—in a hurry. I described the visibility after I was in the water.

Result

The trial ended on December 19, 1945. On January 7, 1946, the Navy Department office of the chief of naval operations Washington issued the NIG's Final Report. The Facts Section, Routing Instructions 8, stated that evidence had been received about at least four Japanese submarines in the area on offensive missions. "The responsibility for not passing on this information . . . appears to lay with Captain Naquin. . . ." The report concluded: "The failure of Captain Naquin prevented the information from reaching the routing officer and Captain McVay. It may be considered a contributory cause to the loss of the *Indianapolis.*"

The report also concluded, however, that McVay "failed to exercise due diligence . . . by his failure to zigzag at night during partial moonlight and good visibility." It noted that he might have been "lulled into a false sense of security through lack of intelligence of enemy submarine activity, which message was on board the *Indianapolis.* . . ." No details were given. Obviously, the ULTRA message was not sent, and none of the shore officers testified to sending a warning.

The report criticized the failure of communication which delayed the rescue effort. That responsibility extended "from the Commander-in-Chief, Pacific . . . and into the bureaus of the Navy Department."

On February 20, 1946, Forrestal approved the court-martial panel's decision. McVay was acquitted of the abandonment charge but found guilty of the zigzag charge. He was sentenced to lose 100 numbers in his temporary grade of captain and 100 numbers in his permanent grade of commander. The panel and Ryan recommended clemency.

Three days later, the Navy Department issued a press release at a news conference held by the new Chief of Naval Operations Admiral Nimitz. "Narrative of the Circumstances of the Loss of the USS *Indianapolis*" omitted two paragraphs that had been in the first draft submitted by Vice Admiral Forrest Sherman to his superiors three days before publication. The first had stated that the secret intelligence about the four submarines on offensive missions known to Captain Naquin was not passed down to the operation officer or routing officer at Guam. This paragraph concluded: "For this failure, Captain Naquin has been held responsible."

The second omitted paragraph had confirmed that McVay was not informed of the four submarines—but a new paragraph had been inserted that stated McVay visited the Office of the Port Director, Guam and that the navigator obtained routing instructions with information of possible submarines along the route. The press was given the final version. Lech, *supra*.

After Navy Department review, Forrestal remitted McVay's sentence and restored him to duty. Forrestal cited McVay's combat duty; his awarding of the Expeditionary, China Service, Silver Star, and Purple Heart medals; and the unanimous recommendation of clemency by the court. McVay's career was over. When he retired from the Navy in June 1949, he received a "tombstone" promotion to rear admiral. This increased his pension allotment. But his conviction remained. Morison, *supra*; Kurzman, *supra*; Newcomb, *supra*.

No one will ever know whether zigzagging might have prevented the sinking of the *Indianapolis* once it appeared on the horizon alone in the intermittent moonlight. McVay accepted the court-martial decision without complaint. Continuing to receive correspondence from embittered relatives of injured and deceased members of the *Indianapolis* crew, he grew more despondent. On November 6, 1968, one day after opening another vituperative letter, he committed suicide outside his home in Litchfield, Connecticut. The 70-year-old McVay shot himself in the head with his Navy-issue .38 caliber revolver.

Afterword

The Letters of Reprimand and Admonition which were given to the shore officers were later withdrawn by Secretary of the Navy Forrestal, leaving their military records unblemished. Naquin was never censured. He later became a rear admiral and died at age 85 in 1989. Forrestal became the first secretary of defense. He resigned because of illness and committed suicide in 1949.

Giles McCoy, a Missouri osteopath, organized the first survivors reunion in 1960 in Indianapolis. McVay attended, worried about his welcome, but the men saluted and cheered. They swarmed around Gwinn, thankful that he had spotted them in the water. They called him their "angel" and made him an honorary member of their organization.

In 1974, Hashimoto was the captain of a merchant ship bound for America with a cargo of automobiles when his ship struck a Liberian freighter in Japan's Inland Sea. Several crew members were killed. A court found him negligent, and he was forced to resign. He became a Shinto priest in Kyoto. On December 7, 1990, *Indianapolis* survivors met Hashimoto at Pearl Harbor. He said: "I came here to pray with you for your shipmates whose deaths I caused." Giles McCoy replied, "I forgive you." Stanton, *supra.*

In 1999, Hashimoto wrote to Senator John Warner, chairman of the Senate Armed Services Committee, concerning pending legislation to exonerate McVay: "I have met many of your brave men who survived the sinking of the *Indianapolis*. I would like to join them in urging that your national legislature clear their captain's name." Hashimoto died in 2000 at age 91. Kurzman, *supra*; www.ussindianapolis.org.

After McVay's death, the *Indianapolis* Survivors Organization worked diligently to restore McVay's reputation. Hunter Scott, an 11-year-old from Pensacola, Florida, impressed by Quint, the shark hunter who mentioned the *Indianapolis* in the movie *Jaws*, wrote about the disaster for a sixth grade history fair. Scott's project helped draw media attention and support from Florida Congressman Joe Scarborough. Senator Bob Smith and Senator John Warner joined the effort to pass a congressional resolution vindicating McVay. It was signed by President William Clinton in 2000. Paul Murphy, firecontrolman third class on the *Indianapolis* and Survivors Organization chair, said: "We feel as though Congress whitewashed things a little bit, but at least it has been recognized that Captain McVay was wrongfully accused."

In July 2001, Senator Smith persuaded Secretary of the Navy Gordon R. England to direct the Navy Department to amend McVay's naval record to exonerate him of any wrongdoing in the loss of the *Indianapolis* and the lives of those who died. The general court-martial conviction remains. No verdict of a general court-martial has been overturned in U.S. military history. www.ussindianapolis.org.

The Survivors Organization remains active, but age is depleting its numbers. On December 31, 2005, Murphy e-mailed: "There are 89 survivors still living today, all in their 80s and 90s, several in very poor health."

"Nine cruisers had been lost in battle during the war, several under questionable circumstances, but not a single commanding officer had been court-martialed. For the other 436 combatant vessels lost, not a single court-martial resulted," wrote Richard F. Newcomb, *supra*. As to McVay's court-martial: "Never, at least for a century, had the United States Navy subjected a commanding officer to a general court-martial for losing his ship to enemy action," observed S.E. Morison. Morison, *supra*.

This chapter is dedicated to Lieutenant William A. Aitken, aviator, USN, WW II, and Lieutenant William J. Aitken, RN, aboard three ships torpedoed, WW I.

SECTION VI

The Prejudice Trials

Abigail Adams famously wrote to her husband in 1776, "In the new code of laws, I desire you would remember the ladies and be more generous and favorable to them than your ancestors." The ladies were not remembered. Women could not vote until the Nineteenth Amendment to the Constitution was ratified in 1920.

Constitutional amendments ending slavery were passed after the Civil War. Prejudice continued. Whistler and Joyce wanted artistic freedom. Oscar Wilde went to jail. Henry Ford promoted anti-Semitism, but Rosa Parks became a symbol of the civil rights movement.

20

Schumann v. Wieck
The Battle for Clara

The love story of Clara and Robert Schumann has become a musical legend: Robert, the dashing composer, and Clara, the brilliant pianist, overcame the objections of her controlling father to enter an idyllic if ill-fated marriage.

Reality is somewhat more complicated. Robert Schumann, early in his career, wanted to marry the young Clara Wieck. Clara was torn between her love for Robert and her loyalty to her father, Friedrich Wieck, a highly regarded piano teacher and an acquaintance of Beethoven. Wieck had early recognized Clara's talent and had devoted himself to establishing her as a superstar.

Robert and Clara were married in 1840, but not before an acrimonious trial pitted Robert against Wieck, in a struggle with Clara as the prize.

The background was nineteenth-century Leipzig in Saxony, a male-dominated society in which Wieck was notable for his encouragement of Clara to compose music as well as to play the piano. This was in an era when the father of composer Felix Mendelssohn's talented sister, Fanny, wrote to her on her twenty-third birthday, "You must . . . prepare more earnestly and eagerly for your real calling, the only calling of a young woman—I mean the state of a housewife." N. Reich, *Women's Philharmonic* CD, Notes.

This was also the era in which *Neue Zeitshrift für Musik (New Review for Music)*, a journal of which Robert was the editor, commented that Clara's music did not really merit a review "since we are dealing with the work of a woman." P. Ostwald, *Schumann, The Inner Voices of a Musical Genius* (1985).

After Clara's parents divorced, her father retained custody. He began her piano training when she was five years old. Clara was nine when she made her debut at the Leipzig Gewandhaus in 1828, the same year she met Robert Schumann. He was 18 and studying with her father.

By 1835 Clara was acclaimed throughout Europe as a phenomenally gifted child prodigy. Her admirers included Goethe, Mendelssohn, Chopin, and Paganini. That year, Clara and Robert exchanged their first kiss. Although Clara was only 16, Robert assumed her father would give them his blessing. He did not.

Wieck, who had watched Robert's fickle passions and unstable mood swings, wanted to spare Clara from disappointment. Moreover, he had seen other young women with promising careers give them up under the pressure of combining marriage and career. He worried that Robert would squander Clara's money. He disliked Robert's indulgence in drink. Most of all, he was unwilling to lose control of his creation, his amazingly talented daughter, the flower of Europe.

Wieck took Clara to Dresden in 1836 to isolate her and to intercept Robert's letters. His action, of course, drew the lovers together. Clara smuggled a letter to Robert planning a meeting in Dresden. He wrote to Clara expressing his love. Wieck, discovering the meeting, told Clara he would shoot Robert if he ever approached her again. He wrote an enraged letter to Robert that marked the beginning of a four-year battle over Clara.

No word passed between Clara and Robert for more than a year. Then Wieck announced that at Clara's next Leipzig concert, a month before her eighteenth birthday, she would play three variations from Robert's symphonic etudes.

Robert wrote to her on the day of the concert, August 13, 1837, and proposed marriage. The next day, she accepted. On her birthday, Robert wrote to Wieck, asking for his friendship and consent. Wieck refused both and arranged a concert tour for Clara to Dresden, Prague, and Vienna. "Am I not a weak girl?" she wrote to

Robert. "I have promised my father to be happy and for a few years yet to live for art and for the world."

In Vienna, Clara won enormous acclaim. By royal edict, she was given the honorary title of "imperial concert pianist." A Viennese pastry was named after her. A poem written by Austria's leading dramatic poet, Franz Grillparzer, was called "Clara Wieck and Beethoven" and immortalized the performance of an 18-year-old girl. J. Bowers & J. Tick, eds., *Women Making Music* (1986).

The struggle continued. Clara was unable to defy her father. Robert was depressed by the situation and by his relative failure to succeed financially. He warned Clara that he was suffering from "mental illness" and needed to be dealt with protectively.

Clara was in Paris in 1839 on a tour Wieck had planned as the climax of his and Clara's career. He had sent her with her nanny for a six-month stay, hoping to demonstrate her need for his help. She triumphed alone.

But Wieck continued to cause trouble. Clara learned of her father's secret correspondence with Robert, in which her father demanded a list of conditions for his consent to her marriage, including withholding from Clara the money she had earned, her renunciation of her father's estate, and legal certification of Robert's income. R. Taylor, *Robert Schumann, His Life and Work* (1982).

Although Robert remained her lifelong love, Clara was still reluctant to give up her ties to her father—and to his teaching. "Do you know what I long for, above all else? A music lesson from my father . . . ," she said in a letter to Robert on June 27, 1839. B. Harding, *Concerto, the Story of Clara Schumann* (1962).

Robert saw this as a danger signal. He insisted Clara decide: They would part forever, or she would allow him to apply for legal consent to marry before she became of age. Clara agreed to marriage and, after consulting with a French attorney, M. Adolphe Delapalm, signed an affidavit that Robert had prepared. Robert gave the affidavit to his lawyer in Leipzig, Herr Wilhelm Einert, with the suggestion he attempt an out-of-court settlement. If that failed, Robert told Einert to file a complaint against Wieck in the Saxony trial court seeking a court order granting legal permission for him to marry Clara.

On July 16, 1839, Robert filed a complaint against Wieck. What follows here is a chronology of the legal proceedings of this extraordinary trial as outlined in S. Sadie, ed., *The New Grove Dictionary of Music and Musicians* (1980), and the Ostwald and Taylor books mentioned above. Whoever won the trial would determine Clara's future.

Three days after the filing, the court ordered the parties to discuss arbitration. In August 1839, Clara returned to Leipzig. Pursuant to a court order, Archdeacon Rudolf Fischer made two attempts to effect an arbitration. Wieck did not appear at the first session, and he was late for the second. He stated he would never agree to the marriage.

On September 17, Wieck tried to reach a settlement in the Leipzig court. His demands were exorbitant: Clara would forfeit her earnings for the prior seven years and receive a settlement of two-thirds of Robert's capital. The proposal was refused. Next, the case came before the Court of Appeal of Saxony. Wieck did not appear at preliminary hearings to determine whether there was a chance of a mutually acceptable solution.

In October, Wieck failed to appear for the official hearing but claimed that, because he had not attended the meeting of the conciliation tribunal in September, the proceeding had never taken place. Einert, presenting Robert and Clara's case, pointed out how dishonest that claim was. The hearing was continued to mid-December. Robert's health declined. He fell into a depression and did no creative work.

On December 14, 1839, Wieck filed another verbose appeal unassisted by counsel. This stalled the proceedings. Again, he failed to appear. The court was asked two questions: Do Clara and Robert have sufficient assets for a successful marriage, and do they have the personal capacity for a happy union?

Wieck, who had observed Robert for 10 years, stated the following: Robert could not support himself; had squandered his inheritance; had "made a mess of his work as editor of *Neue Zeitshrift für Musik*; was "lazy, unreliable and conceited"; drank excessively; and was a mediocre composer whose music was "unclear and almost impossible to perform."

Wieck attacked Clara, claiming she was untrained to be a housewife and had unrealistic expectations about the support Robert could provide. He also stated that her career would suffer if she traveled with Robert, who "was incompetent, childish, unmanly, in short totally lost for any social adjustment"; could not "speak coherently or write legibly"; would "always get in her way"; and would insist that Clara give music lessons, which she was unsuited to do. N. Reich, *Clara Schumann, the Artist and the Woman* (1985).

On December 18, 1839, the parties again appeared in court. Wieck lost control. The president of the court silenced him. Judgment was set for January 4, 1840. In the meantime, Clara and Robert spent Christmas with Clara's mother in Berlin. On January 4, 1840, the court dismissed Wieck's charges, except for the charge of alcoholism.

On January 26, Wieck filed a legal disputation. He also privately distributed lithographed copies of his original charges to the couple's friends. He circulated printed copies of his legal testimony in every city where Clara was scheduled to play.

On January 31, Robert sought to strengthen his position by conferring with Dr. G.A. Keferstein about receiving a Doctor of Philosophy degree from the University of Jena without an examination or thesis because of his achievements as composer, writer, and editor.

On February 13, Felix Mendelssohn agreed to testify for Robert and Clara. Robert filed a refutation that included the following items: an assertion that he could support Clara; a listing of his assets (12,688 thalers—actually, he was exaggerating, because he included 4,000 thalers Clara had saved); a submission of a letter from Wieck praising Robert's character and inviting him to be the godfather of Wieck's daughter Cecilie; and a claim that Wieck had been one of his drinking friends. (He asked the court to reserve his right to sue Wieck for defamation of character and did, successfully, a year later. Wieck was sentenced to 18 days in prison. There is no evidence that Wieck ever served this sentence.)

Several weeks later, Robert submitted a letter from Baron von Fricken that stated, "Is old Wieck still so stiff-necked? What could have caused him to become so angry with you? Before 1834, he was so excited about you and, so to speak, brought up his daughter for you." Robert also submitted the degree he had now received from the University of Jena.

On March 28, the High Court of Appeal of Saxony confirmed the January 4, 1840, judgment. Wieck had the burden of proof to show that Robert was a heavy drinker but on July 7 failed to produce evidence of this. On August 1, legal consent to the marriage was granted by the court. Ten days later, Wieck's allotted time to file an appeal expired. Robert and Clara were free to marry, and marriage banns were published on August 16.

Clara and Robert were married in the village church at Schonfeld near Leipzig on September 12, 1840, one day before Clara's

21st birthday. Clara confided in her diary, "A new life now begins, a beautiful life, a life wrapped up in him whom I love above all things and above myself."

Afterword

The Schumanns made peace with Wieck. On December 15, 1843, Wieck wrote to Robert, assuring the composer of his respect for his talent and fine achievements.

Early in their marriage, Robert and Clara studied music and literature together. Clara inspired Robert to compose a torrent of brilliant piano pieces and lieder. These vocal compositions featured the poems of Goethe, Heine, Byron, and Burns. According to Harold Schonberg, "Fantasiestücke," Schumann's great work for solo piano, is one of the pieces upon which all romantic piano music rests. His piano works are exuberant, poetic, introspective, grand, and intimate. And, although he achieved success in many musical forms, the 16 songs of "Dichterliebe" rank with Schubert's "Winterreise" as the finest of the song cycles. D. Aitken, *The Faust Legend in Romantic Song* (1981).

Wieck was correct in predicting that Clara would have difficulty maintaining her artistry. Robert needed quiet while he composed, so it was difficult for her to practice. He accompanied her on a trip to Russia but found it difficult to be merely Clara's husband. Tours were arranged for Clara because money was tight, but she was often unable to complete them because of pregnancies. She gave birth to eight children, seven of whom survived infancy. Clara accepted her new role. She believed that a composer was more important than an interpreter. Robert's needs came first.

By 1853, Clara was composing again. On Robert's forty-third birthday, she presented him with her new work. "The first songs I have written for seven years and three piano pieces," she recorded in her diary. "Robert was pleased with them."

Then, tragedy struck. Robert, long suffering from periods of depression, attempted suicide in 1854 and was confined to an asylum at Endenich because of mental illness. He died there in 1856.

With the help of close family friend Johannes Brahms, 14 years her junior, Clara pulled herself together, farmed out the children, and began to tour. She prospered and enjoyed a successful career that spanned more than 50 years. Clara had played the first performance of Robert's Piano Concerto in A minor at the Leipzig Gewandhaus on January 1, 1846, and she continued to be Robert's greatest promoter. Her concerts prominently featured works by him and by Brahms.

As a pianist, Clara Schumann was indisputably of the highest rank. According to *The New Grove Dictionary*, she was considered the most important "classical" pianist of the nineteenth century. H.C. Schonberg, *The Great Pianist* (1963). Her talent was held to rival that of Chopin and Liszt. Clara's compositions, including "Trois Romances," "Sonata in G Minor," "Variations on a Theme of Robert Schumann," "Romance in A Minor," and "Soirées Musicales," are currently available on CD.

Clara's friend Fanny Mendelssohn was finally permitted to appear in public as a pianist at a Berlin charity concert in 1838, and two books of her songs were subsequently published. In 1842, during a visit to Buckingham Palace by Fanny's brother, Felix, the young Queen Victoria sang "Italy," a song not by Felix but Fanny—one of the numbers written by his sister that Felix had incorporated into his published works. When he explained the situation, the queen and her consort looked considerably surprised.

Felix always insisted that Fanny was his superior as a pianist. Critic Henry F. Chorley heard her play in a family matinee and said that if she had been born poor and had to earn her living, she would have become as great a pianist as Clara Wieck Schumann. H. Kupferberg, *The Mendelssohns* (1972).

Friedrich Wieck's long life ended October 6, 1873, at the age of 88. He never found another student with Clara's brilliance. Clara wrote in her diary after her father's death, "Although we disagreed on many points, this could never affect my love for him, a love which all my life long has been heightened by gratitude." *The New Grove Dictionary, supra.*

Clara died in 1896. Johannes Brahms, who had loved and admired Clara for more than 40 years, died in 1897.

Tip: A great, bad 1947 movie, *Song of Love*, starring Katharine Hepburn as Clara, Paul Henreid as Schumann, and Robert Walker as Brahms is worth a search on MGM/UA Turner Home Video.

21

Whistler v. Ruskin
A Question of Art

Art: What is it? In 1877, the American artist James McNeill Whistler thought he knew. He exhibited a painting titled "Nocturne in Black and Gold: The Falling Rocket" with other Whistler paintings in London's Grosvenor Gallery. John Ruskin, England's preeminent art critic and a professor of fine arts at Oxford, thought he knew. Not impressed by Whistler's "Nocturne in Black and Gold: The Falling Rocket," he wrote, "The ill educated conceit of the artist so nearly approaches the aspect of willful imposture. I have seen and heard much of cockney impudence before now, but never expected to hear a coxcomb ask two hundred guineas for flinging a pot of paint into the public's face." R. Anderson & A. Koval, *Whistler, Beyond the Myth* (1995). Whistler bristled and sued.

Whistler was born in Lowell, Massachusetts, in 1834 and raised in tsarist Russia. Following a family tradition, he entered the United States Military Academy at West Point in 1851. After failing a chemistry course, he was discharged. Later, he commented, "If silicon had been a gas, I would have been a general." Anderson & Koval, *supra.*

In 1855, he went to Paris to paint. The artistic world he entered was a cauldron of new and imaginative ideas. Whistler, a friend and admirer of Monet, Manet, Degas, and Cézanne, became famous as an artist who created both impressionistic and abstract paintings. He was an expatriate in London.

Ruskin was the self-acknowledged champion of traditional and representational English painting of the Victorian age. He extolled the Pre-Raphaelite movement, a retreat to a mystical, romantic medievalism predating the geometric perspective of Raphael. J. Mass, *Victorian Painters* (1984). The trial, although legally a libel action, marked a clash between two artistic visions.

Whistler believed in artistic freedom. He named his abstractions of twilight scenes *nocturnes*. His portraits were *arrangements* and *harmonies*. His work helped clear the way for contemporary art. He viewed the trial as a forum. Moreover, Ruskin's charges that Whistler's work was sloppy and overpriced sharply curtailed Whistler's income.

On August 4, 1878, Whistler filed a notice of action for libel against Ruskin. Avoiding a trial by apology or compromise was out of the question. "It is war to the knife between them." *Irish Times*, November 1878. Whistler demanded general damages of £1,000 and costs.

Ruskin fired back: This was his opportunity to declare his artistic philosophy. He wrote to Edward Burne-Jones, "It's mere nuts and nectar to me, answering for myself in Court. It will enable me to assert some principles of art economy which may get sent all over the world vividly in a newspaper or two." Anderson & Koval, *supra*. Ruskin believed that art should have a moral purpose, that it should be carefully crafted, and that it should be finished. In his opinion, art should appeal entirely to the eye, not to the imagination.

Both parties petitioned for a special jury and shared the cost. At the time, special jurors could only be males who owned property of a certain value, who had graduated from Oxford or Cambridge, or who held a comparable pedigree. Serjeant John Parry and William Petheram represented Whistler. The judge was Sir John Huddleson, addressed as Baron Huddleson. Sir John Holker, Q.C., and Charles Bowen represented Ruskin. The trial lasted two days.

Day One. On November 25, 1878, at 10:30 AM, the trial began with great alacrity in the court of Exchequer Chamber in Westminster Hall. American writer Henry James stated,

The London public is never left for many days without a *cause célèbre*. The latest novelty is Mr. James Whistler's suit for damages against Mr. Ruskin. Mr. Whistler's conspicuity, combined with the renown of the defendant and the nature of the case, has made the affair the talk of the moment.

H. James, *The Painter's Eye* (1956).

Although suffering from a breakdown and incapable of testifying, Ruskin seemed unperturbed. He wrote to his American friend Charles Eliot Norton, "I believe the comic Whistler trial is to be decided today." J. Ruskin, *The Works of Ruskin*, Vol. 37 (1919).

The celebrity status of the adversaries and the issue of the new nonrepresentational art made the trial a popular event. Every seat was occupied. The London press—the *Daily News*, the *Globe*, the *Morning Advertiser*, the *Morning Post*, the *Evening Standard*, the *Telegraph*, and *The Times of London*—covered the case. (The following statements and testimony appeared in contemporaneous news accounts and the following sources: G. Fleming, *James Abbott McNeill Whistler: A Life* (1991); Anderson & Koval, *supra*; D. Holden, *Whistler: Landscapes and Seascapes* (1969).

Serjeant Parry opened for Whistler:

Gentlemen of the jury, Mr. Ruskin holds perhaps the highest position in Europe and America as an art critic. It is surprising that he could so traduce someone as to lead him into a court of law to seek damages. And after hearing the case, I think you will conclude that indeed great damage has been done . . . [Whistler] was an untiring worker in his profession . . . [and maintained] an independent position in art . . . Now it may be that his ideas will seem eccentric. But this is no reason to treat him with contempt and ridicule. He should be given the highest respect as a man who has followed his theories with earnestness and enthusiasm and has worked untiringly in his profession . . . There is no doubt that those words [the libelous statement] have been injurious and hurtful. This cannot be considered as privileged, bona fide criticism. To speak of a man as an imposter would not be tolerated elsewhere, so why should it be tolerate[d] here?

Next, Whistler testified:

Petheram: What do you mean when you call a picture a "nocturnal"?

Whistler: I mean to indicate an artistic intent, divested of any outside anecdotal interest. Since these pictures are night pieces, I chose the word "nocturne."

Petheram: What does the "arrangement" mean?

Whistler: It means a planned arrangement of lines and colors.

Petheram: What is your aim in painting a picture?

Whistler: For me a picture is a problem to solve, and I use any incident or object in nature to bring about a symmetrical result.

Whistler's testimony centered around the impressionist reveries painted in the London twilight and darkness: "Nocturne in Blue and Silver: Old Battersea Bridge" and "Nocturne in Black and Gold: The Falling Rocket."

Petheram: Do you use musical titles because you want to show a connection between painting and music?

Whistler: No, I have never intended to show any connection between the two arts.

Petheram: Before your "nocturnes" went to the Grosvenor Gallery, had they been sold?

Whistler: All but one.

Petheram: For how much?

Whistler: One hundred and fifty and two hundred guineas.

Petheram: Which one was unsold?

Whistler: The "Nocturne in Black and Gold: The Falling Rocket."

Petheram: What was its price?

Whistler: Two hundred guineas.

Petheram: Since the publication of Mr. Ruskin's criticism, have you sold any "nocturne"?

Whistler: Not at the same price as before.

Sir John Holker began his cross-examination. His goal was to convince the jury that Whistler had not finished the paintings, suggesting that the prices were absurd based on the time Whistler had spent painting them. Holker also sought an admission that Ruskin had the right to criticize Whistler. He began by slowly establishing a foundation:

Holker: What is the subject of the "Nocturne in Black and Gold: The Falling Rocket"?

Whistler: It represents fireworks at Cremorne.

Holker: Is it a view of Cremorne?

Whistler: If it were called a view of Cremorne, it would disappoint the viewers. It is not a view of Cremorne. It is simply an artistic arrangement of colors.

Holker: It was for the sale of 200 guineas?

Whistler: Yes.

Holker: You thought that this was a fair price?

Whistler: Yes.

Holker tried to humiliate Whistler by comparing the actual price to the price the average juror would consider reasonable.

Holker: Is 200 guineas what we who are not artists would call a stiffish price?

Whistler: Very likely.

Holker moved on to questions concerning Ruskin's artistic vision. Clearly, Whistler's paintings were not within Ruskin's aesthetic equations. Holker attempted to tighten the noose.

Holker: Do you know that Mr. Ruskin believes an artist should give fair market value for money and not just endeavor to get the highest price?

Whistler: Very likely, that's his view.

Holker: Do you know that it is Mr. Ruskin's view that an artist should not allow a picture to leave his hand if he can improve it?

Whistler: Yes, that's very likely.

Holker: Is the "Nocturne in Black and Gold: The Falling Rocket" a finished picture?

Whistler: Yes.

Holker: Is it a picture of two colors?

Whistler: No. Every color in the palette is in it, as in every painting of mine.

Holker: Was it the only picture at the Grosvenor that was for sale?

Whistler: Yes.

Holker: Did you send it there to be admired?

Whistler: No, that would have been an absurdity on my part.

Holker: Have you heard that your pictures exhibit eccentricities?

Whistler: Yes, very often.

Holker: You don't expect that your pictures are not to be criticized, do you?

Whistler: No, not at all. I just don't want them to be overlooked.

307

Holker believed the artist's assertion that the paintings were finished put Whistler in an untenable position. The jurors would view the paintings, and they could decide whether the paintings were finished. The impressionistic combination of blue, gray, and black would refute Whistler's claim. Holker sought to persuade the jury that a canvas was not finished until its entire surface presented a completely realistic picture. It must tell a story: Nothing should be left to the imagination; the narration must be complete. Since Holker had successfully induced the audience to respond with hilarity, it was likely that the jury had already been persuaded. Holker questioned Whistler's prices:

> *Holker:* As for the "Nocturne in Black and Gold: The Falling Rocket," how long did it take you to knock it off?
> *Whistler:* I beg your pardon[?]
> *Holker:* I was using an expression which is rather more applicable to my profession.
> *Whistler:* Thank you for the compliment. I knocked it off in a couple of days.

Courtroom laughter incited Holker to proceed further into Whistler's price:

> *Holker:* And for the labor of two days you asked for 200 guineas?
> *Whistler:* No. It was for the knowledge gained through a lifetime.

The hilarity became so intense that the judge intervened and stated, "This is not an arena for applause. If it happens again, I shall have the courtroom cleared." Holker continued with questions about Ruskin's right to criticize Whistler's paintings:

> *Holker:* You know that many critics entirely disagree with your views?
> *Whistler:* It would be beyond me to agree with critics.
> *Holker:* You don't approve of criticism?
> *Whistler:* I don't in any way disapprove of technical criticism by a man whose life has been spent in the art which he criticizes. But I put as little value on the opinion of a man whose life has not been so passed as you would if he expressed an opinion on a matter of law.
> *Holker:* What is the subject of the "Nocturne in Blue and Silver: Old Battersea Bridge," the picture that you gave to Mr. Graham?

Whistler: It's the moonlight scene on the Thames near Battersea Bridge.

This picture was in the anteroom. Holker wanted it in court. Parry would agree if the jury could also see a group of pictures hanging in the Westminster Palace Hotel. Baron Huddleson initially decided the jury could see only those pictures that had been at the Grosvenor Gallery show. Parry responded, "Since the plaintiff has been charged with being an imposter, he has the right to show the jury the kind of work he has done." The court ultimately agreed.

Failed Representation

The T-shaped *Battersea Bridge* was brought into court and placed on an easel. Holker pursued Whistler about the representational aspects of the paintings. If a picture must tell a story, an abstraction or an impressionistic arrangement of colors could not do it. It failed to meet Ruskin's definition of a finished painting.

Holker: What does that picture represent?
Whistler: Battersea Bridge in the moonlight.
Holker: Is this a correct representation of Battersea Bridge?
Whistler: I don't intend it to be a portrait of the bridge. It is a moonlight scene, a harmony of color.
Holker: Is that mark on the right of the picture a firework?
Whistler: Yes.
Holker: What is the peculiar mark on the frame?
Whistler: It's there to balance the picture. The frame and the picture together are a work of art.

Baron Huddleson was befuddled. He asked Whistler,

Huddleson: Which part of the picture is the bridge?
Whistler: Your Lordship is too close to the picture to perceive the effect which I intended to produce. The spectator is supposed to be looking down the river toward London.
Huddleson: Is that a barge beneath the bridge?
Whistler: Yes. I am very much flattered at your seeing that.
Huddleson: Are these figures on top intended to be people?
Whistler: They are whatever you would like them to be.

During the luncheon recess, the jury took a three-minute walk to the Westminster Palace Hotel to see Whistler's paintings. After the recess, Parry did not object when Holker asked that the "Nocturne in Black and Gold: The Falling Rocket," which was small enough to be passed around the jury box, be inspected by the jurors. Holker pressed Whistler on whether the painting was representational:

Holker: This is Cremorne?

Whistler: The picture represents a distant view of Cremorne, with a falling rocket and other fireworks.

Holker: Is that a finished picture?

Whistler: Yes.

Holker: What is the peculiar beauty?

Whistler: I'm afraid it would be impossible for me to explain to you, although [I] dare say I could do so to a sympathetic listener.

Holker then ended his cross-examination with what he thought was a pivotal question:

Holker: Would you be willing to place your reputation on that picture?

Whistler: Yes, as I would upon any of my other pictures.

Parry's redirect was terse:

Parry: Did you intend the "Nocturne in Black and Gold: The Falling Rocket" to be a representation of a place?

Whistler: No, it is my aesthetic impression of the scene.

This ended Whistler's testimony. Afterwards, William M. Rossetti testified as an expert witness on Whistler's behalf. Following preliminary questioning, Rossetti was asked for his opinion about Whistler's art:

Parry: What is your opinion of the "Nocturne in Black and Gold: The Falling Rocket"?

Rossetti: It is an effort to represent something indefinite. As a representation of the night, it must be indefinite. It represents darkness mingled with and broken by the brightness of fireworks.

In cross-examining Rossetti, Holker attempted to show that he was not a competent witness because he was not a painter. Holker questioned him about whether he regarded the painting as a thing of value.

Holker: Mr. Rossetti, are you a painter?
Rossetti: No, I am not.
Holker: Is that painting a gem?
Rossetti: No.
Holker: Is it an exquisite painting?
Rossetti: No.
Holker: Is it eccentric?
Rossetti: It is unlike the work of most painters.
Holker: Has there been much labour bestowed upon it?
Rossetti: No.

Holker next raised the question of price:

Is 200 guineas a stiffish price for a picture like that?

Rossetti asked the judge if he had to answer this question. The judge told Rossetti to respond:

Rossetti: I think 200 guineas is the full value of the picture.
Holker: Would you give 200 guineas for it?
Rossetti: I am too poor to give 200 guineas for any picture.

The artist Albert Moore was Whistler's next witness. As with Rossetti, Moore was asked for his opinion after introductory questioning concluded:

Holker: What is your opinion of the two pictures produced in court?
Moore: I consider them to be beautiful works of art. I wish I could do as well. For one thing, he has painted the air, which very few have attempted. I think the atmosphere in the bridge picture is very remarkable. As to the Cremorne picture, I think the atmospheric effects are marvelous. It is a wonderful work of art.
Holker: Is 200 guineas a reasonable price for the picture?
Moore: As prices go, it is not unreasonable. Considering his position, you wouldn't expect Mr. Whistler to work for one hundred pounds any more than you gentlemen would. If I were rich, I would buy the picture myself.
Holker: Are Mr. Whistler's pictures eccentric?
Moore: I should call it originality. What would you call eccentricity in a picture?

Whistler's last witness was William Gorman Will, an Irish playwright and artist. His testimony was redundant. Holker began his opening statement but was interrupted by Baron Huddleson, who said, "The condition in which the court is now might be called 'nocturne.' As it is four o'clock, this court will adjourn until tomorrow morning at halfpast ten."

Day Two. The next day, Holker stated Ruskin's position:

The question which you will have to decide . . . is not whether these pictures are of great merit or of no merit, but whether Mr. Ruskin criticized them fairly, honestly, and bona fide. A critic has a perfect right to indulge in ridicule and to use strong language. The only question is whether he has been fair. I will endeavor to show that Mr. Ruskin did not overstep the bounds of moderation. For years he has devoted himself to the study and criticism of art. He has written books upon art, and since 1869 he has been [a] professor of fine arts at Oxford. He has the greatest love and reverence for the subject. He expects an artist to be devoted to his profession and pose more than a few flashes of genius. He holds that an artist should desire not simply to be well paid, but should also want to give the purchaser something that is worth his money. He believes also that no work should leave an artist's hands which can reasonably be improved.

Since Mr. Ruskin entertains these views, it should not be wondered that he subjected Mr. Whistler's pictures to severe criticism, even ridicule. If he honestly believed what he wrote, he would have neglected his duty if he hesitated to express his opinions.

Gentlemen, you have seen the pictures. If they had been exhibited to you before Mr. Whistler's elaborate disquisition, would you not have thought them strange and extravagant? If you had gone to the Grosvenor Gallery and had seen one of them valued at 200 guineas, would you not have said, "That price is absurd"? Mr. Whistler says they are beautiful works of art. Mr. Ruskin was of a different opinion, and he did not commit a misdemeanor, or a breach of the duties and privileges of an Englishman, when he disputed Mr. Whistler's view of his own productions.

Gentlemen, you have examined the "Nocturne in Blue and Silver: Old Battersea Bridge." You saw a good deal of colour,

312

and you probably thought it would have been better if some of it hadn't wandered onto the frame. As for the structure in the middle, you probably asked, "Is that a telescope or a fire escape? If it's a bridge, and those figures on top are human beings, how in the name of fortune will they ever get off?"

Now in the Cremorne picture, there is the blackness of night with some fireworks coming down and a blaze at the bottom, perhaps a bonfire. That is all there is.

I do not deny that Mr. Whistler has done some very good things, but these pictures are strange fantastical conceits not worthy of being called works of art. Artists whom I almost had to drag into court will say that they are not worthy of admission into any gallery.

As to the alleged libel, the defendant has the right to criticize; that is his business. But, my learned friend says, one must not prevent Mr. Whistler from earning a living. Why not? In fulfilling his duty, is Mr. Ruskin obliged to be tender? Then it was said, "You have ridiculed Mr. Whistler's pictures." Well, Mr. Whistler should not have subjected himself to ridicule by exhibiting such productions.

Mr. Ruskin's language, it is said, was strong, but an action cannot be brought against a man for strong language. If a critic thinks a painting is a daub, he has a right to say so. True, Mr. Ruskin called Mr. Whistler a coxcomb, but as an artist, not as a man. What is a coxcomb? According to the dictionary, it carries out the old idea of a licensed jester who has a cap on his head with cock's comb on it and goes about making jests. If that is the definition, Mr. Whistler should not complain. His pictures are an amusing jest. I do not know when so much amusement has been afforded to the British public as by Mr. Whistler's pictures. The old meaning of coxcomb has been well carried out by him.

Gentlemen, I ask you not to paralyze the hand of one who has given himself wholly to the art he loves. If you decide against Mr. Ruskin, he will cease writing. It will be an evil day for art in this country if he is prevented from indulging in legitimate criticism, and if critics are forced to indulge in nothing but fulsome admiration.

313

Edward Burne-Jones, a leader of the Pre-Raphaelite movement, was the first defense witness. He was an artist who, like Ruskin, believed in finished, narrative painting. Ruskin's junior counsel, Charles Bowen, asked Burne-Jones what constituted an artistic painting:

> *Bowen:* How important are finish and completeness to the merit of a painting?
>
> *Burne-Jones:* I think that nothing short of perfect finish should be allowed to artists. They should not be content with anything that falls short of what is essential to the work.
>
> *Bowen:* What is your judgment of the "Nocturne in Blue and Silver: Old Battersea Bridge"?
>
> *Burne-Jones:* The colors are beautiful, but form is as essential as color[,] and the picture is totally and bewilderingly formless.
>
> *Bowen:* What about its composition and detail?
>
> *Burne-Jones:* It has none whatsoever.
>
> *Bowen:* Does it show the finish of a complete work of art?
>
> *Burne-Jones:* Not in any sense whatever. It is a sketch.
>
> *Bowen:* What is your opinion of the "Nocturne in Black and Gold: The Falling Rocket"?
>
> *Burne-Jones:* I think it has less merit than the other one.
>
> *Bowen:* In your opinion, is it a work of art?
>
> *Burne-Jones:* No, I cannot say that it is.
>
> *Bowen:* Why not?
>
> *Burne-Jones:* I never saw a successful picture of the night. This is only one of a thousand failed efforts to paint the night.

Bowen introduced a painting by Titian of Andre Gatti, a doge of Venice:

> *Bowen:* Is that a genuine Titian?
>
> *Burne-Jones:* Yes. I have no doubts whatsoever about it.
>
> *Bowen:* What can you say about its finish?
>
> *Burne-Jones:* It is a perfect example of the highest finish that all true artists have aimed at.

Ruskin's last witness was William Frith, a well known painter and a member of the Royal Academy:

> *Bowen:* In your opinion, do the pictures of Mr. Whistler that were brought into court have any merit?
>
> *Frith:* I should say not.

314

Bowen: Is the nocturne representing fireworks at Cremorne a serious work of art?

Frith: Not to me.

Bowen: What about the other picture?

Frith: It has beautiful colours, but no more than in a piece of wallpaper.

Bowen: Are composition and detail important in a picture?

Frith: Very important. Without them, a picture cannot be called a work of art.

Ruskin never appeared. There had been several continuances because of his health. Finally, on June 8, 1878, Ruskin's solicitor sent to Anderson Rose, Whistler's solicitor, a physician's certificate stating that Ruskin was "totally unfit to take part in the pending action." Glasgow University Library, Special Collection. This thwarted Parry's plan to cross-examine Ruskin. Once testimony was completed, summations ensued. Bowen spoke for Ruskin:

> The issue is not the merits of Mr. Whistler's pictures, nor whether you think a nocturne is worth 200 guineas. The issue is whether Mr. Ruskin's comments, strong though they may have been, were fair and honest criticism. A critic must not indulge in personal malice. But he is not bound to wait with bated breath. He may say what he likes if he does honestly without leaving the subject matter before him. Mr. Ruskin's criticism was of this nature. I hope that no English jury will do anything to chain honest criticism, thereby irreparably damaging the future of art in this country.

Serjeant Parry responded for Whistler:

> Mr. Ruskin's [defense] comes to this: "I shall say what I please, and nobody must ever interfere." It is to be hoped, however, that you gentlemen will tell him that he does not have this power.

> I am astonished that someone in his position would use such language. This was not fair criticism; it was a personal attack. A pretended criticism on art which is really a criticism of the artist and holds him up to ridicule is not permissible. Can such words as "throwing a pot of paint in the public's face" be considered fair, bona fide criticism?

Gentlemen, if you find in favor of Mr. Ruskin, you will tell the world that Mr. Whistler is a willful imposter. And Mr. Whistler was called a "cockney." This means that he is dirty and disagreeable. This is not criticism. It is defamation. . . .

Mr. Ruskin cared not whether his decree injuriously affected others and loftily declined to discuss his judgment or to justify himself before a jury . . . he is a man who exceeds the fair limits of criticism and allows personal feeling to carry him too far . . . This is the language of a libellous mind, utterly indifferent to others' feelings but gratifying to its own vanity.

Mr. Ruskin might delight in the reflection that he is a smart, a pungent, and a telling writer but he must not be allowed to trade in libel. The works of Mr. Whistler are open to fair and honest criticism. He has not shrunk from any public investigation; but his detractor has. . . . Is he to be expelled from the realm of art by the man who sits there as a despot? I hope the jury will say by its verdict that Mr. Ruskin has no right to drive Mr. Whistler out by defamatory and libellous accusations.

The judge gave his summation:

It is for you gentlemen to decide whether the defendant used his powers fairly and honestly, or whether he went beyond the work itself. If a critic honestly expresses an opinion in a work, even with strong language, he should be protected. But if he denounces the individual whose work he is criticizing, he is not entitled to protection.

If a critic feels he is dealing with a charlatan and an imposter, he may use strong expressions about his work but not about his personal character. If you think that Mr. Ruskin's language was honest and bona fide, even though strong, you must find for him. But if you think the words were not fair and bona fide, the plaintiff is entitled to your verdict.

Then there is the question of damages. If you decide for the plaintiff, you must also decide whether the insult was so gross as to call for substantial damages, or whether it is a case for slight damages, indicating that the case ought not to have come into court.

The jury deliberated from 2:50 PM to 4:10 PM. Whistler won, but the jury awarded only one farthing. Baron Huddleson rendered a judgment without costs.

Whistler wanted his solicitor to appeal, but Rose told Whistler that Ruskin might have a better right to appeal because the judge had instructed the jury not only that Ruskin's criticism should have been fair and honest but also bona fide. Honesty should have sufficed.

Three days after the trial, the Fine Arts Society began a subscription to defray Ruskin's trial expenses of £400 because of Ruskin's "lifelong honest endeavor to further the cause of art." On May 8, 1879, Whistler went bankrupt because he could not pay his trial costs: His debts were £4,641; his assets were £1,924. P. Hesketh, *The Man Whistler* (1952).

Ruskin resigned from his Slade professorship at Oxford. The official reason was ill health, but, in a letter to Dean Liddell, he stated:

> The Professorship is a farce if it has no right to condemn as well as to praise. There should have been no question possible between a university teacher and a man like Whistler, and I certainly cannot take the trouble to judge on any point of art if a scamp who belongs in a workhouse or jail can make me pay half a year's income to lawyers. Ruskin (1919).

Whistler had the farthing he received as damages made into a watch fob. He wore it until his death in 1903.

Whistler influenced twentieth-century artists including Pablo Picasso, Henri Matisse, Mark Rothko, Gustav Klimt, and the Vienna Secession movement.

In December 1878, Whistler published a pamphlet titled *Whistler v. Ruskin: Art and Art Criticism.* Whistler said it was to provide "an unbiased report of the law suit to go down to posterity" and "to expose the empty pretensions of art criticism." He said that Ruskin was "a representative of the tribe of art critics who, in their ignorance, would make and unmake the reputation of artists with an ignorant public." The trial was the "opening skirmish" of the war "between the brush and the pen." By January 1879, the pamphlet was into its sixth edition.

Today, Whistler's paintings appear at numerous renowned venues, including the Freer Gallery of Art, the Smithsonian Institution, and the National Gallery of Art in Washington, DC; the Art

Institute of Chicago; the Fogg Art Museum in Cambridge, Massachusetts; the Isabella Stewart Gardner Museum and the Museum of Fine Arts in Boston; the Taft Museum in Cincinnati; the Glasgow Art Gallery in Glasgow, Scotland; and the Frick Collection, the Metropolitan Museum of Art, and the New York Public Library in New York City. "Nocturne in Black and Gold: The Falling Rocket" is on display at the Detroit Institute of Arts. "Nocturne in Blue and Silver: Old Battersea Bridge" hangs at the Tate Gallery in London. "Arrangement in Grey and Black: Portrait of Painter's Mother" (also known as "Whistler's Mother") resides at the Louvre.

22

Sir Edward Carson Cross-Examines Oscar Wilde

The first duty in life is to assume a pose. What the second is, no one has yet discovered.

———Oscar Wilde

Oscar Wilde, England's famous playwright with the rapier wit, was accused of "posing" as a sodomite by the eighth marquess of Queensberry, whose name is forever associated with amateur boxing rules. This was in 1895 in Victorian England.

Lord Alfred Douglas, Queensberry's third son, was Wilde's inseparable companion. Queensberry disliked the arrangement. Douglas disliked Queensberry. Egged on by Douglas and disregarding advice from friends including George Bernard Shaw, Wilde took the matter to court.

Wilde could have impaled Queensberry with words in a drawing room comedy, and Queensberry might have found satisfaction in a punch-out with Wilde in a boxing ring, but the courtroom belonged to Edward Carson, Q.C., M.P. Carson was Queensberry's barrister. He had been Wilde's classmate at Trinity College. Carson's cross-examination of Wilde is considered a legal triumph. For Wilde, the results were tragic.

Yet Wilde remains as popular as ever as a major playwright and a master of sophisticated banter. In that sense, Wilde has had the last word.

Act I: Happiness

Oscar Wilde was brilliant. No one disputed that. He was born in Dublin in 1854 to Sir William Wilde, a womanizing doctor, and his eccentric wife Jane, who, writing as "Speranza," was an Irish nationalist poet. Oscar Fingal O'Flahertie Wills Wilde grew up to be a classical scholar, studying at Trinity College and then at Magdalene College, Oxford, where he was one of the very few who won two Double Firsts. He also received the prestigious Newdigate prize for poetry. Influenced by John Ruskin and Walter Pater, Wilde became a champion of aesthetics and developed a flair for flamboyant attire and a distaste for conventional morality. R. Ellman, *Oscar Wilde* (1985).

Wilde's wit and love of language emerged early. When he was 16, at his first ball at Dublin Castle, he asked an unmarried woman to dance. She said, "Do you think I'm going to dance with a child?" Wilde's reply: "Madame, if I had known you were in that condition, I never would have asked you." M. Nicholls, *The Importance of Being Oscar* (1980).

Wilde was Oxford's most notorious undergraduate. Talk of his aesthetic cult of "art for art's sake," with its symbols of peacock feathers, sunflowers, blue china, and velveteen breeches, reached London. When Gilbert & Sullivan's producers wanted to stage *Patience* in America, they realized that since the comic opera was intended to ridicule aesthetes, it was necessary to display an aesthete. So they invited Wilde to lecture there.

The large man with flopping hair and quotable epigrams arrived in New York on January 2, 1882. Asked by the customs authorities whether he had anything to declare, he replied, "Nothing but my genius." His tour was a triumph. Wilde met Walt Whitman, Oliver Wendell Holmes, Henry Wadsworth Longfellow, Louisa May Alcott, and Ulysses S. Grant. He continued his lectures in England and Scotland. Oscar Wilde's reputation was established. J. Laver, *Oscar Wilde* (1963).

Needing money and ridiculed by moralists, Wilde considered marriage. Pretty Constance Lloyd possessed artistic inclinations

320

and modest income. They were married on May 29, 1884, and were soon the parents of two sons, Cyril, born in 1885, and Vyvyan, a year later. Romance had vanished. Oscar remained fond of Constance and delighted by his sons, for whom he wrote two children's books, *The Happy Prince* and *A House of Pomegranates*. But he was ready to return to the company of beautiful young men.

All went well for a while. His play *Lady Windermere's Fan* was a great success. *A Woman of No Importance* began rehearsals in March 1893. By June, Wilde was consumed with passion for Oxford undergraduate and aspiring poet Lord Alfred Douglas, known as Bosie, whom Wilde first met in 1891. Douglas was demanding, expensive, reckless, and unfaithful. He introduced Wilde to a world of transitory pleasure. Wilde's third comedy, *An Ideal Husband*, was staged in London on January 3, 1895, and his last and most famous play, *The Importance of Being Earnest*, opened on February 14, 1895.

But lurking in the background was John Sholto Douglas, the pugnacious, bellicose, and alarming marquess of Queensberry. He was an eccentric Scottish nobleman devoted to sports and atheism. A loud bully divorced from his wife, estranged from his children, and fiercely obsessed with separating his son from Oscar Wilde, Queensberry threatened to disown Douglas if he did not stop seeing Wilde.

In June 1894, Queensberry arrived at Wilde's door with a prizefighter and threatened to thrash Wilde if he appeared again in a public restaurant with Douglas. Wilde's famous reply: "I don't know what the Queensberry rules are, but the Oscar Wilde rule is to shoot on sight." M. Holland, *The Real Trial of Oscar Wilde* (2003).

Attempting to upset the reception of *Earnest*, Queensberry tried to enter the theater carrying a "floral arrangement" of turnips and carrots but was stopped at the door. This bouquet was inspired by Gilbert's lyrical description of Wilde in *Patience*: "Then a sentimental passion of a vegetable fashion must excite your languid spleen. An attachment à la Plato for a bashful young potato or a not-too-French French bean!"

Finally, Queensberry left his calling card at the Albemarle Club, with the words "To Oscar Wilde—posing as somdamite" [*sic*]. The hall porter placed it in an envelope, and Wilde received the card ten days later. At Douglas's insistence, Wilde decided to sue. Alfred Douglas was obsessed about testifying against his father, but his testimony would have been ruled irrelevant. A writ was served on Queensberry for criminal libel. Queensberry appeared in court and was ordered to stand trial.

Act II: *Wilde v. Carson*

Wilde could never have imagined that his quest for justice would lead not only to the trial against Queensberry but also to two subsequent criminal trials with Wilde as a defendant, followed by his bankruptcy and finally a prison sentence, all within two months.

When the trial against Queensberry began on April 3, 1895, at the Central Criminal Court known as the Old Bailey, the jury's duty was to determine whether Wilde had "posed" as a sodomite. If they decided that Wilde had not, Queensberry would be guilty of libel. Queensberry's burden was to present a written plea of justification proving that his words were true and were published for the public's benefit.

Justice R. Henn Collins, another Dubliner, presided. Former Solicitor-General Sir Edward Clarke, Q.C., M.P., was Wilde's barrister. Wilde assured Clarke and his solicitor, Charles Humphries, that the charges were false. Queensberry had already retained Wilde's previous solicitor and friend, Sir George Lewis, who later commented that knowing of blackmail attempts against Alfred Douglas, he would have advised Wilde to tear up the card and take no action.

Queensberry retained as his solicitor Charles Russell, son of England's Lord Chief Justice, Lord Russell of Killowen. His barrister was Edward Carson. Carson had been appointed Queen's Counsel both in Ireland and England. While Russell collected statements from men who claimed they had sexual liaisons with Wilde, Carson read Wilde's work. He divided his cross-examination between homosexual references in Wilde's writing and sexual contacts with young men in his life. Carson was well prepared.

In direct testimony, Wilde told the jury about his background. He spoke of the pinnacle he had reached as England's leading playwright. *The Evening News* claimed Wilde "almost lolled in the witness-box." Then came his first misstep.

> *Clarke:* I think you are thirty-eight years of age?
> *Wilde:* I am thirty-nine years of age.

Cross-Examination

When Clarke sat down and Carson began his cross-examination, he took immediate advantage of Wilde's gaffe. Wilde's attempt to minimize the age difference between himself and Douglas threatened his credibility.

> *Carson:* You stated at the commencement of your examination that you were thirty-nine years of age. I think you are over forty, isn't that so?
>
> *Wilde:* I don't think so. I think I am either thirty-nine or forty—forty my next birthday. If you have my certificate there, that settles the matter. [*Carson held up a copy of Wilde's birth certificate*]
>
> *Carson:* You were born, I believe, upon the 16th of October, 1854?
>
> *Wilde:* Yes, I have no intention of posing for a younger man at all. I try to be correct in the date.
>
> *Carson:* It makes you somewhat over forty.
>
> *Wilde:* Very well.
>
> *Carson:* May I ask you, do you happen to know what age Lord Alfred Douglas was or is?
>
> *Wilde:* Lord Alfred Douglas, I think, was twenty-four his last birthday. I think he will be twenty-five his next birthday.
>
> *Carson:* May I take it that when you knew him first he was something about twenty or twenty-one?
>
> *Wilde:* Yes.

Holland, *supra*; H.M. Hyde, *Oscar Wilde* (1948).

Literature

Carson turned to questions of morality and literature. First, he tried to show Wilde's guilt by association. Wilde had just written a list of "Phrases and Philosophers for the Use of the Young" for the *Saturday Review*. He sent them for use in *The Chameleon*, a new Oxford undergraduate magazine, but the first issue also contained a tasteless, perhaps blasphemous story entitled "The Priest and the Acolyte," written by John Bloxam, the editor. In these excerpts from the cross-examination, Wilde defended his words as art, while Carson attempted to establish Wilde's standard of morality.

> *Carson:* "The Priest and the Acolyte" was a scandalous novel. . . . You are of the opinion, I believe, that there is no such thing as an immoral book?
>
> *Wilde:* Yes.

Carson: May I take it that you think "The Priest and the Acolyte" was not immoral?

Wilde: It was worse. It was badly written. [Laughter]

Carson questioned Wilde's depiction of corruption in *The Picture of Dorian Gray*, published in the July 1890 issue of *Lippincott's Monthly* magazine and in 1891 as a separate novel. It had engendered an indignant reaction and foreshadowed Wilde's own impending tragedy. Gray, too, had experimented with sexual alliances with both women and men. The plot was well known: Dorian Gray's portrait becomes increasingly grotesque as he commits each of his sins, while Dorian Gray, himself, remains unchanged. When he furiously stabs his portrait, it reverts to its original condition, but Gray dies. His body, when found, is shockingly corrupted and decayed. When *Dorian Gray* was attacked in the press, Wilde's defense was that a "work of art must never be judged by any standards of morality, or by any ethical code with which it has nothing in common." Nicholls, *supra*.

Clarke had warned the jury that to attribute the vices of Dorian Gray to Wilde would be strange because the character is shown by Wilde to be a vicious creature. Wilde had testified in direct examination that the picture became Dorian's conscience and that "by trying to kill his own soul the man directly dies." But Carson used quotations from the *Lippincott* edition to press Wilde on his moral views:

Carson: [Quoting *Dorian Gray*] "I quite admit that I adored you madly." Have you ever adored a young man, some twenty-one years younger than yourself, madly?

Wilde: No, not madly.

Carson: Well, adored him?

Wilde: I have loved one friend in my life.

Carson: You asked me to take your own phrase, "adored."

Wilde: I prefer love—that is higher.

Carson: Never mind going higher. Keep down to the level of your own words.

Carson: Then, you never had that feeling you depict here?

Wilde: No, it was borrowed from Shakespeare, I regret to say. [*Laughter*]

Carson: "I have adored you madly, extravagantly."

Wilde: Yes.

Carson: Have you ever extravagantly adored?

Wilde: Do you mean financially or emotionally?

Carson: Financially? Do you think we are talking here of finance?

Wilde: I don't know what you are talking about.

Carson: Don't you?

Wilde: You must ask me a plain question.

Carson: I hope I shall make myself very plain before I am done. "I was jealous of everyone to whom you spoke." Have you ever been jealous?

Wilde: Never in my life.

Carson: "I wanted to have you all to myself." Did you ever have that feeling?

Wilde: No. I should consider it an intense bore.

Carson: A man never corrupts a youth?

Wilde: I think not.

Carson: Nothing he could do would corrupt him?

Wilde: If you are talking of separate ages—it is nonsense.

Carson: No, sir. I am talking common sense.

Wilde: I do not think one person influences another.

Carson: You don't think flattering a young man, making love to him, in fact, would be likely to corrupt him?

Wilde: No.

Letters

Carson next turned to letters written by Wilde to Alfred Douglas, which had found their way into the hands of a blackmailer.

Carson: You would think, I suppose, Mr. Wilde, that a man of your age to address a man nearly twenty years younger as "My own boy" would be an improper thing?

Wilde: Not if I was fond of him. I don't think so.

Carson: You adore him?

Wilde: No, I loved him. [*Wilde claimed the letter to Douglas was a sonnet*]

Carson: Your sonnet is quite lovely. "It is a marvel that those red rose-leaf lips of yours should be made no less for music of song than for madness of kissing."

Wilde: Yes.

Carson: Do you mean to tell me, sir, that was a natural and proper way to address a young man?

Wilde: Yes, I think it was a beautiful letter. It is a poem. I was not writing an ordinary letter. If you ask me whether it is proper you might as well ask me whether *King Lear* was proper or a sonnet of Shakespeare was proper . . . it was written with the object of making a beautiful thing.

Carson: But apart from art?

Wilde: I cannot answer any question apart from art.

Carson: Suppose a man who was not an artist had written this letter to a handsome young man, would you say it was a proper and natural letter?

Wilde: A man who was not an artist could never have written that letter. [*Laughter*]

Carson: Why?

Wilde: Because nobody but an artist could write it.

Carson: Supposing a man had an unholy and immoral love towards a boy or young fellow . . . and he addresses him in the language that would perhaps be used in a love letter—he might use that language.

Wilde: He certainly could not use such language unless he was a man of letters and an artist.

Carson: I can suggest, for the sake of your reputation, that there is nothing very wonderful in this "red rose-leaf lips" of yours.

Wilde: A great deal depends on the way it is read.

Carson: "Your slim gilt soul walks between passion and poetry." Is that a beautiful phrase?

Wilde: Not as you read it, Mr. Carson. When I wrote it it was beautiful. You read it very badly.

Carson: I do not profess to be an artist and when I hear you give evidence, I am glad I am not. [*Laughter*]

Carson: Was that the ordinary way in which you carried on your correspondence?

Wilde: No, But I have often written to Lord Alfred Douglas, though I never wrote to another young man in the same way.

Carson: Have you often written letters in the same style as this?

Wilde: I don't repeat myself in style.

Carson: Here is another letter which I believe you also wrote to Lord Alfred Douglas. Will you read it?

Wilde: I don't see why I should.

Carson: Then I will. "Dearest of all boys, your letter was delightful, red and yellow wine to me; but I am sad and out of sorts. Bosie, you must not make scenes with me: they kill me . . . Shall I go to Salisbury? There are many difficulties. My bill here is forty-nine pounds for a week." [*Laughter*] Is that an ordinary letter?

Wilde: Everything I wrote is extraordinary. I do not pose as being ordinary, great heavens! Ask me any question you like about it.

Carson: Isn't that a love letter?

Wilde: It is a letter expressive of love.

Carson: Is it the kind of letter a man writes to another man?

Wilde: It was a tender expression of my great admiration for Lord Alfred Douglas. It was not, like the other, a prose poem.

Witnesses

Wilde was safe while discussing literature. But now Carson was on the attack. He began asking Wilde questions about young men, mostly of the lower classes, whose anticipated testimony could destroy him. Wilde became the hunted, not the hunter.

Carson began with Alfred Wood. Wilde testified he met Wood through a friend named Alfred Taylor. Carson asked whether Wilde had immoral practices with Wood. Wilde denied any impropriety. Carson established that Wilde gave Wood supper and money. When Wood came to blackmail him with letters Wilde wrote to Douglas, Wilde gave him money to go to America.

Carson moved on, questioning Wilde about his relationship with Edward Shelley.

Carson: At the time were Messrs. Elkin Matthews and John Lane, of Vigo Street, your publishers?

Wilde: Yes.

Carson: Did you in February 1892 become fond of their office boy?

Wilde: I deny that that was the position held by Mr. Edward Shelley, to whom you refer. He was not an office boy.

Carson: What age was Mr. Shelley?

Wilde: I should think about twenty.

Carson: I suggest to you he was eighteen.

Wilde: It is quite possible.

Carson: A good-looking boy?

Wilde: No, I wouldn't call him so—an intellectual face.

Carson: He was selling books in a shop?

Wilde: I regarded him as a gentleman.

Carson: Did you ask this lad to dine with you?

Wilde: Oh, yes, he often dined with me.

Carson: Was that for the purpose of having an intellectual treat?

Wilde: Well, for him, yes. [*Laughter*] We dined in my own sitting room, and there was one other gentleman there.

Carson handed Wilde writing paper, telling him to write the name of the other guest.

Carson: On that occasion did you have a room leading into a bedroom?

Wilde: Yes.

Carson: Did you give him whiskey-and-sodas?

Wilde: I suppose he had whatever he wanted. I do not remember.

Carson's questioning led to Wilde's insistence that although Shelley dined and drank in Wilde's private suite and Wilde gave him money, no improper behavior resulted.

Carson: Did you think this young man of eighteen was a proper or natural companion for you?

Wilde: Certainly.

Carson next moved to Alfonso Conway.

Carson: Did you become intimate with a young man named Conway?

Wilde: Oh yes, at Worthing.

Carson: Did he not sell newspapers at the kiosk on the pier?

Wilde: No, it is the first I have heard of his connection with literature. [*Laughter*]

Carson: What was he?

Wilde: He led a happy, idle life.

Carson: He was a loafer, in fact?

Wilde: He seemed to me to be just enjoying life.

Carson: Was his conversation literary?

Wilde: On the contrary, quite simple and easily understood. He had been to school, where naturally he had not learned much.

Carson established that Conway was about eighteen. Wilde denied kissing Conway or having familiarities with him. Carson produced a signed photograph of Wilde and a cigarette case and a silver-mounted walking stick, all of which Conway had accepted from Wilde

Carson: Did you take the lad to Brighton?

Wilde: Yes.

Carson: And provide him with a suit of blue serge?

328

Wilde: Yes.

Carson: And a straw hat with a band of red and blue?

Wilde: That, I think, was his unfortunate selection.

Carson: You dressed this newsboy up to take him to Brighton?

Wilde: I did not want him to be ashamed of his shabby clothes.

Carson: In order that he might look more like an equal?

Wilde: Oh, no, he could not look like that. [*Laughter*]

Carson asked what Wilde and Conway were doing in Brighton. Wilde said they had stayed a night at the Albany Hotel with a sitting room and two bedrooms and had eaten at a local restaurant.

On the second morning, Carson cross-examined Wilde about Alfred Taylor. He suggested that Taylor procured young rent boys. Carson created a picture of heavily draped, perfumed rooms in which Taylor gave tea parties.

Carson: Did he use to do his own cooking?

Wilde: I don't know. I don't think he did anything wrong.

Carson: I have not suggested that he did.

Wilde: Well, cooking is an art.

Carson: Another art? [*Laughter*]

Carson: Wasn't Taylor notorious for introducing young men to older men?

Wilde: I never heard that in my life. He has introduced young men to me.

Carson: Were the young men all of about twenty years of age?

Wilde: . . . I like the society of young men. I delight in it.

Charles Parker was next in Carson's lineup.

Carson: Then may I take it that Charles Parker was one of the ones you became friendly with?

Wilde: Oh, yes.

Carson: Did you know that Parker was a gentlemen's servant out of employment?

Wilde: No.

Carson: But if he were, you would still have become friendly with him?

Wilde: Yes. I could become friendly with any human being I liked.

Carson: How old was he?

Wilde: I do not keep a census.

Carson: Never mind about a census. Tell me how old he was?

329

Wilde: I should say he was about twenty. He was young and that was one of his attractions, the attraction of youth.
Carson: He was seventeen.
Carson: Was he a literary character?
Wilde: Oh, no.
Carson: Was he an artist?
Wilde: No.
Carson: Was he an educated man?
Wilde: Culture was not his strong point. [*Laughter*]

Carson questioned Wilde about meeting Charles Parker and his brother, William Parker, at Taylor's and immediately taking them to a fancy restaurant.

Carson: Did you know that Parker was a gentleman's valet and the other a groom?
Wilde: I did not know it, but if I had I should not have cared. I didn't care twopence what they were. I liked them. I have a passion to civilize the community.
Carson: What enjoyment was it to you to entertain grooms and coachmen?
Wilde: The pleasure to me was being with those who are young, bright, happy, careless, and free. I do not like the sensible and I do not like the old.
Carson: Was it a good dinner?
Wilde: Kettner's is not so gorgeous as some restaurants but it was Kettner at his best.
Carson: Was there plenty of champagne?
Wilde: Well, I did not press wine upon them.
Carson: You did not stint them?
Wilde: What gentleman would stint his guests?
Carson: What gentleman would stint the valet and grooms?
Clarke: [*Objection*]
Carson: Do you drink champagne yourself?
Wilde: Yes. Iced champagne is a favourite drink of mine—strongly against my doctor's orders.
Carson: Never mind your doctor's orders, sir.
Wilde: I never do. [*Laughter*]

Carson questioned Wilde about another youth, Freddie Atkins, a bookmaker, an idle fellow whom Wilde claimed to have taken to Paris as a favor to a friend. Carson moved on to Ernest Scarfe,

330

whom Wilde met through Taylor. Wilde admitted dining with Scarfe and giving him the customary cigarette case, but he denied kissing him or having indecencies. The next name Carson introduced was twenty-five-year-old Sydney Mavor. Wilde claimed to have met him through the same man who had sent him to Paris with Atkins. [This was Maurice Schwabe, whose name had been shielded. Schwabe was the nephew of Lady Schwabe. Her husband, the Solicitor-General Sir Frank Lockwood, later conducted the Crown's prosecution of Wilde in his last trial.] Mavor dined and stayed a night with Wilde at the Albermarle. Again, Wilde denied indecencies. Mavor received the ubiquitous cigarette case.

The Wrong Answer

For the third time, Carson hit Wilde with the kissing query. This time it was Walter Grainger, a sixteen-year-old Oxford resident. But Wilde, overconfident, could not resist a flippant reply. Wilde stumbled. He never recovered.

Carson: Did you know Walter Grainger?
Wilde: Yes.
Carson: What was he?
Wilde: A servant at Lord Douglas's rooms in Oxford.
Carson: Did you ever kiss him?
Wilde: Oh, no, never in my life; he was a peculiarly plain boy.
Carson: He was what?
Wilde: I said I thought him unfortunately—his appearance was so very unfortunately—very ugly—I mean—I pitied him for it.
Carson: Very ugly?
Wilde: Yes.
Carson: Do you say that in support of your statement that you never kissed him?
Wilde: No, I don't; it is like asking me if I kissed a doorpost; it is childish.
Carson: Didn't you give me as the reason that you never kissed him that he was too ugly?
Wilde [*Warmly*]: No.
Carson: Why did you mention his ugliness?
Wilde: No, I said the question seemed to me like—your asking me whether I ever had him to dinner, and then whether I had kissed him—seemed to me merely an intentional insult on

your part, which I have been going through the whole of this morning.

Carson: Because he was ugly?

Wilde: No.

Carson: Why did you mention his ugliness? I have to ask these questions.

Wilde: I say it is ridiculous to imagine that any such thing could possibly have occurred under any circumstances.

Carson: Why did you mention his ugliness?

Wilde: For that reason. If you asked me if I had ever kissed a doorpost, I should say, "No! Ridiculous! I shouldn't like to kiss a doorpost"? The questions are grotesque.

Carson: Why did you mention the boy's ugliness?

Wilde: I mentioned it perhaps because you stung me by an insolent question.

Carson: Because I stung you by an insolent question?

Wilde: Yes, you stung me by an insolent question; you make me irritable.

Carson: Did you say the boy was ugly because I stung you by an insolent question?

Wilde: Pardon me, you stung me, insult me and try to unnerve me in every way. At times one says things flippantly when one should speak more seriously, I admit that, I admit it—I cannot help it. That is what you are doing to me.

Carson: You said it flippantly? You mentioned his ugliness flippantly; that is what you wish to convey now?

Wilde: Oh, don't say what I wish to convey. I have given you my answer.

Carson: Is that it, that that was a flippant answer?

Wilde: Oh, it was a flippant answer, yes; I will say it was certainly a flippant answer.

Carson: Did ever any indecencies take place between you and Grainger?

Wilde: No, sir, none, none at all.

Holland, *supra*; Hyde, *supra*.

Partial transcripts existed of Wilde's case against Queensberry (*Regina v. Queensberry*), but they were incomplete until 2000 when Merlin Holland, Wilde's only grandson, assisted the British Library's preparation for the centenary celebration of Oscar Wilde. A longhand manuscript of the complete Queensberry trial, possibly commissioned by Queensberry, was brought into the library for exhibition. The transcript was published, with an introduction by Holland, in *The Real Trial of Oscar Wilde*.

When Carson began his powerful opening statement, telling the jury they would hear from witnesses who said they had improper sexual experiences with Wilde, Clarke interrupted him. He announced to Carson and the court that Wilde would no longer proceed. Clarke tried to salvage Wilde's reputation by suggesting that the court agree to a verdict that would not require Wilde to admit that Queensberry's insult was correct. Carson and the court refused. The jury quickly responded to the court's instruction and gave a verdict that Queensberry's putative libel was true; that it was published for the public's benefit; and that Queensberry was "not guilty" of libeling Wilde. Only three days after it began, Wilde's defamation trial was over. Queensberry was triumphant. Wilde's reputation was in shambles. Holland, *supra*.

Hoping to stem the damage, Wilde gave a statement, which the *Evening News* published:

> It would have been impossible for me to have proved my case without putting Lord Alfred Douglas in the witness-box against his father. Lord Alfred Douglas was extremely anxious to go into the box, but I would not let him do so. Rather than put him in so painful a position I determined to retire from the case, and to bear on my own shoulders whatever ignominy and shame might result from my prosecuting Lord Queensberry.

Act III: Tragedy

It was Queensberry's turn. Wilde had given up pursuing Queensberry. But Queensberry had not given up pursuing Wilde. Russell, at Queensberry's insistence, took the file he had compiled to the director of public prosecutions. From there, the file was rushed to the House of Commons and presented to the attorney-general, the solicitor-general, and the home secretary. The three immediately ordered an application for Wilde's arrest. It was granted that afternoon, and Wilde, refusing to flee to France, was arrested that evening at the Cadogan Hotel.

Wilde and alleged procurer Alfred Taylor were charged with "committing acts of gross indecency with other male persons" under the Labouchere amendment to the 1885 Criminal Law Act.

The Act's primary purpose was to raise the age of consent for girls from age 13 to 16. Although the charge was a misdemeanor, no bail was permitted. Even Carson tried to end the attack on Wilde, appealing to the solicitor-general, who replied, "I would, but we cannot: we dare not: it would at once be said both in England and abroad, that owing to the names mentioned . . . we were forced to abandon it." Holland, *supra*; H.M. Hyde, *Carson* (1953).

Now Wilde was a criminal defendant, prosecuted by the Crown. His trial ended in a mistrial when the jury failed to reach agreement as to whether he had committed gross indecency. The Crown moved rapidly to a second trial. Clarke defended Wilde for no fee. This time Wilde's ignominy was total. On May 25, 1895, he was found guilty of gross indecency and given the maximum sentence. Wilde was taken to Holloway Gaol, then to Wandsworth Prison, and finally to Reading Gaol in Berkshire. Nicholls, *supra*.

Afterword

During his two-year sentence at hard labor, Wilde wrote "De Profundis," a long letter to Douglas expressing his dismay that Douglas had abandoned him. He also wrote *The Ballad of Reading Gaol*, in which he dwelled on the inhumanity of capital punishment. After his release on May 19, 1897, he moved to Paris. Wilde never returned to England. He was 46 years old when he died at the Hotel d'Alsace on November 30, 1900.

During Wilde's trial, his two sons were sent to Switzerland. Constance left England after Wilde's conviction and joined the children a week later. When a hotelier in Switzerland refused her booking because she was a "Wilde," she changed the family name to Holland. She established an allowance for Wilde on condition he not see Douglas, but that ended when Douglas joined Wilde in France and then journeyed with him to Italy. Their reunion did not last.

Constance underwent surgery and died at age 40 in Genoa on April 7, 1898. After his conviction, Wilde did not see his sons again. Cyril was killed in action in World War I. Vyvyan died in 1965. H.M. Hyde, *Oscar Wilde: The Aftermath* (1963).

Sir Edward Carson was a lifelong Ulster Unionist. In England, he was elected to Parliament in 1892 and was solicitor-general from 1900 to 1905. During World War I, he served as attorney-general, first lord of the admiralty, and as a member of the war cabinet. Carson became a baron in 1921 and died in 1935.

Alfred Douglas later married and converted to Catholicism. He wrote widely against homosexuality. In 1923 he was prosecuted and convicted for criminally libeling Winston Churchill. He claimed Churchill accepted a bribe for writing a misleading report about the World War I Battle of Jutland. Douglas was sentenced to six months in Wormwood Scrubs jail. He died on March 20, 1945. Wolfenden Report (1957); B. Belford, *Oscar Wilde: A Certain Genius* (2000).

On November 30, 1950, the 50th anniversary of Wilde's death, a graveside ceremony was held for him at the Père Lachaise cemetery in Paris.

Readings around the world of Wilde's work were planned for his 150th birthday. The Andrews Clark Library at UCLA holds the most complete collection. In March 2004, the library announced the acquisition of two manuscripts never before available to scholars. One is a 280-page student philosophy notebook from Wilde's Oxford days, and the other is the manuscript of *Without Apology*, a book written by Lord Alfred Douglas and published in 1937. B. Levine, "Oscar Season Starts Early for UCLA," *Los Angeles Times*, March 17, 2004.

After Wilde's conviction, his plays were banned and his literature shunned, but his popularity revived soon after his death. His works remain popular. The contemporary playwright Tom Stoppard refers to Wilde in *The Invention of Love*. The TV cast of *Frasier* performed a reading of *The Importance of Being Earnest*, and Kelsey Grammar called the *Frasier* series "an homage to the writing of Oscar Wilde." Levine, *supra*.

CNN reported that officials in Rhea County, Tennessee, were considering a ban on homosexuals, compelling them to leave the county or face criminal prosecution. Rhea County was in the news in 1924 when it was the site of the Scopes "Monkey Trial" in which Clarence Darrow, pitted against William Jennings Bryan, defended the teaching of evolution. Commenting on the latest controversy, a local woman resident exclaimed, "We are back to the days of Oscar Wilde." CNN, Mar. 18, 2004.

Wilde's *Ballad of Reading Gaol* provides this summary of his legal experience:

I know not whether Laws be right,
Or whether Laws be wrong;
All that we know who lie in gaol
Is that the wall is strong.
And that each day is like a year,
A year whose days are long.

23

United States of America against One Book Entitled *Ulysses* by James Joyce

Who ever anywhere will read these written words?
———*Ulysses*, James Joyce

Homer's epic *The Odyssey* tells the story of Ulysses's adventures returning home to Ithaca from Troy. James Joyce's epic *Ulysses* tells the story of Leopold Bloom's adventures in Dublin on June 16, 1904. Yet, the journey of Joyce's novel as a defendant in the American legal system, culminating in the trial of the *United States of America v. One Book entitled Ulysses by James Joyce*, is as remarkable as a work of fiction.

Joyce began writing *Ulysses* in Trieste in 1914. Once Italy entered World War I, he continued his work in Zurich where he lived with his wife Nora and children Georgio and Lucia in self-imposed exile from his Irish homeland. There, almost penniless and receiving financial help from grants, benefactors, and fellow writers such as William Butler Yeats and Ezra Pound, he wrote about Ireland. Fear by publishers that his novel would be considered obscene prevented its publication not only in Ireland, but in England and America as well. E. O'Brien, *James Joyce* (1999).

Rarely is a book a defendant. But there it was. Unlike Homer's *The Odyssey* in ancient Attica, James Joyce's *Ulysses* stood in the dock in New York in 1921, and again in 1933.

The 1921 Trial

In February 1918, Ezra Pound sent the manuscript of Episode 1 of *Ulysses* to Margaret Anderson and Jane Heap of the *Little Review* in America. They printed the first installment in March 1918 and continued printing further sections despite Pound's warning that they might have problems with the censors. The United States Post Office deemed the work "filthy" and seized all available copies. The published installments of *Ulysses* that were posted in the mail were intercepted and burned. Nevertheless, Anderson and Heap continued publishing and mailing serializations of *Ulysses*. R. Ellman, *James Joyce* (1982).

In 1920, John S. Sumner, secretary of the New York Society for the Prevention of Vice, charged the *Little Review* with publishing obscenity. A summons was served on the Washington Square Bookshop for selling a copy of the magazine. The censors were particularly incensed by Episode XIII ("Nausicaa"), involving Bloom's reaction upon seeing Gertie McDowell's lingerie.

Both Anderson and Heap were charged with publishing "indecent matter" and tried in the New York State Court of Special Sessions before three judges. The trial began February 14, 1921. John Quinn, defense counsel, analogized Joyce's work to Picasso and Braque's cubism, claiming that the published episode, if disgusting, was not "indecent." The prosecutor vehemently disagreed, whereupon Quinn, pointing to the prosecutor's angry face, retorted:

> There is my best exhibit. There is proof that *Ulysses* does not corrupt or fill people full of lascivious thoughts. Look at him! He is mad all over. He wants to hit somebody. He doesn't want to love anybody. . . . That's what *Ulysses* does. It makes people angry. . . . But it doesn't tend to drive them to the arms of some siren.

Ulysses was a "beautiful piece of work, in no way capable of corrupting the mind of a young girl," said John Cowper Powys, who testified as an expert witness.

Anderson and Heap were, nevertheless, found guilty of publishing "obscenity" and fined $50. Publication was discontinued.

They were both threatened with prison. To prevent this, Quinn "certified" that the Nausicaa episode was the most "obscene."

Leaving the courtroom, Quinn admonished Anderson, stating, "And now for God's sake don't publish any more obscene literature." Anderson replied, "How am I to know when it's obscene?" Quinn, puzzled, responded, "I'm sure I don't know, but don't do it."

The *New York Times* commented that *Ulysses*, although dull, was not immoral, but the use of certain "realistic" words was deplorable and deserved punishment. The decision ended the possibility of further publication of *Ulysses* in America.

Finally, *Ulysses* was published by Sylvia Beach of Shakespeare & Company Bookstore, 12 Rue de l'Odeon, Paris. Bereft of capital and publishing experience, Beach advertised advance subscriptions at 150 francs each. Subscribers included G.B. Shaw, William Butler Yeats, Ezra Pound, Ernest Hemingway, and André Gide. One thousand copies were printed by February 1922.

In October 1922, Harriet Weaver, using Beach's plates, published 2,000 copies of *Ulysses* for the Egoist Press in London. Five hundred copies were sent to New York and were promptly seized by the United States Post Office. In 1923, England banned any further publication or circulation. Joyce's *Ulysses* was now banned in the English-speaking countries of the United Kingdom, the United States, and Ireland.

A German translation was published in 1927. A French translation was published in 1929. Spanish and Japanese translations followed. Censors in England and America, however, continued to reject *Ulysses*.

Avid readers who bought *Ulysses* despite the ban included Winston Churchill.

So strong was the official aversion, that *Ulysses* was placed on the obscenity list in America by the United States Customs Service. In 1928, an American judge claimed that "only a casual glance" was enough to convince him that *Ulysses* was "filled with obscenity of the rottenest and vilest character." Hope for *Ulysses*'s legal entrance into America remained bleak.

The Seizure

In 1933, when the trial of the *United States of America v. One Book entitled* Ulysses *by James Joyce*, No. A 110-59, finally took place in the United States District Court for the Southern District of New York: (1) legally unprotected "obscenity" included anything indecent, and (2) the United States Post Office and the United States Customs Service determined what was "obscene." M. Moscato & L. Le Blanc, eds., *US v Ulysses* (Documents) (1984).

Other writers had faced similar challenges. Theodore Dreiser's *The Genius* was suppressed in 1920, the same year James Branch Cabell's *Jurgen* was declared "indecent." Under political pressure, D.H. Lawrence agreed not to reprint *Women in Love* and *A Young Girl's Diary*.

The parched literary thirst for *Ulysses* continued to intensify in America. Copies were sent clandestinely through the mail, and American tourists routinely purchased copies in Paris and brought them home. Finally, Bennett Cerf of Random House, excited by the prospect of legalizing the sale of *Ulysses* in America, obtained the rights to publish the book and devised a plan.

His financial fear was that if Random House published *Ulysses* and it was banned under the obscenity act by the United States Post Office and the United States Customs Service, thousands of unread and unpaid for copies would languish in their warehouse. A test case was the answer.

Ulysses was carried to New York so the United States Customs inspector would open it, read it, and reject it.

Cerf recalled years later that there was unanticipated difficulty persuading the Customs agent "actually" to seize *Ulysses*. On a humid summer day, a passenger from England alighted from the *Aquitania* with the famous contraband in his luggage, pursuant to Cerf's scheme. The Customs agent was anxious to get the passengers through the line. He was stamping all the baggage without opening and inspecting it. When the passenger arrived with *Ulysses* in his suitcase, the Customs agent began to stamp his luggage without looking at it. The passenger became frantic and said, "I insist that you open that bag and search it." The Customs agent refused, replying, "It's too hot."

The passenger repeated, "I think there's something in there that's contraband, and I insist that it be searched." The Customs agent, now annoyed, opened the passenger's bag and saw *Ulysses*. The Customs agent remained unmoved, however, saying, "Oh, for God's sake, everybody brings that in. We don't pay any attention to it." The passenger persisted, "I demand that you seize this book." The Customs Chief was called to the scene. He thought that seizing *Ulysses* was ridiculous, but because the passenger who was carrying *Ulysses* was legally correct, the Customs agent was compelled to seize it. He did so on May 8, 1932. That copy of *Ulysses* was later introduced into evidence in the trial.

Ulysses's next stop was at the United States Attorney's Office in Manhattan, where it awaited legal proceedings under Section 305 of the Tariff Act of 1930, 19 U.S.C.A. 1305(a). The Act "prohibited from importing into the United States from any foreign country . . . any obscene book. . . ." *Ulysses,* according to the United States Post Office and the United States Customs Service, was "obscene."

America's classic obscenity case was filed in the United States District Court in Manhattan. The firm of Greenbaum, Wolff & Ernst in New York was retained by Random House. Morris Ernst, a leading obscenity lawyer, and Alexander Lindley represented *Ulysses* in the trial. Nicolas Atlas and Samuel Colemen represented the United States. The case was continued several times because Ernst wanted Judge John Woolsey to hear the case. Woolsey loved literature. Ernst knew Woolsey would understand the genius of Joyce. Woolsey presided at the trial. Ellman, *supra.*

Ernst and Atlas agreed to have the case heard without a jury. Woolsey continued the case through the summer while he read *Ulysses*. Finally, on November 25, 1933, the parties appeared in a small, oval courtroom at the Association of the Bar of the City of New York. The trial began.

After the parties gathered in the courtroom, a prosecutor claimed the United States was helpless to proceed against *Ulysses* because "the only way to win is to refer to the great number of four-letter words used by Joyce." The prosecutor declared that he was unable to do this.

Ernst, perplexed and surprised, asked why the prosecutor was not able to state these putative vulgarities in court. "Because there is a lady in the courtroom" responded the prosecutor. In the packed courtroom, there was a woman present.

Ernst responded, "But that's my wife; she is a schoolteacher. She has seen all these words on toilet walls or scribbled on sidewalks by kids who enjoy them because they are forbidden."

The 1933 Trial

After this exchange, the United States of America proceeded, contending that *Ulysses* clearly was a threat to America and should be banned because of: (1) the use of four-letter words that were clearly unmentionable in polite society, and (2) the glaring and blatant frankness of Joyce's technique in using a stream of consciousness in the portrayal of characters such as Stephen Dedalus and Leopold and Molly Bloom.

Ernst took the offensive early:

Counsel: Judge, as to the word "fuck," one etymological dictionary gives its derivation as from facere: "to make—the farmer fucked the seed into the soil." This, your Honor, has more integrity than a euphemism used every day in every modern novel to describe precisely the same event.

Judge Woolsey: For example. . . .

Counsel: Oh—"They slept together." It means the same thing.

Judge Woolsey: (smiling) But, Counselor, that isn't even usually the truth!

Ernst then explored Joyce's stream of consciousness, declaring that *Ulysses* was Joyce's "dramatic incisive attempt to record those thoughts and desires which all mortals carry within themselves."

In response to the judge's query whether he had read *Ulysses*, Ernst said he tried to read it in preparation for the trial. He continued, "While lecturing in the Unitarian Church in Nantucket on the bank holiday. . . ." Suddenly, Woolsey interrupted, asking, "What has that to do with my question? Have you read it?"

Ernst responded:

While talking in that church I recalled after my lecture was finished that while I was thinking only about the banks and the banking laws I was in fact, at the same time, musing about the clock at the back of the church, the old woman in the front row, the tall shutters at the sides. Just as now, Judge, I have thought I was involved only in the defense of the book—I must admit at the same time I was thinking of the gold ring around your tie, the picture of George Washington behind your bench and the fact that your black judicial robe is slipping off your shoulders. This double stream of the mind is the contribution of *Ulysses*.

Woolsey quietly replied:

Now for the first time I appreciate the significance of this book. I have listened to you as intently as I know how. I am disturbed by the dream scenes at the end of the book, and still I must confess that while listening to you, I have been thinking at the same time about the Hepplewhite furniture behind you.

Ernst responded:

Judge, that's the book.

The Decision

On December 6, 1933, Woolsey issued his opinion:

I hold that *Ulysses* is a sincere and honest book, and I think that the criticisms of it are entirely disposed by its rationale. . . . The words which are criticized as dirty are old Saxon words known to almost all men, and, I venture, to many women, and are such words as would be naturally and habitually used, I believe, by the types of folks whose life, physical and mental, Joyce is seeking to describe. In respect to the recurrent emergence of the theme of sex in the minds of his characters, it must always be remembered that his locale was Celtic and his season Spring. . . .

I am quite aware that owing to some of its scenes *Ulysses* is a rather strong draught to ask some sensitive, though normal, persons to take. But my considered opinion, after long reflection, is that whilst in many places the effect of *Ulysses* on the reader undoubtedly is somewhat emetic, nowhere does it tend to be aphrodisiac. *Ulysses* may, therefore, be admitted into the United States. Moscato & Le Blanc, eds., *supra.*

The result of the trial was immediately cabled to Joyce in Paris. So many well-wishers clogged Joyce's telephone that his daughter Lucia had the telephone line disconnected twice. Joyce expressed his pleasure in a letter to T.S. Eliot on December 18, 1933, writing:

Dear Eliot:

Thanks for your letter but the U.S. ban does not "seem" to be lifted. It is lifted. I have here counsel's brief (100 printed pp) and the judge's ruling, about 12 pages. He states that his ruling is as legally valid as a decision by judge and jury, both parties having agreed to have the case tried before him alone. He orders that his ruling be filed. Three-fourths of the text was published in the *N.Y. Herald Tribune* of 7 December. The U.S. Attorney-General immediately after the decision, stood up and said he accepted the judge's ruling with great satisfaction and that the state would not appeal from it to a higher court. The defendant, Cerf, then said he would publish the book with an account of the proceedings (I suppose like the edition definitive of Madame Bovary) on January 19 next. . . .

En somme, one half of the English-speaking world has given in. The other half, after a few terrifying bleats from Leon Britannicus, will follow—as it always does. I am sorry you are not coming over. Anyhow, I wish you a Happy Christmas and good luck in the coming year.

Sincerely yours,
James Joyce

And in a letter to Michael Healy on December 20, 1933, Joyce wrote:

I hope things will go better now after the U.S. decision. It took me about 13 years to bring it off. England will follow, as usual. Ireland scarcely matters as there is a negligible market there for anything of this kind.

Because of the fear of piracy, typesetters were busy ten minutes after the decision. One hundred copies were published in January 1934. In February, the floodgates opened. Thirty-five thousand copies had been sold by May 1934.

The Appeal

The U.S. Attorney, George Medalie, was satisfied, and it appeared that *Ulysses* would legally reside in America without further litigation. But Medalie was succeeded by Martin Conboy before the expiration of the three-month period during which an appeal could be filed. The United States Post Office and the United States Customs Service were not pleased with the result. Conboy continued their efforts to protect America from *Ulysses* by appealing to the United States Court of Appeals for the Second Circuit.

In the appellate brief, Ernst presented Joyce's background, his influence, and an analysis of *Ulysses*, stating:

Joyce belongs to that distinguished company of Irish authors which includes such men as Padraic Colum, . . . James Stephens, Sean O'Casey, William Butler Yeats and George Bernard Shaw. . . . He has exerted a profound influence on world letters—possibly a greater influence than any man before him. There is not a single modern psychological novel worthy of mention which does not bear some trace of the Joycean method.

It is not often that an author, within the span of his lifetime, sees a work of his acclaimed as a classic. Joyce is such an author. He stands as a kind of Colossus of creative writing, dominating his age. He is a genius of the first rank.

Ernst then quoted encomiums about Joyce from eminent writers and critics.

Stuart Gilbert, distinguished American critic, says: ". . . the genius of James Joyce has an Elizabethan quality, an universality, a gift of reconciling classical, modern and romantic that, Shakespeare excepted, renders it unique."

"His prose works," says Rebecca West, "prove him beyond argument a writer of majestic genius."

"No living author," says Paul Rosenfield, "brings a vocabulary either as crisply, sharply, pungently used, or as vast. Joyce possesses a relatively unlimited knowledge of the resources of the English language. . . . It is no petty achievement to have attained with serio-comedy the level upon which Swift and Flaubert stand, and long will stand."

"When it comes to psychology or realism, beside Joyce Balzac is beggared and Zola bankrupted," says Shane Leslie in the *Quarterly Review*, October 1922.

"In *Ulysses* there is evident," according to J. Middleton Murray, noted English critic, "a genius of the very highest order, strictly comparable to Goethe's or Dostoyevsky's."

"He is," Gilbert Seldes writes in the *Nation*, "possibly the most interesting and the most formidable writer of our time. . . . Among the very great writers only two can be named with him for the very long devotion to their work and for the triumphant conclusion—Flaubert and Henry James. He has scored a victory of the creative intelligence over the chaos of uncreated things and a triumph of devotion, to my mind one of the most significant and beautiful of our time."

Finally, Ernst quoted Edmund Wilson:

". . . this austere, almost pedantic writer," says Wilson in the *New Republic*, "soars to such rhapsodies of beauty as have probably never been equalled in English prose fiction." (December 18, 1929).

345

"It is monstrous to suppose that a man of Joyce's stature would or could produce a work of obscenity."

Ernst then historically analyzed *Ulysses* and its influence:

Dante wrote the Divine Comedy, and Balzac the Comedie Humaine. It remained for Joyce to write the Comedie Intellectualle.

In some respects *Ulysses* defies accurate description. Although fictional in form, it is not a novel. It is a vast edifice of episode superimposed on episode, a panorama of all the aspects, moods, excesses and torments of the human mind. Despite its heroic proportions, it deals with but one day in the life of Leopold Bloom (Ulysses), advertising solicitor. All the action unfolds itself in Dublin. . . . All the emotions and attributes find their place here. There is birth, love, death, adultery, greed, sloth, drunkenness, anger, chicanery, intrigue, religion, philosophy, spiritual torture, childish ignorance, nationalism, lechery, madness, this list is infinite. Expressing these emotions, hundreds of characters hold forth in the streets, public houses, cemeteries, shops, libraries, newspaper offices, hospitals, brothels and churches. With this infinite variety of material . . . the author conceives a certain order and in doing so he creates a new form of the novel. . . . The real genius of the book . . . is implicit in the complete revelation and development of two characters, two of the greatest, saddest, most tragi-comic portraits in the entire annals of literary achievement—Stephen Dedalus and Leopold Bloom.

Yet, it is neither Dedalus nor Bloom who is the hero of *Ulysses*. The real protagonist is the mind. The arena is not Dublin, but the human skull.

Joyce has patterned his book after Homer's *Odyssey*, but he has not sought to make a parallel perfect. Whatever discrepancies exist are unimportant. In one significant respect there is a kinship between the two books: the *Odyssey* is a record of journeyings in a physical world; *Ulysses* is the epic of the coursing of the stream of consciousness.

Louis Golding, writing in *The Nineteenth Century*, April 1933, thus indicated the stature of Ulysses:

Among great works of prose we find none that compares in kind with *Ulysses*. When we seek works which compare with it in scope, we cannot stop this side of the *Inferno*, *Hamlet* and the *Odyssey*, each of which, in point of fact, has the closest bearing on the developing history of Stephen Dedalus and Leopold Bloom during the eternal eighteen hours of the day on which the action of *Ulysses* occurs.

Woolsey's decision was upheld by a split vote in the United States Circuit Court of Appeals for the Second Circuit. Two Hands of justice, Learned and Augustus, affirmed, stating, "Art certainly cannot advance under compulsion to traditional forms." Justice Martin T. Manton dissented. The case was not appealed to the United States Supreme Court. Americans have been able to enjoy *Ulysses* legally ever since. Moscato & Le Blanc, *supra*.

The confiscated copy of *Ulysses*, the only evidence presented at the trial, was donated to Columbia University on May 21, 1935, by Bennett Cerf, who stated:

The impeccable copy that we had imported was already in the tattered, dog-eared condition in which you now find it. Obviously, everybody in the Customs Department spent some time on this erudite volume. The District Attorney had also gone to the trouble of marking with a heavy cross every line of the book that he considered pornographic. This marking will undoubtedly be of great help to Columbia students who, I hope, will have a chance to examine this volume in the years to come.

Afterword

A *New Yorker* critic wrote on January 27, 1934, that:

James Joyce's *Ulysses* stands among the dozen or so greatest literary works of all time. Like most books of magnificent stature, it is a whole literature in itself.

Justice Martin T. Manton, the dissenting judge, later was convicted of corruption in office on an unrelated charge and served a prison sentence.

Joyce thanked Ernst for his legal victory in a letter dated October 18, 1937:

Dear Mr. Ernst:

By a post boat a few days ago I sent you a copy of the (still highly-priced) trade edition of *Ulysses* with a few words inscribed which are a very meager return for the great service you have done to me and it. The reason I did not send you a copy before is that, until I had the pleasure of meeting Mrs. Ernst and yourself here and of talking with you, I had no idea that you were "my" lawyer, that is, enlisted almost voluntarily and from conviction for the general and particular causes you sustained so brilliantly: Evidently I was in error; and I hasten to repair my bevue [error].

Thank you for the copy of the book about the censorship law. I shall send this on to my London lawyer when I have read it. . . .

Sincerely yours,
James Joyce

On October 27, 1931, Joyce had written to Harriett Weaver that if America ever lifted the ban ". . . England will follow suit as usual a few years later. And Ireland 1000 years hence." Joyce, himself, never set foot in America. Cerf had tried to persuade him to visit, but Joyce was afraid of boats.

When the German Army marched into Paris in June 1940, Joyce and his family moved again to Zurich. He had arrived in Paris for a one-week visit and had stayed for 20 years. On January 10, 1941, Joyce was hospitalized for a perforated duodenal ulcer. Surgery was unsuccessful. He died on January 13, 1941. Although *Ulysses* finally became legal in England in 1937, at the time of Joyce's death *Ulysses* still was banned in Ireland. Now, of course, despite Joyce's pessimistic prediction, the celebration of Bloomsday has become an ample source of Dublin's pride and prosperity.

Virginia Woolf, who had been hostile towards *Ulysses*, wrote in her *Diary* on January 15, 1941: "Then Joyce is dead: Joyce about a fortnight younger than I am. I remember Miss Weaver, in wool gloves, bringing *Ulysses* in typescript to our tea table at Hogarth House."

Nora, Joyce's wife, survived him by ten years. She called him "my poor Jim." Nora said that she had "been married to the greatest writer in the world." She never read *Ulysses*.

Paul Lewis in the *New York Times* on July 20, 1998, reported:

Ulysses, that sprawling, difficult, but uniquely original masterpiece by James Joyce, has been voted the finest English-language novel published this century by a jury of scholars and writers.

The book—in which an immensely long account of a single day in the lives of a group of Dubliners becomes a metaphor for the human condition and the author experiments with language almost to the point of unintelligibility—heads the list of 100 novels drawn up by the editorial board of Modern Library, which has been publishing classic English-language literature at affordable prices since 1917 and is now a division of Random House. . . .

Ulysses was banned in the United States as obscene from 1920 to 1933, when the ban was lifted by a Federal judge, John M. Woolsey, who called the book "a sincere and serious attempt to devise a new literary method for the observation and description of mankind."

"As I am, As I am. All or not at all."

Ulysses
James Joyce

24

Pride and Prejudice
The Dark Side of Henry Ford

Henry Ford was an American phenomenon. Raised on a farm in Dearborn, Michigan, he was a mechanical genius who, by 1914, "put America on wheels." Lauded for high wages for workers, the assembly line, and low-priced cars, Ford became one of the world's richest men. But he wanted more. Despite his limited education, Ford intended to use his influence.

The paternalistic Ford was always confident that he knew best. He sent a "peace" ship to Europe in 1915 in an attempt to end World War I. The effort failed. He self-published a series of antismoking pamphlets, which he titled *The Case Against the Little White Slaver*.

In a reprint of Ford's antismoking pamphlets, David L. Lewis of the University of Michigan noted that as a visionary and crusader, Ford "championed birds, peace, Prohibition, . . . waterpower, village industries, old-fashioned dancing, reincarnation, exercise, carrots, wheat, soybeans, plastics, hard work, and hiring of the handicapped, and attacked Jews, jazz, historians, 'parasitic' stockholders, alcohol, rich foods, meat, overeating, . . . lipstick, rolled stockings, horses, cows, pigs, and chickens." Labor unions later were added to the attack list.

But two trials shaped Ford's future. The dark period of Ford's life began when a 1919 defamation trial by Ford against Colonel Robert McCormick's *Chicago Tribune* exposed his ignorance of history and wounded his pride. Ford had bought his own newspaper, the *Dearborn Independent* (*Independent*), to promote his views. It began as a progressive, pacifist weekly. With the *Chicago Tribune* trial, Ford's era of idealism ended. Backed by his powerful personal secretary, Ernest G. Liebold, he used the *Independent* to rail against Jewish influence in international banking and national culture. The second trial, in which Aaron Sapiro sued Ford for defamation, ended Ford's anti-Semitic campaign. He apologized in 1927. Yet the articles continued to be published by others, promoting anti-Semitic prejudice throughout the world. R. Hofstadter, *The Age of Reform* (1955).

The Chicago Tribune Trial

In the first trial, Ford sued McCormick's *Chicago Tribune* for $1 million. The trial was a major media event. It began on May 12, 1919, with Judge James G. Tucker presiding in the circuit court of Macomb County, Michigan. The setting was the spa town of Mount Clemens. Press coverage became intense when a cross-examination by *Tribune* lawyer Elliott Stevenson exposed Ford's inability to answer basic questions about American history. Ford's education had been based on a series of McGuffey *Readers* that promoted moral values based on Protestant Christian ethics.

The lawsuit arose from a description of Ford in the *Chicago Tribune*. When President Woodrow Wilson activated the National Guard in June 1916 to defend the Mexican border, a reporter from the jingoistic *Tribune* questioned a Ford aide about Ford's antiwar reaction. The aide replied that employees responding to duty would lose their jobs and would not receive Ford's help. This was wrong, but without checking with Ford officers, the *Tribune* published a story called "Flivver Patriotism." It was followed by an editorial headlined "Ford Is an Anarchist," which charged that if Ford meant to follow this policy, he should move his factories to Mexico, and that Ford had revealed himself as not merely an ignorant idealist but an anarchistic enemy of the nation that protected his wealth.

Ford was livid. Had Ford's lawyers sued because of the words *anarchist* and *anarchistic*, they would have won because those words were already legally considered libelous per se. They could have held the court to a strict limitation of evidence and conducted a short trial. But they cited the entire editorial, allowing admission of evidence that Ford was an "ignorant idealist" and "unpatriotic." A. Nevins & F.E. Hill, *Ford: Expansion and Challenge* (1957).

During the cross-examination, Ford defended his view that war was murder. He insisted that "over preparedness" was the root of all war. "Anything that contemplates more than defense is over preparedness," he claimed. The better way was "to educate people. To teach them to think for themselves." "You call yourself an educator," Stevenson jabbed. "Now, I shall inquire whether you were a well-informed man, competent to educate people." The door was open.

He began by reminding Ford that he had once told a *Tribune* reporter, "History is more or less bunk." Ford retorted, "I did not say it was bunk. It was bunk to me . . . I did not need it very bad." But that day on the stand, Ford failed Stevenson's history quiz, which included these questions:

Q: Have there been any revolutions in this country?
A: There was, I understand.
Q: When?
A: In 1812.
Q: In 1812, the Revolution?
A: Yes.
Q: Any other time.
A: I don't know.
Q: You don't know of any other?
A: No.
Q: Don't you know there wasn't any revolution in 1812?
A: I don't know that. I didn't pay much attention to it.
Q: Don't you know that this country was born out of a revolution in 1776? Did you forget that?
A: I guess I did.

Ford's lawyer, former Congressman Alfred Lucking, protested, but Judge Tucker insisted that Ford submit to an inquiry as to all things that would go to make an "ignorant idealist." Stevenson continued his questioning:

Q: Did you ever hear of Benedict Arnold?
A: I have heard the name.
Q: Who was he?
A: I have forgotten just who he is. He is a writer, I think.

Lucking protested again: "Outrageous, cruel, a shame to subject such a man to such an examination." Stevenson asked Ford several times to read something. Ford refused, saying he forgot his spectacles. Stevenson confronted Ford:

> Q: I think the impression has been created by your failure to read . . . that you could not read. Do you want to leave it that way?
> A: Yes, you can leave it that way. [*Ford continues*] I am not a fast reader and I have hay fever and I would make a botch of it.

When Ford finished his testimony he vowed never to return to a courtroom.

In his summation, Lucking attacked Stevenson's vilification of Ford's character. He reminded the jury that Ford's factory was one of the "Wonders of the World." The jury reached a verdict: "We find for the plaintiff in the case and award Henry Ford nominal damage of six cents."

The *New York Times* announced that Ford "had not passed the examination of his intellectual horizons." Other urban publications agreed. But rural Americans continued to treat Ford as a folk hero. C. Gelderman, *Henry Ford, The Wayward Capitalist* (1981).

Citizen Ford

Meanwhile, critics found Ford's *Dearborn Independent* colorless and dull. The *Detroit Times* called it "the best periodical ever turned out by a tractor plant." E. G. Pipp, former managing editor of the *Detroit News*, was appointed editor, with complete control except for "Mr. Ford's Own Page," a weekly feature on which Ford collaborated with William J. Cameron, a *Detroit News* editorial writer. Liebold, Ford's watchdog and implementer, became general manager, with complete responsibility for Ford's column. In a conference, staff member Joseph O'Neill suggested that the newspaper "find an evil to attack, go after it and stay after it . . . name names and tell actual facts," concluding, "Let's have some sensationalism."

O'Neill may have been surprised at the subject Ford chose for his crusade. A 91-week anti-Semitic series began on May 22, 1920, with a front cover article entitled "The International Jew: The World's Problem." Editor Pipp believed the attack on Jews was encouraged by the prejudiced Liebold. Anti-Semitic sentiments were not uncommon in America's heartland, and Ford found it easy to believe that "an international Jewish banking power" had started World War I and kept it going. He felt "good" Jews would be happy about the exposé of the "international" types. Ford claimed that he first learned about the activities of the "International Jews" from journalist Herman Bernstein on the peace ship, but Bernstein denied Ford's allegations and later sued him for defamation.

Leo M. Franklin, the leading rabbi of Detroit, was Ford's friend and neighbor. He had been a guest at Ford's Fair Lane home in Dearborn. In response to the articles, Franklin returned a car that Ford had given him. According to Pipp, Ford, oblivious to Franklin's reaction to the article, called and asked, "What's wrong, Dr. Franklin? Has something come between us?" Ford also admired Albert Kahn, the famous architect who designed most of his buildings. Within the company, industrial jobs were not closed to Jews, but they were never employed in Ford offices. W.C. Richards, *The Last Billionaire* (1948).

Pipp resigned. Cameron, who took his place, was assigned to research Jews and reported "what a wonderful race they were" and how little he had known of their "magnificent history." Yet he did not stop the attack and eventually joined the anti-Semitic campaign. D.L. Lewis, *The Public Image of Henry Ford* (1976); Nevins & Hill, *supra.*

The *Independent* not only tagged Jews in world governments but Jews in American finance, copper production, theater, motion pictures, baseball, bootlegging, and song writing. Articles included "Jewish Exploitation of Farmers' Organizations," "Jewish Gamblers Corrupt American Baseball," "Jewish Jazz Becomes Our National Music," "The Jewish Associates of Benedict Arnold," "How the Jewish Song Trust Makes You Sing," and "Jew Wires Direct Tammany's Gentile Puppets." The *Independent* anointed Bernard Baruch a "Jew of Super-Power." This anti-Semitic onslaught was the most far-reaching in American history. Dearborn Independent, *The International Jew*, 3 vols. (1920–1922).

Ford's weekly linked these charges to the notorious fiction *The Protocols of the Elders of Zion*, which depicted a conspiracy of Jews seeking world domination. In an article in the 1955 *American Jewish Yearbook*, Oscar and Mary F. Handlin wrote:

Everywhere in Eastern and Central Europe the old regimes have been pulled down by Bolsheviks eager to destroy established institutions. Was it not possible that identical covert forces moved the wild groups of Anarchists, Wobblies, Socialists and other disturbers of order in the United States? A Congressional committee heard evidence that it was the East Side Jews who had created the Russian Revolution, and many a man began to reflect that perhaps it was true, as prophetic novelists had already suggested, that the Jewish conspiracy operated on both fronts, through the international bankers and through the international revolutionaries.

Thus was the explanation advanced by a vicious little volume that began to circulate widely through the nation in the 1920s. *The Protocols of the Elders of Zion* gave the details of a meeting . . . at which the whole design had presumably been planned. All the frightening images were present: the mysterious powers of the Rabbis, the gold standard, the great bankers, the insidious radicals. The obvious forgery of the *Protocols* had actually been perpetrated earlier in the century by the Czar's secret police. But it was now accepted literally by thousands of gullible Americans along with a vast array of other racist and anti-Semitic writings imported from Europe.

The French branch of the Okhrana, the Russian secret police, produced the *Protocols* manuscript soon after the first Zionist Congress in Basel, Switzerland, in 1897. The 24 *Protocols* contain materials from at least two sources. Herman Goedsche in his 1868 pulp fiction novel *Biarritz* told of Jewish world conquest in structure and words often identical to the *Protocols*. A chapter in *Biarritz* describing a midnight meeting of Jewish leaders was published separately in an 1872 pamphlet called "The Rabbi's Speech." Sir John Retcliffe, Goedsche's nom de plume, became Sir John Readclif, an English diplomat. "The Rabbi's Speech" was later used shamelessly to authenticate the *Protocols*. N. Cohn, *Warrant for Genocide* (1996).

In 1921, Philip Graves of the London *Times* discovered that an 1864 book by Maurice Joly, *The Dialogue in Hell between Machiavelli and Montesquieu*, a political satire directed against Napoleon III, was not only plagiarized but falsified in the writing of the *Protocols*. Paragraph-by-paragraph comparisons show the Jewish elders mouthing Joly's rendition of the words of Machiavelli. B. Segel, *A Lie and a Libel* (1995).

A revised version of the *Protocols* was published in 1905. Sergei Nilus, a mystic and Nietzsche admirer, linked the Jewish star with the seal of the Anti-Christ. The 1918 Russian Revolution sent Czarist allies packing, and soon the Nilus *Protocols* reached Western Europe. With the backing of a doctor at the U.S. War Department, in 1920 Boris Brasol, a Russian emigré, helped with the translation in America. The transcript was turned down by the *New York Herald* as a "clumsy falsification," but soon the *Protocols* came to the attention of Liebold, and publication of excerpts was assured. N. Baldwin, *Henry Ford and the Jews* (2001); Dearborn Independent, *supra*, vol. 1.

The *Independent's* circulation leaped from 70,000 in 1920 to 900,000 in 1926. It was largely distributed through Ford car dealers, who often sent it to names in local telephone directories in order to meet the subscription quotas. Reprints were used by the Ku Klux Klan, and 3,000 copies were sent by Ford to friends. D. Brinkley, *Wheels for the World* (2003); Lewis, *supra*; H.E. Quinley & C.Y. Glick, *Anti-Semitism in America* (1979).

With Ford's diatribes gaining attention, the Dearborn Publishing Co. combined four volumes of articles from the *Independent* and published them in pamphlet form, again titled *The International Jew*. The individual volumes were "The World's Foremost Problem" (1920); "Jewish Activities in the United States" (1921); "Jewish Influence on American Life" (1921); and "Aspects of Jewish Power in the United States" (1922). Liebold did not copyright the pamphlets.

Then, as suddenly as they had begun, the articles ended. Although Ford had lost his run for election to the U.S. Senate in 1920, he was considering a presidential campaign. In 1924, an enthusiastic young German politician named Adolph Hitler was jubilant, telling a *Chicago Tribune* reporter: "I wish I could send some of my shock troops to Chicago and other big American cities to help in the elections. . . . We look to Heinrich Ford as the leader of the growing Fascist movement in America. . . . We have just had his anti-Jewish articles translated and published. The book is being circulated in millions throughout Germany." Baldwin, *supra*; Brinkley, *supra*; F.R. Bryan, *Beyond the Model T: The Other Ventures of Henry Ford* (1997).

Ford, a Republican, eventually supported Calvin Coolidge, but *The International Jew* continued to attract international attention. Adolf Hitler lauded Ford as a man of great vision. In *Mein Kampf*, he wrote: "It is Jews who govern the stock exchange forces of the American Union. Every year makes them more and more the

357

controlling masters of the producers in a nation of one hundred and twenty million; only a single great man, Ford, to their fury, still maintains full independence." Ford was the only American Hitler mentioned in his American edition. A. Hitler, *Mein Kampf* (1925).

Sapiro v. Ford

On April 12, 1924, a new series of 20 articles began in the *Independent*. Aaron Sapiro was a Chicago lawyer who had obtained his law degree from Hastings Law School in San Francisco in 1911. He had become famous by organizing cooperative associations for farmers based on commodity rather than geography. Sapiro incorporated 90 cooperatives in America and Canada. They permitted farmers to pool their crops and spread sales throughout the year rather than be forced to sell at harvest time. He had created cooperatives for southern cotton planters, Canadian wheat farmers, and California fruit growers. Sapiro organized a wheat-marketing cooperative for financially troubled Midwestern farmers.

Although Bernard Baruch enthusiastically supported Sapiro's program, the Department of Agriculture warned farmers against participating in the cooperatives. Kentucky and Illinois politicians claimed Sapiro was manipulating the farmers. It was an explosive issue. "I don't believe in cooperation," Henry Ford said. "What can cooperation do for farmers? All it amounts to is an attempt to raise the price of farm products." Baldwin, *supra*; Gelderman, *supra*; Lewis, *supra*.

The *Independent* began attacking Sapiro, claiming he was cheating his clients. The articles warned farmers, "A band of Jew-bankers, lawyers, moneylenders, and agencies, fruit-packers, professional office managers and bookkeeping experts is on the back of the American farmer." The newspaper claimed that all cooperatives would be combined into an international monopoly dominated by Jews. B.M. Baruch, *Baruch: The Public Years* (1960); Nevins & Hill, *supra*; Richards, *supra*; Quinley & Glick, *supra*; Gelderman, *supra*.

Sapiro sued Ford. Neither the *Independent* nor its editors or writers were made parties. Sapiro's lawyers included William Henry Gallagher and Judge R. S. Marx of Detroit. Senator James A. Reed of Missouri, Ford's lead counsel, was assisted by Ford company lawyer C. B. Longley and five Detroit lawyers. The trial began on March 15, 1927, in the U.S. District Court in Detroit, before Judge Frederick S. Raymond.

The parties disagreed on the evidentiary parameters. Reed claimed that the evidence should be limited to the alleged libel directed at Sapiro. Gallagher argued that Ford had attacked all Jews. "There is no use in trying to pull the wool over our eyes and tell ourselves this is only an attack on Aaron Sapiro and that he personally and individually is being libeled," he said. Richards, *supra*.

Reed's retort was that the Jewish people were not plaintiffs and that Sapiro could not demand damage for the injured people and then keep the damage award for himself. The court ruled for Ford. Evidence was limited to the personal attacks on Sapiro. Sapiro initially alleged 141 libels but reduced the number to 54.

Louis Marshall, a New York lawyer and president of the American Jewish Committee, wrote on March 29, 1927:

> I must say that there is much loose thinking on this subject. It is the ordinary action for libel brought by Mr. Sapiro on the theory that the *Dearborn Independent*, under the control of Ford, has by its publications injured him in his business as a lawyer and as the organizer of agriculture cooperatives.
>
> The court has eliminated from consideration the infamous charges made by Ford against the Jews. No action could be brought by the Jews, as such, and Sapiro could not represent the Jews in fighting for honor, because an action in a representative capacity cannot be maintained. Whether this ruling is correct or not is immaterial at the present juncture. All that I desire to point out is that the action is a personal action of Mr. Sapiro. It is nobody else's business. If he was injured to the extent of a million dollars, he has the right to seek redress. . . . Personally I am sorry that the action was brought, because it has given Mr. Ford the publicity which he has craved ever since he embarked upon his attack of the Jews.

L. Marshall, *Champion of Liberty* (1957).

Reed relentlessly cross-examined Sapiro, attempting to show that he had charged exorbitant fees. Ford's major witness was W. J. Cameron, the *Independent*'s editor. Cameron testified for six days and stated he was solely responsible for the content. He denied discussing any article concerning Jews with Ford or sending him copies of articles before publication. He never saw Ford read a copy. Whether anyone read the articles to Ford was never asked.

Ford's defense was that he had no role in anything that appeared in the *Independent*. Ford's lawyer told the court that Ford had never heard of Sapiro before the trial began. But James M. Miller, a surprise witness and a former Dearborn Publishing Co. employee, testified that Ford told him that he wanted to have Sapiro exposed. Nevins & Hill, *supra*.

After Ford's *Chicago Tribune* testimony debacle, Sapiro's lawyers were eager to cross-examine Ford. He did not want to testify and avoided being subpoenaed. Finally, a process server found him while he was watching airplanes at Ford Airport. The night before Ford was scheduled to testify, he was driving alone on Michigan Avenue in Dearborn. His car was sideswiped and forced down a 15-foot embankment near the River Rouge. It struck a tree. Ford claimed that, dazed and bleeding, he made his way home.

Two days later, his surgeon had him removed to the Henry Ford Hospital. The authenticity of Ford's accident has been questioned. Ford Hospital physicians and employees confirm Ford's injuries. But Harry Bennett, pugnacious chief of security during Ford's union-breaking days, claims Ford was never in the car. In any case, he never testified. H. Bennett, *We Never Called Him Henry* (1951); Nevins & Hill, *supra*.

The trial then took a startling turn. When Gallagher, Sapiro's lawyer, asked the judge to appoint a disinterested doctor to examine Ford, Ford's lawyers submitted 14 affidavits acquired by Bennett and signed by his subordinates, charging Sapiro had hired an agent to bribe jurors and that a juror had accepted a suspicious package.

The juror, Mrs. Cora Hoffman, denied the charge to a *Detroit Times* reporter, telling him that she believed Ford's lawyers did not want the case to go to the jury. Judge Raymond exonerated her and criticized the *Detroit Times*'s "depraved journalism." But, under the law, the judge was compelled to declare a mistrial. The case was adjourned for six months. Gelderman, *supra*; Nevins & Hill, *supra*.

With Ford determined not to testify, his lawyers used this hiatus to settle the case. Ford agreed to pay Sapiro $140,000 in legal fees and court costs, to create a scholarship fund for a needy orphan, and to issue a retraction and apology. *N.Y. Times* (July 19, 1927); Baldwin, *supra*. The statement was prepared by four individuals: two of Ford's friends, Joseph Palma of the New York office of the U.S. Secret Service and Earl Davis, former assistant U. S.

Attorney General, and two of Sapiro's friends, Nathan Pearlman, former Congressman and a vice president of the American Jewish Congress, and Louis Marshall. The apology and retraction were drafted by Marshall.

Ford signed the statement without reading it. Palma cautioned that the retraction was "pretty strong" and that Ford should read it carefully. "Joe, no matter how strong it is, it could not be too strong," Ford replied, saying he wanted to undo a great wrong. He added, "Let the Jews judge me by my acts in the future." He told Palma to deliver the statement, dated June 30, 1927, to journalist Arthur Brisbane and ask Brisbane to make it public. In addition, on July 7, 1927, Ford published in the *Independent* a personal apology to Sapiro and a formal retraction of all charges against the Jewish people. Marshall, *supra*; Gelderman, *supra*.

Ford also settled with Bernstein, the peace ship journalist who had become editor of the *Jewish Tribune*, stating, "I sincerely regret any harm that may have been occasioned to the people of that great race and am anxious to make whatever amends are possible." *N.Y. Times* (July 25, 1927).

Ford's Apology

For some time past I have given consideration to the series of articles concerning Jews which since 1920 have appeared in the *Dearborn Independent*. Some of them have been reprinted in pamphlet form under the title *The International Jew*. Although both publications are my property, it goes without saying that in the multitude of my activities it has been impossible for me to devote personal attention to their management or to keep informed as to their contents. It has therefore inevitably followed that the conduct and policies of these publications had to be delegated to men whom I placed in charge of them and upon whom I relied implicitly.

To my great regret, I have learned that Jews generally, and particularly those of this country, not only resent these publications as promoting anti-Semitism, but regard me as their enemy. Trusted friends with whom I have conferred recently have assured me in all sincerity that in their opinion the character of the charges and institutions made against the Jews, both individually and collectively, contained in many of the articles which have been circulated periodically in the *Dear-*

361

born Independent and have been reprinted in the pamphlets mentioned, justifies the righteous indignation entertained by Jews everywhere toward me because of the mental anguish occasioned by the unprovoked reflections made upon them.

This has led me to direct my personal attention to this subject, in order to ascertain the exact nature of these articles. As a result of this survey I confess that I am deeply mortified that this journal, which is intended to be constructive and not destructive, has been made the medium for resurrecting exploded fictions, for giving currency to the so-called *Protocols of the Wise Men of Zion*, which have been demonstrated, as I learn, to be gross forgeries, and for contending that the Jews have been engaged in a conspiracy to control the capital and the industries of the world, besides laying at their door many offenses against decency, public order, and good morals.

Had I appreciated even the general nature, to say nothing of the details, of these utterances, I would have forbidden their circulation without a moment's hesitation, because I am fully aware of the virtues of the Jewish people as a whole, of what they and their ancestors have done for civilization and for mankind and toward the development of commerce and industry, of their sobriety and diligence, their benevolence and their unselfish interest in the public welfare.

Of course there are black sheep in every flock, as there are among men of all races, creeds and nationalities who are at times evildoers. It is wrong, however, to judge a people by a few individuals, and I therefore join in condemning unreservedly all wholesale denunciations and attacks.

Those who know me can bear witness that it is not in my nature to inflict insult upon and to occasion pain to anybody, and that it had been my effort to free myself from prejudice. Because of that I frankly confess that I have been greatly shocked as a result of my study and examination of the files of the *Dearborn Independent* and of the pamphlets entitled *The International Jew*.

I deem it to be my duty as an honorable man to make amends for the wrong done to the Jews as fellow-men and brothers, by asking their forgiveness for the harm that I have unintentionally committed, to retracting so far as lies within my power the offensive charges laid at their door by these publications and by giving them the unqualified assurance that henceforth they may look to me for friendship and good will.

It is needless to add that the pamphlets which have been distributed throughout the country and in foreign lands will be withdrawn from circulation, that in every way possible I will make it known that they have my unqualified disapproval, and that henceforth the *Dearborn Independent* will be conducted under such auspices that articles reflecting upon the Jews will never again appear in its columns.

Finally, let me add that this statement is made on my own initiative and wholly in the interest of right and justice and in accordance with what I regard as my solemn duty as a man and as a citizen.

Marshall, *supra*.

Despite Ford's protestations of innocence, muckraking author Upton Sinclair wrote, in *The Flivver King*, "unfortunately for Henry's record, he has published an autobiography, a book entitled *My Life and Work*, in which, speaking in the first person, he had espoused the entire anti-Jewish campaign, and summed up and endorsed the worst of the charges."

Liebold said that the anti-Semitic articles "were prompted largely by Mr. Ford" and that "he kept in touch with every phase." Liebold claimed that when he warned Ford about the possibility of a suit by Sapiro, Ford replied "that would be just what he wanted." Ford stopped publication of the *Dearborn Independent* in 1927. Liebold later insisted that Ford's prejudice continued after the apology. Nevins & Hill, *supra*; E. Liebold, *Reminiscences* (1953); S. Watts, *The People's Tycoon* (2005).

Afterword

On December 21, 1927, Marshall wrote to Ford:

Today's European mail has brought me a copy of the issue of December 7, 1927, of the *Volkischer Beobachter*, published in Munich by the notorious Adolf Hitler. He is one of the most virulent anti-Semites that the world has ever known. A few years ago he was convicted of an attempt to stir up a revolution in Bavaria and was imprisoned for a considerable period. He cooperated with Ludendorff in an effort to overthrow the

German Republic. He and his followers have resorted to libel, slander and violence of the most pernicious character, and throughout the civilized world he was regarded as a menace to society.

In this number appears a translation of your letter addressed to Theodore Frisch, of Leipzig, [editor of *Der Hammer*] which bears the date November 1, 1927, in which you demanded . . . that he desist from the publication and circulation of the *International Jew* and from the use of your name and that of the Dearborn Publishing Company. . . . It also contains what purports to be a letter dated December 1, 1927, addressed to you by Theodore Fritsch.

So far as it is published it is merely a repetition of the falsehoods which he and his followers have been circulating for years past. It also contains the most absurd statement as to the reason why you wrote the historical document which you forwarded to me on June 30, 1927. He is seeking to make it appear that you were forced by Jewish bankers to make reparation for the anti-Jewish articles published in the *Dearborn Independent*.

On February 21, 1928, Marshall wrote to the president of a German society of Jewish citizens, stating, "There is no doubt that anti-Jewish propagandists will continue to use much of this voluminous material and to this extent the harm done is irreparable." Marshall, *supra*.

On July 30, 1938, Ford's 75th birthday, he was the first American awarded the Grand Cross of the German Eagle, Hitler's highest honor for non-Germans. Ford claimed he accepted it in the name of the German people and not because of sympathy with the Nazis. R. Bassel, *Nazism & War* (2004); *Detroit News* (July 31, 1938).

Once World War II began, Ford returned to his technical skills to supply America's massive war effort. He retained Albert Kahn to design a huge factory at Willow Run, where 60,000 Ford workers mass-produced B-24 Liberator bombers, airplane engines, jeeps, trucks, tank engines, tanks, and tank destroyers. Brinkley, *supra*.

The Red Army liberated the Majdanek concentration camp in Poland on June 22, 1944. Uncut films of this Nazi extermination camp were shown in the River Rouge auditorium in May 1945. They showed how 200,000 Jews were killed in the gas chambers. Ford, horrified, realized the possibility of a connection between the Nazi atrocities and his anti-Semitic articles. He broke down. According to historian Carol Gelderman, "The shock caused a certain disorientation from which he never recovered." Ford died two years later. I. Gutman, *Encyclopedia of the Holocaust* (1990); Gelderman, *supra*; Lewis, *supra*.

In 1946, Baldur von Schirach, leader of the Hitler Youth and Gauleiter of Vienna, was convicted of crimes against humanity by the International Military Tribunal at Nuremberg. Von Schirach's mother was American. His paternal great-grandfather, a Civil War Union Army officer, lost a leg at the Battle of Bull Run. Von Schirach had joined the Nazi Party when he was 17 after reading *The International Jew*. At his trial he testified: "You have no idea what a great influence this book had on the thinking of German youth. The younger generation looked with envy to the symbols of success and prosperity like Henry Ford, and if he said the Jews were to blame, why naturally we believed him." He served his 20-year sentence. R.E. Conot, *Justice at Nuremberg* (1983); J.E. Persico, *Nuremberg* (1994); R.A. Martin, *Inside Nuremberg* (1993); Lewis, *supra*.

Edsel Ford, Henry's only child, had vehemently opposed the articles and gave generously to Jewish causes. Under the leadership of Edsel's son, Henry Ford II, the Ford Motor Co. was finally considered a friend to the Jews. Because of Henry Ford II's commitment to Israel, the Anti-Defamation League of B'nai B'rith gave Ford its American Heritage Award in 1980. Philip Slomovitz, editor of the *Jewish News* in Detroit, noted, "Henry Ford II has done a great deal to atone for the sins of his grandfather," and Richard Lobenthal of the Anti-Defamation League in Detroit said, "Every Jew I know who knew him told me . . . that he didn't have an anti-Semitic bone in his body." An example of the Ford Motor Co.'s continuing commitment was the sponsorship of the first screening of Steven Spielberg's *Schindler's List*, commercial-free, on national network television. Brinkley, *supra*; 2000 Anti-Defamation League website.

The *Protocols* continue to be distributed by Arab organizations and governments overseas. *The International Jew* also has domestic admirers. One recent Internet posting referred to Ford as follows:

> This text is a tribute to a great man's genious [sic] and desire to do the right thing for America and the world. Although much-maligned, its detractors—most of them close to or associated with the Jewish cabal of One World Dictatorship—have been unable to prove Henry Ford's ideas, facts, and

365

discussions to be incorrect. This, however, has never stopped the elitists who own much of our presses—90% of our media—just as Mr. Ford said they did.

Available at www.jewwatch.com.

The *Protocols* continue to be debunked. Under the headline "Frame by Frame, a Monstrosity Dismantled," *New York Times* writer Peter Edidin recently wrote:

> *The Protocols of the Elders of Zion*, which the *Encyclopedia Britannica* calls a "classic of anti-Semitism," turns 100 this year. It is one of the most successful pieces of conspiracy propaganda ever written. That success is puzzling. First, it is a preposterous work. . . . Second, the *Protocols* have repeatedly been exposed as a fraud.

Edidin also described a new graphic novel, *The Plot:* "The final work of Will Eisner, the eminent illustrator and writer, . . . mixes comic-style dramatizations from the lives of those with roles in the *Protocol's* history and quotations from actual documents." Edidin quoted Eisner's widow, Ann, as saying that Eisner hoped to reach people "the scholarly work could not. He wanted ordinary people to be able to understand that the *Protocols* are a forgery." *N.Y. Times* (April 17, 2005).

The books that provided much of Ford's education no longer appear in classrooms, but McGuffey *Readers* were the principal textbooks in American schools from 1836 to 1921. Henry Ford collected first editions. He reprinted all six *Readers* and distributed them to students. In 1934, Ford had William Holmes McGuffey's log-cabin birthplace moved to Greenfield Village, his outdoor museum. In 1936, Ford was an associate editor of a collection of McGuffey favorites, ranging from "Mary Had a Little Lamb" to Shylock's acceptance of defeat in Shakespeare's *Merchant of Venice.* Baldwin, *supra.* The collection is available for reading at the Benson Ford Library in Dearborn, Michigan.

25

Rosa Parks
An American Icon

I did not get on the bus to get arrested. I got on the bus to go home.

———Rosa Parks

In Montgomery, Alabama, a fine film of water covers a metal disk inscribed with key events and the names of 40 people killed in the struggle for civil rights between 1954 and 1968. This is sculptor Maya Lin's Civil Rights Memorial. Rosa Parks's name appears on the list. Her famous bus ride igniting the black boycott of public transit occurred nearby. She is a survivor.

The State Capitol of Alabama is across the way. Here, Jefferson Davis was sworn in as president of the Confederacy in February 1861; his house across the street served as headquarters during the first months of the Confederacy, when Montgomery was its capital. The rotunda in the Capitol commemorates more recent history, with murals of governors including George Wallace and a statue of his wife, former Governor Lurleen Wallace. The newly completed Troy State University Montgomery Rosa Parks Library and Museum and the Frank M. Johnson, Jr., Federal Building and

United States Courthouse are a few steps away. Rosa Parks's state court file is available at the clerk's office in the circuit court of the Montgomery County Courthouse. A pretty clerk, absorbed in talk about her birthday, took the file from a shoe box and copied pages for us.

Rosa Parks's Arrest

On December 1, 1955, reaction to Rosa Parks in Montgomery was not so benign.

At about 5 PM, Rosa Parks, a 42-year-old seamstress, walked to Court Square and waited for the Cleveland Avenue bus. She had just left work at the Montgomery Fair Department Store and entered the bus for her regular ride home. After paying her fare, Rosa Parks recognized the driver, James F. Blake, who 12 years before, after she had paid her fare, had told her to leave the bus even though it was raining and re-enter by the rear door. Bus drivers were known to do this after African-Americans paid the fare, and drive away before they reached the rear door.

The first 10 rows of seats on every Montgomery bus were reserved for white passengers only, and this right was sacrosanct. If the seats were filled, blacks in the next row had to give up their seats to the white passengers. The bus drivers were white and legally empowered to allocate seats and enforce the segregation laws. They had police power to carry sidearms.

After Rosa Parks boarded the bus, the seats filled rapidly. Twenty-two blacks were seated in the "colored" section in the rear. Fourteen whites were seated in the white section in the front. Rosa Parks sat next to a black man, in an aisle seat in the first row directly behind the white division. Two black women occupied the two seats across the aisle from her.

At the next stop, the bus driver picked up several white passengers, who filled the remaining seats in the white division. A white man was left standing. Blake told the four black passengers sitting in the row immediately behind the white division to leave their seats and go to the back of the bus. "Move, I want those seats." Four seats would then be available for the lone white man. No one moved. Blake, increasingly impatient, said, "You better make it light on yourselves and let me have those seats."

The two black women across the aisle from Rosa Parks left their seats and walked to the back. Rosa Parks shifted her legs so the black man sitting beside her could leave his seat; she then moved into his vacant seat next to the window. There she remained, looking across the street at the Empire Theater, where *A Man Alone* starring Ray Milland was advertised in neon on the marquee.

Now there were three seats available. But the white man remained standing. Blake, livid, walked toward Parks and looked down at her: "Are you going to stand up?" The chatter on the bus subsided. "No," she said. There was silence; then her answer exploded into America's greatest civil rights movement.

Blake told Rosa Parks she was in the white division, and the white division was wherever he said it was. Parks had to move. Blake had legal discretion to "separate the races." Rosa Parks was on a bus. Seated in no-man's land. She vividly recalled the event:

> People always say that I didn't give up my seat because I was tired, but that isn't true. I was not tired physically, or no more tired than I usually was at the end of a working day. I was not old, although some people have an image of me as being old then. I was 42. No, the only tired I was, was tired of giving in.
>
> The driver of the bus saw me still sitting there, and he asked was I going to stand up. I said, "No." He said, "Well, I'm going to have you arrested." Then I said, "You may do that." These were the only words we said to each other. I didn't even know his name, which was James Blake, until we were in court together. He got out of the bus and stayed outside for a few minutes, waiting for the police.
>
> As I sat there, I tried not to think about what might happen. I knew that anything was possible. I could be manhandled or beaten. I could be arrested. People have asked me if it occurred to me then that I could be the test case the NAACP had been looking for. I did not think about that at all. In fact if I had let myself think too deeply about what might happen to me, I might have gotten off the bus. But I chose to remain.

Rosa Parks, *My Story* (1992).

Blake called his supervisor on the radio and asked for instructions. His supervisor asked, "Did you warn her, Jim?" He said he did. The supervisor responded: "Well, then, Jim, you do it. You got to exercise your powers and put her off, hear?" Blake told Rosa Parks not to move until he returned with regular Montgomery police officers. D. Brinkley, *Rosa Parks* (2000).

Blake came back with officers F.B. Day and D.W. Mixon. Together, they arrested Rosa Parks in her seat, led her off the bus, put her in their police car, and drove her to the South Ripley Street Jail. There, she was booked, fingerprinted, and jailed.

Clifford Durr, a white lawyer, and his wife, Virginia Durr, a white civil rights activist who had employed Rosa Parks as a seamstress, along with E.D. Nixon, former president of the state and local NAACP chapters and a Pullman porter, went to the jail and had Rosa Parks released on bond. Her arrest and incarceration were reported on page nine of the *Montgomery Advertiser*: "Negro Jailed for 'Overlooking' Bus Segregation."

Rosa Parks was initially charged with violating a city ordinance that gave bus drivers police power to enforce racial segregation. At City Attorney Eugene Loes's request, however, the warrant was amended. Parks was charged with violating Section 54, Title 14, Code of Alabama 1940, and Section 301(31n), which called for "Separate Accommodations for White and Colored Races":

> All . . . transportation companies . . . shall at all times provide equal but separate accommodations on each vehicle for the white and colored races. . . . The conductor . . . of the transportation company in charge of any vehicle is . . . required to assign each passenger to the division of the vehicle designated for the race to which the passenger belongs.

The First Trial

Rosa Parks answered ready for trial on December 5, 1955, in a city hall courtroom at 103 North Perry Street. Her lawyers were 25-year-old Fred Gray, one of only two black lawyers in Montgomery and only the second black lawyer admitted to practice in Alabama, and Charles Langford, also a black lawyer. No legal training was available for African-Americans in Alabama at that time, and Gray was a graduate of Western Reserve Law School. Judge John B. Scott presided. City Attorney Loes appeared for the city of Montgomery. The courtroom's 100 segregated seats for spectators were filled.

The driver, James F. Blake from Seman, Alabama, testified that there was a vacant seat in the colored division of the bus. Otherwise, his testimony was consistent with Rosa Parks's account. Two white women witnesses corroborated Blake's testimony that a vacant seat was available in the colored division. But Rosa Parks had refused to sit there. The prosecution did not argue the availability of a vacant seat in the colored division. Instead, they alleged that the state segregation law gave bus drivers such as Blake unlimited power of enforcement.

When the prosecution rested, Parks pleaded not guilty. She did not testify. Gray unsuccessfully challenged the constitutionality of the Alabama bus segregation law. Rosa Parks was found guilty of refusing to yield her seat to a white man even though there were three adjacent vacant seats available. She was fined $10 plus $4 in court costs. Gray filed an appeal in the Montgomery Circuit Court.

Rosa Parks's arrest created a crisis—and an opportunity for Montgomery's African-American community. Parks was a member of the NAACP, and the organization planned to take action. A bus boycott boiled to the top of the list. That evening, approximately 4,000 people attended a meeting at the Holt Street Baptist Church. A 26-year-old pastor, Martin Luther King Jr., of the Dexter Avenue Baptist Church, had been nominated that same morning as president of the Montgomery Improvement Association, organized as the official boycott organization. King addressed the crowd:

Mrs. Rosa Parks is a fine person. And since it had to happen I'm happy it happened to a person like Mrs. Parks, for nobody can doubt the boundless outreach of her integrity. Nobody can doubt the height of her character, nobody can doubt the depth of her Christian commitment and devotion to the teachings of Jesus . . . And just because she refused to get up, she was arrested. . . .

You know, my friends, there comes a time when people get tired of being trampled over by the iron feet of oppression . . . tired of being flung across the abyss of humiliation where they experience the bleakness of nagging despair. There comes a time when people get tired of being pushed out of the glittering sunlight of life's July and left standing amidst the piercing chill of an alpine November.

Now let us say that we are not here advocating violence. We have overcome that. . . . The only weapon we have in our hands this evening is the weapon of protest. . . . My friends, don't let anybody make us feel that we ought to be compared in our actions with the Ku Klux Klan or the White Citizens Councils. There will be no white persons pulled out of their homes and taken out to some distant road and murdered.

There will be nobody among us who will stand up and defy the Constitution of this nation. We only assemble here because of our desire to see right exist.

Right here in Montgomery when the history books are written in the future, somebody will have to say, "There lived a race of people, fleecy locks and black complexion . . . who had the moral courage to stand up for their rights. And thereby they injected a new meaning into the veins of history and of civilization." And we're gonna do that. God grant that we will do it before it's too late.

Quoted in T. Branch, *Parting the Waters* (1988).

Parks's conviction for refusing to give up her seat to a white man stirred the black people of Montgomery. They would not use the buses. The Montgomery bus boycott had begun.

The Second Trial

Because approximately two-thirds of the passengers who used buses in Montgomery were black, the boycott caused a severe financial loss to the Montgomery Bus Co. The city of Montgomery struck back. On February 21, 1956, Rosa Parks and 89 other blacks including Martin Luther King Jr., were indicted by a grand jury. Parks's case was *State v. Rosa Parks*, No. 7409. The indictment read:

Rosa Parks . . . did without just cause or legal excuse for so doing, enter into a combination, conspiracy, agreement, arrangement, or understanding for the purpose of hindering, delaying, or preventing Montgomery City Lines, Inc., a corporation, from carrying on a lawful business, to wit, the operation of a public transportation system in the City of Montgomery, Alabama.

The indictment led to a charge against Parks for participating in a conspiracy to boycott Montgomery's bus system under a long-forgotten 1921 anti-labor statute prohibiting boycotts that violated Chapter 20, Title 14, Section 54, Code of 1940:

Two or more persons who, without a just cause or legal excuse for so doing, enter into any combination, conspiracy, agreement, arrangement or understanding for the purpose of hindering, delaying, or preventing any other persons, firms, corporations, or association of persons from carrying on any lawful business shall be guilty of a misdemeanor.

Rosa Parks now faced a contradiction. She had been insulted, arrested, jailed and convicted for refusing to move to the rear of a municipal bus. Now she was criminally charged for refusing to use the same buses, presumably so she could be insulted, arrested, jailed, and convicted again. Although the trials were set for March 19, the state aggressively proceeded only against King. On March 21, 1956, he was convicted. He was fined $500 plus court costs. The judge said he spared King a harsher sentence because King urged nonviolence.

Montgomery's authorities desperately fought the boycott. To stop drivers from transporting blacks, police officers followed buses and monitored bus stops. Any black driving a car was an immediate suspect. Anyone assisting blacks came under intense scrutiny. One driver, Jo Ann Roberson, was ticketed 17 times in several months for minor traffic violations: one for driving too fast, one for driving too slow. A black taxi driver was arrested when police discovered two men in the back seat—one white, the other black.

The Third Trial

After talking to Clifford Durr, the Montgomery Improvement Association decided to file a federal lawsuit so a constitutional challenge to Alabama's bus segregation laws could be made without waiting for Rosa Parks's appeal from her December 5, 1955, conviction to proceed in the Montgomery Circuit Court.

On February 1, 1956, Fred Gray filed an action entitled *Browder v. Gayle*, 142 F.Supp. 707 (1956) under Title 28, U.S.C. § 2284, which provided for injunctive relief for civil rights violations before a three-judge panel in the U.S. District Court for the Middle District of Alabama. The plaintiffs were four women and all persons who had suffered indignities on the buses. They claimed the "segregation" law under which Parks had been convicted on December 5, 1955, was unconstitutional. Robert Carter, an NAACP lawyer, joined Gray.

The defendants were the city of Montgomery, state of Alabama, Board of Commissioners, Montgomery Chief of Police, Alabama Public Service Commission, Montgomery City Lines, Inc., and two bus drivers.

The three judges were Frank M. Johnson, Jr., Richard Rives, and Seyborn H. Lynne. All were white. The African-Americans sought relief under the Privileges and Immunities Clause, the Equal

Protection Clause, and the Due Process Clause of the Fourteenth Amendment of the U.S. Constitution. The case was heard on May 11, 1956. The court determined that Blake, the bus driver, was "an officer of the State of Alabama empowered to enforce segregation laws on Montgomery buses." And he could use a handgun to do it.

The court further found that C.C. (Jack) Owen, president of the Alabama Public Service Commission, admitted that on April 24, 1956, he sent a telegram to the National City Lines of Chicago, of which the Montgomery City Lines, Inc., was a subsidiary. The communication included the following statements:

> As President of the Alabama Public Service Commission, elected by the people of Alabama, sworn to uphold the segregation laws of this state, which include all forms of public transportation, I hereby defy the ruling handed down by the United States Supreme Court ordering desegregation on public carriers. Alabama state law requiring segregation of the races on buses still stands. All public carriers in Alabama are hereby directed to strictly adhere to all present existing segregation laws in our state or suffer the consequences.

This was not helpful to the Alabama Public Service Commission. Its motion to dismiss was denied.

The pivotal issue was whether the statutes and ordinances "requiring the segregation of the white and colored races on the common carrier motor buses in the City of Montgomery and its police jurisdiction are unconstitutional and invalid." Alabama relied on *Plessy v. Ferguson*, 163 U.S. 537 (1896). Separate but equal had been the law since 1896.

In *Plessy*, a black man, Homer Adolph Plessy, boarded a train in Louisiana and took a "whites only" seat. The conductor told him to go to the "colored" railroad car. Plessy refused. He was immediately arrested and tried by Judge John H. Ferguson in the Criminal District Court for the Parish of Orleans for violating an 1890 statute, An Act to Promote the Comfort of Passengers, which decreed: "All railway companies carrying passengers in their coaches in this State, shall provide equal but separate accommodations for the white, and colored races, by providing two or more passenger coaches for each passenger train, or by dividing the passenger coaches by a partition so as to secure separate accommodations." Passengers refusing to cooperate with railroad officials in implementing this statute were subject to a $25 fine or a sentence of up to 20 days in jail.

Plessy argued that this statute violated the Equal Protection and the Privileges and Immunities Clauses of the Fourteenth Amendment, ratified in 1868:

> All persons born or naturalized in the United States, and subject to the jurisdiction thereof, are citizens of the United States and of the State wherein they reside. No state shall make or enforce any law which shall abridge the privileges or immunities of citizens of the United States; nor shall any state deprive any person of life, liberty, or property, without due process of law; nor deny to any person within its jurisdiction the equal protection of the laws.

His argument was unavailing to both Judge Ferguson and the Louisiana Supreme Court—and to the U.S. Supreme Court, where his lawyer Albion Tourgee argued that the "separate but equal" clause in the Louisiana statute was unconstitutional because it was "coincident with the institution of slavery." Tourgee stated:

> [T]he object of such a law is simply to debase and distinguish against the inferior race. . . . Its object is to separate the Negroes from the whites in public conveyances for the gratification and recognition of the sentiment of white superiority and white supremacy of right and power. . . . Justice is pictured blind and her daughter, the Law, ought at least to be color blind.

J.W. Johnson, ed., *Historic U.S. Court Cases,* 2nd ed. (2001).

However, Plessy lost again. On May 18, 1896, Justice Henry Billings Brown announced the U.S. Supreme Court's majority opinion of the Fourteenth Amendment's meaning:

> [T]he object of the amendment was undoubtedly to enforce the absolute equality of the two races before the law, but in the nature of things it could not have been intended to abolish distinctions based upon color, or to enforce social, as distinguished from political equality, or a commingling of the two races upon terms unsatisfactory to either. Laws permitting, and even requiring, their separation in places where they are liable to be brought into contact do not necessarily imply the inferiority of either race to the other, and have been generally,

if not universally, recognized as within the competency of the state legislatures in the exercise of their police power. . . .

But, in determining the question of reasonableness, [the Legislature] is at liberty to act with reference to the established usages, customs and traditions of the people, and with a view to the promotion of their comfort, and the preservation of the public peace and good order. . . . We cannot say that a law which authorizes or even requires the separation of the two races in public conveyances is unreasonable. . . .

We consider the underlying fallacy of the plaintiff's argument to consist in the assumption that the enforced separation of the two races stamps the colored race with a badge of inferiority. If this be so, it is not by reason of anything found in the fact, but solely because the colored race chooses to put that construction upon it.

Although "separate but equal" bus seats in Montgomery were constitutional and would remain so until the *Browder v. Gayle* decision in 1956, Justice John Marshall Harlan foretold *Plessy*'s future in his dissent:

But [e]very one knows that the statute in question had its origin in the purpose . . . to exclude colored people from coaches occupied by or assigned to white persons. . . . The fundamental objection, therefore, to the statute is that it interferes with the personal freedom of citizens. . . .

Our constitution is color-blind. . . .

In my opinion, the judgment this day rendered will, in time, prove to be quite as pernicious as the decision made by this tribunal in the Dred Scott case. . . .

The thin disguise of "equal" accommodations for passengers in railroad coaches will not mislead any one, nor atone for the wrong this day done.

After *Plessy*, the "separate but equal" formula remained the rigid and implacable bedrock of segregation laws. Although the *Plessy* concept of "equal" was consistently challenged in the "separate but equal" equation, the "separate" concept remained inviolate.

Fifty-eight years later, Justice Harlan's prescient dissent proved correct. On May 17, 1954, in *Brown v. Board of Education of Topeka*, 347 U.S. 483 (1954), Chief Justice Earl Warren galvanized a unanimous 9-0 U.S. Supreme Court by reading his ringing rejection of

Plessy's "separate but equal" principle: "In the field of public education the doctrine of 'separate but equal' has no place." Historian Alfred Kelly called Warren's opinion remarkable both for its simplicity and "for the extraordinary fashion in which it avoided all legal and historical complexities." A.H. Kelly & W.A. Harbison, *The American Constitution* (1955).

Brown was a victory for American idealism. And a victory for African-Americans in their quest for racial justice. *Brown v. Board of Education* was now the law of the land. Thereafter, "equal" stood alone. It became the sole benchmark in deciding the constitutionality of segregation laws. But the state of Alabama adamantly disagreed and argued that the *Brown* decision did not give African-Americans the right to pick their own bus seats. *Brown* involved public education, not public transportation.

Brown did not expressly overrule *Plessy v. Ferguson.* But its sharp, emphatic language was clear: ". . . anything inconsistent with this decision is overruled." On June 5, 1956, the *Browder v. Gayle* decision gave Parks and all African-Americans the "equal" right that whites had always had, to sit in any vacant bus seat. Rosa Parks's right was "equal." Not "separate." "Equal." This time she won.

Judge Frank M. Johnson, Jr., was the decision's architect. A 1943 graduate of the University of Alabama Law School and a classmate of George Wallace, Johnson entered World War II as a second lieutenant and landed in Normandy on June 11, 1944, five days after D-Day. After the war, he returned home and practiced law. In January 1956, President Eisenhower appointed him to the federal bench. On January 31, 1956, the U.S. Senate affirmed the appointment. J. Bass, *Taming the Storm* (1993). By a 2-1 majority, Judges Johnson and Rives decided the *Plessy* "separate but equal" decision had been "impliedly, even though not explicitly," overruled by the *Brown* decision. And that

> there is no rational basis upon which the separate but equal doctrine can be validly applied to public carrier transportation within the City of Montgomery and its police jurisdiction.
>
> We hold that the statutes and ordinances requiring segregation of the white and colored races on the motor buses of a common carrier of passengers in the City of Montgomery and its police jurisdiction violate the due process and equal protection of the law clauses of the Fourteenth Amendment to the Constitution of the United States.

Browder v. Gayle, 142 F. Supp. 707 (M.D. Ala. 1956).

Plessy's "separate but equal" principle, Alabama's basis for segregated busing laws under which Parks was convicted, was unconstitutional.

Judge Lynne dissented, claiming that although the *Brown* decision held that "in the field of public education the doctrine of 'separate but equal' has no place, that principle did not apply to public transportation practices which under the laws here attacked have resulted in providing the races not only substantially equal but in truth identical facilities."

Judge Johnson later commented: "I don't think segregation in any public facility is constitutional. [It] violates the equal protection clause of the Fourteenth Amendment. . . . That's all I had to say. It didn't take me long to express myself. The law was clear. The law will not tolerate discrimination on the basis of race." S.J. Rowe, *The Alabama Lawyer* (1991).

The Appeal

On November 13, 1956, the U.S. Supreme Court affirmed the U.S. District Court for the Middle District of Alabama's decision in *Gayle v. Browder*, 352 U.S. 903 (1956). Rosa Parks had a constitutional right to sit in any vacant seat on the bus she had boarded on December 1, 1955, in Montgomery, Alabama. And in any vacant bus seat in America thereafter.

On December 20, 1956, the U.S. Supreme Court order declaring Montgomery's segregated seating unconstitutional was served on Montgomery city officials. African-Americans boarded Montgomery buses again after 381 days—and they sat where they wanted. But not without violent and brutal rancor from racists.

The door was now open. The Supreme Court widened its *Brown* umbrella to include the *Gayle v. Browder* "public transportation" case, as it was doing in other segregated public facility cases, by affirming lower court decisions without opinion. See, e.g., *Baltimore v Dawson*, 350 U.S. 877 (1955) (public beaches); *Holmes v. Atlanta*, 350 U.S. 879 (1955) (public golf courses).

On December 21, 1956, Rosa Parks sat in an integrated Montgomery bus for the first time. James F. Blake, the bus driver who had her arrested, was on the same bus. Her comment: "He didn't react at all [pause]. Neither did I." *Montgomery Advertiser* (1982).

Afterword

In 1967, the Alabama House of Representatives voted to ask the U.S. Congress to impeach Judge Johnson.

In 1992, the Alabama House of Representatives voted unanimously to praise the decision of Congress to name the federal courthouse for Judge Johnson. On May 22, 1992, at the naming ceremony, a black legislator, Alvin Holmes, read a unanimous House resolution commending Congress for naming the U.S. Courthouse in Montgomery for Johnson. Holmes told Johnson, "We will never forget your contribution to this nation." J. Bass, *Taming the Storm* (1993).

Rosa Parks lost her job after her conviction. She received numerous death threats. Parks and her husband Raymond moved to Detroit, Michigan, in August 1956. Rosa Parks received 10 honorary degrees, including one from Shaw College and an honorary Doctor of Humanities degree from Wayne State University in 1975. Her Mount Holyoke College honorary degree included this citation: *"When you led, you had no way of knowing if anyone would follow."* Twelfth Street in Detroit was renamed Rosa Parks Boulevard in her honor. Raymond Parks died in 1977.

On July 2, 1964, Rosa Parks was an honored guest in the White House when President Lyndon Johnson signed H.R. 7152 into law: the Civil Rights Act of 1964. Johnson said: ". . . those who are equal before God shall now also be equal in the polling booths, in the classrooms, in the factories, and in hotels, restaurants, movie theaters, and other places that provide service to the public." T. Branch, *Pillar of Fire* (1999).

On August 6, 1965, President Lyndon Johnson signed the Voting Rights Act of 1965. Alabama had no elected black officials when Parks was arrested in 1955. In 1975, Alabama had 200 black officeholders.

In 1988 Rosa Parks was interviewed by the *Chicago Tribune*: "Back then we didn't have any civil rights. It was just a matter of survival . . . of existing from one day to the next. I remember going to sleep as a girl hearing the Klan ride at night and hearing a lynching and being afraid the house would burn down." She considered this the reason she fearlessly pursued the court proceedings and the boycott, saying, "I didn't have any special fear. It was more of a relief to know . . . that I wasn't alone. If I was going to be fearful, it would have been as far back as I can remember, not just that separate incident."

In November 1991, Judge Frank Johnson was interviewed by Stephen Rowe:

Q: In the Montgomery bus case, the majority opinion by Judge Rives and you extended the Supreme Court's *Brown* decision. In a sense new law was created. What is the proper role of lower courts in taking this type of action?

A: The use of the word "extended" and your phrase "new law was created" are both wrong. Lower court judges in the federal system have a duty and an obligation to follow the law. . . . Supreme Court decisions in the federal system are binding on all lower court judges.

The court of appeals judges, district courts, magistrates, everyone in the federal judiciary system. Judge Lynne—I have a lot of respect for Judge Lynne—in that case dissented because he said the Supreme Court hadn't specifically overruled *Plessy v. Ferguson.*

Well, the Supreme Court had in concept overruled *Plessy v. Ferguson.* They had overruled any public institution that discriminated on the basis of race. Why should we have sat back and let the Montgomery bus system and the Alabama bus system continue to discriminate on the basis of race when that concept had been very definitively decided by the Supreme Court of the United States?

I think you're abandoning your duty if you say, "Well, I think you're right, but I'm going to deny relief and let you file a petition for certiorari to the Supreme Court of the United States and let them decide this specific issue as to whether the concept applied in *Brown* is applicable to public transportation." Judges shouldn't do that. So, we didn't make new law.

Some judges have a different concept. Judge Lynne, for example. I tried cases before him when I was a lawyer. I prosecuted when I was a U.S. Attorney, and he's a great judge, but that's a position that I don't think judges should take. I never have. Of course, Judge Rives obviously felt the same way.

The Supreme Court is not set up to decide every case, every issue. They're set up to give some guiding principles to the lower courts to apply specifically. That's what they did in *Brown* and that's what we did in the bus desegregation case. . . .

Q: What kind of stress did the reaction to these decisions impose on you and your family? What kind of danger did you think you were in?

A: You don't ever know that. You just speculate on it. It was a little harder here as the *Montgomery Advertiser* and the *Alabama Journal* were owned by a family referred to as the "Hudson family." They were very reactionary as far as the civil rights movement was concerned.

They editorialized on me at least once a week, very adversely and critical of me. That makes it harder for your family. It stirs up adverse feelings in people who don't think for themselves, but just believe what they read in the paper. You don't ever know what the danger is.

The United States Marshal service provided some protection at my home at night, particularly when I was off in court. My mother's house was bombed. She lived about six blocks from where my wife and son and I lived. I don't think there's any question but that her house was chosen for that bombing either by error, thinking it was mine, because they were listed in the telephone book, or because they found that there were marshals at my house, and they just did that for intimidating purposes. But you can't tell what the dangers were. We're in the same situation now as far as this Judge Vance murder is concerned. All you can do is speculate.

All the judges on this court, the active judges, received death threat letters the same day that bomb was mailed, written on the same typewriter as the bomb was addressed with. So you don't know. . . . It's worse on some judges than it is on others.

You don't ever get accustomed or acclimated to it. But, you can't let it slow you down or stop you from working or carrying out your regular schedule because they've accomplished a substantial part of their mission if you allow them to do that.

Rowe, *supra.*

In November 1995, Parks was interviewed on the 41st anniversary of the U.S. Supreme Court decision banning segregation in public transportation. Rosa Parks said, "I was willing to risk whatever happened to me to let everyone know that this treatment of our people had been going on much too long." K. Abdul-Jabbar and A. Steinberg, *Black Profiles in Courage* (1996). Rosa Parks was awarded the Presidential Medal of Freedom in 1996, and in 1999, the U.S. House of Representatives by a 424-1 vote awarded her the Congressional Gold Medal.

Judge Frank M. Johnson Jr., was appointed to the 11th Circuit Court of Appeals by President Jimmy Carter. When he retired after 37 years on the federal bench, Johnson said, "My only aspiration has been, and will continue to be, to remove myself from the passions of the moment in order to render the fairest interpretation of the law that I am capable of." Bass, *supra*.

On December 1, 2001, about 45 years after Rosa Parks's arrest, the Troy State University Montgomery Rosa Parks Library and Museum opened in Montgomery, at 251 Montgomery Street—the same corner where the Empire Theater had been located.

Rosa Parks's home in Montgomery has been placed on the National Register of Historic Places. *New York Times*, January 17, 2002.

Bus driver James F. Blake died in Montgomery at the age of 89. Kem Holley, the children's minister at Morningdew Baptist Church, recalled that "Mr. Blake was a kind and gracious man, always had a smile on his face and always loved everybody." According to his obituary in the *Montgomery Advertiser*, Rosa Parks offered her condolences to his family through the Rosa and Raymond Parks Institute for Self-Development in Detroit. Jon Thurber, *Los Angeles Times*, March 26, 2002.

Alabama State Bar Gavel Passes to Fred Gray as First Black President. Another historic event in Alabama's legal history occurred as the Alabama State Bar welcomed its first African-American president, Fred D. Gray, internationally known Tuskegee civil rights attorney, at the meeting's Grande Convocation on Saturday, July 20, 2002. (Press release, Montgomery, Alabama, July 22, 2002).

When President Bill Clinton, speaking before Congress, looked up at Rosa Parks seated next to Hillary Rodham Clinton, he said, "She is sitting next to Hillary but she doesn't have to sit there; she can sit wherever she pleases." *Rosa Parks's Story*, NBC, February 2002.

Maya Lin's Civil Rights Memorial, located at 400 Washington Avenue in Montgomery, includes this inscription: "*1 Dec. 1955 Rosa Parks arrested for refusing to give up her seat on a bus to a white man.*"—Montgomery, AL

Rosa Parks died on October 24, 2005, and on November 2 of that year, she was buried in Detroit's Woodlawn Cemetery. Ten miles away in Elmwood Cemetery lies Henry Billings Brown, who died the year Parks was born. U.S. Supreme Court Justice Brown wrote the *Plessy v. Ferguson* opinion that provided constitutional protection to the "separate but equal" doctrine, which Parks defied while helping end racial segregation. T. Broad, "Henry Billings Brown," *The Supreme Court Historical Society Quarterly* (2006).

BIBLIOGRAPHY

MAKING A NATION

1. The King Who Lost His Head: The Trial of Charles I

America's Constitution, A.R. Amar (2005)
Charles I, C. Carlton (1941)
Great World Trials, E.W. Knappman, ed. (1997)
The Green Flag: The Most Distressful Country, R. Kee (1972)
A History of England, J.N. Larned (1900)
A History of England, J. Thorn, R. Lockyer & D. Smith (1961)
A History of Western Philosophy, B. Russell (1945)
Imagining the Law, N. Cantor (1997)
The Last Days of Charles I, G. Edwards (1999)
Leviathan, T. Hobbes (1651)
On the Laws and Customs of England, Henry of Bracton (c. 1265)
The Story of Civilization, vol. 7, W. & A. Durant (1961)
The Stuarts, J. Miller (2004)
The True Law of Free Monarchies. James VI & I (1599)
World's Great Trials, B. Axner & E. Sagarin (1985)

2. James Wilson: An Unknown American Founder

The American Constitution, A.H. Kelly & W.A. Harbison (1955)
"Before *Marbury*: *Hylton v. United States* and the Origins of Judicial Review,"
    Journal of Supreme Court History, R.P. Frankel Jr. (2003)
A Brilliant Solution, C. Berkin (2002)
Chisholm v. Georgia, 2 Dall. 419 (1793)
The Declaration of Independence, C. Becker (1969)
Dr. Bonham's Case, 8 Co. 113b, 118a, 77 Eng. Rep. 646, 652 (1610)
Founding Fathers, M.E. Bradford (1994)
The Great Rehearsal, C. Van Doren (1948)
A History of the English-Speaking Peoples: The Birth of Britain, W.S. Churchill
    (1956)
Hylton v. United States, 3 Dall. 409 (1796)
James Wilson, C.P. Smith (1956)

Justices of the United States Supreme Court, 1789–1969, vol. 1, R.G. McCloskey (1969)
Justices, Presidents and Senators, H.J. Abraham (1999)
Miracle at Philadelphia, C.D. Bowen (1986)
The Philosophy of Law in Historical Perspective, C.J. Friedrich (1963)
The Political and Legal Philosophy of James Wilson, 1742–1798, M.D. Hall (1997)
Records of the Federal Convention of 1787, M. Farrand, 4 vols. (1911–37)
Signers of the Constitution, R.G. Ferris & J.H. Charleton (1986)
Sources of English Constitutional History, C.S. & F.G. Marcham, eds. (1937)
Story of the Declaration of Independence, D. Malone (1975)
The Supreme Court Justices, C. Cushman, ed. (1993)
U.S. Constitution, Articles, I, II, III
Wesberry v. Sanders, 376 U.S. 1 (1964)
Works of James Wilson, B. Wilson, ed. (1804)
Who Was Who During the American Revolution, Historical Society of Pennsylvania (1976)
Writs of Assistance in Lechmere's case, Quincy Rpts., 51 (Mass. 1761)

3. The 1798 Sedition Act: President's Party Prosecutes Press

The American Constitution, A.H. Kelly & W.A. Harbison (1955)
The American Experience, S. Chase, www.pbs.org (2000)
"Congressional History of the 1798 Sedition Law," *Journalism Quarterly*, J.D. Stevens (1966)
"Fracas in Congress," B. Neff, *Essays in History* 41 (1999)
Freedom's Fetters, J.M. Smith (1956)
Great American Trials, E.W. Knappman, ed. (1994)
Journal of the Supreme Court History, vol. 28, no. 3, G. R. Stone (2003)
The Life of John Marshall, vol. II, A. Beveridge (1916)
Lincoln and Chief Justice Taney, J. Simon (2006)
Make No Law, A. Lewis (1991)
State Trials of the United States, F. Wharton (1849, reprinted 1970)
Thomas Jefferson, A. Mapp Jr. (1987)

4. Signed, Sealed, but Not Delivered: *Marbury v. Madison*

The Adams-Jefferson Letters, L.J.F. Cappon, ed. (1959)
The American Constitution, A.H. Kelly & W.A. Harbison (1955)
"Before *Marbury*: *Hylton v. United States* and the Origins of Judicial Review," *Journal of Supreme Court History*, R.P. Frankel Jr. (2003)
Cases in Constitutional Law, R.F. Cushman (1975)
Commonwealth v. Caton (1780)
Constitutional Law, P.G. Kauper (1954)
The Democratic Republic, M. Smelser (1968)
The Federalist Papers, R.P. Fairfield, ed. (1966)
A History of the Supreme Court, B. Schwartz (1993)
Holmes v. Walton (1799)

Jefferson: A Life, W.S. Randall (1993)

Jefferson Papers, 1751–1826 (Manuscript Collection, Library of Congress)

John Marshall: Definer of a Nation, J.E. Smith (1996)

The Lees of Virginia, P.C. Nagel (1990)

The Life of John Marshall, A.J. Beveridge (1919)

Marbury v. Madison, 1 Cranch 137 (1803)

Memoirs, Correspondence and Private Papers of Thomas Jefferson, T.J. Randolph, ed. (1829)

Origin of the American Revolution, B. Knollenberg (1965)

The Papers of John Marshall, C.F. Hobson, ed. (1990)

A People's History of the Supreme Court, P. Irons (1999)

The Political and Legal Philosophy of James Wilson, 1742–1798, M.D. Hall (1997)

The Rights of the British Colonies Asserted and Proved, J. Otis (1765)

Rutgers v. Waddington (1784)

Scott v. Sandford, 60 U.S. (19 How.) 393 (1857)

The Supreme Court and Its Great Justices, S.H. Ash (1971)

Thomas Jefferson, J. Appleby (2003)

Thomas Jefferson, S.G. Brown (1963)

Trevett v. Weeden (1787)

U.S. Statutes at Large, 1, 73; 1 Annals of Cong. 2d Sess. 2245

What Kind of Nation, J.F. Simon (2002)

Writs of Assistance in Lechmere's Case, Quincy Rpts. 51 (Mass. 1761)

DIVIDING A NATION

5. Justice Benjamin Curtis and *Dred Scott*

The American Constitution, A.H. Kelly & W.A. Harbison (1955)

American Insurance Company v. Canter, 1 Pet. 511 (1828)

American Judicial Tradition, G.E. White (1988)

American National Biography, J.A. Garraty & M.C. Carnes (1999)

An Autobiography of the Supreme Court, A.F. Westin (1963)

Circuit Court Reports, vol. 1, B.R. Curtis

Commonwealth v. Aves, 18 Pick. 210 (Mass. 1836)

Conflict of Laws, J. Story (1834)

Dred Scott Case, D.E. Fehrenbacher (1978)

Justices, Presidents and Senators, H.J. Abraham (1992)

Lincoln, D. H. Herbert (1995)

A Memoir of Benjamin Robbins Curtis, B.R. Curtis Jr., ed. (1879)

The Metaphysical Club, L. Menand (2001)

Prigg v. Pennsylvania, 16 Pet. 611 (1842)

Scott v. Sandford, 60 U.S. (19 How.) 393 (1857)

Slave Catchers, S. Campbell (1970)

Somerset v. Stewart, Lofft 1, 98 Eng. Rep. 499 (K.B. 1772)

Strader v. Graham, 10 How. 82 (1850)

The Supreme Court and Judicial Review in American History, K.L. Hall (1985)
United States v. Morris, 26 Fed. Cas. 1323 (case no. 15,815; C.C.D. Mass. 1851)
We, the Jury, J. Abramson (1994)

6. The Long, Strange Case of Dr. Samuel Mudd: The Lincoln Assassination

All the Laws but One, W. Rehnquist (1998)
Blood on the Moon, E. Steers Jr. (2001)
Doctor Samuel A. Mudd and the Lincoln Assassination, J.E. McHale Jr. (1995)
Ex parte Milligan, 71 U.S. 2 (1866)
Ex parte Quirin, 317 U.S. 1 (1942)
Great American Trials, E.W. Knappman (1994)
His Name Was Mudd, E.C. Weckesser (1991)
The Life of Samuel A. Mudd, N. Mudd (1975)
Mary Surratt: An American Tragedy, E.S. Trindal (1996)
Nazi Saboteurs on Trial, L. Fisher (2003)
A Pictorial History of the World's Great Trials, B. Aymat & E. Sagarin (1983)
The Riddle of Dr. Mudd, S. Carter (1974)
Samuel Alexander Mudd and His Descendants, R. Mudd (1982)
The Trial, E. Steers Jr., ed. (2003)

7. The Unusual Judah P. Benjamin

Digest of the Reported Decisions of the Superior Court of the Late Territory of New Orleans and the Supreme Court of the State of Louisiana, J. Benjamin & T. Sliddell (n.d.)
Dred Scott v. Sandford, 60 U.S. (19 How.) 393 (1857)
Fortnightly Review LXIX (March 1898), "Reminiscences of Judah Philip Benjamin," C. Pollack
Journal of Confederate Congress, Feb.-Mar. 1862
Judah P. Benjamin, P. Butler (1907, reprinted 1980)
Judah P. Benjamin, the Jewish Confederate, E.N. Evans (1988)
Judah P. Benjamin, R.D. Meade (1943, reprinted 1975)
McCargo v. New Orleans Insurance Company & Lockett v. Merchants' Insurance Company, 10 Robs. La. Rpts. 202, 339 (1842)
Oral Statement, F. Brummett (2007)
"SS *Judah P. Benjamin*," www.usmm.org/libertyships.html (2007)
United States v. Castillero, USDC(ND-Cal), No. 420
United States v. McRae, Law Rep 8 Eg 69 (1869)
V, H, Davis, letter (1898)
Statesmen of the Lost Cause, B.J. Hendrick (1939)

PASSION AND MURDER IN AMERICA

8. The Life and Death of George Wythe: "I Am Murdered"

American Aristides, I.E. Brown (1981)

Commonwealth v. Caton, 4 Call 5 (1782)

Decisions of Cases in Virginia by the High Court of Chancery, with Remarks upon the Decrees by the Court of Appeals Reversing Some of Those Decisions, G. Wythe (n.d.)

George Wythe, R.B. Kirtland (1986)

George Wythe of Williamsburg, J. Blackburn (1975)

George Wythe, Teacher of Liberty, A.T. Dill (1979)

Great American Trials, E.W. Knappman, ed., (1994)

A History of the Supreme Court, B. Schwartz (1993)

The Honorable George Wythe, O.L. Shewmake (1950)

Hudgins v. Wright, 1 Hen. & Munf. 123 (1804)

Jefferson Papers, 1751–1826 (Manuscript Collection, Library of Congress)

Marbury v. Madison, 1 Cranch 137 (1803)

The Murder of George Wythe, J.P. Boyd (1949)

"Notes for the Biography of George Wythe" (Manuscript Collection, Library of Congress)

Serene Patriot: A Life of George Wythe, W. Clarkin (1970)

The Two Parsons, G.W. Munford (1884)

9. The Trial of Levi Weeks: Hamilton and Burr for the Defense

Aaron Burr, M. Lomask (1979)

Alexander Hamilton, R. Chernow (2004)

Alexander Hamilton, H.C. Lodge (1898)

"The Defense of Levi Weeks," *A.B.A. J.* 63, L. Baker (June 1977)

Essays: The Laws of Evidence, J. Morgan

History of the Republic in the Writings of Alexander Hamilton, J.C. Hamilton (1864)

The Intimate Life of Alexander Hamilton, A.M. Hamilton (1910)

The Law Practice of Alexander Hamilton, vol. 5, J. Goebel Jr. & J.H. Smith, eds. (1981)

Life and Times of Aaron Burr, J. Parton (1858)

"The Original 'Dream Team,'" *Crime Magazine*, D. Lane (1998)

The Trial of Levi Weeks, E.F. Kleiger (1989)

10. Wild Bill Hickok: The Two Trials of Jack McCall

The American Cowboy in Life and Legend, B. McDowell (1972)

Deadwood: the Golden Years, W. Parker (1981)

Directive from A.G. Alfonso Taft to J.H. Burdick, File No. F-307, Records Group 204 (February 19, 1877)

The Last West, R. McKee (1974)

They Called Him Wild Bill, J. Rosa (1964)

The West: An Illustrated History, G. Ward (1996)

11. Justice Stephen Field, Justice David Terry, and Sarah Althea Hill

Allegeyer v. Louisiana, 165 U.S. 578 (1897)

The American Constitution, A.H. Kelly & W.A. Harbison (1955)
Bonanza Inn, O. Lewis & C.D. Hall (1939)
Brandenburg v. Ohio, 395 U.S. 444 (1969)
Constitutional Law, W. Lockhart, Y. Kamisar, J. Choper & S. Shiffrin (1986)
David S. Terry of California, A.R. Buchanan (1956)
The Growth of American Constitutional Law, B.F. Wright (1942)
Historic U.S. Court Cases, J.W. Johnson, ed. (1992)
In re Neagle, 135 U.S. 1 (1890)
The Justice and the Lady, R.H. Kroninger (1977)
Make No Law, A. Lewis (1991)
Nebbia v. New York, 291 U.S. 502 (1934)
Personal Reminiscences of Early Days in California, S. Field (1877)
The Rivals, A. Quinn (1994)
Sarah & the Senator, R.H. Kroninger (1964)
Sharon v. Hill, 26 Fed. 337 (1885)
Sharon v. Sharon
Slaughter-House Cases, 83 U.S. 36 (1873)
Stephen J. Field: Craftsman of the Law, C.B. Swisher (1930)
The Supreme Court in United States History, C. Warren (1924)
"W. Sharon," *Online Nevada Encyclopedia* (2007)
Whitney v. California, 274 U.S. 357 (1927)

12. Mountain Meadows Massacre

American Massacre, S. Denton (2003)
Blood of the Prophets, W. Bagley (1950)
The Mountain Meadows Massacre, J. Brooks (1962)
People v. Lee et al., USDC (1875)
People v. Lee et al., USDC (1876)
A River Running West, D. Worster (2001)
Utah, the Right Place, T. Alexander (1995)
www.pbs.org/weta/thewest/people (2007)

DEFENDING IRISH REBELS

13. A Punctuation Mark: *Rex v. Casement*

Famous Trials: Roger Casement, H.M. Hyde (1964)
Hatred, Ridicule or Contempt, A Book of Libel Cases, J. Dean (1953)
The Black Diaries of Roger Casement, P. Singleton-Gates and M. Girodias (1959)
The Green Flag: A History of Irish Nationalism, R. Kee (1972)
Joyce v. D.P.P., 1 All. E. R. 186 (1946)
New York Times Magazine (August 13, 1916)
Notable British Trials: The Trial of Sir Roger Casement, H.M. Hyde (1960)
Rebels: The Irish Rising of 1916, P. De Rosa (1990)
Rex v. Casement, 1 K.B. 98 (1917)

Rex v. Keyn, 2 Ex. D 63 (1876)
Rex v. Lynch, 1 K.B. 444 (1903)

14. The Spelling Game: Russell's Cross-Examination of Pigott

The Art of Cross-Examination, F.L. Wellman (1962)
The Green Flag: A History of Irish Nationalism, R. Kee (1972)
A History of Our Own Times from 1880 to the Diamond Jubilee, J. McCarthy (1897)
Ireland, R. Kee (1982)
The Life of Lord Russell of Killowen, R.B. O'Brien (1901)
Random Records of a Reporter, J.B. Hall (1930)

FIGHTING NAZI INJUSTICE

15. Hans Frank: Hitler's Lawyer

Das Dritte Reich und die Juden; Dokumente und Aufsätze; L. Poliakov & J. Wulf, eds. (1955)
Documents of Destruction, R. Hilberg (1971)
Documents on Nazism, J. Noakes & G. Pridham (1975)
The Encyclopedia of the Holocaust, L. Snyder (1976)
The Encyclopedia of the Third Reich, C. Zentner & F. Bedurftig (1991)
The German Dictatorship, K. Bracher (1970)
Germany 1866–1934, G. Craig (1978)
Hans Frank Diary, S. Piotrowski (1961)
Histoire de l'antisemitisme, L. Poliakov (1985)
Hitler, I. Kershaw (1998)
The Holocaust in Romania, R. Ionid (2000)
In the Shadow of the Reich, Niklas Frank (1991)
In the Sight of the Gallows, H. Frank (1953)
Inside Nuremberg, R. Martin, M.D. (2000)
Judenrat, I. Trunk (1972)
Justice at Nuremberg, R.E. Conot (1984)
Justice Not Vengence, S. Wiesenthal (1989)
Kommandant in Auschwitz, R. Höss (1958)
The Nazi Dictatorship, I. Kershaw (2000)
Nazi Germany and the Jews, vol. 1, S. Friedlander (1998)
Nuremberg, J. Persico (1995)
The Nuremberg Mind, F.R. Miale & M. Selver (1975)
Nürnberger Dokumente, 2233-C-PS
Nürnberger Dokumente, CA, IV
Nürnberger Dokumente, NG-2886
Oral Statement, P. Burg (2001)
The Order of the Death's Head, H. Hohne (1970)
Ordinary Men, C. Browning (1992)

Polish White Book: German Occupation of Poland, Poland Ministerstwo Spraw Zagraniczych (1942)
The Rise & Fall of the Third Reich, W. Shirer (1960)
Spiegel Special, V.P. Longerich (2001)
Wittgenstein's Poker, D. Edmonds & J. Eidinow (2001)
World's Great Trials, B. Aymar & E. Sagarin (1985)

16. The Ardeatine Caves

The Battle for Italy, W.G.F. Jackson (1967)
The Battle for Rome, R. Katz (2003)
The Butcher of Lyon, B. Murphy (1983)
Death in Rome, R. Katz (1967)
Hitler's Generals, C. Barnett (1989)
Klaus Barbie and the U.S. Government, A.A. Ryan (1983)
Mussolini's Italy, R.J.B. Bosworth (2006)
Oral History, E. Epstein (2006)
OSS RG 226, CIA, doc. 7459 (October 11, 1943)
Soldat zum das letzten Tag [*Soldier to the Last Day*], A. Kesselring (1958)
The Wehrmacht, W. Wette (2006)
www.CNN.com

17. Massacre at Oradour-sur-Glane

Das Reich, M. Hastings (1981)
Martyred Village, S. Farmer (1999)
Massacre at Oradour, R. Mackness (1988)
War Diary Oberkommando Wehrmacht (1944)
Occupation: The Ordeal of France, 1940–1944. I. Ousby (1998)
Oradour Centre de la Memoire (1946)
The Practice of Justice, W.H. Simon (1998)
(*Proces d'après-guerre*) Theolleyre, www.answers.com/topic/erich-priebke (2007)

18. Exodus: The Trial

Auschwitz in England, M. Hill & L.N. Williams (1965)
Convoy to Auschwitz, C. Delbo (1965)
Dering v. Uris and Others, 2 W.L.R. 1298 (1964)
Encyclopedia of the Holocaust, I. Gutman (1990)
Exodus, L. Uris. (1958)
Kalendarium der Ereignisse im Konzentrationslager Auschwitz-Birkenau 1939–1945, D. Czech
Nazi Doctors, R.J. Lifton (1986)

19. Zigzag: The Sinking of the USS *Indianapolis*

Abandon Ship!, R.F. Newcomb (2001)
All the Drowned Sailors, R.B. Lech (1982)

Candide, Voltaire (1759)
Chronology of the War at Sea, 1939–1945, J. Rohwer & G. Hummelchen (1992)
Congressional Resolution (2000)
Fatal Voyage, D. Kurzman (1990)
History of U.S. Naval Operations in World War II: Victory in the Pacific, S.E. Morison (1960)
History of the US Navy, vol. 2, R.W. Love Jr. (1992)
In Harm's Way, D. Stanton (2001)
The Last Great Victory, S. Weintraub (1995)
Narrative of the Circumstances of the Loss of the USS Indianapolis, Navy Dept. Press Release (February 23, 1946)
Oral History, L. Haynes (1995)
Oral Statement, P. Simon (2006)
Sunk: A History of the Imperial Japanese Navy in World War II: M. Hashimoto (1954)
To Shining Sea, S. Howarth (1999)
The United States Navy in World War II, S.E. Smith (1966)
Voices from the Pacific War, www.ussindianapolis.org: *Bluejackets Remember*, B.M. Petty (2004)
http://history.navy.mil/faqs/faq30=1.htm

THE PREJUDICE TRIALS

20. *Schumann v. Wieck:* The Battle for Clara

Clara Schumann, *The Artist and the Woman*, N.B. Reich (1985)
Concerto: the Story of Clara Schumann, B. Harding (1962)
The Faust Legend in Romantic Song, D. Aitken (1981)
The Great Pianist, C. Schonberg (1963)
The Mendelssohns, H. Kupferberg (1972)
The New Grove Dictionary of Music and Musicians, S. Sadie, ed. (1980)
Robert Schumann, His Life and Work, R. Taylor (1982)
Schumann: The Inner Voices of a Musical Genius, P. Ostwald (1985)
Women Making Music, J. Bowers & J. Tick, eds. (1986)
Women's Philharmonic CD Notes, N. Reich

21. *Whistler v. Ruskin:* A Question of Art

The Man Whistler, P. Hesketh (1952)
The Painter's Eye, H. James (1956)
Victorian Painters, J. Maas (1984)
James Abbott McNeill Whistler: A Life, G. H. Fleming (1991)
Whistler, Beyond the Myth, R. Anderson & A. Koval (1995)
Whistler: Landscapes and Seascapes, D. Holden (1969)
Whistler v. Ruskin: Art and Art Criticism, J.M. Whistler (1878)
The Works of Ruskin, vol. 37, J. Ruskin (1919)

22. Sir Edward Carson Cross-Examines Oscar Wilde

Carson, H.M. Hyde (1953)
The Ballad of Reading Gaol, O. Wilde (1896)
The Importance of Being Oscar, M. Nicholls (1980)
Oscar Wilde: A Certain Genius, B. Belford (2000)
Oscar Wilde, R. Ellman (1985)
Oscar Wilde, H.M. Hyde (1948)
Oscar Wilde, J. Laver (1963)
Oscar Wilde: The Aftermath, H.M. Hyde (1963)
The Real Trial of Oscar Wilde, M. Holland (2003)
Regina v. Queensberry
Without Apology, A. Douglas (1937)
Wolfenden Report (1957)

23. United States of America against One Book Entitled *Ulysses* by James Joyce

Diary, V. Woolf (1941)
James Joyce, E. O'Brien (1999)
James Joyce, R. Ellman (1982)
New Yorker (January 27, 1934)
The Nineteenth Century, L. Golding (April 1933)
Ulysses, J. Joyce (1922)
US v Ulysses (Documents), ed. M. Mosato & L. Le Blanc (1984)
USA v. One Book Entitled Ulysses by James Joyce, No. A 110–59 (USDC; 1933; S. Dist., N.Y.)

24. Pride and Prejudice: The Dark Side of Henry Ford

The Age of Reform, R. Hofstadter (1955)
American Jewish Yearbook, O. & M.F. Handlin (1955)
Anti-Defamation League website (2000)
Anti-Semitism in America, H.E. Quinley & C.Y. Glick (1979)
Baruch: The Public Years, B.M. Baruch (1960)
Beyond the Model T: The Other Ventures of Henry Ford, F.R. Bryan (1997)
Champion of Liberty, L. Marshall (1957)
The Dialogue in Hell between Machiavelli and Montesquieu, M. Joly (1864)
Encyclopedia of the Holocaust, I. Gutman (1990)
The Flivver King, U. Sinclair (1937)
Ford: Expansion and Challenge, A. Nevins & F.E. Hill (1957)
Henry Ford and the Jews, N. Baldwin (2001)
Henry Ford, The Wayward Capitalist, C. Gelderman (1981)
Inside Nuremberg, R.A. Martin (1993)
The International Jew, 3 vols., Dearborn Independent (1920–1922)
Justice at Nuremberg, R.E. Conot (1983)
The Last Billionaire, W.C. Richards (1948)

A Lie and a Libel, B. Segel (1995)

Mein Kampf, A. Hitler (1925)

Nazism & War, R. Bassel (2004)

Nuremberg, J.E. Persico (1994)

The People's Tycoon, S. Watts (2005)

The Public Image of Henry Ford, D.L. Lewis (1976)

Reminiscences, E. Liebold (1953)

Warrant for Genocide, N. Cohn (1996)

We Never Called Him Henry, H. Bennett (1951)

Wheels for the World, D. Brinkley (2003)

25. Rosa Parks: An American Icon

The American Constitution, A.H. Kelly & W.A. Harbison (1955)

The Alabama Lawyer, S.J. Rowe (1991)

Baltimore v. Dawson, 350 U.S. 877 (1955)

Black Profiles in Courage, K. Abdul-Jabbar and A. Steinberg (1996)

Browder v. Gayle, 142 F.Supp. 707, 717 (1956)

Brown v. Board of Education, 349 U.S. 294 (1955)

Gayle v. Browder, 352 U.S. 903 (1956)

"Henry Billings Brown," *The Supreme Court Historical Society Quarterly*, T. Broad (2006)

Historic U.S. Court Cases, 2nd ed., J.W. Johnson, ed. (2001)

Holmes v. Atlanta, 350 U.S. 879 (1955)

My Story, R. Parks (1992)

Parting the Waters, T. Branch (1988)

Pillar of Fire, T. Branch (1999)

Plessy v. Ferguson, 163 U.S. 537 (1896)

Rosa Parks, D. Brinkley (2000)

Rosa Parks' Story, NBC (February 2002)

State v. Rosa Parks, No. 7409 (1955)

Taming the Storm, J. Bass (1993)

INDEX